C000259131

Pragmatics and Grammar

When using language, many aspects of our messages are left implicit in what we say. While grammar is responsible for what we express explicitly, pragmatics explains how we infer additional meanings. The problem is that it is not always a trivial matter to decide which of the meanings conveyed is explicit (grammatical) and which implicit (pragmatic). *Pragmatics and Grammar* lays out a methodology for students and scholars to distinguish between the two. It explains how and why grammar and pragmatics combine together in natural discourse, and how pragmatic uses become grammatical in time. This textbook introduces students to a major topic within current pragmatics research, and discusses prominent questions addressed by scholars interested in grammar/pragmatics relations. Based on natural linguistic examples, providing more persuasive data, it addresses how we should tease grammar and pragmatics apart in controversial cases.

MIRA ARIEL is a Professor in the Linguistics Department at Tel Aviv University, Israel.

CAMBRIDGE TEXTBOOKS IN LINGUISTICS

General editors: P. AUSTIN, J. BRESNAN, B. COMRIE, S. CRAIN,
W. DRESSLER, C. EWEN, R. LASS, D. LIGHTFOOT, K. RICE,
I. ROBERTS, S. ROMAINE, N.V. SMITH.

Pragmatics and Grammar

Pragmatics and Grammar

MIRA ARIEL

Tel Aviv University

CAMBRIDGE UNIVERSITY PRESS
Cambridge, New York, Melbourne, Madrid, Cape Town, Singapore, São Paulo, Delhi

Cambridge University Press
The Edinburgh Building, Cambridge CB2 8RU, UK

Published in the United States of America by Cambridge University Press, New York

www.cambridge.org
Information on this title: www.cambridge.org/9780521559942

© Cambridge University Press 2008

This publication is in copyright. Subject to statutory exception
and to the provisions of relevant collective licensing agreements,
no reproduction of any part may take place without
the written permission of Cambridge University Press.

First published 2008

Printed in the United Kingdom at the University Press, Cambridge

A catalogue record for this publication is available from the British Library

ISBN 978-0-521-55018-5 hardback
ISBN 978-0-521-55994-2 paperback

Cambridge University Press has no responsibility for the persistence or
accuracy of URLs for external or third-party internet websites referred to
in this book, and does not guarantee that any content on such
websites is, or will remain, accurate or appropriate.

For the love of my life

Contents

Tables

Preface

Pragmatics and Grammar is neither about pragmatics, nor about grammar. It is about the complex relationship between grammar and pragmatics. Grammar is defined as a set of codes, and pragmatics as a set of nonlogical inferences derived on the basis of these codes. Here are some of the main questions we seek to elucidate.

First, what does pragmatic inference do that grammar cannot? In other words, what aspects of the interpretation of an utterance should be seen as pragmatic rather than semantic? How much of the interpretation should we attribute to pragmatics? Should the role of grammar in this process be minimized or maximized? Given that the concept of pragmatic inference may involve more than one subtype, we have to ask which kind of pragmatic inference best accounts for any given pragmatic interpretation. Some inferences constitute part of the information explicitly conveyed, in that they contribute, along with the coded meanings, to the truth conditions of the proposition expressed. If so, once we've ascertained that a putative interpretation should be analyzed as a pragmatic inference, we must also determine whether the inference is best viewed as a conversational implicature or as part of the proposition expressed. The classification carries cognitive and interactional implications.

We also address a puzzle which is frequently overlooked in discussions of the grammar/pragmatics interface. The fact is that our current grammar is very often our pragmatics (of the past) turned grammatical. If grammar and pragmatics are absolutely distinct from each other, as suggested by standard analyses, how can we account for grammaticization and semanticization? There must be some way for pragmatic interpretations and distributional patterns to penetrate through the grammar/pragmatics divide to become part of the grammar. We explain how this penetrability is possible while maintaining the validity of the grammar/pragmatics division of labor.

Finally, we examine various synchronic levels at which the grammar/pragmatics interface operates. In addition to the level of conveyed meaning (a representation of the linguistic meaning augmented by all pragmatic inferences), researchers have identified a basic-level meaning which is not as maximal as the conveyed meaning, yet not as minimal as the linguistic meaning. This is the representation we focus on, and once again we ask how minimal/maximal it should be. As we shall see, both minimalist and maximalist basic-level representations play a role in accounting for how language works for communication. We end by noting that the same basic-level synchronic interpretation may also be responsible for the diachronic grammaticization and semanticization.

There is a narrative development to this textbook. The first chapter introduces the issues and the terms needed for later analyses. Part I splits linguistic acts into separate grammatical (encoded) and pragmatic (inferred) components. Part II presents evidence for an intimate association between the two. Finally, part III brings codes and inferences back together, as we consider interface levels where codes and inferences combine.

Acknowledgments

The research that led to this book was conducted at Tel Aviv University and at UC Santa Barbara. I deeply appreciate the feedback I received on parts of this book from colleagues at both universities, Rachel Giora, Tal Siloni, and Sandra Thompson especially. It's also a pleasure to thank François Recanati and Guy Deutscher, whose comments were most helpful to me.

One person deserves special mention, Tanya Reinhart, my advisor, my colleague, my friend. Tanya read the chapter on reflexives, gave me constructive comments, generously reassuring me that it was quite all right for me to criticize her theory. How sad it is for me, indeed for all of us, to no longer have her.

Several generations of bright and enthusiastic students at Tel Aviv University read various drafts of this textbook. Their questions and challenges made classes a fun time and helped me clarify my ideas to myself, and hopefully to the readers too. I thank Ofir Zussman for his meticulous bibliographical searches, Tamar Holoshitz of Harvard University for her help with the production of the example appendix for this book (available online), and Aviah Morag for help with the index. I thank Jack Du Bois for permission to use the Longman Spoken American Corpus (LSAC), which was compiled under his direction at UC Santa Barbara, and for early access to portions of the Santa Barbara Corpus of Spoken American English (SBC).

I am honored to have had Bernard Comrie as my series editor. His care(fulness) and wide knowledge saved me from some embarrassing mistakes, and his wisdom and patience made my book into the textbook I wanted it to be. Andrew Winnard has been a most helpful and encouraging editor, and Sarah Green, Jodie Barnes, and Kay McKechnie extremely professional, as well as considerate and patient with me. Last, I owe a great debt to Jack Du Bois for all the sound advice he gave me, for listening to me talk about this book to no end, and above all, for his love and friendship.

How to use this book

Pragmatics and Grammar lays out the issues regarding both the division of labor between grammar and pragmatics, and the levels in which grammar and pragmatics interface. The topic holds significance for philosophers and for linguists, especially for those with an interest in semantics, pragmatics, grammaticization and semanticization, and functional explanations for language. The book asks which phenomena should be classified as grammatical and which as pragmatic; if classified as pragmatic, what type of inference should be assumed; how pragmatic inference turns into grammatical code (grammaticization); what the minimal relevant basic meaning in discourse ('what is said') is; whether grammar is pragmatically motivated or arbitrary; and other related questions. This book offers a unified approach to the diverse questions in pragmatics and grammar by framing the issues in terms of codes versus inferences, as well as codes accompanied by inferences. Combining reanalysis of the standard problems with a new approach to naturally occurring discourse examples of language use, the book is innovative in grounding pragmatic, semantic and grammatical issues in empirical, sometimes statistical, evidence drawn from spoken corpus research.

The book is intended for upper-level undergraduates, graduate students, and researchers who have an interest in pragmatics, grammar, and the connection between them. It is suitable for a course on the grammar/pragmatics interface, on pragmatics, and on grammaticization/semanticization. While it should preferably be used in the sequence presented for a grammar/pragmatics interface course, courses with a more specialized focus can make a more selective use of the parts, each of which is designed to stand on its own. A course in pragmatics or semantics can focus on chapters 1, 2, 3, 4, and 7. A course specializing in grammaticization or semanticization can begin with chapter 1, proceed directly to part II (chapters 4, 5, and 6) and end with part III. Of course, I hope that practitioners of any of these fields will explore the full range of issues in the rest of the book. Researchers writing on the grammar/pragmatics division of labor should offer accounts which can also enable the crossing of pragmatic inferences into the grammar in a grammaticization process (discussed in part II), and similarly, researchers focusing on grammaticization/semanticization should argue for the grammaticization of some pragmatic phenomenon based on a solid grammar/pragmatics distinction (here offered in part I).

Transcription conventions

The following conventions are used in most of the transcribed examples in this book, i.e. those taken from conversations in the Santa Barbara Corpus of Spoken American English (SBC, see Du Bois and Engelbretson, 2004, 2005; Du Bois *et al.*, 2000; Du Bois, Chafe *et al.*, 2003). Transcriptions have been slightly simplified for ease of reading.

Santa Barbara Corpus of Spoken American English	
SYMBOL	MEANING
JILL:	speaker label
New line	intonation unit*
...	pause, medium or long (untimed)
..	pause, short (less than 0.2 seconds)
@	laugh (one symbol per pulse)
@you're @kidding	laughing words
[ ]	overlapping/simultaneous speech
[2]	overlapping speech (2nd pair)
.	final intonation
,	continuing intonation
?	appeal/question intonation
—	truncated intonation unit (em dash)
wor–	truncated/cut-off word (en dash)
(H)	breathe (in)
(Hx)	exhale
(TSK)	click (alveolar)
(COUGH)	vocalisms (various)
###	unintelligible (one symbol per syllable)
#you're #kidding	uncertain hearing of words
((WORDS))	transcriber comment
<VOX>	voice of another

Note: In most cases, speaker names have been changed to preserve anonymity.

* When the intonation unit is too long, it is carried over to the next line and indented using a hanging indent.

Other symbols and abbreviations:

??	unacceptable string
~	invented example
ACC	accusative
F	feminine
M	masculine
PL	plural
PRS	present tense
SG	singular
morpheme-morpheme	bound morpheme boundary
morpheme.morpheme	two glosses per single object-language element
morpheme:morpheme	a morphological division indicated only in the gloss
morpheme=morpheme	clitic boundary
1, 2, 3	first, second, third person

Other sources commonly used:

The Longman Spoken American Corpus (LSAC)

Lotan 1990: A Hebrew transcript of a conversation between an Israeli businessman and several income tax clerks (all males)

Note: Where the original non-English expressions are not crucial for the point being made, only English free translations of the examples are cited in order to facilitate reading. The original examples and their glosses can be found at www.cambridge.org/9780521559942.

1 Introduction: Grammar, pragmatics, and what's between them

Pragmatics has been notoriously hard to define. Or rather, it has proven quite impossible to reconcile between the patterning of phenomena assumed to be classical pragmatic topics (deixis and reference, speech acts, conversational and conventional implicatures, presuppositions, functional syntax) and the common set of definitions for pragmatics (most notably, context dependency, inferentiality, nontruth conditionality and others). In order to resolve the delimitation problem of the field we are forced to first abandon the expectation that all the definitional criteria converge on classifying some phenomenon as pragmatic (or as grammatical). In other words, we cannot expect that any given pragmatic phenomenon will simultaneously meet all the criterial definitions for pragmatics (and vice versa for grammatical phenomena). For example, while deixis is pragmatic in that it is context-dependent, it cannot meet the nontruth-conditionality criterion (for it contributes a truth-conditional meaning).

In addition, we must give up on what I have elsewhere called the topical approach to pragmatics, which assumes that all aspects of some phenomenon (e.g. of deixis, of presupposition, etc.) uniformly belong in pragmatics, or else, that all of them uniformly belong in grammar (see Ariel, forthcoming and chapter 2). Any specific instance of language use is neither wholly grammatical nor wholly pragmatic. To pick deixis again, it combines grammatical aspects (there is a grammatically specified difference between *I* and *this*) with pragmatic aspects (pinning down who the speaker is, what object *this* denotes). Hence, instead of struggling to find just the right set of definitions which would include all and only the canonical list of pragmatic topics (a mission impossible – see Levinson, 1983), we must choose one criterion to define pragmatics. We cannot even expect it to apply to all (aspects) of the topics on the classical pragmatic list (see Ariel, forthcoming). Perforce, a single criterion will offer a consistent division of labor between the grammatical and the pragmatic.

Now, if we can only choose one criterion for drawing a consistent and coherent grammar/pragmatics division of labor, which criterion should we opt for? This book, along with researchers such as Sperber and Wilson (1986/1995), adopts the code/inference distinction as the basis for the grammar/pragmatics division of labor. Why pick the code/inference distinction (as opposed to any other criterion, e.g. truth conditionality)? The simple answer is that we cannot afford not to adopt this distinction, given the nature of grammar. Whatever else grammar may be, there can be no controversy about it consisting of a set of codes. The essence of grammar is a set of conventional associations correlating specific forms with their

1

obligatory or optional, rule-governed positioning, meaning, and distributional patterns. Whether or not it is in addition devoted, for example, to truth-conditional interpretations remains to be seen.

At the same time, grammar obviously falls quite short of meeting our communicative needs. There is a consensus today about the underdeterminacy of grammar, i.e. the fact that our coded messages never exhaust the meaning we intend to convey (see especially Carston, 2002a, and see also Levinson, 2002a: 8). This is where pragmatics comes in, enriching our encoded messages with pragmatic, i.e. plausible inferred interpretations (as opposed to formal, logical deductions). Grammar and pragmatics always go together. You can't have one without the other for effective communication.

This book is about the complex relationship between grammar and pragmatics, that is, between codes and inferences involved in human communication. The relationship is not unidimensional. It has a few facets, and each one of them needs to be examined. Naturally enough, researchers interested in the grammar/pragmatics division of labor have focused on the complementarity between the two competencies. Such research seeks to establish the precise borderline between codes and inferences. Indeed, this is one important facet of the relationship between grammar and pragmatics, and part I is devoted to this topic. We try to resolve a number of intriguing questions, all of which have the same format: given a certain correlation between some linguistic form and some interpretation or use conditions, should it be grammar or should it be pragmatics that accounts for it? In other words, is the correlation encoded or is it derived by plausible inferences? Now, up till recently, all inferences were automatically seen as conversational implicatures. Relevance theoreticians have proposed that not all pragmatic inferences are implicatures, however. If so, every interpretation we view as a pragmatic inference needs to be further classified as to which type of inference it is.

But there is much more to explore about the relationship between grammar and pragmatics. Codes and inferences must make contact in diachronic change. Research by functional and historical linguists (e.g. Bybee *et al.*, 1994; Traugott and Dasher, 2002) has convincingly demonstrated that, historically, pragmatic inferences routinely become grammatical conventions (via the processes of grammaticization and semanticization). In fact, most, if not all, of our synchronic grammar is the product of our diachronic extralinguistic regularities, which have turned grammatical. If so, any analysis of the grammar/pragmatics divide must also meet the challenge of the penetrability of this divide: grammar is not only distinct from pragmatics, it is also its product. Part II addresses this facet of the relationship between grammar and pragmatics.

The final chapter of this book (part III) brings together these two very different approaches and research traditions. We discuss grammar/pragmatics interfaces, i.e. representational levels where the two combine. Synchronically, we have at least two such levels, conveyed meanings and basic-level meanings. We hardly touch on the first type of representation, despite the fact that it consists of the linguistic meaning plus all the conversational implicatures generated by the speaker (but see section 1.2 below). The reason is that here, although semantics and pragmatics combine, they remain interactionally independent of each other. There is also no controversy regarding this interface level. We focus on the basic, minimal meaning level which the speaker is necessarily seen as committed to. This interactionally significant (synchronic) meaning is an integrative level, where codes and inferences are intimately woven together to form one proposition. Here codes and inferences are in fact so well integrated that it's not clear that they are separable (for cognitive and discoursal purposes). We consider proposals as to how to define this meaning representation, namely, minimally (i.e. with as few inferences as possible), or maximally (incorporating a substantial inferential contribution). The conclusion we reach is that this hybrid-level meaning is minimalist (à la Grice) on some occasions and maximalist (à la Sperber and Wilson) on other occasions.

Now, although this basic-level interpretation has been proposed as a synchronic, real-time representation, we end the book by entertaining the possibility that it also serves as the input for semanticization and grammaticization. In other words, it is possible that the synchronic basic-level grammar/pragmatics hybrid representation is not only the significant meaning level in terms of the ongoing interaction, it is also the diachronic arena where pragmatics may turn grammar. After all, linguistic change must occur in real-time discourse. If this is true, the most significant grammar/pragmatics interface level both synchronically and diachronically is the basic interactional interpretation, where codes and inferences co-mingle, regardless of the fact that they are arrived at via quite distinct cognitive processes.

Let's begin our introduction now, which will prepare the ground for the whole book. We set out from the now well-accepted assumption that we always communicate by combining codes (grammar) with inferences (pragmatics). We introduce the basic facts about inferencing in section 1.1. We briefly outline the Gricean mechanism for generating inferences (conversational implicatures) in section 1.2, and we define and distinguish between codes and inferences in section 1.3. Section 1.4 introduces pragmatic inferences other than conversational implicatures. We end with section 1.5, where we introduce the two challenges facing research into the grammar/pragmatics relationship: drawing the code/inference distinction on the one hand, and accounting for the process whereby inferences cross over and become codes on the other hand.

1.1   On inferring

We get more for our words when they are embedded in natural discourse context. Here are two examples where it is quite clear that we need to read between the lines:

(1) a.   LEWINSKY$_1$: . . . See my mom's big fear is that he's ((President Clinton – MA)) going to send somebody out to kill me.
((PART OMITTED))

	TRIPP:	Oh, my God. Don't even say such an asinine thing. **He's not that stupid. He's an arrogant ... but he's not that stupid**.

TRIPP: Oh, my God. Don't even say such an asinine thing. **He's not that stupid. He's an arrogant ... but he's not that stupid**.

LEWINSKY$_2$: Well, you know, **accidents happen**.

(Nov. 20, 1997: *New York Times*, Oct. 3, 1998)

b.   REBECCA$_1$:   So you can testify to two of [em].

RICKIE$_1$:   [Yeah].

REBECCA$_2$:   That's why I had you come up,

becau[se],

RICKIE$_2$:   [Yeah],

REBECCA$_3$:   ... um,

... that's great.   (SBC: 008)

While the above exchanges are natural enough, and easy to interpret (for their participants, at least), there is something strange about each of them. (1a) seems to involve irrelevant responses: why is Clinton's intelligence (Tripp's response) relevant to the fear of Lewinsky's mother that he will have her killed (a topic raised by Lewinsky$_1$)? And what is the relevance of the occurrence of accidents (Lewinsky$_2$'s response) to Clinton's intelligence (discussed by Tripp)? It seems that while there is a connection between Lewinsky's and Tripp's contributions above, it is not explicitly stated. It is inferred. Tripp intends to convey that since Clinton is intelligent he won't have Lewinsky killed, because killing her would be a stupid act (probably since he would be caught and get into even deeper trouble). Lewinsky then retorts that he may indeed have her killed, except it would be made to look like an accident (so he may not be caught). We similarly need to enrich Rebecca$_2$'s contribution in (1b), since her sentence is cut off in the middle. What is the reason that Rebecca (a prosecuting attorney) had Rickie (a sexual abuse victim preparing to testify against her sexual abuser) come up to her office? Given the specific context, we can assume that it must be the fact that Rickie can testify to two cases of sexual abuse by the defendant, as opposed to other witnesses who "only" experienced one sexual abuse from him. In the light of what has already been said in the exchange, this reason is quite obvious, and hence need not be explicitly mentioned. The addressees can easily infer it. The exchanges in (1) are quite typical of natural interaction. Communication begins with the coded message, but it never ends there. Inferences are an inherent part of it.

The most basic goal of pragmatic theories is to provide an account for how we go about interpreting such everyday exchanges. This is the goal informing Grice (1989), as well as Horn (1984 and onwards) and Sperber and Wilson (1986/1995 and onwards), all following Grice. We here briefly present only Grice's pragmatic theory, because our purpose in this chapter, indeed in this book, is served by demonstrating that there is at least one pragmatic theory which can account for additional interpretations we get people to infer when we speak. In fact, all pragmatic theories are in this sense Gricean. They all assume that every act of communication is actually **inferential**, because the addressee is required to **infer** the speaker's intention from whatever evidence is available to him (the linguistic code constituting only one important source of information).[1] At the same time, this chapter also serves as an introduction for later chapters, where disagreements between theorists will be discussed. These revolve around the role of particularized and generalized conversational implicatures, and the Relevance-theoretic concept of explicature, all here introduced.

Natural discourse is a **cooperative** activity. It's not a random collection of independent utterances (see Mann and Thompson, 1986). What makes discourse coherent? What expectations do we have from interlocutors' utterances? The idea is that whatever those expectations may be, they cannot be fulfilled by our coded messages exclusively. It is only when we (also) consider inferred interpretations that we can ultimately explain how discourse works. In order to produce and interpret appropriate pieces of discourse, speakers must rely on the many inferences which accompany those codes. This is why codes and inferences are so intimately connected with each other. And this is why discourse coherence and inferencing are co-dependent on each other as well. Let's examine briefly Grice's (1975, 1989) proposals on how to account for both the nature of discourse and the mechanism responsible for the derivation of pragmatic inferences.

No doubt, one of the most important features of human discourse is that we assume that speakers' utterances are somehow **relevant** to us. This is why we are led to interpret the following two statements as related, in fact, as constituting a contrast:

(2)   The father was appointed chief of staff, the daughter refused to enlist (in
           the army).   (Originally Hebrew, *Hair* headline, April 25, 2002)

Each statement by itself is quite irrelevant to the addressees. The readers of the newspaper need not be informed that someone's father has been appointed chief of staff. They know the man by name, and they know he was appointed. The fact that some daughter refused to serve in the army is equally irrelevant. However, with the two pieces of information taken together, the headline becomes highly relevant: it turns out that the Israeli chief of staff himself (who had spoken about the importance of serving in the army) has a daughter who refused to serve. To see that we indeed expect discourse to be relevant, note what happens when Darryl can't see Pamela's utterance as relevant:

(3)   PAMELA: I guess it's j– looking at my mother,
                   too,
                   I n– ——
                   (Hx)
           DARRYL: . . . **What does that have to do with** why you're reading a book
                   on death?   (SBC: 005)

---

[1] Indeed Tomasello (1999) argues forcefully that children's ability to view others as intentional agents (an ability which emerges at nine to twelve months) is a prerequisite for language, and something that animals lack.

Darryl's question shows that the default assumption is that interlocutors produce relevant utterances. Since he fails to find relevance, he asks about it. So, an important requirement on speakers is that they be relevant. This is what Grice's maxim of Relation ("Be relevant!") is about.

Next, let's examine Grice's maxim of Quantity. We expect utterances to be **informative**. Here's a case where Joanne finds one of Lenore's utterances (the one marked bold) not informative enough. She then asks for an elaboration:

(4) JOANNE: ... (H) He's got iron,
              with his mul[tiples].
     LENORE: [Well,
              I] have iron too,
              but th– some of it isn't absorbable.
              this is very absorb[able iron.
     JOANNE: **What do you mean absorbable**.
     LENORE: (H) it's good for your anemia.   (SBC: 015)

Of course, Joanne knows what *absorbable* means (semantically). But she can't get enough relevant information from Lenore, presumably because she is missing some background information that Lenore is taking for granted, something to the effect that absorbability is an important issue for the effectiveness of iron pills. In this sense, Lenore's contribution was not informative enough, and hence is not quite appropriate.

A third maxim proposed by Grice is the maxim of Quality. We naturally assume that our interlocutors tell us the **truth**. This is why when Pete in (5) realizes he's about to say something he is not sure is true (that salad spinners did not exist when they were growing up), he stops short, and asks his friends whether it's true or not:

(5) PETE: I don't think they ever —
            .. **did they actually exist back then**?   (SBC: 003)

Grice's maxim of Quality instructs speakers not only to tell only the truth, but also to avoid saying that which they lack evidence for. Pete is abiding by this maxim.

Finally, according to Grice's maxim of Manner, utterances should be constructed in an optimal style or **manner**. They should be brief and clear. Here's a case where the speaker was not clear enough (in the turn marked bold), and caused a problem for his addressee. She has to ask him about his intended message therefore:

(6) W: M!
     M: I'm coming!
     W: Watch out along the way.
     M: Why?
     W: **Sandy!**
     M: ((Looks around, doesn't see Sandy, the dog))
        What?
        She vomited?   (Aug. 5, 2006)

While on other occasions it may be enough to use an NP utterance and trust the addressee to complete the missing propositional information (see *Iraq* standing for 'the American war and occupation of Iraq' in (13) below), this was not a successful act in (6). This is then a violation of Grice's maxim of Manner.

The problems we detected in the discourses in (3)–(6) provide evidence for how proper discourse usually proceeds. The four Gricean maxims mentioned above characterize what Grice (1975, 1989) suggested are cooperative communicative principles. According to Grice, natural discourse reflects the application of the Cooperative Principle, which instructs speakers to "make your conversational contribution such as is required, at the stage at which it occurs, by the accepted purpose or direction of the talk exchange in which you are engaged" (Grice, 1975: 45). This cooperative (some prefer rational – see Kasher, 1976) behavior translates into abiding by the four maxims we've mentioned: **Quantity** (informativeness), **Relation** (relevance), **Quality** (truthfulness), and **Manner**. Speakers are expected to provide just the right amount of information (neither too much nor too little – Quantity), the information should be relevant (Relation) and true (Quality), and it should be optimally phrased, namely, the utterance should be as brief and clear as possible (Manner). As we saw in the above examples, whenever any one of these maxims was violated (or about to be violated), there was some breakdown in the communication, and speakers hastened to query about it, so as to somehow remedy the problem. I should add, however, that examples (3)–(6) were not at all easy to find. Most of the time, discourse does proceed rather smoothly, according to the Gricean maxims above.[2]

Now, what's all this got to do with the question of codes and inferences? A lot, according to pragmatists. The argument is that we simply cannot comply with the cooperative principle, nor with the four maxims, by subjecting just our coded, explicit messages to these principles. As already exemplified in (1), we must take into account inferences in order to see how speakers go about cooperating with each other. If we restrict ourselves to examining only codes, we will find quite a few violations of the Gricean proposal, ones which are not accidental lapses (performance errors), like the exceptional examples in (3)–(6). The violations we are about to examine below (section 1.2) do not cause any communication problems. This is so because they are intended, and they give rise to inferences which then show that speakers were cooperative after all. Inferences serve discourse when codes fail. Still, why is it that we don't communicate by codes alone? Why don't we make sure that our codes fully abide by the four Gricean maxims? Wouldn't it be clearer and more efficient to communicate this way? Why divide up our communicative task between two modes? For example, why didn't the newspaper choose as its headline the Hebrew counterpart of 'The father was appointed chief of staff **but his** daughter refused to enlist (in the army)' (instead of (2))?

---

[2] See Grice (1975, 1989) for a detailed outline of the theory.

First, explicating everything we wish to convey to the addressee would considerably slow us down. Following Levelt (1993), Levinson (2000a) has convincingly argued that our production mechanisms are far too slow to allow for an efficient, fully explicit mode of communication. Many pieces of information which constitute an integral part of our messages are better left to inferencing, because human beings are very apt at drawing inferences. Actually pronouncing out loud these assumptions would take a long time and effort on the speaker's part, and at the same time would waste the addressee's time in superfluous decoding. Many inferences are faster for the addressee to compute than for the speaker to form a verbalizing plan and to articulate with words. Here's a relevant example (and see again (1)):

(7)   HAROLD: that . . really hot tap danc[er]$_i$.
        JAMIE: [Oh] that kid$_i$.
        MILES: **... He$_i$ was actually here two weeks ago,
                 and I missed him$_i$.**   (SBC: 002)

In fact, what Miles is conveying to his interlocutors is that 'He, i.e. **the tap dancer**, was actually here, i.e. **in this town**, two weeks ago **for a public performance**, and I missed **that performance with** him.' But Miles can skip stating explicitly that the dancer gave a performance (see how much longer the explicit version is), because we can very easily infer it. The same applies to the deictic (*here*) and the anaphoric expressions (*He*, *him*, and see again (1b)). Leaving part of the message to inference can be an efficient step, then.

In addition to effort saving as in (7), speakers have a variety of reasons for preferring an implicit over an explicit mode for some interpretations. There is an interactional difference between explicit and implicit messages. Consider the following:

(8) a.   The Americans know Netanyahu, who is actually Benjamin Nitai.
                          (Originally Hebrew, Reshet Bet radio, Jan. 11, 2006)
    b.   She had an uncle who predicted that she will be a musician and a genius.
           And she always said, well, at least I became a musician.
                          (Originally Hebrew, Reshet Bet radio, Mar. 17, 2006)

The implicit message in (8a) is that Israeli Knesset Member (and former prime minister) Netanyahu is not quite a patriotic Israeli, possibly, that he cannot be trusted as a leader. In order to arrive at this conclusion, we need to rely on a host of background assumptions: as is well known (to Israelis), years before he became a politician, Netanyahu had left Israel and lived in the US for quite a number of years, where he changed his name from the Israeli-sounding *Binyamin Netanyahu* to the American-sounding *Benjamin Nitai*. On the assumption that the name one adopts testifies to the national identity one aspires to, there is possibly an even stronger message here, that Netanyahu is not actually loyal to Israel but, rather, to the US. No wonder Knesset Member Ronnie Bar-On (the speaker in (8a)) prefers an implicit over an explicit mode. As we point out below, one can always deny what one did not say explicitly.[3] Next, consider (8b). Being a musician certainly does not preclude being a genius. Yet, it's clear that Drora Chavkin (the *she* cited in the example) implied that she was not a genius. But she didn't quite say it. There is a difference between explicitly stating some information and conveying it by triggering an inference (a self-humoristic effect in this case). So, the answer to our question of why rely on inferences rather than on decoding is that (a) inferences save on time and effort (sometimes), and (b) they are indirect.

1.2   Generating implicatures

We need a "science of the unsaid," as Levinson (2000b) calls inferential pragmatics theories. Grice's (1975, 1989) idea was that we use the same four maxims that inform our cooperative behavior in general as guiding principles in inference drawing as well. Interlocutors' working assumption is that cooperative speakers do abide by the maxims. If so, should they seem to violate one of the maxims, and blatantly so, rather than take it as a breakdown in the communication (as is done in the atypical (3)–(6)), addressees assume that there was a special speaker communicative intention behind the maxim flouting. That communicative intention is a pragmatic inference, based on what was said explicitly and contextual assumptions the speaker intends the addressee to consider in the computation of the inference. Those inferences which fall under the communicative intention of the speaker are what Grice termed **conversational implicatures** ((8a) triggers a particularized conversational implicature, (8b) a generalized conversational implicature – see below). Let's consider a few examples to see how the mechanism of speaker-generated implicatures works.

Consider (8) again. We can now explain why it is that speakers generated the specific implicatures we noted above. In both cases we have violations of the maxim of Quantity. The speaker in (8a) provides too much information. While vaguely relevant to the topic, Netanyahu's American name constitutes superfluous information at the current stage of the discourse. Once the addressee figures that the speaker is being cooperative, and that he has a specific intention in being too informative, the way is paved for deriving the implicature that the added information is relevant in that if Netanyahu has an American name, he may have an American identity and loyalty. Similarly, in (8b), where Chavkin provides too little information (confirming the prediction about her becoming a musician, but remaining silent on the question of her being a genius). Assuming that this is no accident (or performance error), the speaker is seen as avoiding the second question, thereby implicating nonconfirmation.

---

[3] Note that unlike the inferred conclusion specified above, that Netanyahu cannot be trusted, the background assumptions leading to this inference are not spelled out not because the speaker wants to be indirect about them, but because he doesn't want to articulate that which can be more easily inferred (the efficiency motivation alluded to before).

Ironical interpretations are more often than not implicatures generated because Quality (truthfulness) has been flouted:

(9)   S: I'm going upstairs now to the regional committee's office . . . to see
                what's going on. **Only nine years** they've had it, no less ((it = S's
                application for a building permit)).   (Lotan 1990: 4)

Obviously, for a builder, as S is, to wait nine years to get a building permit is not a short time. He doesn't really mean '**only** nine years,' which conventionally implicates that one would have expected it to take longer. Since Quality was breached, but the speaker is taken as cooperative, he is taken to intend to implicate something, in this case, that he means quite the opposite of a short, negligible waiting time: nine years is much too long for the committee to delay its decision about a building permit.

Next, the following is a case where relevance is flouted, the speaker, a job candidate anxious to get the job, generating an implicature, which renders her reply relevant after all (and see again (1a)):

(10)   Boss: You have small children. How will you manage long hours?
           HD: I have a mother.   (Originally Hebrew, June 14, 1996)

Surely, the fact that HD has a mother does not seem a relevant answer to the boss's question about how she will be able to stay at work after regular hours. But since we assume that HD is cooperative, we see the flouting as an indication that she is generating an implicature, in this case, that 'her mother will take care of her children when she needs to stay late at work.'[4]

Manner violations too can serve as a basis for implicature generation, as can be seen in (11a):

(11) a.   Let us look at the **racial, or rather, racist** themes in the argument for
           population control.
                     (Pohlman, *Population: A clash of prophets*; Du Bois, 1974; ex. 8)
     b.   ~Let us look at the **racist** themes in the argument for population control.

(11a) is a case of a repair, where the speaker corrects himself. Supposedly, he said *racial* when he really meant *racist*. When we compare the original (a) version with the contrived (b) version, it's quite clear that (a) is not as brief as (b). Now, in spontaneous conversation, we might see this as a performance error, and not attribute any significance (implicatures) to the repair. But since the example is taken from a carefully edited written source, argues Du Bois (1974), we cannot ignore the fact that the writer here chose the longer over the shorter version. We then attribute to the writer additional implicated interpretations, perhaps that he is not comfortable in asserting an unmitigated version of his strong term (*racist*).

---

[4] We are here glossing over the need to access just the right contextual assumptions for generating the intended implicature. For example, in the case of (10) one could theoretically render HD's utterance relevant by assuming that her mother will come to replace her at work when she has to work late. Of course, this is not what she implicates.

Or, consider the following example. Readers are advised that the Hebrew counterpart of 'lower one's profile' has a very salient collocational meaning: 'get a lower military health rating from a doctor (so as to avoid serving in a fighting unit in the army)':

(12)   bou   le=horid   profil!
        come:2PL   to=lower   profile!
        'Come lower your profile!'
                              (Hebrew, ad for Gym Center in Tel Aviv, summer 2005)

The salient interpretation (a lower health rating) does not make any sense in a gym ad, however. If anything, one would expect to get a higher health profile following workouts at the gym. In order to see the ad as relevant, we have to re-process the utterance, and come up with a different interpretation, that the profile we need to reduce (flatten, rather) is our body profile, our fat etc., not our army health rating. So the writers here use an ambiguous term, whose automatically accessible interpretation ('Lower your military health rating') is precisely the one not intended by them. Note, moreover, that the intended reading ('Come get in shape') is rather difficult to arrive at actually, since it's not simply the literal, compositional meaning of the expression used. (12) manifests an innovative, unconventional use. Just as in English, in Hebrew too we routinely use 'profile' to denote specifically one's facial (rather than body) profile. Why not say then something like 'Come get in shape/ reduce your weight' instead, either one of which is as short, but much clearer and easier to process? The addressors here clearly flout the Manner maxim. It's not in vain, of course. The surprising interpretative change we suddenly realize we need to perform is an added aesthetic effect here (as it is in some jokes). It's hard to explicate this implicature in conceptual terms. Laurence Horn (p.c.) proposes something like, "We're so clever – notice how we got you to misprocess the utterance before forcing you into the correct analysis." Be that as it may, it's clear that (12) has an added value over a straightforward 'Come get in shape,' and this added pragmatic effect justifies the flouting of the Manner maxim. In sum, conversational implicatures are often generated when the encoded meaning seems to violate some Gricean maxim. They then render the speaker cooperative after all. We cannot overestimate the important role of inferences in creating coherent discourses.

1.3   Distinguishing between codes and inferences

Now, so far we've taken codes and inferences simply in their pretheoretical sense. In fact, this is not too different from the way we will use the terms in this book. A linguistic phenomenon is governed by a code if the form–function correlation involved is **conventional** rather than **derived** by a plausible inference/implicature, based on the relevant context. In the latter case it is pragmatic. But actually, we should first understand why we need to draw this distinction (section 1.3.1). We then discuss how to apply the code/inference distinction (section 1.3.2).

1.3.1   Why distinguish codes from inferences? ▓▓▓▓▓▓▓▓▓▓▓▓▓▓

If both codes and inferences are subject to the same cooperative principle, as we've seen above, why do linguists insist on distinguishing between the two? The claim is that grammatical and pragmatic competencies involve different cognitive processes, which in turn entail different discourse roles. For example, both decoding and inferring are required in interpreting ambiguous expressions. But the processes are quite different. The addressee first needs to access all the linguistic meanings of the ambiguous word, e.g. (i) 'round object . . .' and (ii) 'dancing party' for *ball*, a decoding process, and only then can he select the one appropriate sense intended by the speaker in the specific context, relying on pragmatic inferencing. The same is true for cases where we need to construct implicit and/or innovative interpretations based on the coded meaning and contextual assumptions (e.g. in cases of novel metaphors and ironies). There is ample psycholinguistic evidence for the distinction between coded and inferred meanings, between the working of lexical accessing and the working of inferences based on contextual assumptions (see Giora, 1997; Swinney, 1979). But it is not just psycholinguistically that we detect this distinction. Natural language interactions too testify to the very same distinction between the coded and the inferred. We have noted above that communication efficiency and a special discourse status motivate our relying on implicatures rather than only on codes in order to convey our messages. What is it that characterizes inferences?[5]

The most important feature of inferences is that they are implicit. Being implicit, they function differently from explicitly stated messages (see (8) again). Since they are not explicit, they can always be denied or canceled, that is, the speaker is not necessarily committed to their content. The point is that this noncommittal need not even be marked, and is not perceived as self-contradiction on the speaker's part. Consider the following. In each case, some cancellation is involved. Not surprisingly, in each it's an implicit aspect of the interpretation that is canceled:

(13) a.   On Tuesday night, host Jim Lehrer asked Gen. Myers: "Do you consider Iraq a success from your point of view?" The general replied: "I do **now**, I do. I mean, **I don't know why I said now. I do, absolutely**; **I think it's a success**"

(www.truthout.org/docs2005/071305A.shtml)

b.   W: So you baked this with the chicken?
M: Well,
    Separately.
W: I meant in the same oven.   (Aug. 9, 2006)

Myers' initial response (*I do now* in (13a)) implicates that he didn't think so in the past (*now* constitutes too much information), and by implication that he may not consider the situation in Iraq such a great success. He hastens to cancel this

---

[5] Throughout this book, unless specified otherwise, the term *inferences* means specifically 'pragmatic inferences.'

implicature. And consider (13b), where the relevant inference concerns what it means to *bake this* (potato dumplings) *with the chicken*. M took it to mean 'bake the two **in the same pan**.' This is why she intends W to infer from her *separately* that she baked them in separate pans. W explains that he meant that M baked them at the same time, in the same oven, but not necessarily in the same pan. The inference drawn by M is rather easily canceled here with no feeling that W's first utterance, for which he asks for confirmation, is false.

Other characteristics distinguishing conversational implicatures from encoded meaning according to Grice are separateness from the basic, explicit meaning ('what is said'), nondetachability, calculability, and indeterminacy. Consider (10) again. As HD told her addressees when reporting on the exchange with the boss she cites, the truth was that she indeed had a mother, but her mother in fact never helped her with the children. Did HD say a false thing to the boss, then? She certainly generated an implicature which is false ('my mother will help me with the children'). But her explicit message ('I have a mother') was perfectly true. What is the status of false implicatures? Grice proposed that they have no effect on the truth conditions of the proposition made. In other words, the fact that the implicature is false does not render HD's proposition false.[6] This is so because 'what is said' (the explicit message) and inferences based on 'what is said' (the implicature) are independent of each other.

Next, an interpretation is nondetachable if it's not dependent on some specific form. Under this definition, conversational implicatures are interpretations which would have been generated had the speaker used a different phrasing with a similar enough semantic content. For example, what if HD were to say 'My mother lives right next door to my house,' instead of saying 'I have a mother' (in (10))? Most probably, the same implicature ('my mother will take care of my children when I have to stay late at work') would have been generated (in the same context). This is so because both of these responses are equally irrelevant to the question she is asked, and they lead to the same conclusion when we attempt to see the speaker as cooperative. So, inferences are nondetachable from certain contents, and they are independent of specific forms (except for Manner floutations, of course).

Next, unlike codes, inferences are at least to some extent indeterminate. For example, what is the implicature generated by HD in (10) exactly? Is it, 'my mother will take care of my children when I'm at work late'? or is it, 'my mother helps me out whenever I need help'? It's hard to judge, and it doesn't much matter, actually. Either formulation justifies the speaker's flouting of Relation. Two other features, not originally noted by Grice, but very much in the spirit of his proposal, are that conversational implicatures are universal and reinforceable. To see the first point, note that (10) is originally a conversation which took place in Israel in Hebrew. Yet, English speakers have no problem deriving the relevant implicature from the English translation. This is because no specific linguistic form is

---

[6] See section 7.6 for a somewhat different view and findings.

involved in the triggering of the inference. Provided we share a set of contextual assumptions (e.g. young children cannot be left alone, mothers help their daughters), since the maxims are universal and so are our inferential abilities, speakers of any language should be able to generate the same implicatures.[7]

Finally, since inferences are implicit, they may be reinforced explicitly without causing the speaker to sound redundant. Consider:

(14)   He passed away in the arms of a woman, not his ((wife)).
                                    (Originally Hebrew, *Hair*, Mar. 13, 2003)

First, consider only the first part of the utterance, preceding the comma. Note that even if the writer had not added 'not his ((wife))' we would have understood (by implicature) that 'it's not the man's wife,' because if she were his wife the writer would have said so (it's relevant to indicate the relation between referents). But now, if it's the case that the writer here generates a conversational implicature to the effect that 'the woman is not the man's wife' anyway, why does he go on to also assert this piece of information? Isn't it redundant, given that it is implicated anyway? This is another difference between codes and inferences. Reinforceability, as Sadock (1978) called the ability of implicatures to be asserted explicitly without bringing about a redundancy effect, characterizes inferences, but not codes.[8]

Next, let's examine a few cases where the interlocutors themselves "argue for" the importance of distinguishing between codes and inferences. As argued in Ariel (2002b), only the (coded) semantic meaning can be imposed by (uncooperative) interlocutors in an inappropriate context. Note the following:

(15) a.   A municipal regulation determines that a piece of property which remains **empty** is exempt from city tax for six months. A, a lawyer who has moved into a new office, was astonished when city hall inspectors refused to declare his old office as **empty** because of a few chairs left behind. "What is **empty**," he wondered, "when the floor tiles have been pulled out?". . . . The director of the city income department explained . . . that **formally, empty is empty**, and it's possible to say that even if there is a rag in the office, it is considered **full**.
                (Originally Hebrew, reported in the magazine *Tel Aviv*, May 14, 1993)
     b.   BEN: What are you doing, criticizing me?
             GUS: No, I was just . . .
             BEN: You'll get a swipe round your ear hole if you don't watch your step.
             GUS: **Now look here**, Ben . . .
             BEN: **I'm not looking anywhere!**
                (Pinter, *The Dumb Waiter*, pp. 15–16, quoted from Yus Ramos, 1998: 87)

---

[7] This may appear not to be the case when there are cultural differences. For example, in a culture where young mothers are not allowed to walk on their own at night, the implicature in (10) might be 'my mother will come to escort me home when I work late.' But the universality claim only pertains to the inferential mechanism, not to the background assumptions, of course. The idea is that the implicature is language-independent if it's based on the same content (of linguistic utterances and contextual assumptions).

[8] What is crucial to us at this point is that one can reinforce implicatures by asserting them explicitly. But of course, this reinforcing is also used to generate further Manner implicatures. The repeated message 'not his ((wife))' in (14) underscores the special (embarrassing) circumstances of the man's death.

c.   A: When you come home,
            I'll have the food ready **on the table**.
        B: I'd rather have plates.
        A: What?
        B: I'd rather have plates.
        A: (LAUGH)   (Jul. 27, 2005)

The city hall clerks (15a), and Ben (15b) are not only uncooperative interlocutors, they are downright annoying. They each refuse to interpret some linguistic string (*empty* and *look here* respectively) as it was intended by the speaker. Note, however, that their uncooperative interpretations are fully backed up by the semantic meanings of these expressions. In (15a) the city hall clerks refuse to adapt (loosen up) the concept of 'empty' to the specific context (where *empty* should be interpreted as 'relevantly empty, a few chairs or a rag not counting as relevant'). They stick to an unenriched (strict) coded meaning instead. In (15b) Ben refuses to select the intended linguistic meaning (this is a case of ambiguity). In (15c) B is being playful, but what he does is in principle similar to the noncooperative clerks (in a) and Ben (in (15b)). When A says she'll have 'the food ready on the table,' she intends that the addressee take into consideration the culturally available assumption that one does not serve food directly on the table, and that of course, the food will be served on plates. But since this is not an explicitly communicated assumption, B (a wise-guy speaker according to Ariel, 2002b) can ignore it. He couldn't equally ignore an explicit aspect of A's message, saying, e.g. ??*I'd rather have food*. The point is that while these interlocutors are quite uncooperative, since their choice is consistent with the (or a) semantic meaning of the expression, their utterances cannot be dismissed. So, codes can survive incompatible contexts. What about inferences?

Inferred interpretations cannot be imposed in an incompatible context. Consider the following:

(16)   The goblet (= trophy) is red and it is ours.
                        (Originally Hebrew bumper sticker, spotted Feb. 26, 2007)

A red goblet is a goblet which is red in color. But in this context, red is the color associated with a certain soccer team, rather than the goblet's actual color. The bumper sticker on the car with many positive references to the specific soccer team is interpreted as 'the goblet is inherently associated with the specific team.' Outside this exceptional context, say, in a context where the literal meaning of *red* is appropriate, this special meaning cannot arise, and not even a wise-guy interlocutor can get away with it. We cannot impose a potentially inferred interpretation ('the goblet belongs with the specific team') in a context which is incompatible with it. We can only get away with a contextually inappropriate interpretation if it's supported by some semantic meaning. So wise-guy (im)possibilities provide us with an interactional piece of evidence for the differential role of codes and inferences, as well as with a method of teasing the two apart. The code/inference distinction is not only psycholinguistically real, it is also discourse-real.

1.3.2   How can we distinguish codes from inferences? ▰▰▰▰▰

So far, it looks as though the concepts of coded and inferred meanings are clearly distinguishable. But actual interpretations are not always easily classified as encoded or as inferred. We now come to aspects of the relationship between grammar and pragmatics which lie at the heart of this book. Note that once we assume, as indeed we must, that speakers' use of language makes crucial use of our pragmatic/inferential abilities in deriving additional, implicit meanings, we could perhaps make a case for pragmatics accounting for what is potentially accounted for grammatically. After all, interpretations do not come to us with grammar/pragmatics labels. Hence, in principle, many interpretations could be analyzed either as pragmatic or as semantic. How can we decide?

According to Grice's Modified Occam's Razor Principle, "Senses are not to be multiplied beyond necessity" (Grice, 1989: 47). In other words, we should opt for a maximal application of pragmatic inferences at the expense of grammar (semantics), made minimal. Thus, if we can explain some interpretation (or use conditions) as either a code or as an inference, we are supposed to prefer the latter. The advantage linguists see in such analyses is that they are economical. Since we need to assume pragmatic inferences in any case (accounting for inferences supplementing the codes as in section 1.2 above), if we can use the same mechanism for phenomena which would otherwise require the positing of extra grammatical facts, our analysis is genuinely more economical. The assumption usually is that it is to the speakers' advantage that grammar be minimized, since a big grammar is a burden on our limited memory capacity. So let's consider where we can and where we cannot apply Modified Occam's Razor in order to distinguish between encoded and inferred interpretations.

Contrast (17a) with (17b):

(17) a.   A: Trent wants me to make reservations at the Cattle Company.
            Have you eaten there yet?
           B: No, but I understand it's real good.   (LSAC)
     b.   He is my man **and** he done me wrong
                    (https://tspace.library.utoronto.ca/html/1807/4350/poem35.html)

A's direct question in (17a) is whether there has been an occasion in which B ate at the Cattle Company. Indeed, B answers this direct question (negatively). However, given the background for A's question (A's first utterance), B infers that A actually wants to know whether the Cattle Company is a good place to eat at (an indirectly inferred question). He answers this indirect question too (positively, it would seem). Now, could the indirect question in (17a) be given a grammatical account? There seems to be no way to analyze *have you eaten there?* as (also) encoding 'is this a good place to eat at?' The latter interpretation is too ad hoc and not closely associated with any of the specific morphemes used. Moreover, we can easily account for it as an inference (see again section 1.2). An inferential account seems inevitable in this case.

But what about interpretations which are quite consistently associated with specific linguistic expressions? Deciding between a semantic versus a pragmatic analysis is not invariably so easy. This is true for (17b). It is quite clear that the speaker of (17b) intends us to interpret the line in the famous ballad of "Frankie and Johnny" as conveying a certain relation between the two conjuncts. The fact that 'he is my man' is quite relevant to the fact that 'he done me wrong.' There is a contrast between the states of affairs described in the two conjuncts. *And* in (17b) is interpreted something like 'and despite that.' In cases such as these, it is less obvious that the conveyed contrastive interpretation is pragmatic. A possible account could specify a few meanings for natural language *and*, one of them being 'and despite that' perhaps.

In some cases, then, the main question we need to resolve is whether the interpretation at hand should be viewed as encoded (grammatical) or as inferred (pragmatic). There is indeed more controversy in the field regarding what should be relegated to grammar and what to pragmatics in such nonobvious cases. Should we analyze (17b) as semantically encoding 'He is my man' and 'he done me wrong,' and in addition as used by the speaker to also generate a conversational implicature that 'the fact that he done me wrong contrasts with the fact that he is my man'? Or should we analyze it as semantically encoding 'he is my man and despite that he done me wrong'? Modified Occam's Razor principle supports an inferential status for the contrast interpretation here. We analyze this case, as well as a variety of other cases, in part I, sometimes allotting the use/interpretation to grammar, sometimes to pragmatics.

Here's another case where it's not so easy to draw a grammar/pragmatics division of labor:

(18)   As long as I can remember I have always wanted kids and when we were
            talking about getting married over eight years ago, eight years or something
            I said I'm not willing to marry you unless you allow me to have kids 'cause he
            really didn't want me to have any, **the truth is** they terrify him.   (LSAC)

The truth is constitutes "superfluous" information in (18). After all, Quality instructs us to only tell the truth. It seems quite straightforward to explain this violation as indicating a speaker intention to generate a conversational implicature to the effect that she feels uncomfortable in imparting the information modified by *the truth is* ('they terrify him'). The speaker is only telling her addressee that *they terrify him* because she's obliged to say so by Quality. If so, the relevant interpretation (that the information is socially dispreferred) is pragmatically inferred.

But then, consider the next example, uttered by a bilingual Hebrew/Arabic speaker:

(19)   M: efshar   le=daber im   IM?
                possible   to=talk   with IM?
                'Can I talk to IM?'
            H: **be=emet**,   hi   lo   ba=bayit.
                in=truth,   she not in.the=home
                '**Really**, she's not home.'   (Phone conversation, Feb. 3, 1982)

Now, we could easily explain the use of Hebrew *be-emet* 'truly' here in the same manner. H is providing a dispreferred answer, which she feels uncomfortable with.

She similarly violates Quantity and uses Quality to justify her having to disappoint her addressee. But the problem is that (19) actually sounds quite unacceptable to a Hebrew speaker, as does the English translation to an English speaker. We could perhaps explain the difference in cultural terms, namely, that some dispreferred responses culturally require a different "excuse" in the two communities. But note that substituting *ha=emet hi* 'the truth is' for *be=emet* 'really' significantly improves (19) (and its English counterpart). It seems that the difference between Arabic and Hebrew is that Hebrew restricts such "truth excuses" to *ha=emet hi* 'the truth is,' whereas Arabic can employ a variety of truth-indicating expressions (e.g. *el=saraha* 'sincerely' as well).[9] If so, what seemed to be a perfectly clear example of a pragmatically motivated use of language turns out to be grammatical after all. Each language has selected the expression(s) it allows for this use. Indeed, out of nine cases of *the truth is* in LSAC, seven were used as in (18), i.e. as a discourse marker indicating the unwelcome status of the information imparted by the speaker. So it looks as if the expression is actually grammaticized for the special use in English too (the two other cases are not used as discourse markers, and are probably intoned quite differently). The gradual development of inferred interpretations into fully semantic interpretations provides additional cases which are not easy to classify as grammar versus as pragmatic. We address the question of grammaticization/semanticization in part II.

Summing up our assumptions so far, the most important differences between codes and inferences are that the former are explicit, truth-conditionally relevant, and uncancelable, while the latter are implicit, truth-conditionally irrelevant, and cancelable. Inferences have a variety of important roles in interpreting discourse. First, they serve as background assumptions we need to access in order to properly engage in conversation. These are assumptions the speaker intends the addressee to rely on while processing her utterances, and it is primarily communication efficiency which determines that they be implicated rather than asserted. Such implicatures save on the planning of verbalization as well as on articulation. Second, when implicatures constitute a relevant nonbackground point conveyed by the speaker, their advantage is precisely the fact that they are indirect, not quite determinate, nontruth conditional and cancelable (recall (8)–(13)). They enable speakers to imply things they don't feel comfortable taking full responsibility for, and they let speakers get away with meaning cancellations.[10] But, as we see in section 1.4 (and more so in chapters 2 and 3), not all interpretations fit neatly within this Gricean classification. What if some inference is hard to disentangle from the semantic meaning of the sentence? What if it is truth-conditionally relevant? What if it quite routinely accompanies a specific form? What if it is theoretically inferable but is directly accessed in fact? Researchers don't necessarily agree on how to analyze such "nonprototypical" inferences. It is these types of interpretations that we focus on in this book. We introduce the important types in section 1.4.

---

[9] I thank Lamia Eshak for the information regarding Arabic.

[10] Relevance theoreticians call the first type of implicatures implicated assumptions, and the second type, implicated conclusions. Their discourse roles are obviously different.

1.4   Distinguishing between types of inferences

Although we only considered above the Gricean account for inferences, we must mention two prominent alternatives to the classical Gricean
account, just because they argue for a somewhat different code/inference division
of labor, as well as a different classification of (certain) pragmatic inferences. Both
alternatives seek to reduce the number of conversational maxims. Neo-Griceans
(Horn, 1984, 1989, 2006; Levinson, 2000a) have proposed to divide up the
Quantity maxim into two, one stating that the speaker should say as much as
she can (the Q-Principle), the other (R for Horn, I for Levinson) stating that she
should not state the obvious. This means that addressees are to assume that the
speaker was as informative as she could be (no enrichments warranted), except for
very easily accessible inferences, which she may have left for the addressee to
derive inferentially. Horn argues that these two principles can replace not just
Quantity, but also Relation and Manner maxims.

Relevance theory (Carston, 2002a; Sperber and Wilson, 1986/1995 and
onwards) is even more reductive. It also eliminates the Quality maxim, and instead
of the other three maxims it offers a single principle of Relevance.[11] The idea is
that communicative acts guarantee the optimal Relevance of the utterance produced. To be optimally Relevant, speakers must make sure that their addressees
can derive some contextual implication(s) from the information they conveyed.
Such implications are inferred based on the speaker's explicit message and
contextual assumptions the addressee brings to bear (neither one alone can constitute a contextual implication). Intuitively speaking, for an utterance to be
Relevant, it must make some point which hooks up with some background
assumptions. At the same time, speakers must convey the intended contextual
implication(s) in a way that is least demanding in terms of processing. In other
words, it doesn't do to just flood the addressee with information. That wouldn't
necessarily constitute a Relevant utterance. Rather, the point made must be
presented in such a way that makes it as easy as possible for the addressee to
process it. Relevant utterances are those that strike the right balance between
sufficient contextual implications on the one hand, and minimal processing effort,
on the other hand.

Now, many differences between the three versions of inferential pragmatic
theories pertain to what we can call the purely supplemental role of pragmatics,
where inferences (conversational implicatures) are clearly external to 'what is
said.' They offer different accounts for particularized conversational implicatures.
We will not go into these differences, since we do not concern ourselves with
clear cases of the semantics/pragmatics division of labor in this book. For our
purposes, any one of the theories can provide us with an intuitively satisfying
account of inference generation. But some differences between the theories do

---

[11] Note my use of Relevance in connection with Relevance theory, since their definition of relevance
is more technical, and does not correspond precisely to a pretheoretical concept of relevance.

have implications for the grammar/pragmatics question. We can then move on to the next task of this section, presenting pragmatic inferences other than particularized conversational implicatures, where Relevance theoreticians and (neo)-Griceans disagree. Note that up till now we have treated all inferences as if they were particularized conversational implicatures. But, in fact, the inferences alluded to above are not all of one stripe. Some are particularized conversational implicatures, some are generalized conversational implicatures, and others constitute part of the explicit message.

The neo-Griceans focus on generalized conversational implicatures, such as the one generated by 'a woman' in (14). One could, of course, explain the inference 'not his wife' derived from 'a woman' as a particularized conversational implicature (as we did above). But, in fact, argued Grice, not all conversational implicatures are particularized. Some expressions, such as *a woman*, are routinely used to generate what he called generalized conversational implicatures. As Grice noted, an indefinite NP, such as *a woman*, is often used to implicate that the entity in question is not related to the relevant referent (*he* in the example).[12] The reason is that we expect people to be informative enough, and part of our cultural expectations are that being informative enough includes notification about the connection between entities referred to. So, since 'a woman' is not as informative as 'his wife (daughter or mother),' but the speaker chose it over 'his wife' nonetheless, we see the speaker as having been as informative as he could. Hence, we derive as an implicature that the woman concerned is not the man's wife (daughter or mother). Generalized conversational implicatures are identical to particularized conversational implicatures with one difference. They are generated under normal circumstances. In other words, whereas particularized conversational implicatures require that the context actively contribute towards the derivation of the implicature, generalized conversational implicatures don't make such a requirement on the context. It is enough that context be compatible with such inferences for them to go through. If so, we can understand why they are generalized. They are generated in any context, unless there is a counter-indication, in which case they are canceled, just like particularized conversational implicatures are. We can certainly envision the following variant on (14), where the generalized conversational implicature is canceled:

(20)   ~ He passed away in the arms of **a woman, his own wife**.

Here are a few additional cases of generalized conversational implicatures culled from the examples cited so far. The coreference between all the mentions of *he* and *him* in (1a), all referring to President Clinton, and the interpretation of 'the daughter' in (2) as the daughter of the chief of staff are interpretations based on generalized conversational implicatures according to Levinson (2000a). These are generated based on the R Maxim (for Horn, 1984 and onwards), the

---

[12] As it stands, this is not quite right, for the woman, although not a blood relative, is certainly related to the man in that they were lovers.

I-Heuristics (for Levinson), which instructs the speaker not to state that which is obvious. "The obvious" is a preference for coreference according to Levinson. The same mechanism explains the generalized conversational implicature generated by the speaker of (17b) in connection with *and* ('and despite that'). The inference that Chavkin is not a genius in (8b) is a generalized conversational implicature based on the Q principle, which instructs addressees to be as informative as they can be. Since it would have been relevant to know (also) whether Chavkin was a genius, failing to comment on this topic is interpreted as noncommittal to it (by implicature).

Sperber and Wilson (1986/1995) have challenged the assumption that any pragmatic inference is by definition some type of conversational implicature. Specifically, they have questioned the need for a separate concept of generalized conversational implicature. Instead, Relevance theory distinguishes between particularized conversational implicatures and inferences constituting part of the explicature expressed by the utterance. The explicature is the **intended assumption explicitly conveyed** by the speaker. Sperber and Wilson have forcefully argued that this message is far richer than the encoded meaning. Explicatures are based on the linguistic meaning decoded from the speaker's utterance, but the latter only serves as a starting point for developing the full proposition (or propositional form) the speaker intends to convey. This development heavily relies on inferencing, since coded messages are underdeterminate (see again section 1.1). Many of the interpretations analyzed above as generalized conversational implicatures according to neo-Griceans are analyzed as part of the explicature by Relevance theoreticians.[13] Relevance theoreticians are in the habit of contrasting explicatures with implicatures, but the more relevant comparison is actually between implicatures and those inferences participating in forming the explicature (there is no sense in comparing implicatures with all components of the explicature, because explicatures include encoded meanings as well). I will call those inferences contributing to the construction of the explicature **explicated inferences**: explicated inferences here do not denote inferences that have been made explicit, but rather, inferences which are explicitly conveyed according to Relevance theory, despite the fact that they are full-fledged pragmatic inferences.

The idea is that unlike implicatures, explicated inferences are inferences in the service of developing the logical form, which needs to be completed in order to constitute a truth-evaluable proposition. Here are some examples of sentences requiring enrichment by inferences in order to derive the intended explicature. All were easily found within a very short section of one conversation (SBC: 028). I added what I believe to be explicated inferences in double parentheses in bold:

(21) a.   JILL: Cause I'm pretty late? ((**getting my period**)).
     b.   JILL: so we went .. to go get .. an EPT.
            . . . at– . . pregnancy test.

---

[13] But note that not all generalized conversational implicatures are reanalyzed as part of the explicature. Some are simply frequent particularized implicatures.

JEFF: [#Yeah].

JILL: [And then] .. we d– —

That's ((= **our buying and performing a pregnancy test**)) why we were calling you last night.

c.   JILL: I took that ((= **the pregnancy test result**)) as a pretty good (H) sign ((**that I'm not pregnant**)).

d.   JEFF: How come you've been .. keeping all this ((= **suspense about getting pregnant**)) inside you.

e.   JILL: I didn't mean to not tell you at all ((**that my period is late**)).

f.   JILL: . . . I think I was in a .. bit ((**very much**)) of denial ((**about possibly being pregnant**)).

g.   JILL: You know me and cameras ((**are inseparable**)).

There is nothing exotic about the examples in (21). Yet, the encoded meaning could not possibly represent all of the speakers' intended messages, those they expect their addressees to assess for relevance, or for truth. In most cases the completions are not grammatically induced (that is, they are not triggered by some encoded instruction to do so), but even when they are (e.g. in the interpretation of anaphoric expressions), they are fully inferential and Relevance-guided (in other words, they are not rule-governed), according to Relevance theoreticians. Sperber and Wilson emphasize that the very same mechanism responsible for deriving conversational implicatures is also responsible for the development of the logical forms delivered by linguistic decoding into explicatures. In other words, the derivation of the explicature is Relevance-driven, a process guaranteed to yield an adequate amount of contextual effects for the least possible processing effort. It is considerations of Relevance which help the addressee make the appropriate choices.

Now, since implicatures are communicated inferences too, how can we distinguish between implicatures and explicated inferences? It is no accident that many cases analyzed as generalized conversational implicatures by neo-Griceans are analyzed as explicated inferences by Relevance theoreticians (see especially Carston, 1988, 2002a). In both cases the inferences are nonprototypical implicatures. If so, our previous question concerning the coded versus inferred status of interpretations is just one issue which needs to be resolved. Given that some interpretation is pragmatic, we will also need to ask what type of pragmatic inference it is. For example, once we have established that the added meanings associated with *and* conjunctions as in (17b) are pragmatically inferred rather than grammatically encoded, we will have to decide whether they necessarily are (generalized) conversational implicatures. Could they instead be explicated inferences, part and parcel of the minimally truth-verifiable proposition? Discussing similar examples, Carston has argued that the enriched 'he is my man and **despite that** he done me wrong' is often the explicature developed from this semantic meaning, whereas for neo-Griceans the contrast here is a generalized conversational implicature.

Finally, some interpretations are merely truth-compatible with what the speaker said. They are not intended by her, and inferred only at the addressee's responsibility (Ariel, 2004b; Carston, 2002a). If so, they should not be represented as part of the speaker's intended message, because she did not consider them relevant enough to convey them. Consider the following ad. The preceding context goes on and on about how, nowadays, you can get everything on the phone, using your credit card. Everything but the credit card:

(22)   For the credit card itself for some reason you need to put on your shoes,
            open up an umbrella and drag yourself to the bank and get it.
                                (Originally Hebrew, Reshet Bet radio, March 2007)

Now, clearly, there are many other actions one needs to take in order to get one's credit card. In addition to shoes, one needs to put on clothes as well. One also needs to stand in line, ask for the credit card, sign for it, etc. While at least some of these background assumptions (Searle, 1980) must be meant by the speaker, and some of them are also somehow entertained by the addressee (how else can we make sense of the events described?), the speaker does not intend to convey them. They do not fall under her communicative intention.

Truth-compatible inferences may even be quite uncooperative. One such uncooperative inference was drawn by Ehud Asheri, a journalist, when the Israeli president said that the sexual allegations he was charged with could not possibly be true, because his wife was in the habit of coming into his office. The president implicated that it would be unreasonable for him to sexually harass and/or rape his secretaries when he knew he might be caught by his wife. Of course, the president intended this implicature to serve as an implicated assumption from which one would draw an implicated conclusion that he was innocent. But that's not what the journalist derived from the president's words (*Haaretz*, Sept. 8, 2006). Instead, the inference he drew was that the president's reason for not engaging in sexual harassment is fear of being caught by his wife, rather than respect for women, morality, or the law. Needless to say, while this is a potentially truth-compatible inference from the president's words, it was definitely not the president's intention to convey any such thing. Uncooperative inferences are an extreme case of potential truth-compatible inferences. Others may not be so uncooperative although they involve unintended interpretations. Such potential truth-compatible inferences are then yet a different type of inference we should consider.

Indeed, under some circumstances, the contrastive interpretation in (17b) may not be intended by the speaker, although it is, "objectively" speaking, true, and even compatible with the speaker's own beliefs.[14] As we shall later see, the derivation of such inferences is not mandated by the speaker, and the addressee who infers them does so at his own responsibility (Ariel, 2004b; Carston, 2002a). All in all, once linguists have established that some interpretation is inferred rather than encoded, they still need to determine what type of pragmatic inference it is.

---

[14] Consider the interpretation of (17b) in a context where Frankie is asked to say the first two things that come to her mind about Johnny. While the addressee may infer the contrast inference, he cannot assume that this was the speaker's intention.

1.5   The challenges of a code/inference division of labor

Our goal in this book is to examine the relationship between grammar and pragmatics. It's important to keep in mind throughout the book that the assumption of a grammar/pragmatics division of labor forces us to tackle two challenges, not one. The first challenge is identifying precisely the code/inference divide, as well as deciding which of the types of pragmatic inferences proposed in the literature (implicatures, explicated inferences) are functional (for which cases) in language use. Such questions constitute a well-established line of inquiry among semanticists and pragmatists who focus on questions of the grammar/pragmatics interface. But equally important is a second question which typically has not been addressed by such researchers, namely the challenge posed by grammaticization and semanticization. These processes, which turn previously pragmatic phenomena into grammatical phenomena, have been analyzed by functional typologists, by historical linguists, and by discourse grammarians. Their implications, however, must be taken into account in grammar/pragmatics analyses. We deal with the first challenge in part I and with the second challenge in part II.

There always are some pragmatic inferences which are in the process of crossing over to become grammatical codes. This does not, however, argue against the assumption that at any point in time, most pragmatic inferences are distinct from most grammatical codes, each resulting from a different cognitive mechanism of interpretation, each playing a distinct discoursal role. The overall picture of the grammar/pragmatics relations that emerges from this book reveals a clear division of labor between grammar (code) and pragmatics (inference), whereby the two complement each other. At the same time, despite the clear grammar/pragmatics division of labor, grammar and pragmatics do meet at the ephemeral interpretative levels, the conveyed meaning and even more intimately so at the minimal truth-evaluable propositional level (what Grice called 'what is said'). This integrative interface level, the most crucial representation for interlocutors engaging in discourse, forms the subject of part III.

One caveat must be made before we embark on our grammar/pragmatics analyses. By assuming a code/inference division of labor, no commitment is made that the language user necessarily represents to herself a complete linguistic representation, say, the logical form of the whole relevant proposition, before proceeding to enrich/adapt it or parts of it pragmatically. In other words, the term code is here used to refer to linguistic representations of any size (morphemes, words, phrases, as well as sentences), which have not been affected by inferential adaptation. This assumption follows Recanati (1989, 1995) and Kempson (to appear), and is contra the assumption made by other linguists, that there must be a purely grammatical literal meaning representation which corresponds to the complete utterance (usually assumed to be a single, complete proposition). The complete utterance representation may very well be a combined grammatical/pragmatic representation in most cases.

PART I

Drawing the grammar/pragmatics divide

Introduction

Using an utterance, whether as a speaker or as an addressee, seems to be a smooth, uniform type of activity. As speakers we have one mission, to select some string of words to convey our message, and as addressees we also have one mission, to interpret that string as conveying that very message. A closer examination, however, reveals that two quite distinct procedures are actually implemented in each act. The first comprises encoding or decoding, the second, triggering or drawing inferences. Codes are stipulated conventions associating specifically linguistic expressions with their formal or functional use conditions. Inferencing is not unique to linguistic competence or signs. It is based on our general cognitive abilities in drawing on various assumptions and deriving conclusions based on those assumptions.

Chapter 1 introduced the code/inference distinction between grammar and pragmatics. It focused on interpretations whose pragmatic status is for the most part not in dispute (conversational implicatures). Codes and inferences complement each other according to this approach, each making its unique contribution to our use and interpretation of natural discourse. Part I is devoted to drawing the grammar/pragmatics division of labor for less obvious cases. Chapter 2 focuses on referential expressions, and provides arguments for drawing the division of labor between interpretations and use conditions whose grammatical/pragmatic status is not self-evident. Chapter 3 too discusses the code/inference divide, but adding another question: given that some interpretation is pragmatic (rather than grammatical), what pragmatic status should it receive? As we shall see, some interpretations are implicated, some are explicated, and yet others are only potential truth-compatible inferred interpretations.

2   Distinguishing the grammatical and the extragrammatical: referential expressions

The code/inference definition for the grammar/pragmatics divide places quite a few so-called pragmatic phenomena on the grammar side of the fence. Whenever we observe a conventional correlation between some form and some function we classify the interpretation or use conditions involved as encoded (see also Ariel, forthcoming; Prince, 1988). Whether the function is truth-conditionally relevant or not is immaterial. (This is in sharp contrast with the Gricean classification of conventional implicatures as pragmatic.) But how do we establish that the association at hand is conventional? How can we tell that some interpretation is an inference? Cases where functions can be inferred are pragmatic; cases where inference cannot be invoked must be stipulated as grammatical. But, as will become clear in chapter 2, at least in some cases, it is far from trivial to determine whether the form–function association at hand is conventional or inferred. Even the fact that we can derive some interpretation as an inference does not mean that inferring is actually the means by which interlocutors arrive at the relevant interpretation. Part II later provides an explanation for this phenomenon: recurrent inferences may (gradually) turn into codes. This means that there are bound to be borderline cases.

Referential expressions, mostly definite descriptions and pronouns, have been chosen as subject matter for addressing these questions in chapter 2. We shall discuss three phenomena pertaining to referring expressions. Regarding the first one, presuppositions (section 2.1), the literature has been divided about assigning it grammatical (semantic) versus pragmatic status. We will see that some aspects of the use of presuppositions are semantic, others, pragmatic. A second phenomenon we will discuss, choices among certain referring expressions, would appear to be pragmatic, since it seems that we can explain it by reference to extralinguistic principles (section 2.2). Nonetheless, we will review arguments that a grammatical convention is (also) involved. Other distributional phenomena, Preferred Argument Structure constraints and register-specific referring expressions, might seem likely candidates for conventional grammatical restrictions, but an argument will be made that (for the most part) they are not conventional, and not even pragmatic (section 2.3). Taken together, the three types of case studies teach us that there is no predicting ahead of time whether some putative form–function correlation is encoded, inferred, or neither encoded nor inferred. It takes a detailed analysis to determine whether some meaning and/or distributional pattern is grammatical or extragrammatical.

2.1   Code or inference? Existential presuppositions of definite descriptions

Consider the interpretation of the definite description *the queen* in the following:

(1) a.   **The queen** is bald.   (*Weekend Post*, Aug. 5, 2000)
      b.   ~**The queen** is not bald.

Intuitively, the original (1a) and its negation in (1b) differ on the ascription of baldness to the queen, but not regarding the existence of the queen, which is taken for granted in both utterances. In fact, it's not clear how we could even interpret and assign a truth value to either proposition without assuming as a precondition that there exists a queen (Strawson, 1950, 1964/1974). This is the intuition that philosophers and linguists have sought to explain under the concept of presupposition of definite descriptions. Some researchers reasoned that the presupposed assumption must be part of a common ground between the interlocutors. Let us call this the context satisfaction definition.[1] Others conceptualized the interpretation as an interlocutors' commitment to the truth of the existential assumption. Let us call this the commitment definition. For most cases, either conceptualization is appropriate, for both conditions are simultaneously met. Thus, both examples in (1) seem to be used when the interlocutors share a context where 'the queen' is identifiable, and moreover, they believe she exists.

Researchers have in fact tended to identify Givenness in context (the context satisfaction requirement) with commitment to the truth of the existential belief, assuming that if some assumption forms part of the interlocutors' common ground, it must also be a belief they are committed to. This identification seems justified in many cases (see (1) again), but not in all cases. Once researchers discovered a dissociation between the two, they tended to address themselves to one of these aspects, mostly to the commitment aspect, rather than to the context satisfaction aspect. As we see below, this had implications for the semantics/pragmatics divide regarding presuppositional interpretations. Most researchers now draw a semantics/pragmatics line between presuppositional interpretations in affirmative sentences versus in negative (and other types of) sentences.[2] Presuppositional interpretations are said to be semantic in the former, but pragmatic in the latter.

---

[1] What it means for a piece of information to be part of the common ground, or for interlocutors to share a "cognitive file" (Du Bois, 1980, 2003; Heim, 1983a) is a notoriously difficult question (e.g. Abbott, 2000, 2004; Clark and Marshall, 1981), which I make no attempt to address here (but see section 2.1.2 below). I will refer to this condition interchangeably as context satisfaction, Givenness, and identifiability. These are all terms used in the literature on presuppositions and/or definite reference.

[2] See Atlas and Levinson (1981), Grice (1981), Horn (1985), Kempson (1975), Levinson (1983), Sperber and Wilson (1986/1995), Wilson (1975), Wilson and Sperber (1979), and Carston (1988, 1998b).

Section 2.1.1 discusses the semantics–pragmatics division of labor according to commitment/cancellation approaches, and section 2.1.2 focuses on context satisfaction approaches to presupposition. Section 2.1.3 presents a code/inference division within the interpretations associated with presuppositions, i.e. between the Givenness (context satisfaction) aspect and the commitment aspect of presupposed interpretations. As we shall see, the first is best seen as semantic, the second as pragmatic. But first, a short introduction to the topic is in order.

Originally, presuppositional phenomena received a unified semantic analysis. Based on intuitions about examples such as (1), Frege (1892) and following him, Strawson (1950, 1964/1974), argued that a presupposition is a proposition which is entailed by another proposition, as well as by its negation. As we saw in (1), both the affirmative and the negative statement entail the existence of the entity referred to by the definite description they contain. If so, entailment cannot be the right concept for the relation between propositions containing definite descriptions and the existential assumption associated with them. Rather, a special semantic relation was defined, that of presupposition, according to which the existential assumption is entailed by both the proposition expressed and its negative and interrogative variants (this is Keenan's 1971 definition of presupposition). Indeed, all the negative sentences containing definite descriptions in subject position in SBC (436 cases) confirm these intuitions. The referents of all of these are assumed to exist despite the negative marker.[3] Here are two typical examples:

(2) a.   JOE: (H) **their debt to income** (THROAT) is**n't** a problem,
                .. the,
                (H) uh,
                .. problem as I see it is,   (SBC: 014)
    b.   HAROLD: .. **the bottom ones** [don**'t** have flat noses either].
           PETE: [That's #true they all have b– —
                they all have big] noses.   (SBC: 002)

As the discourses following the two definite descriptions show, only the predicate is denied as holding true of the subject in (2a) and (2b). The referents of the subjects (*their debt ...*, *the bottom ones*) are not affected by negation. The same applies to questions (3). Montoya does not go on to question or deny the existence of the black community:

(3)   MONTOYA: ... Is **the Black community** less powerful today,

                                              (SBC: 012)

In fact, even when we have two potential "cancellation devices" (i.e. expressions indicating a lack of speaker commitment, such as *not* and *if*) in the same clause, the tendency is to still presuppose the existence of the referent of the definite description:[4]

---

[3] I did not, however, systematically check contracted negatives (*n't*). There were 1,258 of those.
[4] Indeed, see Carrel and Richter (1981), where subjects tended to confirm the preservation of presuppositions, even when the assumptions were absurd (e.g. *Randy's talking plant*) or "canceled" – see below.

(4)   CAROLYN: .. #You #mean because .. **if** ... **the people** do**n't** vote,

(SBC: 012)

Presupposed interpretations seem "immune" to negation (and other embeddings), then. But now, consider the following, where the existential assumption does not remain intact under negation:

(5)   The residents also do not run to **the shelters** every time a bombing starts, simply because **there are no shelters** in their villages.

(Originally Hebrew, *Haaretz*, Oct. 27, 1995)

(5) poses a problem for semantic analyses. The writer in (5) is not committed to the existence of shelters. This means that an encoded interpretation, the "presupposition," is somehow canceled. In order to maintain the semantic presuppositional analysis, special cancellation mechanisms had to be posited to make sure that the interlocutors of sentences such as (5) are not seen as assuming the existence of shelters in the relevant villages. These mechanisms had to be semantic, rather than pragmatic, because pragmatic inferences may not cancel semantic meanings.

Karttunen (1973) was the first to devise such a cancellation mechanism. Briefly, Karttunen classified linguistic contexts into three types. "Holes" (e.g. factive predicates such as *regret*) let presuppositions survive (i.e. become presuppositions of the sentence as a whole). Here's a case in point, where the presupposition that 'you have done something' remains when embedded under *regret*, a factive verb:

(6)   A: Then afterwards did you **regret what you'd done**?
             B: No. I haven't yet.   (LSAC)

"Plugs" (e.g. verbs of saying) block all presuppositions (so that they do not form presuppositions of the sentence as a whole). These are cases of canceled presuppositions. Note that the speaker of (7a) could (potentially) go on to utter (b), where the existential presupposition is canceled:

(7) a.   And they **said** that they would give **the records** to me but the thing is (LSAC)
    b.   ~ there are no records.

"Filters" (e.g. conditional sentences) behave either as "holes" or as "plugs," depending on various conditions which need not concern us here.

Crucially, negation is semantically ambiguous between internal and external readings (Karttunen and Peters, 1979). Internal negation typically only denies that the predicate holds of the subject, which, if definite, is taken to still be presupposed. It is a "hole," then. In (2b) above, where negation is taken to be internal, 'the bottom ones' are "presupposed" under negation, and only their 'having flat noses' is denied. The example in (5), however, is said to involve external negation, which behaves as a "plug," canceling the existential presupposition concerning the shelters. The idea was, then, that presuppositions survive unless they are explicitly/semantically canceled. It soon turned out, however, that these cancellation mechanisms are not (only) semantic (see especially Gazdar, 1979; Liberman, 1973). They may be pragmatic.

Faced with the problem of presuppositions (assumed to be semantic) sometimes canceled pragmatically, researchers adopted one of two options. One solution was to abandon the Frege–Strawson intuition and adopt Russell's (1905) proposal according to which the negatives (1b) and (5) do not entail any existential assumptions. If so, canceled presuppositions cases do not involve the defeat of semantic presuppositions by pragmatic interpretations after all. This line was adopted by the researchers in section 2.1.1. Alternatively, one could try to hold on to the original intuition. This was the line adopted by the approaches in section 2.1.2.

2.1.1   Focusing on commitment

Most of the research on presuppositions has focused on the question of the commitment aspect of presuppositions. Linguists took it upon themselves to account for when the existential assumption associated with definite descriptions is or is not attributable to the interlocutors.[5] If the cancellation of a commitment to the existential assumption is sometimes pragmatic, assigning (all) presuppositions a semantic status cannot be right. Semantic meanings should not be cancelable by pragmatic inferences. Nonstable presuppositions must therefore be relegated to pragmatics. However, if some defined subset of presuppositions are stable (i.e. noncancelable), then those presuppositions can be seen as semantic entailments. Kempson (1975), Wilson (1975), Atlas and Levinson (1981), Grice (1981), Levinson (1983), Sperber and Wilson (1986/1995), Horn (1985, 1989), and Carston (1988, 2002a) all reduce presuppositions in affirmative sentences to semantic entailments (as Russell, 1905 had proposed), because they are stable in that context. But presuppositions in negative sentences are reduced to pragmatic inferences, since they are not stable. Indeed, it seems that affirmative sentences always presuppose their existential assumptions, whereas negative sentences do so only in the majority of cases. As pragmatic inferences, of course, their "unstable" behavior regarding interlocutors' commitment in negative sentences can naturally be accounted for.

Consider affirmative sentences first. According to these analyses, the existential assumption is entailed, and indeed, if (1a) were to be denied later, by adding *but in fact there is no queen*, a contradiction would result. This is what is expected of an entailed interpretation, so the analysis explains well why presuppositions are consistently read off affirmative sentences. Now, assuming that the existence assumption is entailed by affirmative sentences means that by definition it cannot be entailed by the corresponding negative and interrogative utterances, since negations and interrogatives (potentially) deny all entailments. Since (5) shows that such a denial is acceptable in negative sentences, an entailment analysis for the existential assumption restricted to affirmative statements is only appropriate. Still, this could not be the whole story. While their semantic analysis eliminates presuppositions in negative sentences, the modern researchers who argue against a semantic concept of presupposition are well aware that in the overwhelming majority of cases, the existential assumptions associated with definite descriptions

---

[5] In fact, the discussions in the literature are more general, but we here focus on definite descriptions.

remain intact in negative and interrogative contexts. They have therefore offered various pragmatic accounts for the prevalent reading in which the existential assumption is preserved under negation. Grice (1981) argues that the existential implication is conversationally implicated in negative sentences (this is a generalized conversational implicature).[6] Thus, while the existence of a black community (in (3)) is not presupposed under his analysis, it is conversationally implicated, which accounts for the common interpretation of such sentences, where the entity is taken for granted.

Under Grice's analysis, then, the existence assumption associated with definite descriptions is entailed in affirmative sentences and therefore behaves as a regular semantic entailment (i.e. no cancellation possible). It is conversationally implicated in negative and interrogative sentences, and is then pragmatic. This is a semantics/pragmatics divide which draws a line between the use of definite descriptions in different types of linguistic contexts. Contexts which necessarily sustain the commitment to the existential assumption entail the existential assumption, whereas in contexts which potentially cancel the commitment to the existential belief, speakers generate these very assumptions as pragmatic implicatures (in the common case).

In order to prove that the existential implication in negative (and other) sentences is indeed a pragmatic implicature, rather than a semantic presupposition, Grice has to prove that it manifests the characteristics of a conversational implicature, rather than of an entailment. Specifically, that it is cancelable, nondetachable, and calculable. We have already seen that presuppositions are cancelable. (5) contains an explicit denial of the existence assumption, and crucially, no feeling of contradiction results. The existence assumption simply evaporates (i.e. it does not count as an assumption the speaker is committed to). This is typical of conversational implicatures, but not of semantic meanings, which bring about self-contradiction when denied by the same speaker. In Grice's (8), it is the (implicit) context which cancels the existential assumption:

(8)   ~((Unlike many, the speaker is known to not believe that there is a
            government appointee in charge of questioning citizens suspected of
            disloyalty. She is addressing a very loyal citizen)):
            Well, **the loyal examiner** will not be summoning you at any rate.

Such smooth cancelability is typical of implicatures, argued Grice (see again examples in (13) in chapter 1).

Next, Grice argued that the implicature is nondetachable, because it is also generated when we use paraphrases:

(9) a.   ~The queen is **not** bald.
    b.   ~It **isn't the case** that the queen is bald.
    c.   ~It is **false/not true** that the queen is bald.

---

[6] For variant, neo-Gricean analyses of presupposition see Atlas (1975), Atlas and Levinson (1981), and Levinson (1983, chapter 4).

A speaker using any of the sentences in (9) would implicate that there is a queen (unless it is somehow canceled), despite the different formulations.[7]

Last, Grice outlines an explanation for how the existential implicature is calculable. He first proposes as a subcomponent of his Manner maxim, the Conversational "Tailoring" Principle, which instructs speakers to "frame whatever you say in the form most suitable for any reply that would be regarded as appropriate" (1981: 189). Challenging or denying a speaker's words is an obviously appropriate response, and hence the speaker should formulate her words in such a way that would make it easy for the addressee to deny what she said. Now, whenever a speaker says *The queen is (not) bald*, three assumptions are actually simultaneously being conveyed (or denied): (i) there is a queen; (ii) there is only one queen; (iii) whatever is queen is bald (Grice here accepts the Russellian analysis of definite descriptions). However, if the speaker is observing the maxims, specifically the Conversational "Tailoring" Principle, she would not use such a phrasing unless it was clear to the addressee which of the three assumptions conveyed he is expected to appropriately object to (potentially). Grice proposes that since the first two assumptions above are taken as common ground, only the third is presented as potentially challengeable. This is why the first and second communicated assumptions are routinely implicated in the negative sentence and it is only the third which is taken to be deniable (or denied). Had the speaker expected a denial of either the first or the second assumption, she would have expressed herself differently, presenting each assumption as a separate conjunct (i) *and* (ii) *and* (iii), rendering their separate denials by the addressee straightforward.

One point where Horn (1985, 1989) disagrees with Grice concerns the discoursal status of "presupposition cancellation." For Grice, "presupposition cancellation" under negation is semantically assumed, and should not constitute a special reading, therefore. Horn believes that "presupposition cancellation" (as in (5) and (8)) does involve a special reading. This is supported by the data quoted above from SBC negative sentences containing definite descriptions. Horn then explains the markedness of the cancellation interpretation by attributing it to a special use of negation.[8] Whereas semantically, argues Horn, negation is a univocal, truth-functional operator, pragmatically, it does not have to be so. An additional, pragmatic meaning it has is metalinguistic, in which case it does not have to be truth-functional. Consider the following examples of metalinguistic negation ((10a) is from Horn, 1985: ex. 21a):

---

[7] This argument is less than convincing, however. Note that while Grice is correct in observing that different formulations can be used to generate the same existential implicature, it is actually only different formulations of the negation marker that are involved. The entity presupposed to exist is consistently coded by the same form (*the queen*, a definite description) in all formulations. The existential assumption is then not actually nondetachable as Grice suggested. It is specifically attached to the definite article. Atlas (2004), on the other hand, argues that since presuppositions are reduced to generalized conversational implicatures, the fact that they are not nondetachable is only to be expected.

[8] Note that Kempson (1975), Wilson (1975), Atlas (1977), Horn (1985, 1989), and Carston (1998b) have forcefully argued against postulating a semantic ambiguity for natural language negation.

(10) a.   Ben Ward is **not a black Police Commissioner** but a Police Commissioner
who is black.   (*New York Times* editorial, Nov. 8, 1983)

b.   RON: Why is there a exclamation point.
((PART OMITTED))
MELISSA: Cause **it's not symphony**,
it's .. <ACCENT +symphony ACCENT>.   (SBC: 019)

What the writer in (10a) is denying is not material which contributes to the truth conditions of the proposition 'Ben Ward is a black Police Commissioner.' Rather, it is an implicature generated by the affirmative sentence which is denied (something like 'there is a relevant category of black Police Commissioners'). In (10b), Melissa is objecting to the destressed pronunciation of the word *symphony*, which she expects her addressees to assume. Horn adopts Ducrot's (1972) concept of metalinguistic negation, which is "a means for objecting to a previous utterance on any grounds whatsoever, including ... the way it was pronounced" (Horn, 1985: 134). Metalinguistic negation is accompanied by a special (contradiction) intonation, and is often a response to a previous utterance. Since it's potentially garden-pathing, it is followed by a rectifying clause (as in (10)).

Horn then proposes to distinguish between an unmarked semantic negation and a marked metalinguistic pragmatic negation. This is how he accounts for the fact that "presupposition cancellation" (as in (5)) is a special and rare interpretative step, called upon only after semantic negation was applied and created an implausible interpretation of some sort. Thus, according to Horn, semantic negation cancels all entailments, the so-called presuppositions included (in agreement with Grice). A pragmatic process then applies, which normally restricts the negation to a denial of the predicate alone (leaving intact the "presuppositional" entailment). This is the prevalent reading, under which "presuppositions" survive negation (i.e. the existence assumption is generated as a generalized conversational implicature for definite descriptions). However, sometimes, and this may only occur after the rectifying clause has been processed, another pragmatic process modifies the original pragmatic interpretation of negation here to a metalinguistic negation, whereby the "presupposition" is canceled.

Carston (1998b, 1999), offers a similar, Relevance-theoretic analysis of presuppositions (see originally Wilson, 1975, Wilson and Sperber, 1979). But under Relevance Theory, the semantic analysis of negation leaves unspecified which constituent is to serve as the focus of negation. It is a pragmatic process which makes this selection. Presuppositions tend to be preserved in negative sentences, despite the wide-scope semantic negation which could potentially cancel them, because they are background assumptions against which the point of the utterance is assessed in both affirmative and negative sentences (Wilson and Sperber, 1979). Uttering something like *The queen is not bald* in order to then go on and deny the existence of the queen does not meet the requirement of Optimal Relevance, since the addressee is required to process *is bald* for no reason. This is a processing effort which is not offset by any contextual implications (see originally Wilson, 1975, relying on Grice's Manner).[9]

As against Horn's postulation of pragmatic ambiguity for negation, Carston cites examples with similar metalinguistic effects, which involve different expressions, such as *I doubt that* (where formal negation is not involved). It is not plausible, she argues, that all of these are pragmatically ambiguous between a descriptive and a metalinguistic reading. And here's a natural example to that effect, where B conveys that *most* is an understatement, not that it's not true (A and B are 54 and 55 years old respectively):

(11)   A: 55 and 54.
            Do you realize that **most** of our life is over?
         B: ((LAUGHS))
            (~ Not most). Hell of a damn lot more than most.   (Apr. 18, 2006)

Rather, the "metalinguistic negation" reading results from applying the same (descriptive) negation to a metarepresentation, specifically, to an utterance used echoically. Echoic uses of utterances occur when some aspects of the utterance are not, originally at least, attributable to the actual speaker, but to someone else. They therefore represent others' representations (this is especially clear in (10b)). The metalinguistic feel that negation has in "presupposition cancellation" cases such as (5), argues Carston, derives from the fact that the attribution to another is not explicitly marked, and must be inferred.[10] As is typical in echoic cases, the speaker uses it in order to convey her own stance. In presupposition cancellation cases, the stance expressed is a denial of the presupposition (in (5), the presupposition made by Israelis that shelters are always available where people need them). But such theoretical differences are not so crucial for the code/inference question we focus on.

Under all of these analyses, the semantics of "presuppositions" has been clearly delineated, and moreover, simplified. We no longer have a special concept of semantic (existential) presupposition. Presupposition has been eliminated altogether, by relying on semantic entailment for affirmative sentences, and on generalized conversational implicatures (for Griceans) or pragmatic aspects of explicatures (for Relevance theoreticians) for negative sentences. All concepts (entailments, generalized conversational implicatures/explicatures) are independently motivated, of course, so a genuine simplification of the grammar has been achieved. Note, however, that a dissociation has been created between what seem to be the same existential assumptions, triggered by the same linguistic expressions (definite descriptions). Some of them (in consistent commitment sustaining contexts – affirmative sentences) are assumed semantic, while others (in potentially

---

[9] Note, incidentally, that since for Relevance theory "presuppositions" are skipped over in the interpretation of negation, surviving presuppositions form part of the explicature, rather than an implicature of the utterance.

[10] I would think that Carston is thinking written language here. Spoken discourse might give at least some indication by intonation, should a presupposition be about to be canceled.

canceling contexts – negative sentences) are assumed pragmatic. It is not clear that such a semantic/pragmatic divide is justified. More on this in sections 2.1.2 and 2.1.3.

2.1.2   Focusing on context satisfaction

The "cancellation" analyses discussed in section 2.1.1 are not without problems. First, the status of the existential assumption in affirmative sentences is not really just that of any entailment. Consider again (1a), except this time, imagine it being said to an Israeli about to get a haircut. The existence of a certain queen is indeed entailed, but the sentence is simply unacceptable (since there is no salient queen to be presupposed). How can (some) entailments be cause for unacceptability? It seems that while entailments in general are indifferent to the Given–New distinction, those associated with definite descriptions are not. Next, note the following:

(12) a.   REBECCA: I haven't seen **the other report**.   (SBC: 008)
      b.   REBECCA: ... do you remember **the date**?   (SBC: 008)

Imagine that Rebecca is addressing you, not Rickie. Of course, the sentences are infelicitous in that they assume that you can identify the referents of *the other report* and *the date*. The fact that the non-Given definite descriptions appear in a negated and an interrogative sentence respectively, each providing an appropriate "canceling" environment, is not enough to render the sentences acceptable. Making sure that the commitment/cancellation aspect is taken care of (you don't assume the existence of *the other report/the date*, and these assumptions are indeed "canceled") is not sufficient to secure an appropriate use of a definite description (Prince, 1978). The Relevance theory account is that such sentences fail to achieve Optimal Relevance, but the infelicity involved in these sentences seems stronger than just an infelicity due to lack of Optimal Relevance. It seems that the recontextualized affirmative (1a) and the negative and interrogative (12) do have something in common. All use the definite description inappropriately. The dissociation between affirmative and negative sentences is not perfect, then. Kadmon (2001: 206) raises a related question. How can it be that presuppositions are assumptions which are taken for granted on the one hand, yet they are canceled? How can one cancel something that's taken for granted?

Such problems are better handled by another strand of "presupposition" theories, ones we can call Context Satisfaction Theories. Karttunen (1974), Karttunen and Peters (1979), Stalnaker (1974), Prince (1978), Heim (1983b), and Ariel (1985) all adopt Context Satisfaction theories. Under these approaches, "presuppositions" cannot be canceled (see also Kadmon, 2001). They must always be satisfied within the context of the utterance. Under these theories, there isn't a separate treatment of presuppositions in affirmative and negative sentences. It is then clear why both (1a) (when addressed to an Israeli at the barber shop) and (12) (when addressed to you) are unacceptable. There are no existential assumptions about some 'queen,' 'other report,' and 'the date' which are common to the relevant interlocutors. If so, even the guaranteed potential for "cancellation" of the unwelcome existential assumptions in (12) does not render the sentence acceptable. The assumption of Context Satisfaction approaches is that all presupposed interpretations must form part of a common ground between the interlocutors, because they are encoded.

Context Satisfaction theorists then need to show that indeed all presuppositions are somehow satisfied/Given in their contexts. Cases such as (1), (2), (3), (4), and (12) (in its original context) straightforwardly meet the context satisfaction condition, for the existence of the "presupposed" entities is assumed by the relevant interlocutors. As argued by Prince (1978), where a first-mention definite NP stands for a specific entity for which we cannot assume a prior existential assumption by the addressee, it is one interlocutors can assume to be Given based on stereotypes (such as 'people have doctors'):

(13)   REBECCA: And where were you going.
          RICKIE: . . . Um,
                      . . to **the doctor**'s,
                      . . in San Francisco.   (SBC: 008)

And see (5) again, where, based on the reality in Israel, Israelis assume that every house has a shelter. Note that the context requirement here is weaker. We cannot require that the existential assumption form part of the context. All that is required is that the discourse entity be Given/identifiable.[11] Where the Givenness of the entity may not be derived from some stereotypic assumption, the context must render the referent identifiable somehow. In (14a), prior context makes it clear that the speaker handles horses' hooves, from which one can infer a specific 'hoof,' and 'leftovers' (in (14b)) can be inferred from not cooking the whole fish:

(14) a.   LYNNE: and like,
                      my first hoof,
                      (H) . . **that horse** would have been,
                      . . lame,   (SBC: 001)
     b.   MARILYN: then I'll cook the whole thing.
                      If not then I'll make ceviche.
                      . . . With **the leftovers**.   (SBC: 003)

Lewis' (1979: 172) suggestion that missing presuppositions automatically "spring into existence, making what you said acceptable after all" must be restricted to such cases (see also Abbott, 2000; Kadmon, 2001: 17–21). If Lewis' accommodation strategy were generally applied by interlocutors, examples like (12) (when uttered to you) should have been acceptable. (15a) is based on the attested b example (inspired by Prince, 1978, ex. 21):

---

[11] Hence, definite descriptions may even refer to New entities, even ones created on the spot (e.g. 'the next water crisis which the state will face,' originally Hebrew, cited in Ariel, 1996). Such cases point to the need to define what we here call the Givenness constraint as a constraint on identifiability (see Chafe, 1994).

(15) a.   ~?? ALINA: .. Would you move,
                             so I can come park **my fire engine**.
      b.   ALINA: .. <VOX Would you move,
                             so I can come park **my car** VOX>   (SBC: 006)

Pretend that Alina is telling you about an incident she had on the street, while trying to park. You don't know anything about Alina, so in principle, it should be just as easy for you to add on the assumption that 'Alina has a car' as 'Alina has a fire engine.' Still, only the attested (b) example, where the unknown entity is stereotypically derivable, is acceptable. Presupposed assumptions must be Given somehow.

But can we justify treating *that woman* in (16) as Given?:[12]

(16)   Well if we have another woman Prime Minister in the near future **that
        woman** would have to rise, in the Conservative Party at least, from
        a position outside the Cabinet, because there are no women in the
        cabinet.   (Bill Heine radio phone-in)

Here we cannot argue that the existence of 'that woman' is assumed by the relevant interlocutors. Yet, the existence of 'that woman' is arguably satisfied in the (local) context – the antecedent of the conditional mentions *another woman Prime Minister*. The same applies to (5). Prior mention provides adequate context satisfaction for definite descriptions, so the Givenness relevant for definite descriptions does not necessarily include commitment to an existential belief. It's a weaker availability/familiarity with a relevant mental representation (see section 2.1.3 below). This is why there is a difference between Commitment approaches and Context Satisfaction approaches.

Context Satisfaction theories account well for the unacceptability of some presuppositions in affirmative sentences (e.g. (1), at the Israeli barber shop). They also account for the unacceptability of some canceled presuppositions (those which cannot be contextually satisfied, as with (12), addressed to you), as well as for the acceptability of other canceled presuppositions (those that are satisfied in context although they are not beliefs entertained by the interlocutors). Basically, where the representation for the "presupposed" entity is somehow Given, a definite description is acceptable, and where it's not Given, it's unacceptable. But then, if both the examples in (2)–(4) and those in (5) and (16) are similarly accounted for by Context Satisfaction theories (the context is equally satisfied in all these cases), what's to distinguish the two types of cases? After all, it must be significant that the interlocutors are committed to the existential assumptions in (2)–(4) but not so in (5) and (16). Karttunen and Peters (1979) here rely on Karttunen's (1973) filtering (i.e. canceling) mechanisms (of plugs and filters) mentioned above. A filtered "presupposition" is then different from a nonfiltered presupposition, although both must be satisfied in the relevant context (or they won't be acceptable). So, just as Commitment theories cannot alone account for all the data – they are missing the context satisfaction

---

[12] Note that the example would work just as well for a definite description (*the woman*).

condition – Context Satisfaction approaches equally need an additional component to handle questions of commitment/cancellation.

2.1.3   Encoded Givenness and inferred commitment

We have surveyed two types of approaches to the question of the presuppositional interpretation of definite descriptions. Commitment/cancellation theories (Carston, 1998b, 1999; Gazdar, 1979a, 1979b; Horn, 1985; Karttunen, 1973; Kempson, 1975; Soames, 1979; Wilson, 1975) account relatively well for when interlocutors are or are not seen as committed to the existential assumption associated with definite descriptions. For the most part, interlocutors are committed to the "presuppositions" in affirmative sentences, but not necessarily so in negative (and other types of) sentences. However, such theories do not provide the condition imposed on both "canceled" and "uncanceled" presuppositions. As we saw above, it is not enough to ensure the cancellation of an assumption interlocutors are not committed to. Commitment theories must be supplemented by the Givenness condition, which specifies that the "presupposed" entity is somehow contextually Given. This condition is indifferent to the type of context (i.e. whether it consistently or inconsistently sustains presuppositions).

Context Satisfaction theories (Heim, 1983b; Karttunen, 1974; Karttunen and Peters, 1979; Prince, 1978; Stalnaker, 1974) do offer a Givenness condition, for they require context satisfaction as a condition on the proper use of any definite description. They thus capture well the intuition that presuppositions are assumptions which are taken for granted. But such theories cannot be purely Context Satisfaction theories in effect. In order to explain the difference between presuppositions interlocutors are committed to and those they are not, they actually incorporate cancellation (filtering) mechanisms into their proposals. So, none of the theories is sufficient by itself. Moreover, as we shall see below, both types of theories fail to predict the lack of commitment to existential assumptions in some (rare) "noncanceling" contexts. The conclusion is that we need an account that would combine the advantages of both approaches, and in addition account for the cases that neither of them can account for.[13]

Combining the insights from the two approaches, let's assume that presupposed interpretations actually comprise two sorts of interpretations: context satisfaction/Givenness and commitment/"cancelability." Often, both interpretations are applicable. Such are the examples in (1), (2), (3), (4), and the original (12). In these cases, the entity referred is contextually Given, and moreover, its existence is a belief attributable to the interlocutors. The convergence between contextual Givenness and committed belief seems natural enough, but it's not a necessity. While beliefs shared by the interlocutors are contextually Given, not all contextually Given

---

[13] Note that Soames (1982) also proposes a synthesis between these two strands of theories, but his goal is to resolve problems with cancellations, not with Givenness. Hence, I classify it as a cancellation theory.

assumptions are attributable as beliefs of the interlocutors. Givenness can be established on one of three bases: our general knowledge store, speech situation salience, and the preceding discourse (Ariel, 1985, 1998a). The first two sources involve Givenness coupled with binding beliefs: what we store as our general knowledge and what we perceive as present in the speech situation we usually believe to be true. But what we have heard in the discourse up to the point where the definite description is uttered is not necessarily information we are committed to (see (16) again). Linguistic Givenness (based on prior mention) does not come with guaranteed commitment. All it confers on the mentioned discourse entity is the weak status of familiarity or identifiability (see Chafe, 1994: chapter 8). We do not automatically commit ourselves to assumptions explicitly or implicitly made in discourse (even if we do not explicitly reject them).[14] In other words, Givenness is potentially a much weaker requirement than commitment to an existential assumption, but it's enough to allow for the proper use of a definite description.

But we have to distinguish between +/− commitment cases too. The cases in (5) and (16) above and (17) and (18) below show that we must distinguish between contextual Givenness and commitment to the truth of the existential assumption. In all of them Givenness is applicable, but not so commitment. (16) is a clear case where the definite description represents a Given entity only because it was introduced in the antecedent of the same utterance. The speaker is definitely not committed to the existence of the (hypothetical) female prime minister he discusses. But mentioning such an entity makes it eligible for being considered Given. In (5), the initial presupposing of 'the shelters' is not based on a specific assumption, but on a stereotypical assumption that wherever people live there are shelters (this is the case in Israel). Hence, we do not necessarily attribute a belief in specific shelters to the writer.

In (17) and (18), our knowledge of "reality" blocks our attributing to the speaker a belief in the relevant existential assumptions. Consider (17), where even in the absence of an explicit "filtering" environment, we only attribute a belief in the existence of demons to the protagonist, not to the speaker (the narrator):

(17)   After the death of her mother- and father-in-law she found herself running a large house, with an old servant at her side, who used to say goodbye to her in the evening . . . and so left her alone to face the nocturnal world swarming with **ghosts and scary figures** . . . In order to master her fears she used to walk by the rooms . . ., and at the same time she used to whisper Koran verses that stuck in her mind in order to keep **the demons** away from her . . . She, whose knowledge of **the world of demons** was larger than her knowledge of the world of people, recognized that she did not live alone in the big house, and that sooner or later **the demons** will not keep away . . .
     (Nagib Mahfuz, *A House in Cairo*, the Hebrew translation, p. 8)

Note that we don't simply cancel all the "presuppositions" in (17), just because it's written in indirect free style. *The death . . ., her mother- and father-in-law, the*

---

[14] Indeed, Akatsuka (1986) draws our attention to the use of conditional antecedents (*If . . .*), which encode speaker uncertainty about information just introduced into the discourse.

rooms, *the big house* are all assumed as part of the narrator's fictional world, and not only the protagonist's. Not so *the demons*, though. Similarly, the interlocutors in (18) do not "presuppose" the existence of a common son (the speaker is a man addressing a woman in Afghanistan, the two of them planning to pretend that they are married with children should they be stopped by the Taliban. The man has forgotten the name of their alleged son):

(18)   What's the name of **our son**?   (*Moon over Sun*, 2002/3 movie)

(17) and (18) pose a problem for both the context satisfaction and the cancellation theories discussed above. What is to block the "presuppositions" here?[15] Recall that both theories assume an attributed belief unless the presupposition is filtered (or canceled) out, which is not the case in either (17) or (18). And what's to block the attribution of a belief in God to an atheist referring to God? Or a belief in imaginary figures to a psychiatrist, referring to the creatures about whom her patient is complaining?, asks Prince (1978).[16] Thus, we can't just combine the two approaches, because neither predicts the lack of commitment in these cases.

(5), (16), (17), and (18) demonstrate that at least in principle, there is a dissociation between the two interpretations commonly associated with definite descriptions (Givenness and commitment). The difference is related to the fact that the two don't have equal status. Definite descriptions can be properly used when commitment to the existential belief is not met, but Givenness is. The opposite is not true. Definite descriptions cannot be used when the commitment aspect is fulfilled but not so the Givenness condition (the cases I have in mind are those where commitment is properly "canceled" but Givenness cannot be assigned, as in (12) addressed to you, rather than to Rickie).[17] This is why the code/inference boundary should draw the line between these two aspects of the interpretation of definite descriptions (and not between types of sentences). Specifically, only Givenness is encoded for definite descriptions. The commitment aspect is inferred. The former is obligatory, the latter optional.[18] Of course, all the canceling contexts described in the literature are very useful for interlocutors in determining whether commitment is to be assumed or not. In fact, as noted by Prince (1978), we even have special devices for avoiding commitment to existential beliefs

---

[15] Since (18) is an interrogative, consider the following variant to see that the cancellation theories cannot account for how it is used:

(i)   I now remember the name of **our son**.

[16] In addition, what's to block an implicature/explicature from (8) that there is a loyal examiner? Commitment must be blocked in negated sentences as well.

[17] Note that since Givenness can be satisfied by our general knowledge store, where for the most part only "true" existential assumptions are held, where an entity is believed to exist (complying with the commitment aspect) it automatically complies with the Givenness condition as well. So these cases can't tell us anything about the potential dissociation of the two conditions.

[18] The commitment inference is a pragmatic inference triggered by the need to establish a basis for the Givenness of the definite description. A most rewarding base (in terms of Relevance) is our knowledge store, where the existential assumption comes with commitment to its truth for the most part.

regarding entities we store in our general knowledge store (see the use of 'their alleged son' just above (18)). Thus, the inference regarding (non)commitment is a by-product of the search to establish a Givenness base. If so, a definite description encodes Givenness, and the addressee needs to ascertain that that's the case. Two Givenness bases (our encyclopedic knowledge store and awareness of salient physical facts) tend to come with commitment, but the third (familiarity due to prior mention in the discourse) does not guarantee it. Note that while linguistic Givenness does not guarantee interlocutors' commitment, it does not automatically rule it out either. We rely on inference to determine whether the interlocutors are supposed to be committed to the existential belief or not.

This means that on this account, the commitment/cancellation aspect, so much a core part of presupposition theories, is not actually directly associated with presuppositions. Indeed, many have proposed that the cancellation criterion (pertaining to commitment) does not in fact test for presuppositionhood. What it tests instead is the distinction between foregrounded versus backgrounded portions of the sentence. Wilson and Sperber's (1979) proposal is based precisely on such a distinction (Ariel, 1985; Kadmon, 2001; Levinson, 1983 agree). The reason why negation is not an appropriate test for presuppositions is that while presuppositions are backgrounded material, not all backgrounded material (which behaves similarly under negation) is presupposed (in that it has to also comply with the Givenness condition).[19] So, a division of constructions into backgrounded versus foregrounded portions, while independently motivated, does not fully coincide with the set of presupposition triggers. For instance, nonrestrictive relative clauses, as in (19a), and temporal clauses, as in (19b), (as well as other forms classified as presuppositional in Keenan, 1971) are backgrounded, and certainly do not constitute prominent elements of their utterances to be targeted by the speaker for the addressee to respond to, but, as argued in Ariel (1985: 150–154) (see also Chierchia and McConnell-Ginet, 1990, Du Bois, 1980), they do not share the cognitive status of "presuppositions" in that they are not constrained by Givenness. Witness the following, where the facts that Moses' father-in-law was a Midian priest (for (19a)) and that everything was hunky-dory (for (19b)) may very well constitute New information in the discourse. Nonetheless, were we to negate the main clauses in (19), the truth of the embedded proposition would have most likely remained intact:

(19) a.   DANNY: ... he becomes a sheep herder,
                       for his father-in-law.
                       ... **Who was a .. a Midian priest**.   (SBC: 030)

---

[19] Abbott (2000) agrees with this claim, but proceeds to argue that that's what all presuppositions are. Presupposed material is that which is not asserted. Since she does away with the Givenness constraint on definite descriptions, New entities introduced as definite descriptions pose no problem for her analysis. Abbott's proposal is that non-Given entities can be presupposed in cases where they need not be asserted. What I here refer to as the Givenness condition is then equivalent to her constraint on what does not have to be asserted. I suspect that identifiability is the condition responsible for what I call Givenness and what Abbott refers to as "not requiring asserting."

b.   MARY: . . . and I lit a match to find out where I was,
               and,
               . . . n– **after everything was hunky-dory,**
               . . then I,
               . . . shut the hood,
               and got back in,   (SBC: 007)[20]

In fact, Kadmon (2001: chapter 11) argues that "resilience" to negation is even characteristic of some conversational implicatures (perhaps the ones analyzed as implicated assumptions by Sperber and Wilson, 1986/1995). Kadmon cites an example similar to the following, where A$_2$ implicates that the stamped envelopes are to be used for sending the payments for the bills discussed:

(20)   A$_1$:   Yeah, you need to pay those bills or they'll charge you a late fee and you can't afford that.
         B: I'm going to pay them today ((PART DELETED))
         A$_2$:   At the post office down town they'll sell you envelopes already stamped.   (LSAC)

Note that even if we negate A$_2$, the negated A$_2$ (*At the post office down town they won't sell you envelopes already stamped*) implicates the same assumption.[21] So, immunity to negation (and to other noncommittal indicators) is characteristic of presuppositions qua background material, not qua presuppositions per se.

Summarizing, we must distinguish between a piece of information being Given/ identifiable and being true. While all definite descriptions must meet the Givenness condition, only a subset (probably the majority) also involve commitment, i.e. the existential assumption is considered true by the interlocutors. Crucially, this truth attribution is mediated by pragmatic inference. It is not grammatically guaranteed. Thus, definite descriptions must meet the Givenness condition in all types of sentences. They (optionally) involve true existential assumptions in addition, depending on contextual inferences. Interestingly, in Ariel (forthcoming: 6.4) I also argue for a distinction between commitment to truth and Givenness, based on another putative presupposition. *Not only*, I argue, displays a complementary dissociation between Givenness and attributed belief: it conventionally commits the speaker to the truth of the proposition it modifies (despite the negation), but it is not restricted to Given information. Givenness is only inferred in that case.

The various analyses of so-called presuppositions demonstrate that it is no trivial matter to determine the cognitive status of the interpretation(s) accompanying "presupposing" linguistic forms (we've here focused on definite descriptions).[22] Most current theories distinguish between a semantic status for the existential assumption in affirmative sentences and a pragmatic status for it in potentially "canceling" contexts, such as negative sentences, because their main

---

[20] Note that *He doesn't become a sheep herder, for his father-in-law who is a Midian priest* leaves the relative clause intact.

[21] But for Kadmon this is proof that such implicatures should count as pragmatic presuppositions, since they tend not to be canceled.

[22] Note that there is currently a debate on what are to be analyzed as presupposing linguistic forms.

goal is to account for the commitment/cancellation aspect of the interpretation of presuppositions. We have here seen evidence for a different semantics/pragmatics dissociation. The suggestion is that what was taken as one holistic interpretation associated with definite descriptions actually comprises two partially independent aspects of the interpretation of definite descriptions. Those researchers who have argued for an inferential (pragmatic) status for (some) presupposition are right regarding the attributable commitment to the existential assumption, and those who have argued for a conventional (grammatical) status for presuppositions are right regarding the Givenness of all "presupposing" expressions. Givenness is encoded (and therefore uncancelable) for presuppositions, while commitment (attribution as a true belief) is inferred (and therefore context-dependent). In other words, instead of a unitary analysis for presuppositions, we here conclude that one aspect of the use of definite descriptions is grammatically encoded, the other, pragmatically inferred. What seem to be one linguistic phenomenon (definite descriptions) require both grammatical and pragmatic analyses.

2.2   Code or inference? The referential marking scale

Chafe (1976, 1994), Givón (1983), Ariel (1985, 1990, 2001) and Gundel *et al.* (1993) have each argued for some scalar arrangement of referring expressions in accounting for their use and interpretation.[23] Let us use the following marking scale to represent this type of activation accounts:

(21)   Full name > long definite description > short definite description > last name > first name > distal demonstrative > proximate demonstrative > stressed pronoun > unstressed pronoun > cliticized pronoun > verbal person inflections > zero[24]

Each referring expression on the marking scale indicates a relative degree of memory activation for the representation the addressee is to retrieve.[25] Top expressions are ones used to indicate lower degrees of activation (where the representations are deemed harder for the addressee to retrieve), whereas bottom forms are used when relatively high degrees of activation are involved (where the representations are deemed easier for the addressee to retrieve). The assumption is that memory nodes are not equally activated at any given time. Some are highly activated, others are only mildly activated, and, in between, the range of activation is infinite in principle. The more activated a memory node is, the easier it is to

---

[23] Gundel *et al.*'s theory, however, only views the bottom expressions as graded. The rest are each characterized as encoding a distinct cognitive status (but see Ariel, 2001 for criticism of this point).

[24] Many subparts of the marking scale above have been supported for different languages (see Ariel, 1990; chapter 4; Givón, 1983; Gundel *et al.*, 1993). It was therefore proposed as universal, although, as we see below, some variation among languages is compatible with its universality.

[25] I have chosen to use the concept of activation in reference to referring expressions here so as to be neutral between the different theories above.

retrieve the mental representation intended. If the marking scale is correct, referring expressions specialize for very many degrees of activation.

The relevant question for us is what the status of the marking scale is. Is it pragmatic, or is it grammatical? As we shall see, the form–function correlations specified by (21) are at least partially encoded. Let's consider first why one might be tempted to consider the activation accounts pragmatic.

As a cognitive concept pertaining to mental representations, degree of memory activation is certainly determined extralinguistically. Why are some nodes more activated than others? Why are some mental representations easier to retrieve than others? Degree of activation is the product of a multitude of extralinguistic factors. First, some mental representations are inherently more accessible. More often than not, discourse topics are more accessible than nontopics. Speech participants (the speaker and addressees) are also usually more accessible than nonspeech participants (third persons). On the other hand, entities which compete over antecedenthood with other entities are less easily retrieved, for all competitors are entertained at the same time and interfere with each other (see especially Clancy, 1980). Another set of extralinguistic factors pertains to the relationship between the (mental representation of the) antecedent and that of the anaphor (the specific referring expression). Tighter relations translate into a higher degree of activation of the antecedent when the anaphoric expression is processed. Discourse entities recently mentioned are more activated than entities not previously mentioned in the current discourse, or ones mentioned after a relatively long interval. Similarly, entities previously mentioned in a discourse unit cohesively linked to the unit where a subsequent reference to the same mental representation is made are more activated. Linguistic structures afford different degrees of activation for discourse entities. This would account for the different anaphoric resolutions for subordinations versus coordinations, for example. Subordinations create higher activation contexts than coordinations. Degree of activation, then, results from a combination of activation factors, and the prediction is that speakers select referring expressions based on the (overall) degree of activation they attribute to the mental representation in the addressee's memory. For detailed argumentation and exemplification see especially Ariel (1990, 2001) and Toole (1996).

There is no doubt that degree of memory activation is an extragrammatical concept. But on the code/inference approach, reference to some extragrammatical concept (here memory activation) does not automatically mean that the use/interpretation is pragmatic rather than grammatical. Rather, we need to establish what the nature of the form–function correlation is. For the most part, the form–function correlations between referring expressions and degree of activation are far from random. There is a clear functional motivation behind the marking scale. The form–function correlations in (21) can be motivated by reference to three only commonsensical coding principles: Informativity, rigidity, and attenuation (see Ariel, 1990; Givón, 1983). The idea is that referring expressions are not randomly assigned their relative degree of activation. Some forms are better suited for retrieving highly activated entities, whereas others are better suited for retrieving entities which are difficult to retrieve. The first criterion, informativity, pertains to the amount of information supplied by the expression, as measured by the content of the lexical items included. The more informative the expression, the lower the degree of activation it indicates (other things being equal). Thus, *the other report* is more informative than *that one*, which in turn is more informative than *it*. Hence, these should be used in contexts where the relevant entity is entertained at different degrees of activation:

(22)   REBECCA: I haven't seen **the other re[port]**$_i$.
          RICKIE: [Yeah],
                     I made **that one**$_i$ through,
                     (H) matter of fact **it**$_i$ was just . . over the phone,   (SBC: 008)

Note that as 'the report' becomes more activated, reference to it is made by less informative expressions.

The second principle, rigidity, distinguishes between expressions which more uniquely identify the intended referent versus those which are not as successful in pointing to a single, or a small number of entities. Consider *Pamela* versus *she*. *Pamela* only picks out those people whose name is Pamela, whereas *she* picks out all female entities. *Pamela* is therefore more rigid than *she*. The same applies to *the report* and *it* (the former being more rigid). Now compare *Bette Davis* with either *Bette* or with *Davis*. *Bette Davis* is more rigid than either one, and last names (e.g. *Davis*) are (in the West) usually more rigid than first names (e.g. *Bette*). Note that there is a large overlap between the predictions of informativity and rigidity. Both predict that *Pamela* should code a lower degree of activation than *she*, and the same for *the report* versus *it*, and *Bette Davis* versus either *Bette* or *Davis* alone. This is not surprising, since the more lexical information is supplied about the entity, the more uniquely it describes it in many cases. However, only rigidity can account for the difference between first and last names (*Davis* is more rigid than *Bette*), and between *Mike* and *this guy* (referring to the same discourse entity in SBC: 006). Each pair of expressions is equally informative, but the first expression in each is more rigid.

Last, the principle of attenuation predicts that less attenuated referring expressions (longer or louder phonetically) code lower degrees of activation than more attenuated referring expressions (shorter or less prominent phonetically). Again, this principle overlaps to a large extent with informativity, because, naturally, in order to supply more lexical information, one usually needs more (longer) wording. Thus, *Bette* and *Bette Davis* are not only distinguished because the second is more informative and rigid than the first, it is also less phonetically attenuated, i.e. it constitutes a larger phonetic unit. But attenuation also predicts differences otherwise not accounted for by informativity and rigidity; for example, the difference between stressed (less attenuated) and unstressed (more attenuated) pronouns. Indeed, findings show that the latter are used when a higher degree of activation is assumed (see Ariel, 1990 for references). The same applies to *the United States* versus *the US*, and to *the newspaper* versus *the paper*. The shorter forms are predicted to occur when a higher degree of accessibility is maintained. Indeed, this is what Ariel (2001) found for the second pair. (23) is one such typical example. It is invariably the case that the fuller form occurs initially, and the shorter one in subsequent mentions:

(23)   REBECCA: .. put **the newspaper** on his lap,
           RICKIE: Y[eah],
           REBECCA: [mas]turbated,
                       and then lifted **the paper** up,   (SBC: 008)

Informativity, rigidity, and attenuation seem to be excellent candidates for a common-sensical and therefore pragmatic use of grammatical resources. Lower activation naturally calls for more informative, rigid, and perhaps also phonetically prominent forms, while more highly activated representations can be accessed by less informative, less rigid, and attenuated forms, all more economical. Moreover, the form–function principles of informativity, rigidity, and attenuation do not only motivate the placement of highly conventionalized referring expressions, such as proper names, definite descriptions, demonstratives, and pronouns on the marking scale as in (21). As befits pragmatically motivated principles, they can also account for less conventional expressions, as well as speakers' innovations. Less conventional referring expressions distinguished by the pragmatic principles are the longer, more informative, and rigid *Gundel et al.* 1993 versus the shorter and less informative *Gundel et al.* The former would be used discourse initially, the latter when the representation of the referent is sufficiently activated. Consider the innovative referring expressions in (24) and in (25):

(24) a.   Or consider . . . a central topic of **Grimshaw (1990)** . . .
     b.   **Grimshaw** orders the arguments . . .
     c.   For the verb *announce*, **she (1990: 4)** suggests . . .
                       (John R. Taylor, *Cognitive Linguistics* 5, 1994, p. 232)

(25) a.   **Knesset member Shoshana Arbeli-Almozlino (Labor)** became very
           energetic . . .
     b.   Last week **Arbeli** increased . . ., and on one day even held . . .
     c.   At the Knesset they say that **Arbeli**'s appetite . . .
                       (Originally Hebrew, *Haaretz* Jan. 14, 1991)

(a)–(c) in (24) and (25) are consecutive sentences. Note how references to Grimshaw and Arbeli-Almozlino have a larger phonetic size initially than in subsequent mentions. However, (24c) and (25b, c) introduce rather nonconventional referring expressions. Academics don't cite works by pronoun + year of publication, and we are not supposed to truncate hyphenated last names. Still, the pragmatic principles can account for the pressure behind the creation of these two innovative forms. In both cases, the writers felt that the conventional form (*Grimshaw 1990, Arbeli-Almozlino*) were too prominent phonetically, and therefore unsuitable for the cases at hand, where the entities are entertained at a relatively high degree of activation.

So far the facts point to a pragmatic status for the activation theories. One could then suggest that the activation accounts offer a set of extralinguistic inferences, connecting between linguistic forms and proper contexts on the basis of cognitively motivated principles, rather than based on coded form–function correlations. Reboul (1997) takes an even more radical position, in effect arguing against the reality of the Accessibility marking scale.[26] Her argument is that by relying on Relevance theory "one can account for the use of referring expressions, if one considers the **semantic content** of such expressions and the relationship between their semantic content and their referring ability" (1997: 91, emphasis added). In other words, according to Reboul, the correlations in (21) automatically follow from the semantics of each of the expressions, supplemented by Relevance theory. Kempson (1984) is such a proposal. Kempson argues for a rather minimal linguistic meaning, common to all referring expressions, by assigning a large role to pragmatic inferencing, guided by the Principle of Relevance. Kempson's definition of definiteness (for both pronouns and definite descriptions) is "presumed accessibility." In other words, in using a pronoun (or a definite description), the speaker indicates that the referent is immediately available to the addressee (note that this is quite compatible with activation accounts). It is then up to the addressee to determine the precise reference/reading, by searching for a referent which would support a proposition yielding sufficient contextual effects for a minimal processing effort (see also Wilson, 1992).

In general, activation accounts are quite compatible with the Relevance-theoretic approach to reference (see Sperber and Wilson, 1986/1995: 296). Relevance theory needs to rely on such theories in accounting for reference resolutions. Recall that Relevance theory considers ease of processing crucial. Ease of processing depends on an appropriate tailoring of the utterance to the addressee's needs. The relevant form–function tailoring here is that defined by the activation accounts. Wilson (1992), who emphasizes the importance of ease of processing in determining reference resolution and acceptability, considers the following example:

(26)   ??~ The room had three doors, all but one of which were closed. I closed
         the door.   (Wilson, 1992: ex. 16)

She notes that although one can figure out which door is referred to (presumably the one that was open), the formulation chosen by the speaker of (26) makes the two closed doors more salient (we expect the speaker to continue talking about those doors), and hence the sentence is infelicitous. According to Relevance theory the addressee must not be put to any unnecessary processing effort (see again section 1.3). Put into activation theory terminology, *the door* does not encode a low enough degree of activation for the closed door. The open door is not salient enough to merit reference by a relatively nonrigid definite description. Note that once we choose a more appropriate referring expression (which encodes a lower degree of activation) the sentence improves:

---

[26] Reboul argues specifically against Accessibility theory (Ariel, 1990), but her arguments are also relevant to other activation theories.

(27)   ~The room had three doors, all but one of which were closed. I closed **that third door**.[27]

Here's a similar case, playing on an attested example. Note how the continuation in (28bi) is much more acceptable than that of (bii), but that of (biii) is OK:

(28) a.   All my linens are in my walk in closet on the floor because she has taken over all but one shelf in the linen closet.   (LSAC)

   b.   i. ~Even they are not enough for her.
         ii. ~?? It is not enough for me.
         iii. ~That one shelf is not enough for me.

(29) makes a similar point regarding the connection bertween the referring expression and the antecedent chosen:

(29)   mitbarer   she=la=uvda   she=**arafat**$_i$ noad   peamim   mispar
         turns.out   that=to.the=fact   that=Arafat$_i$ met   times   number
         im **ha=melex xusen**$_j$ hayta   xashivut   raba.   **arafat**$_i$ hitdayen
         with the=King Hussein$_j$ was.   significance   great.   Arafat$_i$ carried.discussions
         im **ha=melex**$_j$ be=et   **shehiyato**$_i$ be=rabat   amon,   ve=nire
         with the=king$_j$ at=the.time.of his$_i$:stay   in=Rabat   Amon   and=seems
         she=ze$_j$ hicbia   **be=fanav**$_i$ al   ha=dimyon . . .
         that=this.one$_j$ pointed   to=him$_i$ on   the=similarity . . .

         'It turns out that the fact that Arafat met with King Hussein a number of times had
         great significance. Arafat carried on discussions with the king when visiting
         Rabat Amon, and it seems that the king pointed out to him the similarity . . .'
                                                     (Hebrew, *Yediot Ahronot*, Oct. 18, 1984)

Since Arafat is the discourse topic, he is referred to with the higher activation marker, a pronoun. King Hussein, the less activated referent, is referred to with a demonstrative pronoun. Once we substitute a pronoun (*hu* 'he') for *ze* 'this one' in (29), subjects choose Arafat as the referent for the subject of 'pointed.' In terms of activation theories, minimizing processing effort means selecting referring expressions according to the memory activation of their mental representations: highly activated entities receive high activation markers (Arafat receiving pronominal reference), entities entertained at a lower degree of activation are referred to using relatively lower activation markers (Hussein referred to by a demonstrative pronoun).

   Reboul's (1997) argument is that Relevance theory has no need for any auxiliary theory of the activation sort in order to account for reference. But how else can we account for the difference between (26) and (27), as well as the interpretative pattern of (28) and (29)? The distinction between the various referring expressions (which Kempson and Wilson do not address) straightforwardly follows from the different semantic meanings of the various referring

---

[27] Note that I chose *that third door* rather than *the open door* to show that it is not necessarily the content that dictates our choice of referent. It is the more informative expression that guides the addressee in his retrieval of the intended referent.

expressions, according to Reboul. Presumably, it's the semantics of the various expressions which renders them (un)suitable for use in various contexts.

But the fact is that at least for some of them it is not at all clear what that semantic difference would be, unless it was degree of activation. One such case is *this*, *that*, and *it*, and Hebrew *ha=hu* 'that one,' *ze* 'this one,' and *hu* 'he' (as partly exemplified in (29)). Calling the first two deictic and the third a personal pronoun does not really provide a semantic distinction between them, unless we are willing to claim that *this* and *that* only refer to the speech situation, whereas *it* only refers to previously mentioned discourse antecedents. Such a claim would simply be wrong: both *that* and *it* only marginally refer exophorically.[28] (30a) shows a (Hebrew) *this* referring to a previously mentioned antecedent, and (b) shows an English *it* referring to an entity physically present at the speech situation:

(30) a.   S: The sum is not right. **This** is not right.   (Lotan 1990: 1)
     b.   PETE: . . . Oh,
                   it smells like that stuff.   (SBC: 003)

And here is an example where the speaker repairs an *it* to a *that*, certainly not because the semantic content of *that* better picks the entity referred to, and not because *that* is accompanied by some deictic gesture. Rather, *it* encodes too high a degree of activation for the representation of the word *awakened*:

(31)   MELISSA: Well,
                    I'll say awakened$_i$,
                    cause that$_i$'s what I have written down.
        RON: . . . (Sniff)
        FRANK: . . . Just watch,
                    He ((the teacher – MA))'ll put a note by **it**$_i$—
                    . . note by **that**$_i$.
                    . . . I really like that word$_i$ Melissa.   (SBC: 019)

So, it seems that we need some activation theory after all. But is it conventional, or only pragmatic? Note that we cannot actually motivate the differences between *this*, *that*, and *it* based on the three pragmatic coding principles. *This*, *that*, and *it* are equally informative, rigid, and phonetically attenuated. But it is still the case that the distal demonstrative encodes the lowest degree of memory activation, and the pronoun the highest. Worse than that, *the* + NP is as informative and rigid as *this* or *that* + (that same) NP. It is, however, phonetically more attenuated, and is therefore predicted to encode a higher degree of activation than the other two expressions.[29] Of course, the opposite is the case (see Ariel, 1990 for findings). Finally, note that different criteria do not necessarily converge on pointing to a high or a low degree of memory activation: *this incredible film legend* and *Bette Davis* both refer to the same actress (in SBC: 005). Whereas *this incredible film legend* is

---

[28] See Ariel (1998a) and references cited therein.
[29] Historically, *the* is a reduced *that*, the reduction brought about by frequency of use. But, of course, speakers currently have no knowledge of this fact.

lexically more informative and phonetically more prominent than *Bette Davis*, the latter is more rigid. Both are, of course, rather low activation markers, but which is predicted to code a lower degree of activation according to the three pragmatic principles? It's hard to tell.[30] (21) stipulates that the full name is the lower activation marker (based on natural discourse data). The referential marking scale is (at least partly) a conventional system, then. This is why, also, rare names, which are more rigid (e.g. *Bardot*), do not invariably pattern all that differently from nonrigid names (*Smith*) in subsequent mentions.[31] And consider the following example, where despite the nonrigidity of the name *Bush* in this context, it is used as if it were as rigid as the name *Clinton*:

(32)   It is a measure of Mrs King's impact upon our society that four presidents – Carter, **Bush**, Clinton and **Bush** – sat before her flower-draped casket and spoke of her life.   (www.truthout.org/docs_2006/020906z.shtml)

The same is true for short names. Note that speakers don't immediately refer to people named *Bea* or *Guy* by name once they have been introduced into the discourse, although these names are as short as *she* and *he* respectively. Since pronouns encode a high degree of memory activation, whereas names encode a low degree of activation, even attenuated names are replaced by pronouns when the entities are highly activated.

In effect, arguments against Reboul's proposal were already cited in Ariel (1990: 83–86). Many referring expressions do not differ with respect to their conceptual content, but they do signal a different activation degree nonetheless. In addition to *it/this/that*, consider name versus shortened name, full pronouns versus reduced pronouns vs. verbal person agreement markers (in Hebrew, for one, all forms encode exactly the same conceptual information). In fact, given that a speaker can choose between verbal agreement markers, reduced pronouns, and full pronouns, there is no reason (except for activation considerations) for any speaker to ever opt for the fuller forms. First, all three are equally informative and rigid, so their conceptual semantics does not predict any preference for one form over another. But then, Relevance-theoretic considerations predict a preference for the more economical form (verbal agreement), since one can get the same effect (referent accessing) for less encoding. Without the mediation of activation theories, which dictate to speakers to select referring expressions according to the degree of activation they encode (their procedural, rather than their conceptual semantics), no (inferential) pragmatic theory can explain the distributional facts of these expressions in Hebrew.[32] Here are two such relevant cases (from a taped kitchen conversation between husband and wife, Jan. 8, 1987):

---

[30] Perhaps a case can be made that rigidity is the most important form–function principle behind the marking scale.

[31] Note that reference here is potentially to two very famous people, Brigitte Bardot and Will Smith, so it's not the case that Bardot's fame makes her relatively more easily activated in this case.

[32] See also the arguments against Levinson's (1991) neo-Gricean account of reference in Ariel (1994).

(33) a.   **ani**   xoshev ...   **an=oci**   oto   be=yom   sheni,
           I   think   I=will.take.out   it   in=day   second
           'I think I'll print it out on Monday,'
           an=lo   yodea ...
           I=not   know ...
           'I don't know.'
           ani   xoshev she=ulay   **ani**   ectarex   li=nsoa   le=london   be=yom   sheni.
           I   think that=maybe   I   will.have   to=go   to=London   in=day   second.
           'I think I may have to go to London on Monday.'

    b.   **hu$_i$**   diber   im   **nubar$_j$.**   **nubar$_j$**   amar ...
           he   spoke   with   Nubar.   Nubar   said ...
           'He spoke with Nubar. Nubar said ...'
           nubar$_j$ haya ...   **h$_i$=pashut**   diber   **ito$_j$.**
           'Nubar   was ...   he=simply   spoke   with.him.
           'Nubar was ... He simply spoke with him.'
           hu$_j$ xashav   kshe=**hu$_j$** ...
           he thought   when=he ...
           'He thought that when he ...'

Note that the speaker shifts between full pronouns (*ani* 'I,' *hu* 'he') and reduced and cliticized pronominal forms (*an*= 'I,' *h*= 'he'). The interesting point is that these shifts are not random. When some entity is highly activated (when it's a continuing discourse topic), reduced pronouns are used. The shift to full pronouns is made at global discourse topic changes, where the activation of previously mentioned entities can no longer be taken for granted. Note that in (33b) the two referents are first distinguished from each other by a pronoun/name distinction and then by a reduced/full pronoun distinction (when the less activated entity becomes highly activated, a name is no longer appropriate). The reduced pronoun is invariably used to refer to the more highly activated entity. Activation degree is a function of the conceptual semantics of the expression, but it is not invariably a transparently inferred relationship.

Another argument against doing away with a conventional activation concept as mediating the proper use of referring expressions is that there are well-known differences between languages which have the same referential forms. English, Hebrew, and Chinese all have pronouns and zeroes, but they use them under partially different circumstances. If the form–function correlations associating referring expressions with their discourse distributions are purely pragmatic, on the assumption that pragmatics (and degree of activation of various mental representations) is universal, such language-specific patterns are quite surprising. Why does Chinese allow more zero subjects than Hebrew, which, in turn, allows more zero subjects than English?[33] Which contexts count as high enough in activation so as to license a zero subject vary quite dramatically among these

---

[33] Note that despite beliefs to the contrary, English does allow zero subjects:

(i)   REBECCA: What did he do.
           RICKIE: Just looked,   (SBC: 008)

languages (for details, see Ariel, 1990). This is an activation feature which is definitely language-specific, and hence grammatical.

In sum, while there is a universal cognitive basis (defined by activation) tying referential forms with their use, specific grammars translate the cognitive generalization somewhat differently (see Levinson, 1987, 1991 for a similar point regarding a pragmatic universal). There is a role for the specific grammar of the language in determining the degree of activation encoded by specific referential forms (see also Gundel *et al.*, 1993). Hence, despite the fact that the coding principles behind the referential marking scale are universal, highly motivated, and productive, based on the arguments above, the marking scale is (at least partially) a coded form–function system. And so, all in all, a set of generalizations which seemed to be natural candidates for pragmatic status turn out to be (partly) grammatical after all.

2.3 Grammatical or extragrammatical? Discourse function and discourse profile

Next we examine cases which could be misclassified as conventional. They are not, however. The main distinction we are after here is between discourse function (part of grammar) and discourse profile (extragrammatical). **Discourse functions** identify all and only the necessary discoursal conditions obtaining when a certain linguistic expression occurs. In section 2.2 we saw that the discourse function associated with pronouns is high activation, for example, whereas that of definite descriptions is low activation. Based on an empirical study of English VP preposing in discourse, Ward (1990) argued that VP preposing, as in:

(34)   As members of a Gray Panthers committee, we went to Canada to learn, and
         learn we did.   (*Philadelphia Inquirer*, Jun. 16, 1985, Ward, 1990: ex. 2a)

affirms a speaker's commitment to a salient proposition which was explicitly evoked (but not entailed or presupposed) in the preceding discourse. A variant construction with *if* serves to suspend a speaker's belief in an explicitly evoked salient proposition:

(35)   It's really too bad that Joseph left, **if leave he did**.
                  (Robert Stephens to G. Ward in conversation, Ward, 1990: ex. 5b)

These discourse functions should hold true in (virtually) every case these constructions are used. Goldberg (1995) has similarly attributed meanings to syntactic constructions which are not as syntactically marked as the ones initially investigated by pragmatists. Such conventional form–function correlations squarely fall within the grammar under the approach here advocated, although they do not involve truth-conditional meaning aspects.

But how can we tell what it is that the form means and/or what the obligatory conditions on its proper use are? In order to argue for some (encoded) discourse function, researchers typically rely on the discourse profiles of the relevant forms.

Whereas **discourse functions** are those conditions or interpretations which must be present when the form is used, (prototypical) **discourse profiles** also include nonobligatory discourse conditions obtaining when a certain linguistic expression occurs, provided these conditions repeat themselves consistently enough. The rationale behind this method is that specific discourse functions predict specific contexts where the form would be useful.

For example, in order to support the idea that e.g. definite descriptions refer to entities the representations of which are entertained at a relatively low degree of activation, and that pronouns refer to entities which are currently highly activated, the distance between the last and the current mention of some entity by either expression is examined (e.g. Ariel, 1990; Givón, 1983). It turns out that the referential distance for definite descriptions is significantly larger than that for pronouns. Reference to topics, on the other hand, is more characteristic of pronouns than of definite descriptions. So we can say that the discourse profiles of definite descriptions (greater distance from the antecedent, a nonhigh ratio of reference to topics) are compatible with and support the claim about a discourse function of low memory activation. Similarly, for pronouns, the discourse profiles of short referential distance and a high ratio of reference to topics are compatible with and support the assumption of a discourse function of high activation. In other words, (extragrammatical) discourse profiles can be used to support points about (grammatical) discourse functions.

For example, whereas above 80 percent of pronouns find their antecedents in the same sentence or in a previous sentence, over 80 percent of the anaphoric definite descriptions find their antecedent in a nonadjacent sentence, over a third of them coreferential with an antecedent across a paragraph boundary (see Ariel, 1990; Givón, 1983). The same applies to reference to topics. Whereas over 44 percent of the pronouns referred to topic antecedents, none of the definite descriptions in these data did. And whereas nontopical pronouns comprised less than 3 percent of the anaphoric expressions used across paragraphs, definite descriptions contributed 78 percent of those anaphoric expressions (data here are based on Ariel, 1990: 18–19).

Similarly, Prince (1981), in an attempt to argue that unstressed *this* NPs – as in *this German shepherd was coming at me* (Terkel, 1974: 366), cited in Prince (1981: 234) – are indefinite NPs introducing New entities into the discourse, quoted discourse statistics that their behavior (i.e. their discourse profile) conforms to that of indefinites (indefiniteness being their discourse function). Thus, 242/243 of the cases in her data are first-mention, a discourse profile which fits with the expression being indefinite, and 209/243 of the cases are later referred to again, another discourse profile which fits the discourse function she attributes to these NPs – introducing a potential discourse topic – see also Gernsbacher and Shroyer (1989), Givón (1992). Other works using statistical data about discourse profiles in support of claims on discourse functions include Thompson (1990), Gundel *et al.* (1993) and Birner (1994).

Thus, if some form (e.g. definite description) is claimed to carry some function x (e.g. low activation) and if x is predicted to manifest itself in certain (but not other) contexts (e.g. large distance, nontopic antecedents), then demonstrating that those contexts frequently obtain when the form under discussion occurs supports the conclusion that the form encodes that function. In other words, discourse functions are often supported by counts concerning compatible discourse profiles. This is where the problem lies. What's to distinguish between the extragrammatical discourse profiles and the grammatical discourse functions, if both manifest statistically highly significant skewed distributions? Why not say that pronouns and definite descriptions encode their various discourse profiles (e.g. that pronouns are used with a short referential distance and/or when reference to topics is intended, and definite descriptions are used with a large referential distance and when reference is made to nontopics)? Presumably, grammatical codes are obligatory. We therefore expect an absolute correlation between forms and functions. Discourse profiles are not obligatory, and hence the statistical correlations between the forms and the discourse contexts are not expected to be as high. But then, researchers examining natural discourse rarely find 100 percent correlations. The question becomes much more complex.

Section 2.3 examines two cases where these questions are pertinent: Preferred Argument Structure constraints and register-related distributions of referring expressions. In both cases very significant statistical counts are observed for the distribution of referring expressions, but as we shall see, they do not constitute grammatical statements.[34] Such patterns may stand for extragrammatical discourse profiles in some cases (Preferred Argument Structure – 2.3.1), but in other cases, they do not even constitute discourse profiles. Although they are statistically real, they have no implication for language use (some register-specific distributions of referring expressions – 2.3.2).

2.3.1   Preferred Argument Structure as discourse profile

Argument structure is clearly a grammatical phenomenon: different verbs are said to have different argument structures, by which we mean that they select different types of core arguments as obligatory arguments (additional, noncore arguments are always optional). Intransitive verbs, such as *appear*, *swim*, and *relax* require exactly one argument, prototypically the S role (an intransitive subject). Transitive verbs, such as *kiss*, *like*, and *play* require two arguments, an A role (the transitive subject) and an O role (a direct object). Ditransitive verbs, such as *give* and *buy*, require three arguments, an A role, an O role, and an I role (indirect object). One would then expect a purely grammatical distribution of arguments in discourse, but Du Bois (1987, 2003a, 2003b) has found a few intriguing discourse patterns, which he termed Preferred Argument Structure. Preferred Argument Structure (PAS henceforth) restricts the information

---

[34] See also the analysis of possessive NPs in Ariel (2002c).

status (Accessibility/Newness) associated with various arguments in the clause. In other words, argument selection is not wholly determined by the objective content of the speaker's message and the grammatical specifications of the appropriate verb (i.e. what participants the speaker is interested in mentioning with respect to which activities, encodable by specific verbs which best describe these activities and have specific argument structures). After we introduce PAS, we discuss the status of these restrictions: should we claim that different arguments have different discourse functions associated with them, in which case we have a grammatical form–function correlation? Despite his robust findings, Du Bois suggests that this is not the case. PAS is better viewed as a preferred discourse profile, defined over grammatical categories, but not reducible to grammatical rules. They are extra-grammatical, then.

The following examples, all easily culled from SBC: 005, are typical of natural (spoken) discourse in very many languages according to Du Bois (see Du Bois, Kumpf, and Ashby, 2003 for cross-linguistic studies of PAS):

(36) a.   PAMELA: **it**'s really interesting.
    b.   DARRYL: **whoever wrote the book of Zen** wasn't dead either.

(37) a.   PAMELA: it's like **it** pulled **me** under,
    b.   DARRYL: when **you**'re reading **fiction**,

(38) a.   DARRYL: **he** should keep **it** to **himself**.
    b.   PAMELA: **I** could read **you some**.

(36) contains intransitive clauses. (36a) has a pronominal S and (36b) a lexical S. The examples in (37) are two-place transitive clauses. (37a) has pronominal A and O, (37b) has a pronominal A and a lexical O. (38) has three-place argument clauses. In (38a) they are all pronominal, in (38b) A and I are pronominal, while O is lexical. Note that given two- and three-place argument verbs, one would have expected to find many other combinations. This is not what Du Bois discovered. According to Du Bois, S is a free position, namely, it can accommodate either pronominal or lexical NPs. But clauses containing more than one argument are not as free.

First, PAS predicts that speakers will not select more than one lexical NP as a core argument. Indeed, all six examples abide by this restriction: (36a), (37a), and (38a) have no lexical arguments, and (36b), (37b), and (38b) have one lexical argument each. None has two lexical core arguments. Du Bois (1987) then proposed the One Lexical Argument Constraint:

(39)   Avoid more than one lexical core argument.

But there's another regularity in the examples quoted in (36), (37), and (38). Whereas lexical NPs occur freely in the S and O positions (see the three (b) examples), lexical NPs typically don't occupy the A position. Based on such findings Du Bois has formulated the Non-lexical A Constraint:

(40)   Avoid lexical A.

These formal constraints, argues Du Bois, follow from the information status associated with lexical and pronominal NPs respectively. Pronominal forms refer to highly accessible discourse entities. Lexical NPs refer to entities entertained at a relatively low degree of accessibility. Reformulated in pragmatic terms, the two constraints instruct speakers to:

(41) a.   Avoid more than one New core argument.
     b.   Avoid New A.

Once the constraints are defined in pragmatic terms, they are far less mysterious, of course.[35] It is relatively straightforward to motivate the Quantity constraint in (41a). On the uncontroversial assumption that NPs introducing New (or, low accessibility) entities into the discourse are harder to process than NPs introducing accessible (or, rather, highly accessible) entities, it is perfectly understandable why natural language should develop such a constraint. (41a) is a constraint against too heavy a processing load, then. But what about (41b)? Why should the A role be selected for the constraint? Why isn't (41a) sufficient? Du Bois does not address the "why A" question, but he does motivate the choice of some predetermined role as target for the constraint in (41b). As he explains, the role constraint, (41b), stipulates predictable loci (the S and O roles) for (potential) heavy cognitive demand. If addressees can rely on speakers abiding by (41b), they know what they may be expected to allocate more cognitive resources for.

A search for all the occurrences of two indefinite NPs, *a woman* and *a man* in SBC showed that 21/22 cases appeared in S or O roles. In the one example where *a man* occurred in an A role, the expression was interpreted generically, rather than as New. And note that Jill uses (a) rather than (b) in the following, making sure that the New entity is introduced as an O rather than as an A:

(42) a.   JILL: We had **a woman**,
                   um,
                   a physician come and .. talk to us,   (SBC: 028)
     b.   ~ **A woman**, a physician, came and talked to us.

Similar motives lie behind the preference for (43a) over (43b). In her last sentence, Alina reintroduces *the guy with the nice shirt* in an S position, even though she had already introduced him. Since she introduced two more guys at that point, the one she wants to refer to is no longer highly accessible (which is why she uses such an informative referring expression to refer to him). She then refrains from using (b), where an entity which is not highly accessible would occupy an A role. She prefers to repeat her assertion that the guy came in:[36]

---

[35] In fact, it is not clear that we need the formal constraints in (39) and (40), for a theory of referential forms (such as Ariel, 1990; Chafe, 1994; or Gundel *et al.*, 1993) is responsible for the encoding of different types of entities in various linguistic expressions.

[36] I take it that (43a) is a sentential, rather than phrasal conjunction, since each conjunct occupies a separate intonation unit.

(43) a.   ALINA: ... (TSK) And these three guys walk in and,
                          (H) one guy,
                          ... was so geeky,
                          ((5 LINES OMITTED))
                          the .. other guy had a real nice shirt on,
                          and then there was some other geek.
                          (Hx) So **the guy with the nice shirt** .. came in,
                          and started talking to **me**,   (SBC: 006)
    b.   ~ALINA: So **the guy with the nice shirt** started talking to **me**,

PAS constraints have been supported by empirical findings from many diverse languages (Du Bois, 1987; Du Bois, Kumpf, and Ashby, 2003). Consider the following statistics (the data are here quoted from Du Bois, 2003a). In Sakapultek and English 100 percent of the clauses examined had at most one New core argument. Other languages too had very low counts of two New arguments.[37] As for the role selected for New arguments, note that indeed S and O are free positions: Ss present New entities in 21 percent of the cases in English and 55 percent of the cases in Sakapultek. The same is true for 40 percent of the Os in English and 79 percent in Sakapultek. Contrast these ratios with those for As. English and French had no As introducing New entities. In Spanish 99 percent of the clauses did not contain New As, and this was the case in 94 percent of the clauses in Hebrew and Sakapultek. These are no doubt very impressive numbers, in fact, not lower than those cited in counts in support of coded discourse functions (see above and below). PAS patterns seem highly robust, and not just within, but also across typologically different languages. Du Bois proposes it as a universal, in fact.

Now, the question is whether the discourse patterns above constitute conventional discourse functions, in which case they constitute part of the grammar, or prototypical discourse profiles of As, Ss, and Os, i.e. motivated and consistent discourse patterns which do not constitute grammatical conventions. Recall that PAS constraints have been found in diverse languages, where common history, areal influences and typological variety cannot explain the recurrent patterns. Moreover, grammatical categories are clearly implicated in the pattern. First, it is only core arguments that are cognitively constrained by PAS. There are no constraints on the number of optional obliques presenting New entities.[38] Second, the constraints distinguish between different core arguments as well. PAS is then not simply a general cognitive constraint against too many New arguments. It is grammar-sensitive. Still, Du Bois treats PAS constraints only as discourse preferences ("soft constraints"), for certain syntactic distributions for arguments standing for certain types of entities. He insists that the very strong generalizations he proposes are not reducible to grammatical rules.

---

[37] There are more cases with two lexical NPs than with two New arguments, because some lexical NPs are also used to refer to entities which are activated, but not maximally so.

[38] Donohue (2006) has recently argued for a one New adjunct constraint in some Northern New Guinea languages, but as John Du Bois (p.c.) notes, these are serializing languages, which can afford to have this constraint, for they rather freely add verbs, which open up slots for more adjuncts.

Du Bois' position is clearly justified with respect to S and O. S and O cannot be seen as conventionally encoding "Newness," despite the fact that practically all New entities introduced as core arguments occur either in S or in O positions.[39] Du Bois reminds us that Ss and Os often introduce accessible entities, so the correlation here is not a candidate for grammatical discourse function status. But this is not the case for accessible As and for the quantity constraint on the number of New entities (in core positions). Here the numbers seem indistinguishable from those of any encoded form–function association: they are extremely significant although not absolute. As we know full well, linguistic claims are hardly ever substantiated by 100 percent form–function correlations when natural discourse is examined.[40]

The percentages quoted above for PAS are then not quantitatively different from statistical findings cited for linguistic conventions. But there is still a difference between PAS counterexamples and counterexamples to grammatical stipulations. In grammatical cases we can often account for the counterexamples by reference to some competing constraint (see chapter 4), or, it might be due to a performance error (as in the case of *most* – see note 40 again). In the absence of a competing motivation, grammatical counterexamples are not felt to be perfectly natural. This is not true when PAS is violated, as in (44):

(44) a. WALT: ... **My wife** would write **a check for ten dollars**. (SBC: 021)
     b. PAMELA: ... (H) **people who .. had .. technically died,**
         and then have been revived.
         ... (H) Saw .. **relatives** coming for them. (SBC: 005)

Note that each of the examples in (44) introduces two New entities in core argument positions, violating the Quantity constraint. Moreover, each includes a New A, which violates the Role constraint.[41] So PAS is not only not imposed in 100 percent of the cases, there is nothing strange about violating it. The examples in (44) are perfectly natural, argues Du Bois. Such findings point to the non-grammatical status of PAS, despite its very high convention-like occurrence in natural discourse.

As Du Bois reasons, reducing every consistent form–function association to a Saussurian sign function (what we here call discourse function) is a mistake. PAS shows that syntax often offers structure functions, rather than discourse functions.

---

[39] Note that in ergative languages, such as Sakapultek, S and O constitute one grammatical role (the absolutive), which makes it even more tempting to claim that the role encodes Newness.

[40] For example, despite *most*'s lexical meaning ('more than half'), there are subjects who are willing to accept that *most* can denote less than a majority, e.g. 50% (10.9% of the subjects), or 49% (9.4% of the subjects) – see section 3.2. Still, since about 90% only accept values above 50% for *most*, we assume that *most* must denote 'more than half,' despite the lack of unanimity about it.

[41] The reader is advised, however, that it was no easy matter to find such examples. In addition, while *my wife* here presents a New entity to the discourse, some New entities are accessible nonetheless (see the discussion of stereotypic definite descriptions in section 2.1.2). Kin terms are one such category. Three of the four such examples quoted in Du Bois (2003b) introduce generic NPs. Indeed, it seems that PAS is better defined as constraining high-activation-cost arguments, in which case, (44a) at least would not constitute a counterexample.

The function of most syntactic structures, especially of unmarked constructions, is to enable certain meanings/functions, rather than to strictly encode them.[42] Some constructions facilitate (but by no means encode) certain meanings, while others facilitate (but do not encode) other meanings. It is not just S and O that do not encode Newness. Even A does not encode accessibility. Each syntactic role facilitates the processing of NPs denoting certain types of entities. As Du Bois suggests, grammar provides an architectural framework for constructing our messages in what we may term user-friendly ways, even in the absence of encoding relations. Extragrammatical strategies, then, can make crucial use of the grammar without being grammatical themselves. Discourse profiles are not part of (the synchronic) grammar, but it does not mean that they have no role to play in processing utterances.

Recurrent discourse profiles, such as PAS patterns, are important for speakers to master despite the fact that they are not rigid grammatical conventions. Being a cooperative speaker involves more than following grammatical rules and pragmatic maxims. One also needs to abide by recurrent discourse patterns. The special strategies speakers have devised for introducing New entities which avoid PAS violations, as exemplified in (42a), (43a), some of them quite routinized according to Du Bois (2003b), testify that PAS must be psychologically real for speakers (see also Du Bois, 1980, 1987, 2003b). Moreover, as Du Bois emphasizes, it demonstrates that what we are used to thinking of as the arena of unconstrained individualistic freedom of choice (discourse) is actually quite regular. It's not at all the case that what the grammar does not exclude (presenting New entities in any syntactic role) is freely used by discourse participants. Speakers do not use the options made available by their grammar randomly or equally. They consistently opt for certain uses of language over others, and we have a tendency to prefer well-trodden discourse patterns, even if they are not close to 100 percent conventions. Moreover, at least some discourse profiles actually turn grammatical. For example, given the accessibility/Newness status differences between As on the one hand, and Ss and Os on the other, it is not surprising to find that some languages are ergative, classifying Ss and Os as one case (the absolutive). It seems that speakers must store at least some discourse profiles, even before they have grammaticized. We examine such cases in part II.

Now, if PAS principles do not constitute grammatical conventions, are they then pragmatic? Are all discourse patterns pragmatic? Under some approaches to the grammar/pragmatics division of labor they are, because any aspect of language use that's not grammatical is pragmatic. But this is not the view here adopted (and see also Ariel, forthcoming: 9.5). Although all pragmatic inferencing is extragrammatical, not all extragrammatical phenomena are pragmatic. Pragmatic inferencing is just one type of extragrammatical work that goes into language use. So, we need to

---

[42] See Goldberg (1995), for many such cases, but see Prince (1976 and onwards), Ariel (1983), Ward (1990), and Birner (1994) for encoded form–function correlations of constructions.

further ask whether the PAS constraints and the discourse patterns they account for are inferable. If so, they are pragmatic. Haspelmath's (2006b) proposals might support such a view. Haspelmath suggests that the role constraint in (41b) (Avoid New As) can be reduced to a discourse (pragmatic?) tendency. The discourse findings regarding the very high proportions of Given As, he argues, follow from the fact that we tend to talk about human beings (and animates), we tend to talk about their actions (hence the A role), and those human beings we talk about tend to be Given. The consequence of these assumptions is the discourse pattern we find. If Haspelmath is right, then this PAS constraint might be pragmatic.

Note, however, two problems with this proposal (see also Goldberg, 2004). First, one would expect the S role not to be so different from the A role in this respect. Ss too are topical. But, as we've seen, they pattern differently from As. Second, the existence of strategies for avoiding New As (see Du Bois, 1980, 1985 and onwards, and following him, Lambrecht, 1984), exemplified in (42) and (43), suggest that not all potential As would just naturally follow the expected pattern (of being Given).[43] It seems that the initial impetus for the pattern is indeed pragmatically based. If speakers wish to assign prominence to certain entities, they repeatedly refer to them (hence the entities would tend to be Given), and they would tend to assign to them a grammatically prominent role (A or S). But, most probably, the extremely high proportions of Given As found in discourse are an amplification of this pragmatic tendency. It's hard to imagine that just about all of our As would spontaneously be Given. The findings are better seen as discourse profiles, initially created by pragmatically motivated factors, but later on followed by speakers in order to adhere to an already salient discourse pattern. It is in this way that a pragmatic tendency can potentially grammaticize, although we have reviewed arguments against assuming grammatical status in this particular case.

Moving on to the quantity constraint, (41a), this too does not seem to be a pragmatically motivated constraint. First, cognitive processing constraints, rather than pragmatic inferencing, must be behind this constraint.[44] Second, again, it's probably the case that the discourse profile, a salient pattern due to the cognitive motivation behind it, has long been amplified, so that speakers now intentionally avoid introducing some entity and predicating something about it involving another entity within the same clause (see Du Bois, 1987), regardless of whether that would have been a strain on the interlocutors.

The upshot of this discussion is that a functionally motivated pattern may be elevated to the status of a salient discourse pattern, which is neither grammatical nor pragmatic, yet followed by speakers as a strategy. More on this in part II.

---

[43] As Haspelmath correctly notes, such claims need to be checked empirically, of course.

[44] Incidentally, Haspelmath (2006b) attempts to eliminate this constraint as well, arguing that if A is necessarily Given, then of course there cannot be two New core arguments per clause. As John Du Bois (p.c.) informs me, this reductive step is unjustified in view of the fact that the same PAS pattern is observed for ditransitives, where there are three core arguments, and both non-A arguments could theoretically be New. His findings are that they are not.

2.3.2   Genre-related uses of definite descriptions and pronouns: discourse function and discourse profile ▬▬▬▬▬▬▬▬

Genres seem to be prime candidates for the creation of discourse patterns for linguistic forms. According to Miller (1984) (and see also Bazerman, 1988; Swales, 1990), genres constitute recurrent patterns of language use, defined according to social acts or motives. Following Biber *et al.* (1999), we here consider any speech variety associated with some specific situation, goal or context a register, so as to generalize over all specifically situated speech (genres included). Many register-specific distributional facts have been described in the literature. Some of them pertain to referential forms. We should note that the correlations concerned can be statistically highly significant. For example, Chafe (1982) found (among many other things) that first-person references are 13.4 times more frequent in conversations than in written English (this is a 1240 percent difference!). The main question we address in 2.3.2 is whether such formal findings have grammatical status. In other words, given some statistically significant register–referential form correlation, is it conventional (a discourse function) or not? If it is not, we further ask whether it is an extragrammatical pattern (a discourse profile, as PAS probably is), or merely an epiphenomenon, namely a statistical finding which does not reflect a salient discourse profile for speakers.

Based on statistically significant genre differences, Fox (1987: 152) concludes that "there is **no single rule for anaphora** that can be specified for all of English . . . instead, we have a variety of specific patterns which obviously share a number of general characteristics, but which nevertheless differ enough to require **separate formulations**" (emphases added). Lord and Dahlgren (1997: 339) agree, and propose (regarding the distinction between proximal and distal demonstrative distribution) that "These patterns . . . have become part of the tacit **knowledge of the genre**, shared by the writer and reader . . ." (1997: 346, emphasis added). Under this approach, there is a conventional association between referential patterns and specific registers. This would entail grammatical status on our approach. But not all researchers analyze such findings as attesting to a discourse function. Some view them as discourse profiles (extragrammatical on our approach). Chafe (1982), for example, explains all the differences he found between spoken and written English by reference to a few general characteristics of the two registers: speaking is faster than writing, and affords a direct interaction between the speaker and her addressee. The very large gap in self-references between spoken and written English is explained by noting that in general, informal conversations are characterized by a high degree of involvement. Biber *et al.* (1999) too distinguish between grammar and use of grammar.

In section 2.3.2 we again find out that not every statistically significant difference is grammatically significant. While we must recognize some grammatically specified register-specific referential forms, most register-specific styles are discourse profiles, rather than discourse functions (see Ariel, 2002c, 2004a, 2007c). At least some of them are possibly only epiphenomenal, in fact. Their very high frequency of occurrence can be explained without positing a direct link (i.e. code) between the referential form and the register. Instead, the association between registers and referential form choice is mediated by the discourse function associated with the linguistic form on the one hand, and the communicative goals characteristic of the specific register on the other (see Chafe, 1982; Chafe and Danielewicz, 1987). The discourse profiles we see are then the result of an interaction between the (nonregister-specific) discourse functions of referring expressions and the register-specific features of the entities referred to. The idea is that if some register is mainly associated with entities of a certain type, since referential forms are associated with (encoded) discourse functions, the register will tend to have a disproportionate number of a specific referring expression, just because the expression is appropriate for the type of entity commonly referred to. But the claim is that the referring expression is appropriate for the type of discourse entity because of its encoded discourse function. It is not conventionally (directly) specified for the register per se.

Now, the type of entity here intended refers to the degree of activation with which its representation is entertained by the addressee (as assessed by the speaker). As we have seen, referring expressions specialize for (i.e. encode) various degrees of activation for representations of discourse entities (section 2.2). Let us now focus on two referring expressions, definite descriptions and pronouns. Definite descriptions encode a variety of low degrees of activation (mostly depending on how informative they are). Pronouns, on the other hand, encode a high degree of activation. Now, if certain registers render relevant certain types of entities, i.e. of a certain variety of degree of activation, then the same referring expression will be selected by the speaker over and over again, and the data will reflect a highly skewed distribution of referential forms. Still, no grammatical stipulation need be assumed. Let's see whether this is the case.

Here's one striking example, where the statistical counts correlating referring expressions and registers are certainly significant. Compare the prevalence of pronouns and definite descriptions in various registers, as presented in Biber *et al.* (1999). As originally observed by Fox (1987), the ratios of pronouns and lexical anaphors out of all anaphoric expressions are extremely different across different registers; see table 2.1.

Note that pronouns vary between being rather marginal in academic writings (20 percent of all anaphoric expressions) to being predominant in conversations (80 percent of all anaphoric expressions, four times more, proportionately). Repeated (identical) definite descriptions vary between 5 percent for conversation and 40 percent for academic writings (proportionately eight times more in academic writing), and synonymous definite descriptions are proportionately approximately ten times more frequent in newspapers than in conversations (this is my estimate). These are no doubt highly impressive differences. Ignoring the question of how one could possibly formulate a convention based on such high but still nonabsolute findings, contrast the dramatic differences in table 2.1 with the much more mild differences pertaining to the distance

Table 2.1 *The percentage of various expressions out of all anaphoric expressions (adapted from Biber et al., 1999: 237, table 4.2)*

Ref. Exp.	Conversation	Fiction	News	Academic writing
Pronoun	80%	75%	40%	20%
Def, repeated	5%	10%	35%	40%
Def, synonym	<2.5%	5%	20%	10%

Table 2.2 *The referential distance of various referring expressions (in number of words; adapted from Biber et al., 1999: 239, table 4.3)*

Ref. Exp.	Conversation	Fiction	News	Academic writing
Pronoun	15	20	20	20
Def, repeated	30	45	40	40
Def, synonym	35	35	30	35

separating the above referring expressions from their antecedents in table 2.2. Recall that the distance between referring expressions and their antecedents is one of the factors which determine the degree of activation at which the antecedent is entertained. All things being equal, the larger the distance, the less active the antecedent is when a subsequent mention of the same entity is made. More recently mentioned entities tend to be more highly activated in the addressee's memory.

Note that here the difference between the referential distances of pronouns in different registers is significantly smaller (33.3 percent more for the written genres), repeated definite descriptions have a maximal 50 percent difference (between conversation and fiction), and synonymous definite descriptions have a rather marginal difference between the newspapers and the three other genres (16.7 percent). Thus, in terms of the frequency of types of referring expressions, there is great variability between the different registers (the gaps in table 2.1 vary between 300 and 900 percent), but in terms of referential distance, the differences vary between 16.7 and 50 percent. These findings attest that different registers have clear preferences for certain types of entities: conversations prototypically involve highly activated entities, whereas academic writing tends to involve low-activation entities. But crucially, the conditions under which pronouns and definite descriptions are used in the different registers are quite similar, despite the very large gap in their frequency. The referential distance remains rather constant across genres per referring expression. Each obeys the same discourse function in all registers: pronouns encode a relatively high degree of memory activation, definite descriptions encode a relatively low degree of memory activation.

These data show that it is the difference in the nature of the entities referred to (in other cases, it is the special goals of addressors – see Ariel, 2007c) that are responsible for the selection of different referential forms. And while the nature of the entities is directly dictated by the type of register, there is no direct, conventional association between the specific register and the forms frequently figuring in it. In each register, it is the same activation-based discourse functions which mediate between the register-appropriate entities and the resulting linguistic expressions (types of referring expressions). Thus, the different frequencies with which definite descriptions and pronouns are found in different registers can directly be accounted for by their conventional discourse function, and no appeal need be made to the register they occur in. Given the same set of form–function correlations (in our case, those accounted for by the various reference activation theories), the linguistic forms actually selected by addressors may well be consistently different across registers if the functions to be coded (the type of discourse entities) are consistently different.

Biber (1995: 10) notes that associations between linguistic expressions and situations may be either functionally motivated, or conventional. The cases we have reviewed so far have all been cases where the statistically significant differences among registers are functional, and do not entail register-specific conventions for referring expressions. In fact, it's doubtful that native speakers are even (unconsciously) aware of the statistically highly significant pattern revealed in table 2.1. Pronouns and definite descriptions are such frequent referring expressions in all registers that it is highly unlikely that they are associated with specific registers. In other words, unlike the PAS pattern, which seems to be an amplified statistical tendency, speakers following it beyond their motivated needs, the discourse profiles of pronouns and definite descriptions in Biber's data seem to be wholly motivated by their respective discourse functions. This argument was forcefully made by Toole (1996), who had similar register differences among referring expressions in her Australian English data. Once degree of activation was properly calculated, by reference to a multiplicity of activation factors, most of the distributional differences as in table 2.2 disappeared. What Toole did was examine the distribution of referential forms based on a few activation-related factors (distance is just one factor, topicality and competition are others). She found that once activation was assessed on the basis of four activation factors the predictions were much more precise, and the genre-related differences, as reflected in table 2.2 disappeared. It's quite possible that although the findings in tables 2.1 and 2.2 are objectively real, they are epiphenomenal in terms of speakers' competence.

This does not mean that all referring expressions are register-insensitive. Some form–function correlations are register-sensitive. That some such correlations are register-specific may be due to the gradual nature of linguistic change. Most linguistic changes occur in face-to-face conversations, and hence innovations may occur with a higher, even absolute frequency in informal talk. For example, spoken Hebrew first- and second-person verbs in future tense only marginally permit zero subjects (see Ariel, 1990, 2000 for statistics). This is not the case for written Hebrew, where the majority of such cases did have a zero subject. Future tense verbal person-agreement markers are being reanalyzed as nonreferential, hence the need for an overt (subject) referring expression. As expected, this reanalysis primarily affects the spoken register. In this case, then, we can say that written Hebrew has a (high-activation) referring expression which spoken Hebrew has lost, namely, the person verbal-agreement markers in future tense. For this difference to be motivated and possibly epiphenomenal, we would have to assume that written Hebrew has a dramatically stronger tendency to refer to extremely activated discourse entities in future tense than spoken Hebrew. This is not a reasonable assumption. Another example is what I have termed the VIP *mi* construction (Ariel, 1983). This is a very marked referring expression used in conjunction with a proper name, to introduce VIPs into the discourse (see ex. (28) in section 5.3.3). The construction is restricted to journalistic Hebrew.

There are, then, cases where a referring expression is restricted to a specific register in a conventional manner. These are cases where the differential distributions cannot wholly be explained on the basis of the extralinguistic, communicative goals of the addressors in the specific register. Note that Hebrew conversationalists certainly discuss VIPs sometimes. But when they do, they have to use other means for their initial introduction. And first/second verbal agreement markers are a (very high-activation) referring expression in written Hebrew, but they are not in spoken Hebrew (where they are nonreferential agreement markers). The register differences briefly mentioned in the previous paragraph all require specific conventions which are register-dependent. As such, they carry grammatical status. This is not the case for pronouns and definite descriptions, despite the impressive statistics in table 2.1.

Register-related differences between discourse patterns are real and perhaps even pervasive. They can be quite dramatic too. Still, such differences are derivative of speakers' goals more often than not. As such, they do not define discourse functions where an encoded association obtains between the use of some linguistic form and some register. We have here found confirmation for Swales' (1990) argument that genre cannot be reduced to statistical counting of formulas. Neither can (grammatical) discourse functions. Many register-specific discourse profiles can be accounted for by reference to one, register-insensitive, grammatical discourse function. If we assume a grammatical mechanism whereby linguistic forms are selected in accordance with their function, then the same set of conventions will yield the different discourse profiles, since speakers tailor their choice of linguistic expressions to their (register-different) communicative goals. In such cases, the statistical pattern may be, or may be perceived as, a salient discourse profile.

Summing up, chapter 2 was devoted to the grammar/pragmatics division of labor associated with (some) definite NPs. "Be careful with forcing bits and pieces you find in the pragmatic wastebasket into your favorite syntactico-semantic theory," warned Bar-Hillel (1971: 405). We have seen a few examples of the validity of this advice in chapter 2. In section 2.1 we concluded that the commitment aspect associated with definite descriptions is inferred rather than encoded. In section 2.3.1 we discussed Du Bois' point that the distribution of lexical (mostly) definite NPs and pronouns, although highly predictable as to their syntactic role, is not a grammatical fact, and the same goes for the definite description/pronoun distributions across registers (section 2.3.2). Nonetheless, a shift in the opposite direction, of attributing grammatical status to phenomena previously analyzed as pragmatic, is sometimes justified. The Givenness condition on definite descriptions (section 2.1), some of the form–function correlations on the referential marking scale (section 2.2), as well as some (very few) register-specific distributions of referential forms (section 2.3) are grammatically specified.

All in all, while the main point of section 2.2 was that codes are involved where inferences would seem to provide a natural account, and that of section 2.3 that statistically significant patterns (where codes might be expected) may not be grammatical after all, all linguistic phenomena actually invoke both codes and inferences (some are governed by extragrammatical use conventions as well, such as PAS). This point was explicitly made for presuppositions (section 2.1), but is equally true for the various referential theories (section 2.2). While degree of activation and the three coding principles are extragrammatical, the marking scale itself is encoded, at least partially. Most intriguingly perhaps, some highly consistent discourse patterns were seen to be epiphenomenal, namely, neither grammatical nor pragmatic.

We continue discussing the reshuffling of phenomena between grammar and pragmatics in chapter 3. We add an additional set of questions, however, regarding different statuses among pragmatic inferences (implicatures, explicated inferences, and truth-compatible potential inferences).

3 Distinguishing codes, explicated, implicated, and truth-compatible inferences

We have already introduced Grice's "Modified Occam's Razor Principle" in section 1.3: 2: "Senses are not to be multiplied beyond necessity" (Grice, 1989: 47). By the senses not to be multiplied, Grice meant specifically semantic, rather than pragmatic meanings. The received view is that if a linguistic form seems to have more than one interpretation, we should try to avoid positing semantic ambiguity. If at all possible, we should assign a single semantic meaning to the form, and derive the other interpretation(s) pragmatically. All things being equal, then, whenever possible, additional attested meanings should be viewed as pragmatic rather than semantic. This was the position we adopted in section 2.2 when we tried (and failed) to analyze the accessibility-associated distributional patterns of referring expressions as pragmatically inferred rather than grammatically stipulated. Prime examples offered in the literature include *and*, *or*, and *if*, for each of which, following especially Horn (1972), Griceans propose one semantic meaning (their logical operator counterpart), despite the variety of contextual interpretations they manifest in discourse.

Moreover, even if linguistic forms seem to have one invariable meaning (e.g. *but*, *some*, *six*), Griceans still try to minimize their semantics, by analyzing some aspects of their meanings ('contrast' for *but*, the upper bound for *some* and for *six*) as pragmatic.[1] Only part of their meaning is assigned to their semantics ('and' for *but*, 'at least one' for *some*, 'at least six' for *six*). In other words, there is a drive towards a minimalist linguistic code, in conformity with the Radical Pragmatics agenda, proposed in Cole (1981: xi): "many linguistic phenomena, which had previously been viewed as belonging to the semantic subsystem, in fact belong to the pragmatic subsystem" (see also Atlas and Levinson, 1981).

The motivation behind this preference for pragmatic over semantic meanings is theoretical economy: pragmatic meanings are derived by relying on inferential pragmatic theories (such as the ones discussed in chapter 1), which are motivated on independent grounds (because they are needed for accounting for supplemental interpretations, i.e. particularized conversational implicatures). Whatever we can derive by inference, relying on a theory we must assume anyway, is seen as preferable to stipulating an additional semantic fact. The linguistic meaning selected must of course be compatible with all the potential contextual interpretations the expression can receive. For example, whatever semantic meaning we

---

[1] The upper bound on *some* is 'not all,' and on *six*, 'not more than six.'

choose for the numbers (e.g. *six*) has to be able to give rise (with the help of inferencing) to all its contextual readings, i.e. 'six,' 'at least six,' 'exactly six,' 'about six,' and 'at most six.' Applying Modified Occam's Razor Principle, the relevant contextual interpretations are variously analyzed as conventional implicatures (the contrast in *but*), as conversational implicatures (interpretations associated with *and*) or as conveyed meanings (i.e. the combination of the coded with the implicated, in the case of scalar expressions, e.g. 'some but not all' for *some*, 'exactly six' for *six*).

Given these shared assumptions among researchers, one would expect agreement as to the application of the grammar/pragmatics divide. Indeed, there is universal agreement in the field about conversational implicatures being inferred, and hence pragmatic. While there may not be a consensus on the grammatical status of conventional implicatures, nobody disputes the fact that they are conventional. As such, they automatically constitute part of grammar according to the approach adopted here. We applied the same reasoning to the discourse function/ discourse profile controversy discussed in section 2.3. The former (but not the latter), being conventional, falls within grammar.

Still, while all approaches are in principle committed to the code/inference distinction, not all apply it with the same rigor. Gricean pragmatists also rely (to varying extents) on the criterion of truth conditionality for distinguishing grammatical and extragrammatical interpretations, taking truth-conditional meanings as semantic and nontruth-conditional meanings as pragmatic. Not so Relevance theoreticians, who apply the code/inference distinction strictly (this is also the position of this book). No wonder, then, that researchers sometimes differ in their conclusions regarding the status of interpretations in specific cases: what is attributed to semantics by some may be attributed to pragmatics by others, and vice versa. For example, conventional implicatures are considered pragmatic for Grice (e.g. the contrast associated with *but*), because they are nontruth conditional, regardless of their conventionality. But they are (linguistic) semantic for Relevance theoreticians, because they constitute coded meanings, their nontruth conditionality considered irrelevant. Reference and ambiguity resolutions are (linguistic) semantic for Griceans because they are crucial for determining the truth conditions of the sentence, but pragmatic under Relevance theory because they are inferred. We are here concerned with other theoretical differences (but see chapter 7).

On the one hand, chapter 3 is very much a continuation of chapter 2. Here too we first of all explore the grammar/pragmatics division of labor. But whereas the analyses argued for in chapter 2 were theory-neutral for the most part, the ones discussed here are associated with specific pragmatic theories, primarily the neo-Gricean and Relevance-theoretic frameworks. Indeed, we discuss not only candidates for codes versus inferences, but also for the neo-Gricean generalized conversational implicature, for the Relevance-theoretic explicature, and for yet another type of inference, the potential truth-compatible inference. We present cases where practitioners of different theories advocate different analyses. Nonetheless, while the analyses are each anchored within a different pragmatic theory, often enough, it is not the inferential mechanism per se which dictates what the grammar/pragmatics divide should be.

The inferential mechanisms presented in Chapter 1 are at least to some extent independent of the grammar/pragmatics distinction drawn by (neo-)Griceans and by Relevance theoreticians respectively. Consider *six*, for example. Which of the possible contextual interpretations should we pick as its semantic meaning? Proposals in the literature include 'at least six,' 'six,' and 'exactly six,' each outlining a way to derive the other interpretations pragmatically. In principle, any of the inferential theories could provide a pragmatic account for all the attested meanings given any choice of these candidate meanings as the coded one. Indeed, while Horn's original position was that the upper bound on the numbers (e.g. 'no more than six') is an implicature (and this is still Levinson's 2000b position), Horn (1996 and onwards) views it as part of the semantic representation. Very often, it is broader considerations about the nature of codes and the status of various types of inferences that guide researchers' theoretical decisions. These considerations form the focus of chapter 3.

As we shall see, Modified Occam's Razor Principle need not automatically be assumed any more. Carston (2002a: 218/219) expresses some doubts about the justification of the principle, noting that economy/elegance of the theory is not necessarily a reasonable argument for attributing to speakers a certain type of competence. Psycholinguistic experiments (relying on the plausible assumption that semantic meanings are more easily accessible to us than inferred meanings) would serve as a much more solid ground for arguing for what is economical for interlocutors. As Carston reasons, it may in fact be more efficient for speakers to access a few meanings per form and choose one from among them than to access just one meaning and laboriously draw further inferred interpretations from it.[2]

We here therefore rely on Recanati's (1989) "Availability Principle," which states that researchers' analyses must be faithful to pretheoretic intuitions on whether some pragmatic inference is "said" or implicated. We shouldn't analyze as an implicature an interpretation speakers view as inseparable from the semantic meaning, argues Recanati. We discuss the Availability Principle in chapter 7, but I here quote Recanati's (1989: 326) objection to a lower-bound-only semantic analysis of the cardinal numbers, based on this principle:

> Not many people have observed that Grice's theory departs from our intuitions when it is applied to examples such as 'John has three children,' which Griceans take to express the proposition that John has at least three children and to implicate that he has no more than three children. However, there is an important difference between this example and e.g. 'I've had no breakfast today,' which implicates that the speaker is hungry and wishes to be fed. In the latter example, the implicature is intuitively felt to be **external** to what is said; it corresponds to something we would ordinarily take to be 'implied.' In the former case, we are **not**

---

[2] As is argued in part II, routinization of inferred meanings is a regular path for pragmatics to cross over to grammar. The driving force here is not necessarily efficiency. Rather, semanticization is something that happens to us while using language. There's no higher motive behind it.

> **pre-theoretically able to distinguish between the alleged two components of the meaning** of the utterance – the proposition expressed (that John has at least three children) and the implicature (that he has at most three children). We are conscious only of their combination, i.e., of the proposition that John has exactly three children. In this case . . ., the theoretical distinction between the proposition expressed and the implicature does not correspond to the intuitive distinction between what is said and what is implied.   (Emphases added)

For example, the meaning of *six* should be taken as the unified 'six,' rather than as composed of 'at least six' (its semantic meaning) + 'at most six' (the common implicature derived from it).

The main goal of chapter 3 is to illustrate how assigning a particular status to a given meaning is far from trivial, and involves a rather complex set of theoretical considerations. For conjoined clauses (section 3.1), is e.g. the chronological ordering interpretation encoded or inferred? If inferred, is it implicated, explicated, or merely potentially truth-compatible? For *most*, is the upper-bound interpretation (to use a neutral term for interpretations such as 'not all') encoded, explicated, or conversationally implicated (section 3.2)? If the latter, is it a generalized or a particularized conversational implicature? Or is it not even communicated by the speaker, although it is quite a plausible potential inference (a truth-compatible potential inference)? All of the above seems to be the right answer, but under different contextual circumstances.

3.1   *And*-associated inferences

One of Grice's most significant contributions to linguistics is no doubt his proposal to distinguish between semantics and pragmatics in a principled way. An important aspect of the Gricean program was the simplification of semantics which it allowed. Grice's distinction between the semantic 'what is said' and the pragmatic 'what is implicated' enabled semanticists to maintain the assumption that (certain) natural language expressions are semantically identical with their counterpart classical logical operators, despite the fact that their actual discoursal uses are not restricted to this meaning.[3] The differences between their semantic meaning and their interpretations in context have been assigned to pragmatics. One such case is sentential *and* (others are *but*, *or*, *if*). Section 3.1.1 reviews the arguments for the Gricean position that many interpretations associated with *and* are pragmatically derived, rather than semantic. This pragmatic view is now consensual. But there is no agreement on what kind of pragmatic status these inferences should be assigned. Up till recently, pragmatic status automatically translated to implicature status. But with Relevance theoreticians' concept of explicature (see again section 1.4), a pragmatic inference may either be implicated or explicated, and it can even be a truth-compatible interpretation, not intended by

---

[3] 'What is said' is roughly the conventional semantic meaning. See chapter 7 for discussion.

the speaker. As we will find out in section 3.1.2, *and*-associated interpretations can have any of these statuses under different circumstances.

3.1.1   The semantics/pragmatics division of labor in interpreting *and*

The meaning of the logical '&' is clear and simple. Once we equate *and* with '&,' so is the semantic meaning of *and*. For a proposition which consists of two (or more) propositions conjoined by *and* to be true, each conjunct has to be true. If any one of them is false, the whole proposition is rendered false.[4] Thus, for (1) to be true, it must be true that 'The bus lines in Ramle have been privatized' and that 'the residents of the Arab neighborhoods have to walk' (for (1a)), and that 'Ken eats the local food' and that 'Ken gets deathly ill' (for (1b)):

(1) a.   The bus lines in Ramle have been privatized – **and** the residents of the Arab
neighborhoods have to walk.   (Originally Hebrew, *Haaretz*, Aug. 12, 2005)

b.   KEN: (H) So I eat the local food,
and get deathly ill.   (SBC: 015)

To see that, indeed, we can use conjoined sentences in accordance with this minimal semantic characterization, consider the following. First, (2a) shows that *and*-conjoined clauses are compatible with a purpose reading (note that 'we were going to take out the broken radio **in order to** send it back to the factory' in (2a)). Although this reading would have been most natural in (b), it can be blocked. (Bear in mind that Weldon's readers know that Arthur is secretly in love with Helen):

(2) a.   ALINA: we were gonna s– —
take it out **and** send it back to the factory,   (SBC: 006)

b.   Arthur went back to Helen, in London, to enquire about the emerald
pendant. Or shall we say, reader, that he went back to Helen in London,
AND enquired about the emerald pendant.
(Original emphasis, Fay Weldon, *The Hearts and Lives of Men*, 1987, p. 156)

It's clear that Weldon's narrator is offering the alternative, *and*-conjoined formulation precisely in order to question the link (established in the first sentence) between Arthur's going to London and his enquiring about the pendant. *And*-conjoined clauses can then be used when the speaker wishes to avoid any commitment as to the link between the two conjuncts (Blakemore and Carston, 2005; Carston, 2002a: chapter 3). Such uses seem to justify the reduction of *and* to '&.'

But, of course, (2b) is an atypical example. Normally, the truth-functional aspect of an *and* conjunction does not exhaust the speaker's intended meaning in using it. The author of the newspaper headline in (1a) intends the readers to understand more than the separate contents of the two clauses, namely, that the bus

---

[4] Note that some of the examples cited below (e.g. (2a)) show phrasal, rather than sentential conjunction formally. But in each of these cases, the reader can construct a parallel sentential conjunction, where the argument is equally applicable. Indeed, as Huddleston *et al.* (2002: 1280) note, "in the absence of special factors, a subclausal coordination is semantically equivalent to the corresponding clausal coordination."

privatization is the **cause** of the residents of the Arab neighborhoods having to walk. *And* is here interpreted as 'and as a result.' This is why whereas the linear ordering of conjuncts in logical formulas does not matter, we often cannot reverse the ordering of naturally occurring conjuncts. Compare (1a) with (3) which is either incoherent, or else would be interpreted quite differently:

(3)   ~?? The residents of the Arab neighborhoods in Ramle have to walk – and the bus lines have been privatized.

Grice's (1981) "Occamistic" analysis, which assigns the causal interpretation above a pragmatic status (of conversational implicature) contrasts with an alternative semantic analysis, where *and* is taken to be **semantically** ambiguous between logical '&' and 'and as a result' (as well as other meanings). Note a few more actual uses of *and* (and see Huddleston *et al.*, 2002: 1301–1303 for other uses and analyses; Posner, 1980; Schiffrin, 1986, 1987).[5] Once we realize the variety of the contextual interpretations associated with *and*, the semantic ambiguity analysis becomes much less attractive:

(4) a.   M: I'm reminding you that Virginia's coming at eight, **and**
                    we need five or six lemons   (Feb. 23, 2002)
    b.   KEN: your blood's all shot,
                    and you have the liver of a ninety-year-old,   (SBC: 015)
    c.   KEN: He just di- did a blood test,
                    and said,   (SBC: 015)
    d.   JOANNE: [I knew someone who went to Cuba],
          KEN: (H)]
          JOANNE: **and** had to go,
          KEN: [yeah].
          JOANNE: [make] connections through Mexico.   (SBC: 015)
    e.   KEN: when we were there last,
                    we —
                    th– it was just after an election.
                    (H) **And** I got all these great,
                    um,
                    photographs of,   (SBC: 015)
    f.   In attacks less than an hour apart . . . a Palestinian suicide bomber struck at a bus stop near Tel Aviv . . . **and** Israeli helicopters fired missiles . . .
                    (*International Herald Tribune*, Dec. 26, 2003)
    g.   JOANNE: he said you've been blessed with a great body,
                    and here you are . . . fucking it up   (SBC: 015)
    h.   LH: Just got my copies of . . . ((LH's book published)) (Private e-mail correspondence with IS, Dec. 20, 2003)

---

[5] For example, Schiffrin demonstrates how speakers shift between *and*-conjunctions and juxtaposed clauses (without any overt connective) or *so*-prefaced clauses in order to indicate discourse segmentations.

IS: Hey . . . Mazel Tov! **And** on the first day of Hanukkah!

>   (Private e-mail reply to LH, Dec. 20, 2003)

i.   **And** what will Nachum eat?

>   (Originally Yiddish, reconstructed from memory, 1950s)

(4a) seems closest to the semantic analysis of *and* as '&.' Note that we can reverse the order of the conjuncts (*I'm reminding you that we need five or six lemons and Virginia's coming at eight*), without changing the interpretation of the utterance. Moreover, the clauses actually conjoined, *Virginia's coming at eight* and *we need five or six lemons* perfectly fit the minimalist requirement in that the two propositions seem quite irrelevant to each other.

Of course, it's no accident that we do actually get a framing in (4a) (*I'm reminding you*), which connects the two pieces of information (these are two things the addressee needs to be aware of when planning his morning). (4b) is a similar case, also reversible, where the conjuncts are more obviously related to each other, both indicating malfunctioning of the body. For the most part, natural language utterances do not simply lump together true propositions into conjoined sentences, and, as Schiffrin (1986) argues, *and* is the unmarked mode of linking. So, it's not surprising that we tend to read more into *and*-conjoined sentences. The following is funny just because we are forced to see the two conjuncts as relevant (enough) to each other, and as similar in importance ((5) is taken from a cartoon where the husband is reading the newspaper, the wife in tears is holding a cake that didn't rise):

(5)   Husband: shlixuto   shel beiker lo   alta yafe
>   mission:his of   Baker not rose well
>   'Baker's (diplomatic) mission did not rise well (i.e. was not successful).'

>   Wife: ve-gam   lo   ha-ugat   gvina.
>   **and**-also   not the-cake:of cheese
>   'And neither did the cheese cake.'

>   (Hebrew, *Hadashot*, May 17, 1991)

Back to the previous examples, (4c) manifests the familiar case of chronological ordering being reflected in linear ordering: the event depicted first is also the one preceding in time, but (4d), (4e), and (4f) show that this is not invariably the case. The person (*someone*) in (4d) must have first made connections through Mexico and only then did s/he go to Cuba.[6] In (4e), getting all the great photographs must have occurred at some interval of time within the period defined as after an election and not necessarily following that time. The order of events described in (4f) is in fact the opposite of the order of the conjuncts (as is made clear later in the news article). Next, (4g) shows a contrast between the conjuncts (*and* is here roughly substitutable by *but*).

Finally, (4h) and (4i) demonstrate that even identifying the propositions being conjoined requires us to go beyond the logical formula. The *and* in (4h) is not conjoined to IS's first utterance. Rather, it connects to a (nonfinal) sentence in a

---

[6] Alternatively, as Bernard Comrie (p.c.) notes, *going through Mexico* can be interpreted as a subevent included under the event of 'going to Cuba'. But even so, we still don't get the classical chronological reading of one event ending before the next one begins.

previous message from LH to IS. IS's conjunct (only when prefaced by *and*) conveys that 'this auspicious event (you receiving copies of your book) happened on the first day of Hanukkah' (the Jewish holiday of Hanukkah is associated with a miracle and with happiness). This *and* does not even introduce a separate state of affairs. In (i), the question is not conjoined to any linguistic string. Rather, to a contextually salient state of affairs in which the mother-in-law is critically examining the food being cooked by the daughter-in-law (her addressee), implicating that while the food is good enough for the daughter-in-law (and her son from a previous marriage), it is not good enough for the mother-in-law's own son, Nachum (the addressee's husband).

No doubt the relations between the propositions conjoined by *and* are richer than the meaning of the logical '&.' The Gricean position is that *and* be given the minimal semantic meaning of '&,' assuming that the speaker in addition generates a conversational implicature, with any of the effects above (and, no doubt, many others). These would be generated in order to see the speaker as relevant (see Carston, 1988; Grice, 1981; Horn, 2004, 2006).[7] A semantic ambiguity analysis, on the other hand, would entail listing in our mental lexicon all the interpretations associable with *and*, assuming that the addressee will first retrieve all these meanings, and then pick the contextually appropriate one from among them. Since there is such great variability in the sorts of relations we assign to conjoined clauses, it's not even clear that the semantic option is actually viable (Carston, 1988 and onwards). In addition, as Horn (2004) emphasizes, the pragmatic analysis accounts well for the fact that language after language manifests virtually the same range of interpretations for its counterparts of *and*. He points out, for example, that no language uses *and* for an 'and before' interpretation, but all use it for an 'and then' interpretation (linear ordering reflecting chronological ordering). The fact that the same meanings are associated with *and*s in unrelated languages indicates that these meanings cannot be arbitrary. They must be calculable, rather than coded, and inferred ad hoc by reference to some rational principle(s). Semantic ambiguities (e.g. of *bar*) tend to be language-specific.

An important feature of implicatures is cancelability. Note the following, where the chronological interpretation is canceled, and the speaker is not seen as having contradicted herself:

(6)   She was in once with her kids **and** once without but I can't remember which came first.

          (www.thiswomanswork.com/category/the-story-of-my-life/shelter/page/4)

Additional cancellation cases are presented in (7):

(7) a.   What is keeping the two Isaacs ((Shamir and Rabin – MA)) together ((in a unity government – MA)) are two common adversaries: Yassir Arafat **and** Shimon Peres (the ordering is purely accidental).

          (Originally Hebrew, *Haaretz*, Jan. 7, 1990)

---

[7] Since the arguments in favor of a pragmatic analysis for *and*-associated inferences were originally made by Griceans, I here equate between a pragmatic analysis in general and a conversational implicature analysis in particular. The proposal that the relevant inferences are explicated rather than implicated is taken up in section 3.1.2.

b.   MOM: Can I have a smile **and** a look?
      MAYA: Here's a smile (Maya smiles but looks away)
           And here's a look (Maya looks at Mom with a grim face).
                                                           (Jun. 7, 2001)

When we enumerate items on a list conjoined by *and*, the speaker often generates an implicature that the first item is more significant than later items (Cooper and Ross, 1975). Note, however, that the speaker can then cancel this implicature (7a). The addressee can also ignore the speaker's implicature (of simultaneous action) in (7b).

Next, the pragmatic analysis is supported by the fact that adjacent utterances often receive the very same chronological and causal interpretations, in the absence of an overt *and*. This seems to show that the relevant interpretations do not depend on the presence of *and*, and hence should not be analyzed as meanings of *and*. Note that in the *and*-less (8), the writer generates a causal implicature too, that Okon quit his job because of the tension between him and Beinisch. (We can also cancel it, just as we cancel the chronological implicature in (6), which is what the journalist does here):

(8)   Relations between Okon and Beinisch grew tense ((over the Nili Cohen
         episode – MA)). Shortly afterward, Okon left the position of registrar . . . His
         confidants say there is no causal connection between the Nili Cohen episode
         and his leaving.   (*Haaretz* English edition, Feb. 11, 2005)

Indeed, it would seem that the interpretations connecting the two clauses/phrases in (1)–(7) are not necessarily dependent on the presence of *and*. This is why, for the most part, omitting *and* in the above examples does not result in eliminating the effects we discussed. Note (9), a modified version of (1b) above, where the same causal meaning is present:[8]

(9)   ~KEN: (H) So I eat the local food. I get deathly ill.

Posner (1980) and Huddleston *et al.* (2002: 1300) note in addition that the inferred interpretations vary in strength. The temporal sequence understanding is stronger when past events are narrated than when intended future events are described. These are all characteristics of pragmatic inferences and not of semantic meanings. All in all, the interpretations here discussed meet all the criteria for conversational implicatures. They are quite ad hoc (see the variability in interpretations of the conjunctions in (1)–(5)), they seem independent of *and* (nondetachable) and not even language-specific. They are calculable (by reference to the Gricean maxims, say), context-dependent (each context calling for a different implicature), cancelable without affecting the

---

[8] Although this argument is often used by analysts (e.g. Carston, 2002a: 224–225; Huddleston, 1988: 197; Posner, 1980; Wilson and Sperber, 1998), on its own, it is not actually a very convincing argument. Many lexical codes exist for interpretations that could be pragmatically inferred. Thus, one would not want to say that *as a result* has no causal semantic meaning just because adding it to (1), for example, is redundant. Carston (2002a: 259–260) rightly suggests we should be careful in how we use this criterion, then.

truth conditions of the proposition, and vary in the strength with which they are communicated.

Indeed, based on the arguments presented in section 3.1.1, the consensus in the field is that *and* has a minimal semantic meaning, supplemented by a variety of pragmatic interpretations. Most researchers now subscribe to the (basically Gricean) pragmatic view: it is shared by philosophers (Bach, 2004a), semanticists (Chierchia and McConnell-Ginet, 1990; Gamut, 1991), pragmatists (Blakemore, 1987; Carston, 2002a; Horn, 2004; Levinson, 2000b; Sperber and Wilson, 1986/ 1995), functionalists (Chafe, 1988) and conversation analysts (Schiffrin, 1986, 1987; Turk, 2004) alike.[9] Cohen (1971) is one exception, and we argue against his semantic position in section 3.1.2.1.

Before we move on, however, it should be pointed out that there may after all be linguistic semantic aspects to 'and,' above the minimal Gricean meaning. Consider the following from Biblical (10a) and Modern (written) Hebrew (10b), where *ve* 'and' is interpreted as 'when/while':

(10) a. adonay elohim ma titen   li **ve-**   anoxi holex   ariri ...
          Lord   God   what will.you.give me **and-** (=when) I   am.going. childless.
                                                            (Genesis 15: 2)
          'O Lord God, what can you give me, seeing that I shall die childless'.

b. bisvivot 11 ba-boker,   **ve-**   hu ba- xanuto,   bau   shxenim
    around   11 in:the-morning, **and-**(i.e while) he in:the his:shop, came.PL neighbors
    ve-sipru le-samir she- shamu   ba-radio   she-wafa   neecra ...
    and-told to-Samir that- heard.PL on:the-radio that-Wafa had:been:arrested.F ...
    'Around 11 in the morning, while in his shop, neighbors came and told Samir that they heard on the radio that Wafa had been arrested.'   (*Haaretz*, Jul. 1, 2005)

Indeed, as Bernard Comrie (p.c.) notes, such uses have been identified as specific to Semitic languages (although there is a parallel use in Irish as well). The Biblical 'and' also functions as 'then' in conditional sentences, and Cebuano – a Philippine language – can use *og* 'and' for 'if' as well as for 'or' (although it has a word for 'if,' see Haiman, 1985a: 46–56). Such differences may depend on other forms available in the language, as well as on the historical source of the form (see Mithun, 1988). Most intriguing is the following Biblical example, where a reason clause is coordinated (see Kautzsch, 1898: 518, who noted a few such cases, although as a rule, Biblical Hebrew employs other, specialized conjunctions for this purpose):

(11) hava lanu ezrat mi   car   **ve**   shav tshuat   adam.
       give us   help against adversary **and** (i.e. **for**) vain the.help.of man
      'Give us help against the adversary for vain is the help of man.'

                                                            (Psalms 60: 13)

---

[9] Note, however, that some linguists adopt Grice's minimalist semantic approach to *and*, but not necessarily the reduction to the logical '&' (see Carston, 2002a: 254–257; Sweetser, 1990: 90–93).

The Modern Hebrew version of (11) is as unacceptable as the English lite-ral counterpart is. No doubt, there are language-specific distributional facts about 'and.'[10] But we here focus only on those interpretations seen as universally pragmatic.

3.1.2   What pragmatic status?

We have so far reviewed arguments in favor of a pragmatic analysis for the many inferences associated with *and* conjunctions. Griceans assume that these are implicated. But Relevance theoreticians have argued for an explicated status, at least for some of them. In addition, Carston (2002a: 3.5, 3.7) argues that some inferences are only potential inferences, in that they are based on our world knowledge, rather than on speaker intentions. I have proposed to term such inferences potential truth-compatible inferences (see again section 1.4). We now seek to determine the status of *and*-associated inferences. In section 3.1.2.1 we focus on the debate about whether the inferences associated with *and* are implicated or explicated. In section 3.1.2.2 we explain some interpretations as merely truth-compatible inferences.

3.1.2.1   Explicated or implicated?

According to the Gricean position, inferred interpretations must be some kind of implicature. Thus, Grice (1981) proposes that the Manner maxim (dictating to the speaker to be orderly) is responsible for the generation of the chronological sense attached to examples such as (4c) and (12), as a generalized conversational implicature (Horn, 2004; Levinson, 2000b rely on the enrichment R/I-Principle instead; see section 1.4):

(12)   MARY: . . . So I did that,
            . . . **and** I lit a match to find out where I was,
            and,
            . . . n– after everything was hunky-dory,
            .. then I,
            . . . shut the hood,
            and got back in,
            and I started up the engine and,
            (H) both #Gary and #Rita were sitting on the edges of their seat.
            . . . (SWALLOW) **And** I turned around **and** I looked,
            .. **and** I said,
            . . . did I scare you kids?   (SBC: 007)

Recall, however, the variety of senses accompanying *and*-conjoined clauses (see above). It is not clear that we can then privilege just the chronological

---

[10] Sailer (2002) (as cited in Goldberg, 2006: 8) discusses a German-specific use of 'and,' whereby incredulity is conveyed, as in:

(i)   Larry   und   Arzt?!
           Larry   **and**   doctor
           'Larry, a doctor?!'

interpretation with this status. So, particularized conversational implicatures may be a more appropriate status for *and*-associated inferences, but this question is orthogonal to our discussion in section 3.1.2.1. We here focus on the debate between proponents of the classical approach, according to whom these interpretations are (always) conversational implicatures (of whatever sort), and Relevance theory proponents (most notably Carston, 1984, 1988, 1993, 2002a), who argue that they are explicated inferences (at least in many cases).[11]

The first argument used by Wilson (1975) against the implicature analysis is based on Cohen (1971), and hinges on the fact that *and*-related inferences can (sometimes) affect the truth conditions of the proposition they are based on (see, originally, Strawson, 1952: 80). According to the implicature analysis, since implicatures do not contribute to the proposition expressed by the utterance (an assumption accepted by Relevance theoreticians), should the reality behind (12), for example, be that first 'I lit a match' and then 'I did that,' the proposition in (12) should be equally true. It is not clear that this is invariably the case. We have already seen that reversing the order of the conjuncts in (1a) results in a different proposition ((3)). Indeed, this is why the following is meaningful ((13) is a minimally modified version of an attested, originally Hebrew example from a stand-up comedian on Israeli TV, Channel 22, Jan. 28, 2004):

(13)   ~In general I hate all these retarded directions that they have on foods.
            Take, let's say, these frozen schnitzels in the fridge. It says **heat and serve**.
            Aha. It's good you tell me. Because my instinct was to **serve and heat**.

Note that if 'heat and serve' had the same propositional content as 'serve and heat' there would not be much point in uttering (13). Context makes it clear that there should be a difference between the two conjunctions, and the only difference we can come up with is that the temporal order of heating and serving is different. If so, the inferred chronological relations contribute to the truth conditions of the propositions expressed (it so happens that this example is a directive and not a proposition, but it would have worked the same way had we had propositions instead).

Given such examples, and barring a semantic retreat à la Cohen (1971) (in view of the arguments presented in section 3.1.1), we must either allow implicatures to affect truth conditions (against the Gricean original insight), or we need to assign these interpretations some other pragmatic status, which can affect truth conditions. So one reason to view the chronological inferences as explicated rather than implicated is their effect on truth conditions. A putative inference is explicated rather than implicated if it makes a contribution to the truth-conditional content of the proposition it is triggered by.

Researchers often use operator-scope embedding tests, first offered by Cohen (1971) (and employed by Carston, 2002a: chapter 2; Recanati, 1989, 2001), for determining whether what a putative interpretation must have contributed is

---

[11] The question of distinguishing between implicatures and explicated inferences in general is taken up again in section 7.3.2.

truth-conditional or not. If we see that some logical operator has an effect on the inferred interpretation, the inference must have contributed to the truth conditions of the proposition. The rationale behind this test is that logical operators have scope only on explicitly stated materials. If so, when we see a differential patterning of some inferences, such that some of them fall under the scope of logical operators but others do not, we have a basis for distinguishing between the two. Explicated inferences are those which fall under the scope of logical operators, because they have a more direct interactional presence. Implicatures do not. Consider the following (created by embedding (1b) under a conditional):

(14)   ~If I eat the local food **and** get deathly ill I should stop going to Mexico.

Quite clearly, the reason given by the speaker in (14) for stopping going to Mexico is the inferred causal connection between eating the local food and getting deathly ill. This is why it is practically equivalent to (15a), where we embed the enriched proposition under the same conditional. But it is different from (15b), where we embed the reverse order of the constituents under the same conditional:

(15) a.   ~If I eat the local food **and as a result** I get deathly ill I should stop going to Mexico.
  b.   ~?? If I get deathly ill and eat the local food I should stop going to Mexico.

Since the causal inference here falls under the scope of the conditional it is explicated, rather than implicated. Here's an attested example, where the causal interpretation falls under the scope of negation:

(16)   I read somewhere,
          that it's **not** that,
          she fell and broke her hip,
          but,
          she broke her hip and fell.   (Reconstructed from memory, Jan. 30, 2007)

Only if there is a difference between (a) *she fell and broke her hip* and (b) *she broke her hip and fell* (what caused what) can (16) be meaningful, rather than contradictory. And it is meaningful.[12]

   Erteschik-Shir and Lappin's (1979) "Lie Test," which identifies foregrounded information (Dominant is their term), can help us see that the relation between the conjuncts is indeed a potential foregrounded message in these cases. The idea behind the "Lie Test" is that the addressee's response most naturally relates to the foregrounded, rather than the backgrounded material of the speaker's utterance (recall our discussion of some presuppositions as background material in section 2.1). Applying the "Lie Test" here shows that either conjunct, but, crucially, also the connection between the conjuncts can be targeted by the test. Consider (17), where Joanne can utter a, b, or c:

---

[12] But see Saul (2002) for a defense of the original Gricean position. According to Saul, whereas (16) is false, it implicates a (potentially) true proposition.

(17)   KEN: (H) So I eat the local food,
                            and get deathly ill.
              ~JOANNE: That's not true.
                            a.   You don't eat the local food.
                            b.   You don't get deathly ill.
                            c.   The food's got nothing to do with your illness.

Just as Joanne can deny the truth of any one of the conjuncts (as in (17a, b)), she can also deny the inferred causal connection between the two events (17c). This means that the inference is a Dominant interpretation of Ken's utterance, which supports an explicature status.

Levinson (2000b: 198–217) partly concedes this point, and stipulates that implicatures can "intrude" on truth-conditional semantics and sometimes become part of 'what is said.' Horn (2004, 2006) refrains from assigning these interpretations a semantic 'what is said' status (because 'what is said' cannot contain cancelable elements). He explains such cases as "retroactive" accommodation, where what is explicated under Relevance theory is a proposition indirectly communicated for him. His rationale is that addressees perform this reinterpretation only when they have to in order to rescue the utterance from incoherence.[13] In addition, Levinson and Horn believe that these cases are restricted to certain structures (e.g. conditionals, as in (18a)).

Carston (2004a) counters that the phenomenon is not actually restricted to certain "intrusive" constructions. Simple sentences (such as (18b)) exhibit the same "intrusion," which is why (18) is considered a valid argument (in natural discourse). Consider (18a, b) as premises for concluding (18c):

(18) a.   Well, I guess if they call him Randy **and** he answers, he's Randy.   (LSAC)
     b.   Someone called him Randy **and** he answered.
     c.   Conclusion: He's Randy

Nonlogicians, argues Carston, view cases such as (18) as exemplifying a valid argument for concluding (18c). The reason is that we interpret the *and* in both (18a) and (18b) as 'and as a result,' and not only in (18a), as Levinson claims. Note that in the absence of an inferred causal relation between the two conjuncts, the argument would not have followed through, for only if there is a causal connection between someone calling him Randy and him answering is this grounds for concluding that the person is Randy. This shows that the causal inference does affect the truth conditions of "nonintrusive" constructions as well. So, "implicatures" affecting truth conditions are not as restricted as Levinson envisages. And even if they were, it seems odd to assume that the very same pragmatic inference has a different status when embedded under a logical operator. Why should embedding under a logical operator matter to whether the interpretation is or is

---

[13] Bach (2001, 2004a) treats these as implicitures. Unlike implicatures, implicitures are pragmatic inferences which are truth-conditionally relevant, but still count as implicit (see section 7.6 below). As such, implicitures are not all that different from explicatures.

not truth-conditional? Rather, on the Relevance-theoretic view, the embedding test brings to the fore an interpretation that's there anyway.

Indeed, the following conversation between a woman (I) filing a complaint and the policeman (He) writing it down shows that the assumption that *and*-associated inferences in simple sentences are not truth-conditional may be unfounded:

(19)   I: He broke the door open with a kick. Started to act madly. To yell . . .

        HE: (reads) My husband (his name) came into the house **and** broke open the door . . .

        I: Excuse me, I correct his writing. He first of all broke the door open **and then** he came in . . .

        HE: Madam, don't interrupt me and don't teach me how to fill out a complaint . . .

        I: Try to understand, Sir. It's impossible that he first of all came in and then broke the door open . . .

        HE: It's not important. That's how you fill out a complaint.

        I: But **it's not true**, and I won't sign this complaint unless . . .

                                (Originally Hebrew, *Haaretz*, March 26, 1982)

Note that the woman here insists that the officer's putative chronological implicature from *My husband came into the house and broke open the door* renders the whole proposition "not true," which is not an effect that implicatures are supposed to have. Noveck and Chevaux's (2002) subjects had the same intuitions: 71 percent of them refused to confirm that a temporally "backwards" conjunction, such as the "He" version above, was true, when the story they had heard made it clear what the actual temporal sequence of events had been.[14] Eisenberg (2005) has similar results for Hebrew. The following too testifies to an intuition that the causal interpretation is explicated rather than implicated:

(20)   Last Wednesday *Maariv* came out with the banner headline "The literature teacher was fired **and** committed suicide." Some of the characteristics of tabloid media are shrugging off responsibility . . . It can create an unjustified scandal . . . On Wednesday "The literature teacher was fired **and** committed suicide." **A direct causal connection**. An open and shut case. Was fired, and committed suicide.   (Originally Hebrew, *Haaretz*, May 30, 2003)

The journalist here protests against another newspaper's headline, which, according to him, makes a "direct causal connection" between the events. Note that this strong interpretation is derived from an *and* conjunction.

Another Relevance-based argument for including the inferred connections between conjuncts as part of the explicature is the Functional Independence principle. It rests on examples such as (21) (constructed on the basis of Carston's 2002a: 227–228, ex. 227):

(21)   ~LENORE: So that's put you off traveling down there?
        KEN: Well, I eat the local food, **and** get deathly ill.

---

[14] I call "backwards" conjunctions those conjunctions where the linear order is the opposite of the chronological order.

Obviously, Ken is implicating that he is not planning to travel to Mexico. But what is the basis for this implicature? The premise for the implicature must be 'I eat the local food **and as a result** I get deathly ill.' If the basis for this implicature were the bare Gricean '(a) I eat the local food and (b) I get deathly ill' then it's not clear how the implicature could be generated. Only if Lenore understands Ken as explicating a cause and effect proposition can she be justified in inferring an implicated (affirmative) answer to her question from Ken's expressed proposition. According to Griceans, this premise would be an implicature. So what we have here is an implicature (the confirmation) triggered on the basis of another implicature (the causal implicature). Saul (2002) argues that some implicatures may be generated on the basis of other implicatures, in which case the fact that the causal inference is implicated does not block it from serving as a premise in the derivation of a further implicature. Carston objects, arguing that in this case this means that the proposition expressed plays no (direct) role in the generation of the implicated answer. In order to avoid such an unintuitive assumption, Carston suggests that the proposition expressed must include the causal inference, so it has a clear and independent role from that of the implicature.

Based on examples of this sort, Relevance theory advocates have treated the various pragmatic inferences in sentences such as (4) as pragmatic enrichments which form part of the explicit proposition, the explicature. Note that once we accept the Relevance position regarding the status of *and*-associated inferences as explicated inferences, rather than implicatures, we can maintain the original Gricean assumption that implicatures do not affect truth conditions: although the inferences here involved do affect truth conditions, they are explicated and not implicated. Also, the proposition expressed has an independent interactional role in the Relevance-theoretic framework. However, we should note that most probably there is a difference between chronological and causal (or rather, explanation) inferences on the one hand, and other inferences, such as contrast, on the other hand. The former are cognitively basic, and seem to go through almost automatically. For example, Sanders and Noordman (2001) found that causal relations (between adjacent sentences where no overt connective occurs) are read faster and reproduced more accurately than additive (list) relations. This is why Carston (2002a) finds that even when the events depicted are contra stereotypic causal/temporal scripts, we try to impose causal connections anyway (Carston, 2002a: 251, considers ~*Tonto rode into the sunset and he jumped on to his horse* in this connection, which "leaves us with a weird interpretation"). For contrastive interpretations, on the other hand, we seem to rely much more heavily on the contents being contrasted in order to infer a contrastive relation. This is why the modern Hebrew reader is usually surprised to learn that the Biblical interpretation of 'and' is contrastive in the following (note the English official translation: 'I am dark, **but** comely,' Berlin *et al.*, 2004):

(22)   shḥora   ani   **ve**=nava
          black/dark.F   I   and=beautiful.F.   (Song of Songs 1: 5)

Since we no longer assume that being tanned or dark skinned is incompatible with being beautiful, we tend not to infer a contrast here. Such inferences are then not very good candidates for being explicated. Where appropriate, they may constitute implicatures rather than explicatures perhaps. As we see in the next section, not even every causal and chronological inference necessarily constitutes part of the explicature either.

3.1.2.2   Explicated, implicated, and truth-compatible inferences

We have so far considered two types of sources we rely on when forming mental representations in order to match between what the speaker says and the corresponding states of affairs. One obvious source is the semantics of the speaker's utterance (the linguistic code). Another source, uncontroversial by now, is the pragmatics of her utterance, namely, all the inferred interpretations the speaker intends us to draw (both implicated and explicated). But, recall our discussion in section 1.4, where we introduced yet another source we rely on when we try to match between a speaker's utterance and states of affairs, namely, potential truth-compatible inferences. Based on commonsensical assumptions, these inferences too are pragmatic rather than semantic, but unlike implicated and explicated inferences, they are not speaker-intended. They may or may not be meant (entertained by the speaker), but they are definitely not conveyed by the speaker. They must not be represented as part of the speaker's intended message, because the speaker does not intend for us to draw contextual effects from them. As such, they are not Relevant, argues Carston (2002a: 254).

Now, given that interpretations may be either encoded, or pragmatically inferred (as explicatures or as implicatures), or merely (plausibly) truth-compatible with what the speaker is saying, we should once again raise the question regarding *and*-related interpretations, considering the possibility that some of them are only plausibly truth-compatible, rather than actually communicated by the speaker uttering an *and* conjunction. The idea is that some of them are precisely that.

Recall that "backwards" conjunctions are often judged infelicitous, because the original inference disappears (e.g. (3)). Bar-Lev and Palacas (1980) have argued that the "backwards" effect occurs when the second conjunct refers to an event/situation which is temporally or causally prior to the first conjunct. Thus, if Ken first eats, and later and as a result of this he gets deathly ill, placing the result clause before the causing clause counts as "backwards." Nonetheless, such "backwards" linear orders can sometimes be rescued, as in the following, a reversal of (1b), based on Carston's (2002a: 234, ex. 216). (23) is a "backwards" conjunction, but it is still compatible with a causal reading:

(23)   ~Lenore: Is it safe to eat at small towns in Mexico?
        Ken: Well, I get deathly ill,
                and I eat the local food.

Despite the "backwards" ordering of the conjuncts, according to one possible reading, it is the local food which causes Ken's illness.[15] And here's a similar "backwards" case, where a conjunction (24a) seems unacceptable, because the second conjunct explains the first, and is in that sense prior to it. Indeed, reversing the conjuncts (as in (24b)) renders the conjunction acceptable:

(24) a.   ALINA: (H) But there was hardly anybody there.
                        (~?? **and**) It was the matinee, (SBC: 006)

      b.   ~ALINA: It was the matinee,
                        and there was hardly anybody there.

Still, in the right context, the conjoined version in the "backwards" (24a) can become acceptable:

(25)   ~LENORE: Do you know anything about how the new theatre is doing?
            ALINA: Not much. I was there just once. All I can say is that there was
                        hardly anybody there **and** it was the matinee.

Crucially, just as in (23), despite the "backwards" ordering in (25), the speaker is not ruling out the possibility that the explanation for the fact that 'there was hardly anybody there' is that 'it was the matinee.' Carston's point is that, contra Bar-Lev and Palacas (1980), not only can "backwards" orderings be made coherent, such conjuncts do not automatically block causal inferences. What status do these inferences have?

Before we try to answer this question, we should note that the problem is not restricted to "backwards" conjunctions. "Properly" ordered conjuncts too do not guarantee an explicated status for a potentially relevant causal inference (see Blakemore and Carston, 2005):

(26)   ~LENORE: Do you know anything about how the new theatre is doing?
            ALINA: Not much. I was there just once. All I can say is that it was the
                        matinee **and** there was hardly anybody there.

Here, despite the fact that the linear order is "proper," the first conjunct presenting a potential explanation for the fact in the second conjunct, the framing sentence *All I can say is that* warns that the speaker is not committed to a necessary connection between the conjuncts. All in all, then, it seems that "backwards" ordering does not necessarily preclude a causal inference (e.g. (23)), and "proper" ordering (e.g. (26)) does not guarantee it.[16] The idea is that these are only potential truth-compatible inferences or, at best, they are weakly implicated.

Carston (2002a: 3.5.1) draws attention to a subtle difference between examples such as (21) and (23). Although both examples are compatible with a causal interpretation, in (21) it is an explicated inference (see again the arguments in section 3.1.2.1), but not so in (23), where it is only weakly implicated. In (23) and

---

[15] Another interpretation is the denial of a causal relation, 'Even when I get deathly ill I still eat the local food.' But note that the two interpretations receive different intonations.

[16] And see Posner (1980) on how chronological interpretations may or may not be generated depending on a variety of factors.

(25), the speaker seems to intentionally avoid committing to a causal relation between the two conjuncts. In (23) it's because he is being playful, in (25) it's because she truly doesn't know whether there is a causal relation.[17] While a causal inference is not ruled out, it certainly doesn't enjoy the prominent status it has in e.g. (21). For example, Lenore in (25) cannot respond with: *That's not true. The fact that it was the matinee has nothing to do with hardly anybody being there*, just because Alina is not conveying that there is a causal connection between her conjuncts. We can also more comfortably add an explicit negative response to (21) (as in (27a)) than to (23) (as in (27b)):

(27) ~a.   LENORE: Do you think I can eat in small towns in Mexico?
            KEN: No. I eat the local food, **and** get deathly ill.
     ~b.   ?? LENORE: Do you think I can eat in small towns in Mexico?
            KEN: No. I get deathly ill, **and** I eat the local food.

This is so because it is Ken's intention in (27b) to get Lenore to infer the answer by herself, rather than directly and rather explicitly convey it to her. Since his *no* explicitly answers her question, it makes less sense to then have her infer his answer via a weak implicature.

Carston's insight is that the restriction on *and* conjunctions is not that the **state of affairs** in the second conjunct cannot explain the one in the first conjunct, but rather that the second conjunct cannot **function** as an **explanation** for the first conjunct. Whereas Bar-Lev and Palacas' (1980) restriction on conjunct ordering was seen as dictated by possible states of affairs, Carston places her restriction on the **discoursal role** of conjuncts, and not on how the world must be if the conjunction is true. The fact that the (causal) connection is inferable in both (21) and (23) (and we can add in (25)) does not mean that this causal inference must have the same pragmatic status in all cases. Instead, when the linear ordering of the conjuncts reflects the temporal order, the chronological and causal understandings (where applicable) are potentially explicated. When the linear ordering is "backwards" the chronological and causal links may not be conveyed at all. In this case, if derived by the addressee, they count as plausible potential truth-compatible inferences, based on the two facts presented in the conjuncts, combined with our world knowledge about causes and effects. In yet other cases, a weak implicature may be attributed to the speaker (i.e. an intention to weakly implicate the causal interpretation).[18]

What these cases demonstrate is that we must distinguish between states of affairs compatible with speakers' utterances and the interactional status of

---

[17] See also note 14 in chapter 1, for a contrastive interpretation of a conjunction (example (17b) in that chapter) as only a truth-compatible inference.

[18] In Ariel (2007a) I distinguish between two basic strategies in interpreting conjunctions: the relational and the independent strategies. I propose that the difference in the status of the causal inference between (21) and (23) is the difference between a causal inference being derived via the relational strategy (21) versus the same inference derived indirectly, following the application of the independent strategy (23), (26).

such facts. We cannot measure meaning, nor intended pragmatic inference, by consulting the objective reality behind our utterances. This is why Halliday and Hasan's (1976: 235) objectivist view of the nature of the link between conjoined clauses must be rejected: "Each new sentence either is or is not linked to its predecessor, **as an independent fact**" (emphasis added). Meanings depend on speakers' intentions, not (only) on objective facts. Relations between conjuncts do not have to mirror the relations between the states of affairs each of them represents. It's up to the speaker to decide which aspects of reality she intends to convey. Hence, while there may very well be a causal connection between the food Ken eats and the illness he gets according to him in both (21) and (23), these potentially inferable relations do not automatically translate into intentions to convey them. Barwise and Perry (1983: 38) (and see also Ariel, 2002a, 2002b; Du Bois, 1998) have warned against the tendency among semanticists to impose on (linguistic) semantic meanings all the elements necessary for the speaker's proposition to mesh with reality, so that the representation can yield all the logical entailments that necessarily follow from the speaker's statement. The same warning is applicable to our analysis of intended pragmatic inferences. Not every potential truth-compatible pragmatic inference is necessarily intended by the speaker.

(28a), a "backwards" conjunction, is another case in point. (28b) is its reversed version, where the event in the first conjunct is "properly" temporally and causally prior to that in the second conjunct. Here, as in (23), there probably is "objectively" a causal connection between Cathy's wanting Jonathan's address and her calling Alina:

(28) a.   ALINA: So Cathy calls me up,
                   and she wants Jonathan's ph- .. address.   (SBC: 006)
      b.   ~ALINA: So Cathy wants Jonathan's address **and** she calls me up.

It's quite clear from the original surrounding context that Cathy must have called Alina **because** she wanted Jonathan's address. Had she used the reversed version in (28b) she would have possibly explicated this inference. Note, however, that because of the "backwards" order chosen by Alina in (28a), the causal interpretation is not conveyed by her. The conjunction is interpreted as a sequence of temporal events, as they came to be perceived by the addressee (Alina first got the call and then figured out why Cathy called her). But while Alina does not intend a causal reading in (28a), it is not impossible that some addressee might still infer from (28a) that the reason why Cathy called Alina is that she wanted Jonathan's address. It is plausibly compatible with the state of affairs described by Alina's utterance in (28a). The point is that truth compatibility is not enough to justify attributing to the inference an implicated (or explicated) status. The causal connections above are true only of our conception of how the world must be, given that the propositions explicitly expressed are true. They are not part of the conveyed meanings.

Other examples where we see the importance of maintaining a separation between circumstances compatible with true propositions and the meanings actually conveyed by speakers can be seen in the following conjunctions. As

Carston (2002a) notes, the temporal relations between the events depicted in a conjunction are far more complex than has been assumed in the literature. Note (29), where in each there is a slightly different temporal relation. But the question is, do all of these inferable relations constitute intended interpretations?

(29) a.   MONTOYA: (H) American democracy is dying,
                     ... **and** I want you to try to think .. of why.   (SBC: 012)

      b.   MONTOYA: you're an American citizen,
                     and it's your civic duty,   (SBC 012)

      c.   RANDY: I was paying pretty close attention there,
                     and I didn't .. really see much of a problem.   (SBC: 022)

      d.   DANNY: .. now when I was growing up,
                     and I heard this story,   (SBC: 030)

      e.   REBECCA: .. (H) he sits through all the testimony,
                     and he just sort of shakes his head,

      f.   CAROLYN: Get [chalk from the] chalkboard.
            KATHY: [@ @]
            CAROLYN: **And** you just peg it at their face.   (SBC: 004)

      g.   ALINA: we were friends with this one Australian guy,
                     .. **and** he was friends with this other .. idiot from New Zealand,
                                                                (SBC: 006)

In (29a, b) the first conjuncts have started at some point in the past, but in (29a) the partial temporal overlap with the state of affairs in the second conjunct is starting now (for a limited amount of time, presumably), whereas in (29b) the overlap has held ever since the addressees became adults (and will last until they die, presumably). (29c) shows a complete temporal overlap between the two states of affairs in the past, whereas in (29d) there is only a partial overlap between 'growing up' and 'hearing the story.' In (29e) we have a continuous act of sitting, accompanied by periodic acts of head shaking, and in (29f) we can imagine the teacher getting a lot of pieces of chalk from the chalkboard and pegging them at the students all at once, or there can be multiple pairs of single chalk-getting followed by single peggings. In (29g) we understand that there is some overlap between the two states of affairs, but we have no way of knowing if there is a partial overlap between them (in which case, which is the containing state of affairs?) or a complete overlap (by some funny chance). The main point is we don't necessarily care. Most of these examples (29a–f) are grounding conjunctions, where we interpret the second conjunct in view of a background state of affairs, depicted in the first conjunct. At best, should the temporal relations here discussed be inferred, they would be truth-compatible inferences, that is, ones not falling under the communicative intention of the speaker.

As a final example, consider (30a), a *then*less version of the original (30b):

(30) a.   ~We watched the Akaba conference, we hoped for the best, **and** yesterday
           they knocked on our door.

      b.   We watched the Akaba conference, we hoped for the best, **and then**,
           yesterday they knocked on our door.
                          (Originally Hebrew, *Voice of Israel*, Reshet Bet, June 6, 2003)

Although the event in the second conjunct of (30a) is definitely understood as temporally following the event in the first conjunct, this chronological ordering is not the speaker's main point (in both versions, despite the overt *then* in (30b)). Rather, it is the contrast between the family's hopes for peace, triggered by the Akaba peace conference, and the knocking on their door – of the officer who came to tell them that their son had been killed by Palestinians. We must resist the impulse to attribute to the speaker an intention to convey every aspect which is truth-compatible with what she says. In (30a), the speaker's intended inference is contrast, not temporal sequence, although the latter is certainly a truth-compatible inference.[19] As Carston argues, which inferences are intended and which are not can only be decided by relevance considerations.

In sum, following Ariel (2002a, 2002b, 2004b) and Carston (2002a), we distinguish between a pragmatically inferable assumption merely being compatible with some proposition and that same inferable assumption actually functioning as part of the meaning conveyed by the speaker as an explicated inference or as an implicature. *And*-associated causal inferences are potentially explicated, the speaker intending them and assuming responsibility for them (although less explicitly than had she encoded the causal connection with *because*, for example). This is the case in (21), for example. But this is not invariably the case. Mostly in "backwards" ordering cases (where we reverse the ordering the speaker would have used to explicate the inference), should the causal connection be relevant, it is probably intended by the speaker (weakly implicated in this case, according to Carston). This is the case in (23). Should the connection not be relevant, it can still be derived, but only as a truth-compatible inference by a less than perfectly cooperative addressee (this is the case in (25) and (28a)). The main conclusion we must draw from our discussion of *and*-associated inferences is that the very same inference within the same construction (an *and* conjunction) may have quite different cognitive and interactional statuses. It may be explicated, implicated or merely a potentially truth-compatible inference.

3.2 The upper bound on *most*

Using a very sharp Occamistic Razor, Horn (1972 and onwards: 1984, 1989, 1992, 2006) has proposed that scalar expressions (cardinal numbers, quantifiers, gradable adjectives) only have a lower-bound semantic meaning. The upper bound is pragmatically derived. On this proposal, *six* means 'at least six,' *most* means 'more than half,' and *good* means 'at least good.' Pragmatics then contributes the upper bound, namely, 'at most six,' 'not all,' and 'not excellent,' respectively. The common interpretation of such expressions is then a combination of the semantic lower bound with the pragmatic upper bound: 'at least six' and 'at most six,' i.e. 'exactly six' for *six*, 'more than half' and 'not all' for *most*,

---

[19] See Mann and Thompson (1986) for a similar point.

i.e. 'more than half but less than all' and 'at least good but less than excellent' for *good*. A lower-bound only semantic meaning means that scalar expressions are compatible with states of affairs in which higher values, e.g. 'seven,' 'all,' and 'excellent' are (respectively) the case, but not when lower values, e.g. 'only five,' 'a third,' 'fairly good' are the case (respectively). Consider the following exchange:

(31)   A: Okay well so, do you think that's a **good** movie?
         B: **Yeah** that's **excellent**.   (LSAC)

Note that B's *yeah* confirms A's words, although s/he thinks the movie is excellent, not just good. This is so because *good* is compatible with the stronger *excellent*. Had we reversed the adjectives, A using *excellent* and B choosing *good*, we might see B as not quite endorsing A's praise of the movie, for *excellent* is not necessarily compatible with *good*.

We here focus on *most*, which is assumed to literally mean 'more than half.' Whereas its upper bound ('not all') is taken to be pragmatically derived by virtually all researchers, its lower bound (above 50 percent) is semantically given. Note the following headline, where *most* cannot denote less than a majority, its semantic meaning:

(32)   POLL: **Most** Israelis, Palestinians support Geneva accord
                       (*Haaretz* English edition, Nov. 24, 2003)

Indeed, when we read the article we find that *most* here denotes 'more than half': "53 percent of the Israelis and 56 percent of the Palestinians support it." But what about an upper bound on *most*? We were not surprised to read that some 50 percent were denoted by *most* in (32). We would have been surprised, however, had we read on and found instead that 100 percent of Israelis or Palestinians support the Geneva accord. Intuitions here converge. *Most* tends not to denote 'all.' So why not assume that *most* also means 'less than all'? Consider the next example:

(33)   The target date for the meeting is Jan. 17 in Los Angeles, provided **most** of the
         Hall of Famers can make it.
                       (*International Herald Tribune*, Dec. 24–5, 2002, p. 16)

(33) demonstrates that *most* can be compatible with 'all.' Thus, should all the Hall of Famers be able to make it to the meeting on Jan. 17, for sure the writer is proposing to hold it then.

There are, then, two basic facts about the interpretation of *most*: (i) its common interpretation (as in (32)) is upper-bounded, 'all-excluding,' but (ii) it is not invariably incompatible with 'all' (as in (33)). In fact, should it turn out that all Israelis and Palestinians support the Geneva accord, we might be surprised, but the consensus in the literature is that we would not be inclined to judge (32) as false nonetheless. All theories must account for these two types of cases, on which most pragmatists agree. But whereas there is agreement on the interpretations *most* gives rise to, researchers disagree on the status of the "now-you-see-it-now-you-don't" upper bound on *most*.

The neo-Griceans (Horn, 1972 and onwards; Levinson, 2000b) have proposed that the interpretation in (33) is accounted for by *most*'s semantic meaning ('all' is indeed 'more than half'). In (32), however, the writer generates a generalized conversational implicature to the effect that 'not all' (section 3.2.1). Combined with the semantic lower-bounded meaning, the overall interpretation of *most* in (32) is the **conveyed meaning**: 'more than half and not all.' Relevance theoreticians similarly account for (33), and they also agree that the upper bound on scalar quantifiers is pragmatically derived. But they have adopted Carston's (1988 and onwards) position that the upper bound on scalar quantifiers is explicated, rather than implicated (section 3.2.2). Under their analysis, the combination of *most*'s semantic meaning with an explicated ('not all') inference provides the proper interpretation of 'more than half and not all' in (32), this time, as an **explicature**. Finally, I have recently argued that the upper bound has the same semantic status as the lower bound on *most* (Ariel, 2003, 2004b, 2006b). *Most* under this circumbounded (lower- and upper-bounded) analysis roughly means 'a proper subset larger than half', so the upper bound is here **encoded** (note the specification of a **proper** subset), as is the total interpretation commonly associated with *most* (as in (32)). On this account, it is the interpretation in (33) which is pragmatically derived (section 3.2.3). Let's consider the arguments supporting each of these positions.

3.2.1   Implicating the upper bound

As we have seen, *most* is interpreted in one of two ways: 'more than half but not all' (as in (32)) and 'more than half and possibly all' (as in (33)). One possibility is then to posit an ambiguity of meaning. Recall, however, that a semantic solution of ambiguity is in principle to be avoided as much as possible according to Grice's Modified Occam's Razor Principle. Moreover, with scalar expressions, the two interpretations involved are also partly contradictory ('not all' versus 'possibly all'), which renders the ambiguity solution even less attractive. Horn's (1972) insight was that we can use the semantics/pragmatics division of labor to account for these two interpretations in an intuitively satisfying way. The neo-Gricean solution (following Horn, 1972) was to take the lower-bound-only interpretation (as in (33)) as *most*'s semantic meaning, and derive the circumbounded interpretation (as in (32)) pragmatically, by relying on a (generalized) conversational implicature excluding 'all.'

First, Horn's proposal straightforwardly accounts for a variety of cases where *most* is compatible with 'all.' Here are other cases, in addition to (33):

(34) a.   We were very pleased to get such high quality abstracts . . . we seem to cover **most (if not all!)** the central issues being addressed in research on . . .

(Private e-mail, April 16, 2004)

   b.   ~ A: Did **most** of the students pass the tests?
          B: No.   (Horn, 2006: ex. 45)

   c.   ~**Most** Michigan drivers exceed 70 mph, almost/#barely 75%.

(Horn, 2006: ex. 48)

In (34a) we don't take the writer to contradict herself although she mentions 'all' as a possibility when *most* was first stated. *Most* is compatible with all (compare, ??~*most, if not some*). In (34b), argues Horn, the speaker denying *most* is specifically denying its lower bound, so B is committed to '50 percent or fewer' (less than the lower bound specifies), and not to 'either (a) 50 percent or fewer or (b) all' (more than the upper bound specifies). Since it is the semantic meaning which necessarily falls under negation, and since we see that only the lower bound is here negated, it follows that the lower bound alone is *most*'s semantic meaning. (34c) shows that *most* harmonizes with the upwards-oriented *almost*, and cannot cooccur with the negative-oriented *barely*, which again supports the assumption of a lower-bound-only analysis. In addition, *at least most*, considered an impossible combination, is naturally accounted for. If *most* is only lower bounded, there is no point in modifying it by an expression whose function is to create a lower-bounded interpretation. A similar argument accounts for the impossibility of *exactly most*. If *most* is only lower-bounded, it is incompatible with a punctual reading, which is what *exactly* imposes.

Next, imagine the following scenario:

(35)   The catering company manager announced that if anyone would guess how many of the guests would prefer square plates, they would win a dinner set. Dana guessed that **most** of the guests would prefer square plates, Oren guessed that none of the guests would prefer square plates, and Iddo guessed that **80%** of the guests would prefer square plates.

QUESTION: At the end of the event, it was found out that **all** the guests preferred square plates. Who is entitled to the promised prize?

ANSWERS: A. Dana B. Oren C. Iddo D. Nobody

Based on his judgment regarding a parallel example (Horn, 2006: ex. 47a), Horn unhesitatingly awards the prize to Dana. For him, when the state of affairs is that 'all' is true, the person who stated *most* wins, because *most* is compatible with 'all.'

Second, the differential behavior of a quantifier such as *most* and cardinal numbers, such as *six*, can be accounted for. While originally Horn (1972) analyzed the cardinals as carrying the same, lower-bound-only semantic meaning, deriving their circumbounded ('exactly') reading pragmatically, the consensus has since shifted, and Horn too accepts that the upper bound on the numbers has semantic (truth-conditional) status. If that's the case, we expect *most* and the cardinals to pattern differently, for in the case of *most* the upper bound is pragmatic. Indeed, note how it is possible to deny *six* when a higher number is the case. Unlike (34b), B's denial of *six* in (36) is compatible with either a 'fewer than six' (the *most* pattern) or with 'more than six' (which seems impossible for *most*):

(36)   A: Wait, how many, you took **six**?
         B: No you guys got **seven**.   (LSAC)

Going back to the guessing game of (35), Horn's analysis predicts that although 80 percent and *most* are not all that different, when reality is that 'all' is the case, Iddo should not get the prize, for unlike *most*, the cardinal *80 percent* is circumbounded, so 'all' is incompatible with it. Researchers' intuitions tend to go along with Horn's.[20]

We therefore seem to have good reasons for assuming that only the lower bound has semantic status for *most*. In addition, there is a natural, motivated way to derive the upper bound pragmatically from the lower-bound-only semantic meaning. 'Not all' is a calculable conversational implicature from *most*. Here's how (and see section 1.4 again). Given the enrichment, I-Principle, and the fact that *most* is compatible with 'all,' the expectation would be for the most informative interpretation allowed under *most*, which is 'all.' Recall, however, the neo-Gricean Q-Principle, whose role it is to block some I-implicatures. Here are the relevant parts of the Q-Principle. It is the recipient's corollary of the Q-Principle which directly explains why an I-implicature would not be generated (regularly):

(37)   The Q-Principle

> a. *Speaker's maxim*: Do not provide a statement that is informationally
>   weaker than your knowledge of the world allows.
> b. *Recipient's corollary*: Take it that the speaker has made the strongest
>   statement consistent with what he knows . . .   (Levinson, 2000b: 76)

The relevant comparison is here between *most* (contributing to an informationally weaker statement) and *all* (contributing to an informationally stronger statement). According to (37a), the speaker should not state *most* if she's in a position to state *all*. However, should her knowledge of the world not allow her to state *all*, then she must use *most* (provided she is committed to its lower-bounded semantic meaning, of course).[21] Note the following in this connection:

(38)   And um, we're doing a program <unclear> it's called <unclear> and uh it
            has **all** the groups that are Indian, um, culturally focused, well **most** of the
            groups, well **some**, some of the groups <nv_ laugh>.   (LSAC)

As much as the speaker would like to support her claim with the stronger *all*, she is apparently not in a position to do so, and she retreats to *most* (and eventually to *some*). The addressee reasons that since the speaker could just as easily use *all* (it's equally short), but didn't, even though the latter would have been more informative, she does not intend 'all.' So this is how neo-Griceans get to have 'all' as included in the semantic meaning of *most*, but not actually read off *most* in most cases.

Another argument supporting an implicature status for *most*'s upper bound comes from nondetachability, which predicts that given the same content (and

---

[20] For some reason, which I don't understand, Horn actually states that it's not clear who wins a bet involving a cardinal number (Horn, 2006: ex. 47c). The bet may even be void, he claims. I don't see how that follows from his account, when the cardinals have an 'exactly' interpretation, which is only strengthened by the guessing game context.

[21] In fact, if we add *some* to the scale of informativeness here, we can say that a speaker should prefer *most* (the stronger expression) to *some* (the weaker expression).

context) the same implicature should be generated. This is indeed the case when we examine *more than half*. The article whose headline was quoted in (32) begins with the following sentence:

(39)   **More than half** of Israelis and Palestinians support an unofficial peace
        proposal that includes unprecedented compromises for both sides ...
                                        (*Haaretz* English edition, Nov. 24, 2003)

Note that we would have been equally surprised if we later found out that 'all Israelis and Palestinans' support the Geneva accord when they were described as *more than half* (and see Ariel, 2003, 2004b, 2006b, and section 3.2.3 below). Finally, the assumption is that this interpretative process is the default (Levinson) or the normal (Horn) procedure, and that's why 'not all' is a generalized rather than a particularized conversational implicature.[22] Indeed, the majority of the cases where *most* is used are interpreted as upper bounded (91.3 percent in my data of mostly English conversations – see Ariel, 2004b).

Summing up, Q-implicatures negate the applicability of a stronger alternative (*all*), lexically specified on a Horn scale, to the case at hand. For *most*, the implicature generated is 'not all'. We can now re-examine (32) and (33), and analyze them à la neo-Griceans. Both examples start out in the same way. *Most* semantically means 'more than half (possibly all),' but a generalized conversational implicature is generated more often than not, adding 'not all,' and creating 'more than half but not all' as *most*'s conveyed meaning. In (33) and (34a) we have the extra step of implicature cancellation (due to *if not all* in (34a)). Since the upper bound on *most* is implicated under the neo-Gricean approach, its presence in some cases and absence in others is naturally accounted for. Conversational implicatures, generalized ones included, are cancelable in appropriate contexts. When canceled, the upper bound is missing. When present, the upper bound is in force.

3.2.2   Explicating the upper bound

Relevance theoreticians accept the original Horn (1972) lower-bound-only lexical analysis of scalar quantifiers such as *most*. They too derive the upper bound on *most* pragmatically. However, according to Carston (1988, and especially, 1990, 1998a), the upper bound is (often) explicitly communicated, rather than implicated. It is a pragmatic enrichment of the explicit content. Thus, the circumbounded interpretation of *most* in (32) is its explicature. Carston's arguments are aimed at the neo-Gricean approach in general, but relevant to our discussion here are her arguments against the neo-Gricean analysis of scalar implicatures as generalized conversational implicatures (see Hirschberg, 1991, Sperber and Wilson, 1986/1995: 276–278, 1987 for arguments against positing a distinction between generalized and particularized conversational implicatures).

---

[22] Note that since *more than half* does not participate in a Horn scale, it would be a particularized, rather than a generalized conversational implicature in this case.

Carston's main argument is that what are considered default implicatures (for Levinson, 2000b) or implicatures generated in a "normal" context (Horn, 1984 and onwards) are not quite as "default" or "normal" as the neo-Griceans present them. Many cases where at least Levinson would have the speaker generate a 'not all' implicature are cases where no such interpretation need be generated. Carston reminds us that all implicatures are generated subject to their potential Relevance. If 'not all' contributes to the cognitive effects intended by the speaker, then it should be derived, as in:

(40)   One size fits **most**.
                                    (T-shirt label, Longs Drugstore, Santa Barbara, Jan. 2003).

Otherwise it's not. In addition to (33), here are two examples where the upper bound is irrelevant, and is not generated:

(41) a.   I don't know if **most** of the data that you collect will be for Longman.
                                                                                            (LSAC)
     b.   Be respectful of other views; if **most** people disagree with you, there's probably a good reason.   (www.aclu.org/getequal/orga/gettingstarted6.html)

In (41), what is relevant is whether a lot of the data/people are the way the speaker describes them. It's relevant enough if the specified predicates are true of more than half of these. Whether or not 'all' is the case is simply not relevant.

Carston's point is supported in Ariel (2004b) with many examples from spoken and written English and Hebrew. Here is one such example:

(42)   **Most** of the parties at the Knesset are opposed to most of the economic proposals.   (Originally Hebrew, *Voice of Israel* news, April 25, 2002)[23]

In a democracy, once the majority is opposed to some proposal, whether or not all are opposed is irrelevant. Since majority rules, what counts is 'more than half.' Cases such as (41) and (42) show that contra the neo-Gricean assumptions, what is theoretically more informative ('all') is not necessarily more relevant in specific contexts (see also Green, 1995). If 'all' is irrelevant, however, then no Horn scale comparison is performed, and no implicature should be generated under the neo-Gricean analysis either. (41) and (42) are not, as such, counterexamples to the neo-Gricean account. Still, the very existence of such cases, even if only a minority, casts some doubt on the "generalized" nature of the putative 'not all' implicature.

But there are many other cases where a 'not all' implicature is inappropriate. Discourse data, mostly from conversational English, cited in Ariel (2004b) shows that in fact 'not all' is an irrelevant interpretation in the majority (82.7 percent) of cases where *most* is used. Most of the cases found were different from the examples considered by Carston, however. Most cases are such that had the speaker been in a position to commit to 'all,' her statement would have been more informative and quite relevant. Consider the following:

(43)   **MOST** UCSB students have 0 . . . 1 . . . 2 . . . 3 or 4 drinks per week (4000 don't drink at all).   (An anti-drinking ad at UCSB, Feb. 2002)

---

[23] The Knesset is the Israeli parliament.

(43) is part of an anti-drinking poster. Of course, had the university authorities been in a position to claim that all UCSB students have up to 4 drinks a week their statement would have been stronger and more convincing. 'All' here would have been relevant, then. The point is, however, that the fact that 'all' would have theoretically been relevant does not automatically render 'not all' relevant. The reason why it isn't relevant is that we simply do not normally have expectations for universal claims. Since quantified amounts in natural conversations tend not to concern the color of crows (a philosophers' favorite is *all crows are black*), a statement true of most members of some category is considered a very strong statement, one which can serve as a solid basis for drawing relevant implications. In (43), addressees are supposed to be impressed by the fact that a majority of the students do not drink a lot (up to 4 drinks a week). They are urged to follow the example set by this majority. In fact, even advertisers expect to persuade consumers to buy products based on majorities, rather than totalities of happy clients. What all this boils down to is that we should question the almost automatic reliance on the Horn scale when *most* is used, since it wrongly assumes that we forever expect universal claims.

Note that had 'all' been expected every time quantification was involved, the readers of (43) would compare *most* to *all*, and they would have generated a 'not all' implicature. Now, conversational implicatures, generalized ones included, are speaker intended. As argued at length in Ariel (2004b), it is unreasonable to attribute to the addressors of e.g. (43) an intention to communicate 'not all.' Speakers using *most* intend their addressees to only consider the majority reference set profiled. This is the basis for the cognitive effects that addressees are guided to rely on. Speakers definitely do not want addressees to consider the complement set (the 'not all' set) when they use *most*. Indeed, it is an uncooperative addressee who does focus on the complement set. (44) is taken from a cartoon featuring a couple fighting over *most* (Capital letters indicate original boldface):

(44)   A: Why do you always think you're right?
        B: Because I'm RIGHT **most** of the time
        A: **MOST** of the time? Then you admit you're wrong SOME of the time. Wrong! Wrong! WRONG!!
        B: Things are so different at the office.
                    (Beetle Bailey, *International Herald Tribune*, Oct.17, 2003)

B treats *most* as contributing a very strong statement, in fact, one supporting the claim that he is **always** right. Needless to say, he has no intention of implicating 'not all.' A, on the other hand, being uncooperative, hastens to focus on the complement set in order to prove B wrong. Any proposal that the addressors of (43) generate a 'not all' implicature is tantamount to proposing that the exchange in (44) is quite cooperative, that what A does explicitly in (44) we all do implicitly in (43). This is a strange intention to attribute to speakers, whose point in using a *most* utterance is for the addressee to derive contextual implications based **only** on the reference set. After all, the complement set in such cases is the set of counter-examples to their very claim (the students who have more than 4 drinks a week).

It turns out that (43) represents the typical *most* example. The typical case, then, is one where the reference set, and not the counterexamples of the complement set, is the speaker's focus. It would then be strange to ascribe to the speaker an intention to implicate 'not all,' because 'not all' serves as a basis for deriving precisely the opposite implications (if some students have more than 4 drinks a week, so can we, the addressees). If so, 'all exclusion' may be a particularized conversational implicature at best, generated only in specific contexts.

The next argument equally applies against either a generalized or a particularized conversational status for the 'all exclusion' interpretation. As Carston noted, the upper bound on scalar expressions sometimes contributes to the truth conditions of the utterance. Implicatures, of course, are not supposed to affect truth evaluations. Consider the following:

(45) a.   Son, I've found my method is as good as **any** other and better than **most**.
(a character in the Western movie *Shane*, cited by Bob Knight, *International Herald Tribune*, Feb. 6, 2004)

   b.   Regretfully, I can't say **all** Knesset members, but **most** of the Knesset members . . .   (Originally Hebrew, Golda Meir, Feb. 1970, quoted on *Voice of Israel* radio, Feb. 23, 2003)

In order to interpret the examples in (45) as noncontradictory, each as presenting two distinct options, we must interpret *most* as 'more than half and less than all' here. The content, the coherence and the truth-conditions of (45) depend on our assigning *most* an upper bound at the level where truth-conditional content is determined. Levinson (2000b) and Horn (2004, 2006) agree that some examples do show that what they consider to be implicatures affect truth conditions. As mentioned in section 3.1.2.1, Levinson is pushed into accepting exceptions to the definitional feature of implicatures as not affecting the truth conditions of the proposition they are based on. Horn, on the other hand, views such examples as "retroactive accommodation," where the implausible interpretation is the proposition expressed, but then the addressee reinterprets the examples with the 'not all' interpretation playing a truth-conditional role at a later semantic level. In fact, it is only this indirectly expressed proposition which is assessed for truth. Carston, on the other hand, proposes that the added upper bound on scalar quantifiers (she discusses *some*) constitutes a narrowing of the concept, a necessary interpretative process for practically all linguistic expressions (see her 2002a: chapter 5). In fact, the 'some but not all' narrowing of *some* is just one possible narrowing of the vague concept 'some.' Presumably the same applies to *most*.

Experimental results (e.g. Noveck, 2001; Noveck and Posada, 2003; Papafragou and Schwarz, 2005/6) show that at least some subjects refuse to confirm that statements such as *Some elephants have trunks* are true, even though they should have easily canceled the 'not all' implicature, given their world knowledge that in fact all elephants have trunks. If so, the 'not all' inference here has a truth-conditional effect. Hence, it cannot be a conversational implicature. Recall that even if not canceled, implicatures are not supposed to affect the truth conditions of the proposition which served to trigger them. Indeed, although the following implicates that proportionately more women than men wore evening clothes (this was verified with one set of subjects), when a second set of subjects were asked if (46) is false should there have been proportionately more men than women wearing evening clothes, only one subject (4.5 percent) thought it was false (68 percent thought it was true, and 27.3 percent chose 'can't tell'):

(46)   **Most** of the women and **more than half** of the men wore evening clothes.

Implicatures do not affect truth conditions, then. But the upper bound on *most* does seem to have such an effect.

The most convincing argument against an implicature analysis and for an explicature analysis is based on Recanati's (1989) "Availability Principle," which states that researchers' analyses must be faithful to pretheoretic intuitions on whether some pragmatic inference is 'said' or implicated. We have already considered Recanati's (1989: 326) objection to a lower-bound-only semantic analysis of the cardinal numbers based on this principle (see above). Horn (1992 and onwards) accepts this criticism regarding the cardinal numbers, but he insists that the criticism is inapplicable to the scalar quantifiers.[24] But it seems that Recanati's argument naturally applies to *most*. Native speakers only see it as a circumbounded quantity which is larger than half but smaller than all. Bach has recently expressed a similar view regarding the scalar quantifiers:

> A typical claim is that in uttering "Some of the boys went to the party," the speaker implicates that not all of the boys went to the party. But this assumes that the speaker means **not one but two things**, that some of the boys went to the party *and* that not all of them did. Really, though, the speaker means only **one thing**, that some but not all of the boys went to the party.
> (Bach, 2006: 29, emphases added)

Bach's conclusion is that *some*'s circumbounded interpretation is an impliciture, rather than a conveyed meaning comprising a lower-bounded semantics augmented by an 'all-exclusion' implicature. Bach's (1994) implicitures are similar to the Relevance-theoretic explicatures, although he emphasizes that they are implicit interpretations (see section 7.6). Note, however, that an impliciture is distinct from the more basic semantic meaning of 'what is said,' which determines the literal meaning, what the utterance expresses out of context. Still, the intuition behind the "Availability Principle" regarding the inseparability of the lower and the upper bounds on scalar expressions is here echoed.

It seems that Carston, Bach, and Recanati are right on target regarding the upper bound on scalar expressions in general often being explicated/implicitated rather than implicated.[25] I have specifically argued that it applies to *most*. To see that this is the case we need to provide empirical evidence for the claim that the "Availability Principle," applied to *most*, shows the upper bound to be explicated

---

[24] See his objections in Horn (1992) and my counterarguments in Ariel (2004b, 2006b).

[25] But Recanati is only committed to this point regarding the cardinals. He (p.c.) is agnostic regarding the upper bound on the scalar quantifiers.

rather than implicated (i.e. internal and inseparable rather than external to the semantic meaning). Recall that the rationale behind the "Availability Principle" (Recanati, 1989, and see chapter 7 below) is that if a putative inference is not independently available to interlocutors it is part of the explicature. Implicatures, on the other hand, are perceived as external to the semantic meaning, and therefore easily distinguished from it (think of Linda Tripp's implicature in example (1a) in chapter 1: 'he won't have you killed' from her utterance of *he's not that stupid*. No one would confuse 'he won't have you killed' for part of the utterance's direct, explicated, meaning).

In other words, we need to show that speakers' intuitions are such that the upper bound is nondistinguishable from the encoded meaning of *most*. In order to check speakers' interpretations of *most*, Ariel (2004b) constructed a questionnaire which presented subjects with a variety of sentences containing *most*. Subjects were asked to circle all the values that the speaker could possibly intend when she used *most* in the case at hand, even if the answers seemed quite unlikely to them. Not only did I constantly remind my subjects orally that they should select as many answers as they could, the following, written instruction was also read out loud to them before they began filling out the questionnaire:[26]

(47)   It's possible that **several** of the answers are appropriate. In such a case you should choose **all** the answers that the speaker might have considered possible, **even if chances for it are slim in your opinion**.   (Original emphases)

Consider the following questions on the questionnaire:

(48)   **Most** high school students drink alcohol.
        Which of the following cases could the speaker mean?
        A. 80% of high school students   B. 50% of high school students
        C. 100% of high school students   D. 28% of high school students
        E. None of the above.

(49)   An **overwhelming majority** of the students passed the test.
        What percentage of students may have passed the test according to the speaker's sentence?
        A. 97%   B. 98%   C. 99%   D. 100%

Both theories considered so far make the same predictions regarding choices of non-100 percent responses. The lower-bounded semantic meaning of *most* should prevent subjects from picking answers B and D in (48), because they violate the lower bound on *most*. Answers (48A) and (49A–C) abide by the lower-bound restriction, and should be selected by subjects. The theories differ regarding the confirmation of an 'all' value. Given the repeated instruction to the subjects that the more responses the better, including unlikely responses, subjects must have been prompted to also consider the 100% answers (C for (48) and D for (49)).

---

[26] The questionnaire actually tested Hebrew *rov* which translates both English *most* and *majority*. See Ariel (2003, 2004b) for a detailed description of the questionnaires.

Now, on the implicature analysis, these should be circumstances where at least a sizable minority of the subjects are driven to cancel the 'not all' implicature and choose 'all' answers. On the explicature analysis, subjects are expected to be more reluctant to choose the 100 percent value in either question, because the upper bound is inseparable from the encoded lower-bounded meaning. This is what happened. While 29/32 subjects (90.6 percent) picked A (a value of 80 percent) for (48), only 2 (6.25 percent) chose answer C (a value of 100 percent). Note that this rate is negligible. (A similar percentage of subjects chose the semantically impossible answer B with the value of 50 percent.)[27] Similar results were received for the question in (49). Practically all subjects (30, 93.75 percent on average) chose each of the answers in A–C (with values of 97–99 percent), but only one subject (3.1 percent) chose answer D (100 percent). These results are very clear. Despite my efforts, subjects were reluctant to choose the 100 percent value for *most*, presumably because the upper bound is an inseparable part of *most*'s interpretation.

In sum, we have reviewed three types of arguments against an implicature status for the upper bound on *most*. First, the implicature does not seem to be generalized, in that the majority of cases seem not to favor its generation. Of course, it could then be a particularized conversational implicature. But Carston argues for an explicated status for the upper bound on scalar quantifiers instead, because she views it as part of the explicitly communicated message (a pragmatic enrichment, narrowing the broad meaning of the scalar quantifier). In particular, the upper bound contributes to the truth-conditions of the utterance. Levinson, Horn and Bach concur, although they are opposed to assigning the upper bound an explicated status. But the facts are that the upper bound is part of the truth-conditional content of the utterance (at least sometimes according to Levinson and Horn, in the unmarked impliciture according to Bach). Finally, we have applied Recanati's and Bach's argument that the application of the Gricean distinction between the said and implicated to scalar expressions is a theoretical move at odds with speakers' intuitions: speakers can only access the meaning of *most* as one whole. This is what the questionnaire data point to. In section 3.2.3 we take this conclusion one step further and propose that the circumbounded interpretation is *most*'s lexical meaning.

3.2.3   Encoding the upper bound

In section 3.2.2 we reviewed arguments against an implicature view and for an explicature view of the upper bound on *most*. Now, Carston's argument for an explicature view is that the upper bound is a **pragmatic enrichment**. One can argue for a more radical explicature position. We here examine the possibility that *most*'s **lexical** meaning is circumbounded (lower and upper bounded).[28]

---

[27] Calculation of percentages are performed per response, since subjects could circle any number of responses.

[28] See Ariel (2003, 2004b, 2006b).

Table 3.1 *The discourse status of the upper bound on* most *according to the implicature, explicature, and circumbounded accounts*

Interpretation/Account	Implicature	Explicature	Circumbounded
Upper bound	implicated	explicated: pragmatic	explicated: lexical
'All' compatibility	lexical	lexical	pragmatic: explicated or truth-compatible inference

Assuming a semantic upper bound, it is cases where *most* lacks an upper bound (compatibility with 'all') which need to be pragmatically derived. This approach assumes a reversed semantics/pragmatics division of labor. Table 3.1 is a somewhat simplified presentation of the differences between the three positions we are considering.[29]

The first argument for a lexical rather than pragmatic (albeit explicated) status for the upper bound on *most* is that contra prevalent assumptions, pragmatics (whether neo-Gricean or Relevance-theoretic) simply cannot provide the upper bound. Note that the empirical evidence we have reviewed so far leads to a paradox from the point of view of the two pragmatic approaches we have discussed. On the one hand, in support of the neo-Gricean account in section 3.2.1, findings from natural discourse were reported, where the great majority of *most* uses are seen as upper bounded (91.3 percent). On the other hand, in support of Carston's argument that 'not all' is not a **generalized** conversational implicature in section 3.2.2, counts from the same data were cited showing, this time, that 'not all' is not a reasonable implicature on the speaker's part in a great majority of the cases (82.7 percent, see again (42), (43), which are typical *most* examples). How can both these claims be true?

In the absence of an interactionally intended 'not all' interpretation (82.7 percent of the cases), what is the source of the prevalent upper bound on *most*? Both pragmatic theories rely on some sort of 'all'-exclusion pragmatic inference to derive the upper bound. This inference, the discourse data show, is only rarely relevant in actual discourse. If it's not there, it cannot provide the upper bound. But we know the upper bound is there. How can we account for it? The answer is, with an upper bound that is not dependent on pragmatic implicature/enrichment, a lexical upper bound, in other words. On a lexical view, the upper bound is guaranteed to be there even when a 'not all' pragmatic inference is unavailable (the majority of cases). So, the first argument against the pragmatic approaches is that they just cannot account for many of the cases where an upper bound is read off *most*.

---

[29] See the above references, as well as Horn (2006) and Papafragou and Schwarz (2005/6) for a debate on the topic.

The second argument for an encoded view relies on the absolute refusal of subjects to interpret the intended meaning of *most* as including a 100 percent value.[30] Now, we have relied on the "Availability Principle" to argue for the explicature view and against the implicature view of *most*. But note that the principle captures well the distinction between the implicated and the explicated, but it does not distinguish explicated inferences from encoded meanings. After all, both constitute an inseparable explicated meaning. The fact that we found that the upper bound is explicated does not guarantee that it is a pragmatic enrichment. It could very well be an encoded aspect of *most*'s meaning. We need a way to tease apart explicated inferences from encoded meanings, and to decide whether the results we obtained from the application of the 'Availability Principle' to *most* are due to the upper bound being an explicated pragmatic enrichment or an encoded aspect.

In order to distinguish between the explicature and the encoded views we need to see whether the refusal among subjects to accept an 'all' value for *most* is absolute in all contexts. Recall that the upper bound on the Relevance-theoretic view is a pragmatically enriched aspect of the explicature. Pragmatic inferences are not always present (or they can't be distinguished from encoded meanings). If so, we should be able to get the 100 percent value at least in some special cases. In order to view the pragmatic enrichment thesis as empirically viable, we must ascertain that there are cases where subjects are willing to adopt a different explicature (lacking the upper bound). If they absolutely cannot, we will have to conclude that the explicated upper bound on *most* is not pragmatically derived, but actually an encoded aspect of the expression.

In order to pressure subjects into accepting a 100 percent value as a possible speaker-intended denotation for *most*, they were presented with a question where all the specific answers provided (A–D) involved some type of violation. Answer A (100 percent) constitutes a pragmatic violation under the pragmatic approaches reviewed so far (*most* is preferably seen as upper bounded), whereas B–D constitute clear semantic violations (all values are below 51 percent). Note further that the question was chosen so that world knowledge in fact encourages an 'all' interpretation (cohorts are quite regularly students born in the same calendar year[31]):

(50)   **Most** of the students in the class were born in 1970.
         How many students could the speaker mean?
         A. 100% of the students   B. 20% of the students   C. 50% of the students
         D. 49% of the students   E. None of the above.

---

[30] I say absolutely even though there were a few subjects who chose 100 percent value answers for *most*, because these acceptance rates were as low or even lower than those for lower-bound violations. Questionnaire results never achieve 100 percent results. The main finding is that what are taken as unquestionably semantic interpretations induce the same judgments as what have so far been taken as pragmatic judgments.

[31] Note that the Hebrew counterpart of *students* used here was *talmidot*, prototypically used to refer to elementary or high school (female) students, where cohorts are of the same age.

If the upper bound is indeed pragmatic and hence cancelable, subjects should have had no problem. They should have chosen A (rather than B–D), opting for a pragmatic violation over a semantic violation. Indeed, some subjects did just that (9.4 percent). But, more subjects chose C (with the semantically illegitimate value of 50 percent): 15.6 percent. The conclusion seems to be that the upper bound is as semantic as the lower bound. The number of answers violating the semantic lower bound (49 percent and 50 percent) is in fact larger than the number of answers violating the "pragmatic" upper bound (100 percent) across all questions.

A "pragmatic" violation which is even harder for speakers to perform than a semantic violation cannot be a pragmatic violation. We should therefore seriously consider the possibility that it is semantic. To further see if that's the case we can compare questionnaire results for *most* with those for *more than half*. Recall that *more than half* too tends to be interpreted as less than 'all' (see (39) again). In fact, *more than half* favors lower majorities than *most* does, and is less favored for higher values (90 percent, 99 percent, see Ariel, 2004b). Still, in the counterpart of (50), where no semantically viable option was available except for 100 percent, while there was a clear tendency to avoid the 100 percent value (58 percent of the subjects not selecting 'all'), a sizable minority (42 percent) did accept the 100 percent value for *more than half* in that question.

The pressure here for subjects to accept 100 percent values was much more successful than with *most*. In many respects, *more than half* patterns as *most* is expected to on the pragmatic view. The upper bound is indeed a pragmatic matter here. Subjects show a clear preference for avoiding 100 percent values for *more than half* but, when pressured, they are willing to consider the possibility that *more than half* can denote 'all.' This is what we should expect from a pragmatic pattern. For *most*, on the other hand, subjects absolutely refused to do the same under identical circumstances.

We should now check whether the circumbounded analysis of *most* can give rise to the two types of interpretations of *most* we presented at the beginning of section 3.2. It is of course a straightforward matter for the circumbounded view to account for (32). *Most* is simply interpreted according to its lexical meaning here. Since discourse findings show that (32) is the typical *most* example, the majority of cases do not require any inference.[32] Recall, however, (33), where *most* seems to be interpreted as a lower-bound-only 'more than half.' These cases are straightforwardly accounted for by either pragmatic approach, since they assume a lexical meaning without an upper bound. The challenge for a theory which assumes an encoded upper bound is to account for cases where the upper bound seems to be missing. We need to distinguish here between two types of cases. (33) presents one type. To account for (33), the idea is that *most*, just like any scalar term, can be interpreted in the 'at least' reading. Consider the following, a minimally modified version of (33), with a cardinal number (there were fifty-eight Hall of Famers in 2002):

---

[32] But see Ariel (2004b), where I argue that *most* in addition tends to be interpreted as a noteworthy majority.

(51)   ~ The target date for the meeting is Jan. 17 in Los Angeles, provided **thirty** of
              the Hall of Famers can make it.

Note that the fact that the cardinals are considered semantically upper bounded
does not block our interpreting *thirty* in (51) as 'at least thirty,' probably as an
explicature (the speaker in (51) is committed to their proposal should 37 or all 58
Hall of Famers be able to make it). In other words, the fact that some meaning is
semantically circumbounded (lower and upper bounded) does not block an 'at
least' contextually enriched interpretation. This is true for the numbers and it
could equally be true for *most*. Having an upper bound does not entail 'not all.' So
'at least most' can be an ad hoc adjusted meaning of *most*.

But there is another case of truth compatibility between *most* and 'all.' Recall
the accepted intuition that should 'all Israelis, Palestinians support the Geneva
accord,' interlocutors would not judge (32) false. The same intuition informs
Horn's judgments on bets (see the discussion around (35)). In these cases, it is
not the speakers' intentions to convey an 'at least' interpretation, but should 'all'
be the case the statement is not judged false. Here's a relevant question posed to
subjects. I list the number of subjects choosing each response in parentheses:

(52)   The teacher already knows **most** of the students.
              Assuming that the teacher already knows **all** the students, is the speaker's
              claim true?
              Please choose one answer:
              A. Yes (11/15, 73.3%).
              B. No (2/15, 13.3%).
              C. Can't tell (2/15, 13.3%).

Almost three-quarters of the subjects thought that should the state of affairs be that
'all' is true, stating *most* is true. How can we explain this result when the results so
far have been that 93.75 percent of the responses refuse to accept a 100 percent
value for *most*?

The key issue here is a distinction between upper bound and 'all exclusion,' and
between lexical meaning and truth compatibility. There is a tendency in the
literature to conflate each pair of concepts. We should consider the possibility
that *most*'s lexical meaning is upper bounded, but not excluding 'all,' and that
compatibility with 'all' is a truth-compatible potential inference from *most*, rather
than a potential denotation of *most* (as e.g. values of 85 percent or 99 percent are).
Since the upper bound was defined as an 'all' exclusion inference by the pragmatic
approaches, such an interpretation is incompatible with states of affairs in which
'all' is the case. But if we do not define the upper bound as 'all'-excluding, then
most, just like any other linguistic term, can be seen as compatible with higher
values in appropriate contexts. Parts are usually considered true when wholes are
(If 'all my friends are nice,' then 'most of my friends are nice'; If 'this cake is
tasty,' then 'so is a slice of it').

The point is that truth compatibility (with 'all') does not automatically translate
into lexically specified truth conditions (for *most*). Koenig (1991: 140), writing on

the cardinals, warns us not to confuse between two logically independent questions (i) the fact that "Scalar predicates are (at least sometimes) treated discursively as logically **compatible** with a higher value on the scale they evoke" (applied to *most*, this would mean that *most* can be compatible with 'all'), and (ii) "the theoretical claim that the **lexical meaning** of scalar predicates specifies only a lower bound on this scale" (applied here, this would mean that *most* means 'at least more than half, possibly all,' emphases added). There is then a difference between expression X being compatible with a certain state of affairs, and expression X coding that state of affairs. *Most* is certainly compatible with 'all' being the case (on some occasions), but these scalar effects do not necessitate a lexical status. In fact, they are easily seen as language-independent and not even intended by the speaker. The idea is that whereas *most* commits the speaker to asserting something about 'most but less than all,' its use is potentially compatible with states of affairs in which the predicate is true of 'all.'

To support the point about the separation between intended meaning and truth compatibility, here is a question, which concerns *between 70% and 80%*. Note that this expression has an uncontroversially circumbounded lexical meaning:

(53)   Maya is a new teacher, who will start teaching at a school next year. She very much wants to do well at her job. Galit, the principal, tells her that she has decided to assign her to an especially weak class. The following conversation takes place at the beginning of the school year:
GALIT: The Ministry of Education tests will be conducted in six months. It's a good idea to start preparing the students, especially your class. If half of the students in your class pass the tests it'll be an excellent achievement.
MAYA: I promise you that **between 70% and 80%** of the students will pass the tests.
GALIT: Let's hope so. You know that the education system has no provision for bonuses, but if this miracle happens, I will get you a 3,000 sheqel bonus.
Seven months later it turns out that 90% of Maya's students passed the tests.
QUESTION: In your opinion, will Maya receive the 3,000 sheqel bonus?

All 23 subjects answered "yes," which means that a lexically upper-bounded expression can be seen as compatible with a higher value. Just as we do not conclude from such findings that the meaning of *between 70% and 80%* is 'at least between 70% and 80%,' why should we conclude that *most* means 'at least most/more than half'?

If this proposal is on the right track, then speakers should distinguish between the meaning of *most* (upper bounded) and states of affairs which render it true ('all' may be compatible with *most*). This seems to be the case. Note the results for the question in (54), as compared to those for (52). The target sentence is identical in the two cases:

(54)   The teacher already knows **most** of the students.
The speaker's intention is that the teacher already knows:
Please choose one answer:
A. Between 51% and 75% of the students (inclusive) (5/23, 21.7%).
B. Between 80% and 95% of the students (inclusive) (14/23, 60.9%).

C. Between 51% and 100% of the students (inclusive) (2/23, 8.7%).

D. Can't tell (2/23, 8.7 percent).

In (54) once again only a marginal 8.7 percent chose a lower-bound-only inter-pretation, even though the two other options were each only partially true. Why are there so many more responses accepting the 100 percent value in question (52) than in question (54) when the sentence is the same? There is a difference between *most*'s meaning (asked about in (54)) and *most*'s potential compatibility with 'all' (asked about in (52)). These results suggest that while *most*'s meaning is upper bounded, it may be seen as truth compatible with 'all' by inference.

It is clearly the type of question which triggered the radically different responses. 'All' avoidance is a stable and absolute interpretation in meaning questions. 'All' acceptance in truth-compatibility questions is unstable and nonabsolute. For exam-ple, compare the results reported on for (52) (a majority favoring the truth compatibility of *most* with 'all') with those for the question cited as (35).[33] In (35), only a third of the subjects awarded the prize to Dana, who guessed *most*, when in fact 'all' was the case. Close to twice as many subjects actually refused to award the prize to Dana, in effect refusing to see *most* as a true guess when 'all' is the case. In other words, subjects don't take the truth compatibility of *most* with 'all' as automatic. A pragmatic inference determines the plausibility of the judg-ment. Other cases (reported on in Ariel, 2003, 2004b, 2006b) reveal other ratios. Different contexts induce different truth-compatibility judgments from subjects. So results are far from absolute when truth compatibility is concerned.

How should the lexical meaning of *most* be defined according to the circum-bounded approach? What's the meaning of *Most Israelis support the Geneva accord*? Informally, it means that there is a proper subset of Israelis, larger than 50 percent, which supports the Geneva accord.[34] Note that the set must be larger than half of all Israelis on the one hand, and smaller than all Israelis on the other hand (it's a proper subset of all Israelis).

Finally, note that the alleged difference between the cardinals and *most* does not necessarily pertain to the question of an upper bound. Whatever differences there are may derive from the fact that the cardinals are punctual, whereas *most* covers a wide range of values. This is why in the guessing game question in (35), the very same subjects who awarded the prize to Dana (who guessed *most*) also awarded it to Iddo (who guessed *80%*). There was no difference regarding the truth compat-ibility with 'all' of *most* and of *80%*. This is straightforwardly accounted for on the circumbounded analysis, which assigns a lexical upper bound to both expressions.

---

[33] See also Noveck (2001) and Papafragou and Musolino (2003) on how subjects vary within and across experiments on whether they accept 'all' when *some* was used. And see the differences between Papafragou and Schwarz (2005/6) and Ariel (2004b, 2006b) regarding 'all' acceptances for *most*. I explain the latter differences in Ariel (2006b).

[34] The formulation here is more in line with conventional analyses of natural language quantifiers, and represents a slight change from my informal definitions in Ariel (2003, 2004b, 2006b). I thank Kent Bach (p.c.) for prompting me to make this change.

As for (34c), there is no absolute connection between lower-bound-only expressions and *almost*, as can be seen in the following:

(55)   ~A: Between 60% and 80% of Michigan drivers exceed 70 mph.
           B: Yea, almost/# barely 75% .

Between 60% and 80% is no doubt an upper-bounded expression, but still, just like *most* in (34c), it here requires *almost*, and cannot cooccur with *barely*. What seemed like a correlation between lower-bounded expressions and upwards-oriented expressions actually depends on the type of argument one is making with the quantifier. (34c) cannot be used to support a lower-bound analysis for *most*, then.

To conclude section 3.2.3, the proposal is that *most* asserts the applicability of some predicate to a proper subset of entities of some category, the subset constituting more than half. While it may be taken either as explicating 'more than half' (i.e. 'at least most' as in (33)) or merely as compatible with 'all' (as in (35), (52)), these interpretations are mediated by pragmatic inference. All in all, the proposal in section 3.2.3 partly reverses the code/inference relations assumed under the pragmatic approaches of sections 3.2.1 and 3.2.2. The upper bound is encoded on the circumbounded approach; it is inferred on the pragmatic approaches. The lack of an upper bound is accounted for by reference to the encoded meaning on the pragmatic approaches; it is (optionally) pragmatically inferred on the circumbounded view.

3.3   The coded, the inferred, and the truth-compatible

Recall Recanati's (1989) point that there is an important difference between *and*-associated inferences (in "properly" ordered conjunctions) and the upper bound on scalar expressions.[35] For scalar interpretations, the claim for explicature status is even stronger. Here, Recanati reminds us, the pragmatic views take what is prima facie one meaning, and split it into two (a lexical lower bound and an implicated upper bound). Now, Recanati uses his "Availability Principle" to motivate an explicated inference status for the upper bound. But, as mentioned above, we can take the principle one step further, and question whether all explicated meanings that **can** be inferred **are** in fact necessarily inferred. Surely, many interpretations diagnosed as explicatures by the "Availability Principle" are encoded, rather than inferred (all lexical meanings form part of the explicature).

We could perhaps consider a partially "anti-Occam's Razor Principle": in the absence of counter evidence, explicated interpretations should be assumed lexical, rather than inferred. For *and*-related interpretations we have seen that there are good reasons militating against a lexical status. There are far more interpretations than is reasonable for an ambiguous lexical item (see section 3.1.1 again), and the

---

[35] Recanati restricts himself to the cardinal numbers, however.

interpretations are not always there. The upper bound on scalar expressions is different. It can be considered constant, in fact. Even in cases of truth compatibility with 'all' it does not have to be canceled. Where it is potentially canceled (when interpreted as 'at least most') the cancellation may not be different from the ad hoc adjustment involved in the interpretation of any circumbounded lexical items, such as the cardinal numbers. We must leave such discussion for future research.

Still, it is important to always bear in mind the distinction between conveyed (intended) interpretations (whether implicated or explicated) and unintended, truth-compatible potential inferences. This distinction is not only relevant for a restricted set of expressions, such as *and*, the cardinal numbers, and scalar expressions. It's an important distinction for all linguistic expressions. Consider the following (cited in Ariel, 2004b):

(56)   Israel has liquidated **Sheikh Yassin** at 5 a.m. this morning.
         (Originally Hebrew, news headlines, *Voice of Israel*, March 22, 2004)

Note that with the sheikh, Israel also killed a few of his aides, as well as passers-by. Nonetheless, nobody would consider (56) false because of that. 'Killing Sheikh Yassin' is compatible with 'killing Sheikh Yassin, his aides and passers-by.' At the same time, nobody would propose that the semantic meaning of *Sheikh Yassin* is therefore only lower bounded ('at least Sheikh Yassin'). While the meanings we postulate must be compatible with all the states of affairs with which the expressions are compatible, they need not specify each such state of affairs. It's at least possible that analyzing *most* as only lower bounded semantically is an attempt to impose on semantics the reflection of reality which is not part and parcel of the purely grammatical meaning of the expression. Compatibility with 'all' could be merely a potential truth-compatible inference. For *and*, the causal interpretations in "backwards"-ordered conjunctions are similarly only potential truth-compatible inferences. The speaker need not take any responsibility for 'all' compatibility for *most*, nor for the causal inferences in "backwards" *and* conjunctions. The analyses of some interpretations associated with *and* conjunctions and with *most* as unintended potential truth-compatible inferences could be seen as parallel to the analysis of 'Sheikh Yassin's aides and passers-by' as external and lexically irrelevant to the semantics of *Sheikh Yassin*. It's a delicate matter to distinguish the truth-compatible from the encoded.

The goal of chapter 3 has been to show that the decision whether some interpretation is coded or inferred with respect to some linguistic expression does not only depend on whether it's possible to derive it as an inference. All the interpretations we have discussed are such that any pragmatic theory can derive by inference. Moreover, even when there is consensus that some putative interpretation (e.g. causal interpretations with *and*) is inferred rather than encoded, what its inferential status is is not self-evident. We have reviewed arguments for various positions, and for the claim that the status of some inferences may in addition vary in different contexts. Thus, some *and*-associated causal inferences are probably explicated, yet the same inferences may be implicated at times, or they may only be potential truth-compatible inferences. Similarly for the upper bound on *most* on the "lexical" approach in section 3.2.3. Even if it is encoded, it can also in addition be implicated or even explicated (as an 'all' exclusion interpretation – see (40), (45) again). In other words, the discoursal status of some interpretation is not necessarily invariant, given the linguistic expression responsible for it. Turning to "reality" to guide us on semantic meanings may lead us astray, for truth compatibility is absolutely distinct from intended meanings, be they encoded or inferred, implicated or explicated. Ultimately, the theoretical decisions we have discussed here must be based on a complex web of arguments including distributional facts, but crucially, also on what we view as a reasonable encoded meaning, and what we see as a reasonable inference.[36] Should we opt for the Gricean "Occamistic" approach, according to which anything which can be analyzed as an inference should be so analyzed? Or, should we impose some constraints on this reductive approach?

It's not the task of this chapter to decide the issue of the correct analyses of *and* inferences, of *most* and other scalar expressions, and of the more general question of whether we should prefer a "small" ("Occamistic") grammar or a "large" ("anti-Occamistic") grammar. Each of the three approaches presented can account for the data in an insightful way, and each should be considered seriously. Together, they demonstrate the challenge facing linguists engaged in drawing the grammar/pragmatics division of labor. Our main goal has been to lay out the features of each of the approaches, so that linguists keep an open mind when setting out to distinguish the inferred from the coded, the explicated from the implicated and the conveyed from the potentially truth-compatible. The important message of this chapter is that awareness of the variety of analytical concepts must be part of the mental equipment of anybody undertaking work of this kind.

---

[36] There is of course also some dependency between codes and inferences, such that if some aspect of the meaning is coded another must be inferred and vice versa.

Crossing the extralinguistic/linguistic divide

Introduction

Part I has emphasized that natural language understanding comprises two types of interpretations: linguistic codes and pragmatic inferences of various kinds.[1] But, of course, we necessarily combine these two. Indeed, major points of interface between grammar and pragmatics are the ephemeral explicature and conveyed meaning, where coded and inferred meanings are integrated into the ad hoc take-home message (see chapters 1 and 7). Part II is devoted to another, very different arena for a grammar/pragmatics interface, one which has long-range effects, the emergence of grammar out of extralinguistic patterns. We here examine the possibility that grammar is often pragmatics turned code. Should we determine that this is the case (chapter 4), a set of harder questions present themselves: how does pragmatics become code? Where does this grammar/pragmatics interface take place? Does this fact undermine the grammar/pragmatics divide? (chapter 5). Part II is about grammar in the making, exemplified in detail in chapter 6. The argument is that pragmatics, together with other extragrammatical triggers, provides the raw materials and impetus for grammar.

Pragmatic inferences are not the only basis for our future grammar. Other extragrammatical patterns are too. For example, the discourse profiles discussed in section 2.3 (Preferred Argument Structure and genre-associated discourse profiles), although not necessarily

---

[1] See Ariel (forthcoming: chapters 6–8) for many analyses drawing a grammar/pragmatics divide within most classical pragmatic topics.

inferential in nature, can potentially grammaticize. As we see below, since discourse, and more specifically the salient discourse pattern, is heavily implicated in the crossing of pragmatics into grammar, we cannot actually explain the crossing of pragmatically inferred associations into grammar without reference to the more general phenomenon of the extralinguistic crossing over to become linguistic. Part II therefore takes a wider perspective, addressing more generally the linguistic/ extralinguistic divide, one aspect of which is the grammar/pragmatics divide.

Note that we have thus far carefully maintained not only a grammar/ pragmatics separation, but, in addition, the analysis has been purely synchronic, assuming a clear-cut synchronic/diachronic divide. However, as we shall see, especially in chapter 6, at any given time, at least some pieces of grammar are (re)emerging, often out of extragrammatical patterns of use. Indeed, the neat grammar/pragmatics division of labor drawn in part I cannot tell the whole story about the relation between grammar and pragmatics. (Some) aspects of synchronic grammar are intricately interwoven with (some) diachronic processes, and the direct link is provided by extragrammatical factors.[2] Many researchers view such findings as arguing against long-established dichotomies in linguistic theory: the grammar/pragmatics divide, the synchrony/diachrony divide, the competence/performance distinction and the grammar/lexicon division of labor.[3]

Consider the synchrony/diachrony distinction. First, the argument is that synchrony is much better understood by reference to diachrony, where structures are analyzed in relation to the processes that gave rise to them (see Bybee, 2000). Diachrony too cannot be understood without reference to synchronic structure: "There is no way to account for change except by appealing to structures and processes that exist synchronically" (Traugott and Dasher, 2002: 16) (see also Hare and Elman, 1995, Joseph, 1992; Labov, 1973).[4] But these are valid arguments more for the historical linguist and for the typologist, who seek explanations. What about the individual speaker? The main justification for the partial collapse of the synchrony/diachrony divide is that

---

[2] On the intimate connection between diachrony and synchrony, specifically on the traceability of diachrony in synchrony, see Hopper and Traugott (1993/2003), Croft (1990/2003), and chapter 6 and section 7.7 below.

[3] See Langacker (1987), Heine *et al.* (1991b), Tottie (1991), Traugott and König (1991), Sinclair (1992), Croft (1993b), Bates and Goodman (1997, 1999), Bybee (1998), Bybee and Hopper (2001a), (Haspelmath, 1999b), Goldberg *et al.* (2004), *inter alia.*

[4] Note that we are here talking about spotting a diachronic change by analyzing one synchronic grammar, which is different from the traditional approach, whereby two synchronic grammars from different periods are compared in order to establish a diachronic path between them.

there is no diachronic competence from the point of view of the speaker.[5] There is no synchrony versus diachrony, because all there is is language use (Heine, 1997: 4–6). "The real cause of change of (linguistic) conventions is nothing other than ordinary language use" (Hermann Paul, cited in Haspelmath, 1999b: 1066).

The speaker is only competent in her synchronic grammar, but that includes sensitivity to current skewed discoursal patterns, such as we have seen for Preferred Argument Structure in section 2.3.1. Crucially, an integral part of the speaker's linguistic practice is, in effect, participation in linguistic change. Nonetheless, it is typically only the linguist, looking in retrospect, who discovers the diachronic change that took place, even though the individual speaker was actively participating and contributing to it.[6] Diachrony takes place within synchrony. This is why "synchronic polysemy and historical change of meaning really supply the same data in many ways" (Sweetser, 1990: 9). Of course, only a partial collapse of the distinction is here intended. Speakers certainly do not mentally represent **all** older stages of their grammar (e.g. Biblical Hebrew for modern speakers of Hebrew), only current and potential changes.[7] And these, moreover, are not at all represented as such. Rather, they are considered either free or conditioned alternatives (Croft, 1990/2003: 232), or minor rules, each with its own probability of application (e.g. rare, optional, preferred).

Note that the claim about no diachrony for the speaker is not merely a psychological claim, that the speaker is simply not aware that she is participating in linguistic change, just as she is often unaware of speech errors she makes. The point is that the synchronic grammar itself encompasses coexisting layers of conventions, some of them old, some of them new, even when the two sets are incompatible with each other, as when they govern the same form but make different predictions about its use (as we see for English reflexive pronouns in

---

[5] Note, however, that some researchers might prefer to reduce synchrony to diachrony, rather than diachrony to synchrony. Hopper (1987) and Bybee *et al.* (1994: 22) have taken a radical position re the grammar/pragmatics interface, as well as the synchrony/diachrony divide: "we regard 'system' or 'structure' to be epiphenomenal rather than basic to the nature of grammatical substance . . . rather than studying the 'structure' of grammatical expression in a language, we advocate the study of the way that grammatical meaning and expression are attained across languages as a way of understanding the inherent properties of natural language" (Bybee *et al.*, 1994: 22). In practice, however, it is not clear that their research is restricted in this way. And while some change is always in the making, most of grammar is quite stable at any given point in time (see Croft, 2000; Givón, 1999).

[6] This doesn't mean that speakers are completely unaware of historical changes, or of the fact that their language is slightly different from that of older and of younger speakers.

[7] This is contra Heine *et al.* (1991b: chapter 9), who propose, for example, that the diachronic analysis of the body part > spatial expression transfer (as in *back*) is synchronically alive as well. See Traugott and Dasher (2002: 43–44).

section 6.3). This is a panchronic view of grammar, then. There is nothing special or different that the speaker does when she's participating in language change (and she always is). The speaker always does the same thing, which is use her language in context in an effective way for whatever local purposes she may have (see Harris and Campbell, 1995: 72–75; Itkonen, 2002). The claim is, therefore, that even as she is conforming to the "synchronic" grammar of today, the speaker is at the same time also practicing residues of the (different) "synchronic" grammar of yesterday, as well as evolving tomorrow's (different) grammar. Synchrony is where one can locate both (some) diachrony and (some) future change (see Du Bois, 1985, 1987; Newman and Rice, 2004 on the parallelism between discoursal patterns and grammaticization).

Next, although researchers have worried about distinguishing grammaticization from lexicalization and semanticization, as well as from linguistic change in general (see Giacalone Ramat and Hopper, 1998; Traugott, 2004a), our discussion does not require a sharp lexicon/grammar distinction, nor a grammaticization/semanticization distinction.[8] Semanticization (the process leading to the conventionalization of some meaning for some form) and grammaticization (the process leading to a grammatical convention) will be treated in a similar fashion since, for our purposes, both testify to the effect of extragrammatical factors on speakers' linguistic competence.[9] Researchers have also disputed the competence/performance distinction (e.g. Croft, 1990/2003; Haspelmath, 1999b), emphasizing that use (performance) is not so distinct from grammar (competence), since it drives it.[10] In fact, it is performance practices which provide the link between the extragrammatical and the grammatical (see Hawkins, 1994, 2003). Based on current research,[11] it seems that humans, even babies are "a big statistics machine" (Bates, 2001) (see Aslin *et al.*, 1999; Saffran *et al.*, 1996 about infants, children, and adults

---

[8] Bates and Goodman (1999) argue that there is no evidence from brain research for such a distinction, and, accordingly, child language learning research has shown that vocabulary size goes hand in hand with grammatical complexity – see also Snow (1999).

[9] Bybee *et al.* (1994: 4–9) adopt a similar approach, and Himmelmann (2004) too views grammaticization and lexicalization as processes of conventionalization. Recently Brinton and Traugott (2005: chapter 4) too have discussed many points of similarity between the two processes, the most important ones for our discussion being gradualness, unidirectionality, demotivation, metaphorization and metonymization, and above all, context dependency.

[10] We here ignore the phenomenon of performance errors, such as statistically marginal divergences from grammar, which are considered unacceptable by speakers, even though they do constitute part of performance.

[11] See e.g. MacDonald (1993), Bybee (2002), Bybee and Scheibman (1999), Jurafsky *et al.* (2001), the articles in Bod *et al.* (2003b), and references cited therein.

performing statistical learning). The relevant statistics concern discourse patterns relating to form–function correlations. The claim is that we are somehow sensitive to the probability with which a certain form is used for a certain function.

Note, however, that such an assumption is not incompatible with a competence/performance distinction. This "knowledge" concerning probabilities is neither part of grammar nor of pragmatics. Rather, it represents the actual output which results from the interaction of grammar, pragmatics, and sheer frequency of use, with each token used contributing to the strengthening of the representation. In other words, discourse, as we experience it, reflects grammatical patterns (form–semantic function associations), pragmatic patterns (form–inferences associations), as well as the frequency for each association (reflected in skewed patterns of use). Of course, no numerical values are placed on these but, rather, if we see these connections as patterns of activation, then some are very weak or even nonexistent (some form/inference associations, the register differences we have noted for pronouns), some are very strong (conventional), and some are probably intermediate.[12] Our tendency to conform, to use conventional means, makes us select the expressions which conform to salient discourse patterns. In a snowball effect, these use patterns become even more frequent, and they may become our entrenched competence. Bybee and Hopper (2001b: 7) aptly define grammar as "the internalized aggregate of formations from usage." Langacker (1987) similarly sees grammar as cognitive routinization of recurrent patterns of mental activity. We should note, however, that there is more to becoming part of grammar than undergoing a dramatic rise in salience or frequency.

The general picture that will emerge from part II is that salient discoursal patterns with their frequency probabilities constitute the link between the extragrammatical and grammar. Some of these patterns involve grammar/pragmatics interactions, which accounts for how pragmatic inferences turn into grammatical conventions. Part II primarily provides an explanation for how the extragrammatical derives the grammatical. At the same time, once we realize the intimate connection between grammar and pragmatics, we can perhaps better understand why the code/inference distinction is sometimes a challenge to draw, as we saw in part I. Chapter 4 addresses the following puzzles: if codes are conventionalizations of extralinguistic patterns, in what sense are they codes at all? If they are arbitrary (and, hence, coded), in what sense are they pragmatic (motivated)?

---

[12] See Delong *et al.* (2005) and references cited therein for empirical support for subjects' sensitivity to expected versus unexpected patterns.

The answer will be that grammaticization is motivated (extralinguistically), but grammar is not necessarily so. Chapter 5 attempts to answer the question of how and where the extragrammatical becomes grammar. Finally, chapter 6 presents an in-depth analysis of grammaticization processes associated with one form, English reflexive pronouns, relating these processes to the grammar/pragmatics divide question. The overall conclusion will be that grammar is both the product of extralinguistic processes and the enabling trigger for further pragmatic functions.

4　Grammar, pragmatics, and arbitrariness

We briefly discussed specific form–pragmatic function correlations (referring expressions and degree of activation) in section 2.2. As forcefully argued for by Prince (1988, 1998), (some) interpretative aspects traditionally classified as pragmatic do not merely complement the grammar, as would seem to be the case for most of the phenomena examined in part I. Rather, some extralinguistic generalizations regarding forms must constitute part of the grammar (e.g. definite NPs encode Given/identifiable information, Left Dislocated sentences introduce discourse-new entities, and see the many cases discussed in Ariel (forthcoming: chapters 6–8)). How did that come about? Furthermore, researchers are in agreement that the variability of linguistic structures is quite restricted in languages of the world. How can we explain this? The point of this chapter is to argue that these are not accidental facts. Grammars routinely evolve as a response to extragrammatical forces. If so, it should not be surprising that there are linguistic conventions associating linguistic expressions with extralinguistic factors, and that grammatical forms are not infinitely varied. But, then, if grammars evolve out of pragmatically motivated discourse patterns, shouldn't all of grammar be pragmatically motivated? In principle, the answer is that it may very well have been. However, not every linguistic form wears its diachronic pragmatic *raison d'être* on its synchronic sleeve (see note 4 below). Be that as it may, it seems hopeless to argue this claim for all of grammar at any specific point in time. What we present below is therefore a theoretical framework which shows that this claim could very likely be true.

According to some researchers, linguistic structure reflects language use for communication quite directly, and by necessity: "when pragmatic factors become part of grammar, the result is syntax and morphology" (Hyman, 1983: 71–72). We will here discuss changes in grammar motivated by extralinguistic factors, which have led to the emergence of phenomena generally taken to be purely grammatical. Given this picture of grammatical emergence, and given that at least some basic functions tend to be useful for all people (see Haspelmath, 1999a), analyses are often not restricted to single languages. According to Comrie (1983: 87), functional motivations can account for "a significant set of constructions cross-linguistically" (see also Comrie, 2003). By presenting extralinguistic accounts, applicable cross-linguistically, researchers feel that they are offering explanations for what natural languages are like, and not merely descriptions of linguistic phenomena (see Bybee, 1985b; Comrie, 1994a; Du Bois, 1987; Givón, 1984,

1990; Haiman, 1985a, b; Haspelmath, 2004a; Heine, 1997: 10; *inter alia*).[1] But then, a further question must be raised. How come different languages have different grammars?

We begin by addressing the most basic question, namely, whether grammar is extralinguistically motivated. If extralinguistic motivations form the basis for grammar, why do linguistic conventions (sometimes) seem arbitrary? Why are grammars continually evolving, and why are there differences among languages? The argument will be that language change must be motivated, not that language structure necessarily is. Language must be functional for its use, and being functional does not preclude arbitrary form–function correlations. Note that we must distinguish between functionality and extralinguistic motivation. Grammar is functional if it is adequate for its speakers for their communicative purposes. Arbitrary grammatical conventions pose no obstacle for successful communication. In fact, meaningless grammar (syntactic generalizations) is not at all functionless (Du Bois, 2003b).

It's divergence from the current grammar which must be motivated one way or another. Initially, conventions must be motivated, or they don't stand a chance of becoming conventions, because the innovating interlocutor (either the speaker or the addressee) will have no basis on which to initiate them (obviously, people do not convene and decide on new linguistic conventions). Thus, the fact that grammar is as motivated as it is (as we shall see below) is due to the fact that it is a natural historical product. It can only arise in motivated steps. It doesn't have to stay motivated and, in fact, it often doesn't (or, at least not perfectly so), since the cumulative effect of a series of motivated changes may very well lead to arbitrariness. On this view, linguistic arbitrariness is always indirectly brought about.

4.1   Is grammar motivated or arbitrary?

Much of modern linguistics has rested on the assumption that grammar is a self-contained system. If it is autonomous from external forces, it must be arbitrary, for there is no particular reason why grammar must take some specific shape, but not another. Typological studies, however, have revealed universal regularities, which cannot be traced back to common ancestries among languages. If so, either the regularities are due to language-internal forces, or else language is not arbitrary, for it is motivated by extralinguistic forces. Generative grammarians have adopted the first alternative, relegating such consistencies among languages

---

[1] Lambrecht (1994: 11) finds that "The issue which ultimately divides the 'formal' and the 'functional' approach is not so much disagreement about facts but the question of what constitutes explanation in linguistics." I'm not so sure about agreement over facts, but certainly there is a difference in the explanations adopted. For the functionalists external explanations count as explanations, whereas internal ones count as descriptions. The opposite is true for the formalists. In addition, most discourse grammarians reject the generative grammarian's explanation that a genetically specified **linguistic** capacity (UG) is responsible for universal features of language (see Comrie, 2003; Goldberg, 2006; Haspelmath, 2004a; Heine, 1994b: 255; and see below).

to an innate human endowment which is specifically linguistic – Universal Grammar (Chomsky, 1972: 63, and onwards). Comrie (1980: 24) and Haiman (1985a: 7), on the other hand, argue that innateness is merely a name for a set of universals, not an explanation.[2] Functionalists have for the most part adopted the second alternative, seeking external explanations for language structure. In other words, the claim is that natural languages are shaped the way they are because of our general (rather than language-specific) human cognitive capacities, and due to the common use we put language to, namely, communicative acts. The goal of chapter 4 is to argue that grammar is motivated by extragrammatical factors, just because the process leading to grammar necessarily is. At the same time, grammar is partly arbitrary and is not reducible to external motivations. Grammar is therefore distinct from pragmatics and other extragrammatical forces.

This view is shared by many discourse grammarians, historical linguists, and functional typologists, who insist that grammar is externally motivated.[3] Indeed, if extralinguistic factors drive grammar, it is not surprising that linguistic forms are sensitive to extralinguistic factors. But the researchers here discussed do not restrict their claims to the more obvious cases of conventional discourse functions. They have emphasized that, very often, we can trace the creation of grammatical forms in general to external motivations. To the extent that this proposal is valid, grammar is motivated.[4] We should emphasize, however, that external motivations must not be

---

[2] Many have argued against the rationale offered for the innateness hypothesis, the so-called "poverty of stimulus" argument, which stipulates that the input children are exposed to cannot adequately account for their output. Tomasello (2003a), Goldberg et al. (2004), Goldberg (2006), among others, have argued against this assumption based on empirical research on language learning. Statistical pattern extractions from natural language texts, which seem to replicate grammatical structures, also attest that we need not assume innateness in order to account for natural language grammar (see the model of an unsupervised learning of natural language offered by Solan et al., 2005). Other, independent arguments in support of the innateness thesis have not been offered, so, as Hawkins (2004: chapter 1) notes, the innateness hypothesis seems circular: based on linguistic regularities, innate generalizations are posited, which are in turn claimed to explain the very linguistic regularities they were extracted from. Surprisingly, Chomsky too has recently called for external explanations for linguistic properties (Chomsky, 2001 and onwards). These are interface constraints (imposed by the human sensorimotor and conceptual–intentional systems), as well as general (extralinguistic) properties of computational efficiency (economy), which he assumes to be a general biologically evolved property.

[3] See Givón (1979b and onwards), Comrie (1980 and onwards), Hopper and Thompson (1980, 1984), Du Bois (1987), Croft (1990/2003), Heine et al. (1991a), Heine (1993, 1997), Bybee et al. (1994), Bybee and Hopper (2001a), Traugott and Heine (1991), Hawkins (1994 and onwards), Traugott and Dasher (2002), Haspelmath (1999a, 2004a), inter alia.

[4] It remains to be seen whether or not cases which resist such explanations are to be differently motivated. It is quite possible that motivated conventions become less transparent over time (see the discussion below and the history of reflexive pronouns in section 6.2). If such obliterating processes are themselves motivated, then we can argue that all grammar is pragmatically motivated. Hopper and Traugott (1993/2003: 128–129) argue that whenever grammaticization processes can be diachronically traced, grammatical categories arose out of lexical ones, through discoursal use, rather than arbitrarily or from scratch, but, of course, there are grammatical forms, e.g. to, whose origins are simply unknown. Haspelmath (2004b) speculates that only few grammatical morphemes did not evolve out of lexical items through discoursal use (e.g. demonstratives). Goldberg (2006: 167) adopts a stronger position than that adopted here. She assumes that grammar is synchronically motivated, except for occasional cases, which can only be motivated diachronically.

identified with directly communicative functions. In other words, not every external motivation behind some meaning, form or distributional pattern is directly at the service of communication. But the point is that it is external to the grammar.

Let us start with the relatively easy case of a conventional pragmatic function phenomenon. These are grammatical in that they are conventional, although they specify an extragrammatical condition of distribution. If (such) pragmatic statements are part of grammar, can we at least agree that these aspects of grammar are externally motivated? What is the nature of grammatical form–function correlations such as discussed in section 2.2? In support of her argument that the discourse functions attached to syntactic constructions are grammatical, Prince (1988, 1998) actually argues that they are just like any grammatical phenomenon. For her, this means that pragmatic conventions too are arbitrary, language-specific, and unmotivated. We cannot then take it for granted that even these grammatical aspects are externally motivated. But we can argue for it (sections 4.1–4.5).

Let's examine Prince's argument for the arbitrariness of grammatical form–function correlations. Prince is certainly right when she argues that the intuitive feeling we sometimes have regarding the "natural," "inevitable" connection between forms and their extralinguistic functions may be the result, rather than the cause of those form–function correlations. Indeed, Diderot's (1751/1875) and Lancelot's (1660) position, which she quotes from Chomsky (1965: 7), that word order (in the French they spoke) merely reflects the natural order of thought, is no doubt untenable. As we shall see, however, her arguments against Lancelot (1660) do not carry over to more sophisticated views on the question of grammar and external motivations. Let's examine more closely Prince's (1998) arguments for concluding that "the relation between syntactic form and discourse function is no less arbitrary than, say, the relation between phonological form and lexical meaning" (p. 282). As we see below (section 4.2), Prince convincingly demonstrates that Left Dislocations (LDs) are used for three distinct discourse functions: (i) to introduce discourse-new entities, which canonically would have occurred in an inappropriate position for new entities (e.g. subject position); (ii) to introduce entities which stand in a salient partially ordered set (POSET) relation to an already evoked discourse entity; and (iii) amnestying illicit topicalizations (by adding a resumptive pronoun to the topicalized construction).

Prince first argues that the very fact that LDs have three different discourse functions entails that the form–function correlations concerned cannot be motivated. She assumes that a construction is motivated if there is an **iconic** relation between its form and the function it indicates (an iconic relation obtains between forms and their messages when the former resemble the latter – see Haiman, 1985b). For example, it has been argued that when two events are encoded in a conjoined sentence, the first clause (in terms of linear order) encodes the first event (in terms of chronology), and the second clause encodes the later event. In this case, linear order resembles (metaphorically) chronological order, and we can say that there is an iconic relationship between the sentence and the events described in it. Now, argues Prince, the very fact that LD carries three **different** functions means it cannot maintain an iconic relation to its functions, for the same form cannot simultaneously resemble three different conceptualizations.

Moreover, for a construction to be motivated, Prince assumes that there must be a **necessary** connection between its form and its function. Thus, given that some language has some form which is the translational equivalent of a form in some other language, the form–function correlations in the two languages must be the same. Prince expects universal form–function correlations (see also Aronoff, 1987). Indeed, she shows otherwise. For example, Yiddish has an LD construction almost identical to the English LD. However, while it can be used for the second and third discourse functions Prince identified for English LDs, it cannot be used for the first one. Prince found no examples of LDs introducing new-discourse entities in Yiddish, and her attempts to elicit such examples from native speakers were not successful either. The discourse functions of LDs are language-specific then. In Prince (1988) she offers a complementary argument, again based on a comparison between English and Yiddish. This time she sets out from the pragmatic function associated with English *it*-clefts (focusing an instantiation of an open proposition taken as shared information). Although she does find a counterpart construction in Yiddish, specialized for the very same pragmatic function, formally, that structure is quite different from the English *it*-cleft (the Yiddish counterpart of the English *It was they who found Eichmann* is literally 'This have they found Eichmann'). With the arguments regarding LDs and *it*-clefts taken together, Prince demonstrates that there's no necessary association from forms to functions (LDs) and no guaranteed association from functions to forms (*it*-clefts). According to Prince, then, the three functions associated with LDs are cases of constructional homonymy, paralleling lexical ambiguity.

Prince is certainly right about all these seemingly inconsistent facts. Form–function correlations are not necessarily iconic, specific functions are not necessarily attached to some forms, forms are not fully predictable from functions, nor functions from forms. They are even arbitrary to some extent, forms bearing a one-to-many relationship to functions (and vice versa), and they vary across languages. In fact, however, these very same points have been made in the functional–typological literature.[5] If all agree on the facts, how is it that Prince and the researchers here quoted reach opposite conclusions about grammar being motivated/arbitrary?

Discourse grammarians simply don't share Prince's naive concept of motivation. For them, being motivated means that there is a motivated, not an inevitable path of change which has led to the grammatical form.[6] Haiman (1985a), Du Bois (1985), Bates and MacWhinney (1989), and Givón (1979b, 1993) all reject in

---

[5] See Haiman (1985a), Du Bois (1985), Croft (1990/2003, 2000), Traugott and König (1991), Mithun (1991a, 1991b, and, especially, 2003), Hopper and Traugott (1993/2003), Heine *et al.* (1991a), Heine (1997), *inter alia*.

[6] See Ariel (1998c), Comrie (1994a), Craig (1991), Croft (1993a), Du Bois (1987), Givón (1984, 1991), Lichtenberk (1991), Heine *et al.* (1991b: 37–38), Mithun (1991a, 2003), Traugott and König (1991), Langacker (1995), Traugott and Dasher (2002), *inter alia*.

effect the claim in Bolinger (1972:71) about a one-to-one correspondence between forms and functions. Heine *et al.* (1991b) go so far as to claim that "language constantly contradicts this principle, and it does so for good reasons."[7] The following quote from Comrie (1988: 266) reflects the non-naive approach quite clearly (and see Chafe, 1994: 85; Dik, 1986; Nuyts, 1992; *inter alia*):

> syntax is potentially independent of semantics and pragmatics, in the sense that there are many syntactic phenomena in many languages that cannot be given complete or even nearly complete analyses in purely semantic or pragmatic or semantic-pragmatic terms. However, in many instances such syntactic phenomena can be given partial explanation in such nonsyntactic terms; in particular, many syntactic phenomena can be viewed as phenomena semantic and/or pragmatic in origin which have become divorced from their semantico-pragmatic origin, in other words as instances of grammaticalization ...

There is no claim that contexts causally shape grammar, that extralinguistic factors are uniformly encoded, that codes are always transparent, that structures isomorphically or exclusively correspond to extralinguistic functions, that language-internal factors are not involved, or that language does not contain arbitrary facts.[8]

For Prince to argue against this concept of motivated grammar she would have to show that "anything goes," namely that the three discourse functions of LDs, for example, could be served (and are in fact served in some language) by different constructions, e.g. by Right Dislocation or by *it*-clefts, etc. All evidence shows otherwise. For one thing, historical changes are virtually always unidirectional, that is, certain forms (lexical items) may develop new grammatical functions, but these developments are not random nor reversible. Some forms never turn into others. These facts hold for different, unrelated languages (Bybee *et al.*, 1994; Traugott and Dasher, 2002). For example, main verbs may turn into auxiliaries, but the opposite is not attested.[9] Unidirectionality derives from the fact that recruiting lexical items for grammatical purposes is a more reasonable innovative step than the other way round (recruiting a grammatical category for lexical purposes). The impressive findings in the literature regarding the unidirectional nature of grammaticization then attest to the importance of motivation in linguistic change.[10]

---

[7] The good reasons are that polysemy and homophony are an inherent consequence of grammaticization, and hence an integral part of natural languages.

[8] While there are some equations of motivation or function with iconicity, mainly Haiman (1985a: 71) (and see Croft, 1990/2003: 104, Hopper and Traugott, 1993/2003: 207), this is not the common definition of motivation. In fact, Haiman too emphasizes that there is arbitrariness in language, due to competing motivations (see below).

[9] See Givón (1976) Croft (1990/2003: 251–253), Bybee (1994: 12–14), Haspelmath (1999b, 2004b), many of the articles in Traugott and Heine (1991), and Traugott (2002).

[10] Heine *et al.* (1991b: 51) and Hopper and Traugott (1993/2003: 126–128) discuss potential exceptions to the unidirectionality hypothesis, but Heine (2003) notes that such exceptions are idiosyncratic, in that they tend not to be typologically attested. And see Haspelmath (1999b, 2004b) for additional arguments in support of the unidirectionality hypothesis. It is quite conceivable that exceptions (e.g. the creation of a verb out of *up* or German *du* 'familiar you,' *duzen*) can be explained as motivated changes nonetheless (Hopper and Traugott, 1993/2003: 126–128, explain these as lexicalizations rather than grammaticizations, which are not constrained by unidirectionality, but we here do not accept this distinction).

In order to argue for a motivated change in grammar we need to show that each stage of the development can be explained/motivated externally, in that patterns of use are conducive to that development rather than to just any number of others. We need to show that variability is not unlimited, that it is heavily constrained, and not arbitrarily so (see Croft, 2000). But we don't need to show that it was the only step that language could have adopted. Finally, we need to motivate the very arbitrariness we find in language, for the claim is that the creation of grammar must be motivated. This is the goal of sections 4.2–4.5. We address three types of cases which may seem to support the arbitrariness thesis about grammar. In each case, the argument will be that what seems arbitrary from one perspective turns out to be motivated from another perspective. There are reasons why grammar cannot be motivated from every which way one examines it. First, it is a limited good. It cannot simultaneously meet all potential motivated form–function correlations. Second, motivation is not a transitive relation. While the changes from x to y and from y to z may be motivated, the relation between x and z may not be motivated, so cumulative changes often create synchronic arbitrariness. What must be motivated is innovation, the creation of new conventions. Once a conventional form–function association has been established, motivation is not important, for the convention itself motivates abiding by it.

4.2   Multiple motivations per form, or, are they?

The first type of cases we consider are cases which seem arbitrary because there is a one-to-many correspondence between form and function. Thus, the same form, e.g. Left Dislocation, resumptive pronouns, is dictated by apparently different conventions (both in the same and in different languages). But we will see that not only is the relationship between each of the functions and the single form motivated, actually what are taken as different functions reflect one general motivation.[11] In both cases we consider it is (less than a maximal) degree of accessibility for the discourse entity which accounts for the seemingly different contexts calling for the use of LDs and resumptive pronouns (see Ariel, 1990 and onwards, as well as sections 2.2, 2.3 about activation accounts for referential forms). If this is correct, the cases at hand demonstrate that none of the form–function correlations is arbitrary, that in fact, they do maintain a relationship of one form to one function after all, and that the differences between languages are quite restricted. In such cases, then, arbitrariness is at least drastically reduced in magnitude, but what is more crucial is that each step of conventionalization into grammar can be seen as motivated.

---

[11] See Goldberg (2006: chapter 8) for a similar point regarding the seemingly arbitrary association between subject–auxiliary inversion and its many functions (e.g. questions, exclamations, counterfactual conditionals, wishes, comparatives, etc.).

Consider LDs first. Although, as mentioned above, Prince identifies three distinct discourse functions for LDs, Ziv (1994) finds something common to the three distinct LD uses: a relatively low degree of mental accessibility of the entity introduced by the preposed NP. We start by presenting Prince's analysis. Consider the following example of an LD construction:

(1)   My sister$_i$ got stabbed. She$_i$ died. Two of my sisters were living together on 18th street. They had gone to bed, and this man, their girlfriend's husband, came in. He started fussing with my sister$_i$ and she$_i$ started to scream. **The landlady$_j$, she went up,** and he laid her$_j$ out. So sister$_i$ went to get a wash cloth to put on her$_j$, and he stabbed her$_i$ in the back. But she$_i$ saw her death. She$_i$ went and told my mother ...   (*Welcomat*, Dec. 2, 1981, Prince, 1998: ex. 4)

The first discourse function served by LDs is exemplified by (1). Prince argues that the preposed NP introduces a discourse-new entity (new in the current segment, at least), which, moreover, would have been introduced in subject position had the speaker not selected the LD (*The landlady went up*). Such LDs simplify the processing of new discourse entities, because (a) they remove them from positions usually reserved for discourse-old referents, a misleading position for a new discourse entity, and (b) they create a separate information unit (see Geluykens, 1992), appropriate for relatively costly processing (recall also the discussion of PAS in section 2.3). To see the validity of point (a) Prince contrasts the original example with the following:

(2)   ~ My sister$_i$ got stabbed. She$_i$ died. Two of my sisters were living together on 18th street. They had gone to bed, and this man, their girlfriend's husband, came in. He started fussing with my sister$_i$ and she$_i$ started to scream. The landlady$_j$ went up, and he laid her$_j$ out. So **a wash cloth$_k$** sister$_i$ went to get **it$_k$/ one$_k$** to put on her$_j$ ...   (Prince, 1998: ex. 8)

Note that (2) is not as felicitous as (1), because *wash cloth* does not need to move out of an inappropriate position (direct objects accommodate new information rather easily – see section 2.3.1 again). As corroborating evidence that the construction serves to facilitate processing, Prince notes that this type of LD is characteristic of spontaneous conversation (as originally claimed by Keenan (Ochs), 1977).

The second discourse function associated with LDs according to Prince is the marking of a partially ordered set (POSET) inference. Here's a relevant example:

(3)   She had an idea for a project. She's going to use three groups of mice$_{i,j,k}$. **One$_i$** she'll feed them$_i$ mouse chow, just the regular stuff they make for mice. **Another$_j$** she'll feed them$_j$ veggies. And the third$_k$ she'll feed $\neg_k$ junk food   (SH, Nov. 7, 1981, Prince, 1998: ex. 10f).

These LDs are quite different from the simplifying LDs: they are not restricted to unplanned discourse, the preposed entity is not necessarily discourse-new, and the canonical position (indirect object) of the entity in a non-LD structure is not inappropriate for its information status. The discourse function of these LDs is to trigger an inference that the entity encoded by the preposed NP stands in a salient POSET relation to another entity already available in the discourse. This relation is based on their co-participation in a partially ordered set (Hirschberg, 1991). The relevant one for (3) is a set of mice consisting of groups (i, j, k). Thus, the first group of mice stands in a salient relation to e.g. the second and third groups of mice. While in this case the relation is contrastive, in other cases it is something else.

The third function of LDs is to "rescue" a Topicalization which would either be ungrammatical or hard to process. This type of LD is actually a topicalization plus a resumptive pronoun. Topicalizations obey two restrictions. Consider the last sentence in (3), a topicalization. The first restriction is identical to the one on POSET LDs, namely, the preposed NP encodes an entity which stands in a POSET relation to a discourse-evoked entity (or entities). Indeed, the third group of mice stands in a salient relation to the first and second groups. The second function is to instruct the addressee to construct the sentence as a focus and a focus-frame. The focus-frame (she'll feed the third group of mice, which is part of the set of three groups of mice, X) is taken as an open proposition, information available to the addressee. The new information to be processed against this background is *junk food*. Thus, the difference between POSET LDs and topicalizations is the requirement that the focus-frame is available to the addressee. Indeed, by the time the speaker comes to talk about the third group of mice the addressee knows that the mice will be getting some food as part of a feeding experiment. Now, what if the topicalized construction would create a syntactic island violation (e.g. an extraction out of a relative clause)?[12] Speakers should avoid such ungrammatical structures. Prince suggests that the speaker of (4) was actually very likely to choose a topicalized structure. Note that the open proposition here ('I paid X to the individual who gave me the first member of the set of books I had) is information available from the preceding context. An LD was produced because of the syntactic violation which would have otherwise resulted (compare (4a) with (4b):

(4) a.   The book I had I had got from a guy who got it from a guy who got it from a very good call girl . . . The standard procedure was that somebody new gave half of what they got the first time for each member . . . **My first book, I paid half of each trick to the person who gave it to me**.

                                                      (Terkel, 1974: 95, Prince, 1998: ex. 23a)

    b.   ~*My first book, I paid half of each trick to the person who gave – to me.

Thus, argues Prince, LD, which looks like one construction, turns out to have three very different discourse functions.[13]

Now, as mentioned above, Ziv (1994) convincingly argues that the three functions identified by Prince are not an accidental collection of functions. In all

---

[12] Syntactic island violations involve an interpretative dependency between a gap and an element across some syntactic boundary, such as a relative clause.
[13] It remains to be seen whether these LD types all take one and the same form, for we have ignored the intonation of LDs. Prince herself notes that it's possible that at least the first and second LD types receive different intonation patterns.

of them the preposed entity is entertained at a relatively low degree of mental accessibility. LDs are used with new discourse entities, because they offer a structure well suited for the processing involved: a new discourse entity is costly to process (recall PAS in section 2.3.1). Accordingly, the LD construction requires an informative referring expression (a low activation marker): a lexical NP + a copy pronoun is such a referring expression, and, more crucially, LD dedicates a separate unit (possibly a separate Intonation Unit) for that NP. The second discourse function identified by Prince is the introduction into discourse of an entity which is related to a discourse-evoked entity, although again, it has not itself been introduced into the discourse. Such entities are not highly accessible either. The POSET relation is most probably triggered by the content of the introducing NP (e.g. *one* and *another* in (3) above), combined with the preceding context.

Finally, the third discourse function, that of amnestying a topicalization with a resumptive pronoun is obviously motivated by the low accessibility of the entity preposed. Actually, what needs motivation here is the occurrence of a pronoun in a topicalization. In terms of activation, a gap points to high accessibility (see the referential marking scale), which is not available in cases of referential dependency across a syntactic island. A pronoun, on the other hand, encodes a somewhat lower degree of accessibility. In other words, as argued by Birner and Ward (1998: 93–95), what all the three uses of LDs have in common is the highlighting of an NP position, encoded by a low-activation referring expression (a lexical NP), suitable for entities not highly activated. The third case is in addition characterized by a less than maximal accessibility between the preposed NP and the extraction site. The reasons for the low degree of activation vary, of course. Hence, the three types of use characteristic of LDs. In the terminology of section 2.3, we could say that the three uses reflect three discourse profiles compatible with one discourse function of referring to discourse entities not highly activated.

Now, why is it the case that not all cases of low-activation introductions are served by LDs? Recall that Yiddish does not use LDs for the introduction of new discourse entities. In fact, Prince herself provides a motivated reason for the non-use of LDs for that function in Yiddish. Yiddish has another construction it uses for that very function, Subject Postposing. This construction is useful for precisely the same function, because it too removes from initial, subject position a discourse entity addressees do not expect to find presented in initial subject position. Hence, this different form–function correlation is motivated too. Still, the differences between English and Yiddish are to some extent arbitrary, indeed. Why doesn't English make use of a parallel construction? The non-use in English and Yiddish of the respective form–function correlation they lack is partly motivated: they don't need to, they have another, perfectly suitable form–function correlation they can employ. But the facts are also partly arbitrary in that English could have gone the Yiddish way but didn't, and Yiddish could have gone the English way but didn't. The crucial point is that neither language could go just any which arbitrary way. "To the extent that different generalizations are possible, some arbitrariness is possible" (Haiman, 1983: 815). However, while form–function correlations are not fully determinate, they are heavily restricted. And definitely nonarbitrarily so.[14]

Our next example takes up a grammatical phenomenon "proper", the distribution of resumptive pronouns. Here, despite the apparent variability in the use of resumptive pronouns in the world's languages, one cognitive principle can account for the options actually adopted by different languages (Ariel, 1999a). In other words, what seem to be different grammatical conventions are in fact different manifestations (discourse profiles) of one, more general discourse function. Note the following factors, mentioned by researchers writing on different languages, as involved in the decision whether to use a resumptive pronoun (regardless of whether this is grammatically or pragmatically specified): the grammatical role of the relativized position (a direct object in (5)), the complexity of the relative clause, the complexity of the head, the (non)obligatoriness of the relativized argument, whether the relative clause is a negative sentence, whether the relative head is in a syntactic island, how distant the head and the relativized position are from each other, whether the relative clause contains topicalized material, whether the relative clause is overtly marked by some complementizer, whether the relative clause is nonrestrictive or restrictive, and the (in)definiteness of the head NP (for references see Ariel, 1999a).[15]

However, while partially different grammatical distributions seem to characterize resumptive pronouns in different languages, the grammatically specified contexts where they are mandated, preferred, or allowed have something in common. That commonality is an extralinguistic (cognitive) constraint: a relatively lower degree of accessibility of the head of the relative clause at the time when the relativized position is processed. What the contexts forbidding or dispreferring resumptive pronouns have in common is a relatively high degree

---

[14] Bybee *et al.* (1994: 12), who argue for a very strong connection between sources and grammaticized endpoints, propose that very often differences among languages are actually differences between earlier versus later stages of one grammaticization path. This could explain the difference between English and Yiddish LDs, provided we can establish that the grammaticization path of LDs proceeds from the second and third discourse functions to the first one, which hasn't (yet?) happened in Yiddish. I have no evidence one way or another. In addition, they suggest that what sometimes look like cases of single-source forms giving rise to different grammaticizations do not actually constitute single sources, because they enter different constructions, which in turn yield the different grammaticized forms (see also Traugott, 2003). Craig's (1991) analysis of Rama 'go' seems to fit this claim. The form evolved into (i) a temporal marker, (ii) a purposive adposition, and (iii) a conjunction (seemingly a one form/multiple functions case). However, each appears in a different syntactic context (verbal, nominal, sentential). But is it invariably the case that grammaticization is thus restricted? For example, we know that the German counterpart of English *while* developed into a causal, and not a concessive connective (although there is sporadic use of Middle English *while* for causal purposes – Traugott, 2004a). If Bybee *et al.* are correct, then we should find that in the initial stages of semanticization, the English and German temporal 'while's cooccurred with statistically different lexical items, biasing their interpretations in different directions. This is quite plausibly so (see Traugott and Dasher, 2002 about the cooccurrence of *indeed* with *but*, which explains its developing an adversative aspect), but it hasn't been argued for.

[15] Restrictive relative clauses restrict the domain defined by the head, whereas nonrestrictive relative clauses modify the domain defined by the head. Hence, the former constitute a more cohesive unit with the head, allowing for a higher degree of accessibility for the head vis-à-vis the relativized position.

of accessibility of the relative clause head. Resumptive pronouns, like pronouns in general, point to a relatively lower degree of accessibility than a gap. Data from Hebrew relative clauses demonstrated that a combined calculation of a few of these parameters better predicts the occurrence of a resumptive pronoun than any one parameter alone. For example, 97.6 percent of the cases manifesting 4 or 5 of the 5 high-activation factors indeed show a gap, and 83.3 percent of the cases manifesting 4 or 5 of the 5 low-activation factors contained a resumptive pronoun. Consider the following examples, in view of the fact that, in principle, Hebrew direct objects can take either gaps or resumptive pronouns:

(5) a. efshar   li=mkor   et   **ha=menayot**   she=maxarti **0** az   be=mexir
         possible to=sell   ACC   the=shares   that=I.sold   then at=price
         shel   hayom.
         of   today
         'It's possible to sell the shares that I sold then at today's price.'   (Lotan 1990)

    b.   yesh   li   rak   **sheela**   **axat**   she=ani   lo   macliax
         there.is to:me   only question   one   that=I   not   manage
         le=havin   **ota**.
         to=understand   ACC:it
         'I have only one question, which I cannot understand.'   (*Hair*, April 26, 1996)

Note that a gap is selected in (5a), where the head is definite, close by (one content word separating the head from the relativized position), and the relative clause is a restrictive relative clause. These all contribute to a relatively high activation of the mental representation of the relative clause head ('the shares') when the relativized position is reached. In (5b), on the other hand, the head is indefinite, not close by (four content words separating it from the relativized position), and it is a nonrestrictive relative clause. These factors all contribute to a relatively low degree of mental accessibility. Thus, the correlation between indefinite heads and resumptive pronouns is not arbitrary, and neither are the correlations between long distance and the nonrestrictiveness of the relative clause and resumptive pronouns. What seems to be a random collection of grammatical features, each arbitrarily associated with resumptive pronoun choice, turns out to be highly motivated. Resumptive pronouns are used when a relatively lower degree of activation obtains between the relative clause head and the relativized position. If the form–function associations here were arbitrary, it could very well be that, for example, restrictive relative clauses would call for resumptive pronouns and nonrestrictive relative clauses would favor gaps, that obligatory relativized arguments would trigger resumptive pronouns but nonobligatory ones would favor gaps, etc. Different languages could have opposite form–function correlations. Such cases are not attested.

This does not mean that languages have identical distributional patterns for resumptive pronouns, though. Some language variability remains. Languages may very well have different (but not contradicting) discourse profiles: are these tendencies optional or obligatory? Languages vary. For example, according to

Shlonsky (1992), resumptive pronouns are obligatory with indefinite heads in Arabic. This is not so in very many other languages. Are all the factors listed above relevant for all languages? Maybe not. But the main point is that grammatical conventions (and the availability of resumptive pronouns even optionally is also a grammatical convention) are not as arbitrary as Prince would have us think. Each of these conventions is motivated (as it relates to either high or low degrees of memory activation of mental representations for discourse entities).

All in all, as already argued for in section 2.3, different discourse profiles should be distinguished from different discourse functions. What we have seen in section 4.2 is that although differing in their discourse profiles, all languages examined demonstrate sensitivity to the same discourse function – degree of memory activation – when resumptive pronouns/LDs are selected. What are taken by Prince as different discourse functions are not so different then. Crucially, each of the different discourse profiles is motivated, since each involves a nonmaximal degree of activation.

4.3   Motivations competing over forms

In section 4.2 we discussed cases where it would seem that one form serves multiple functions. In fact, we realized that what appear to be different discourse functions are merely different discourse profiles, reflecting one and the same discourse function. There is then no competition between different motivations over one form in such cases after all. Other cases cannot be explained in the same manner. In the cases presented in section 4.3 we have truly different motivations competing over single forms. But once again we will see that in these cases too arbitrariness is heavily restricted, to selecting between equally motivated options. Motivations "compete" with each other over forms, because grammar is a limited good (Du Bois, 1985; Haiman, 1985a; Thompson, 1991). The competition can be over **how much** to encode (e.g. As, Ss, and Os, or just nominatives or just ergatives?). Assuming that economy is opted for, the competition turns on **what** to encode (e.g. ergativity or accusativity?), as well as **how complex** the marking convention should be (a simple, general, e.g. ergative marking of all persons may bring redundancy, while a motivated selective application of the marking system on only some persons introduces complexity – see below).

Now, the first two types of competition (how much, what) are clearly not language-specific. What about the third? It's not so clear that the urge to generalize/simplify grammatical conventions is a specifically grammatical phenomenon either. Take the Korean taboo against marrying a person bearing the same last name (as reported on in the *New York Times*, Sept. 17, 1996). Traditionally, the convention was motivated, aimed at preventing intra-tribal marriages. Last names were indicative of tribal membership, and served as a salient convention for the taboo. However, once the taboo was generalized to any people bearing the same last name (regardless of tribal origin), while the convention became perfectly general and easy to apply in principle, the original motivation (forbidding intra-tribal marriages) was lost (this is a functional overkill – see below), and very many Koreans now face a problem, since 55 percent of the population in South Korea has one of five last names. Generalizing conventions is not specific to language, then.[16] So, one point to note is that it is not just the motivations behind grammar that are extralinguistic, as we see throughout part II, so are the considerations involved in opting for one rather than another type of grammar.

Let's start with case marking. The fact that some languages are accusative while others are ergative may seem quite arbitrary. Recall (section 2.3.1) that ergative languages distinguish between two kinds of subjects. Ergative subjects (As) are subjects of transitive verbs. Subjects of intransitive verbs (Ss) are grouped with direct objects (Os), as absolutives. Nominative–accusative languages (such as English), on the other hand, group subjects of transitive and intransitive verbs (As and Ss) together as subjects, and distinguish these from direct objects, accusatives. If ergativity is well motivated, why aren't all languages ergative? Alternatively, if accusativity is motivated, why aren't all languages accusative? Why would some languages opt for one classification, while others for another? Du Bois (1985) takes it upon himself to explain the seemingly contradicting fact that both ergative marking and accusative marking are functionally motivated. We have already mentioned the discourse motivation behind ergativity in section 2.3.1. Ergatives are overwhelmingly used for entities which are accessible, that is, NPs which are not demanding in terms of processing costs. This is true for virtually all the As in his Sakapultek data (see Du Bois, 1987: table 6). Absolutive, on the other hand, is the role which can accommodate new, costly, discourse referents (although it absolutely does not have to). Indeed, about a quarter of the Sakapultek absolutives present New entities (ibid).

But what about accusative languages? According to Du Bois, they have classified together potentially topical entities. Subjects (As and Ss) tend to be human and relatively agentive, they often serve as (continuing) topics, so they too naturally form a pragmatic class. This is not true for direct objects (e.g. only 3.4 percent of the humans were coded as direct objects in English). In fact, Du Bois (1987) examines the discourse patterning of English (accusative) and Sakapultek (ergative), and finds that they are quite similar, despite the different case systems. He finds that in English too As tend to refer to accessible entities (92 percent of

---

[16] Comrie (2003) goes further than that in externalizing what are considered language-internal processes. He argues that even the fact that grammar is structure-dependent is not exclusive to language. Rather, we need structure in order to cognitively manipulate strings consisting of more than a few items in general. This is why when we memorize a series of numbers or the alphabet we form sub-structures (try reciting the alphabet backwards, and see how hard it is, he proposes). Thus, even structure-dependence, the hallmark of grammar, is but an instantiation of a more general cognitive strategy. Bybee (2001: chapter 2) also emphasizes that linguistic units are categorized in the same manner that nonlinguistic objects (e.g. birds) are. Of course, the grammatical structure itself is language-specific.

As are accessible), whereas new discourse entities are encoded by either direct objects or intransitive subjects (absolutives), thus manifesting the "ergative" discourse pattern. And similarly in Sakapultek too topics are routinely encoded as As and Ss (subjects), which is the "accusative" discourse pattern. (Mithun, 2003 finds this accusative pattern in Yup'ik, another ergative language.) In other words, English and Sakapultek discoursal patterns are both ripe for either type of grammaticization, which means that ergativity and accusativity are in competition.

But actually, couldn't languages have it both ways (i.e. mark all three grammatical roles)? They could, but then they would be compromising yet another motivated feature – economy (see Haiman, 1985a). Languages do not encode each and every potential piece of message, because articulation is very costly. It slows communication down (see the discussion in Levinson, 2000b: 6). Hence, only some motivations can be satisfied. So, the first competition is between maximal case marking and a more economical marking. Once economy wins out, the competition is between the two case systems. Languages choose one option or they choose the other. Which choice it is may be arbitrary indeed (but see section 5.3 for an attempt to account for such conventionalizations). But once again, the choice is between rather limited options. Specifically, no language lumps together As with Os to the exclusion of Ss. It is either the As which form a category of their own (because of their high correlation with high accessibility) or the Os (because of the absence of a correlation with either topicality or accessibility). Ss have no unique discourse profile of their own which would set them apart. Moreover, as noted by Comrie (1978), As and Os cooccur, and hence need to be distinguished from each other. Ss do not cooccur with either As or Os, and, hence, do not need to be distinguished from either. This is how Du Bois explains the choice of a two-way distinction (either between ergatives and absolutives or between nominatives and accusatives) instead of a theoretically possible three-way distinction (between As, Ss, and Os). As Du Bois (1987) analyzes it, languages grammaticize either in the (6a) pattern, or in the (6b) pattern:

(6)   a. **Accusative case marking**   b. **Ergative case marking**

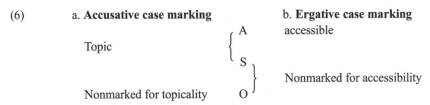

Du Bois further argues that the best support for the proposal regarding competing motivations for ergative versus accusative marking comes from split ergativity cases. Some languages seem to be ergative for some categories but accusative for others. Crucially, the split does not occur randomly. Thus, ergative languages sometimes have accusative markings on their first- and second-person pronouns. The opposite case, whereby only first and second persons are ergative, is not attested. As Du Bois notes, first and second persons, which refer to speakers and addressees, are regularly treated as accessible. The accessible–nonaccessible contrast is here neutralized, then, rendering the ergative marking unnecessary. If this distinction is not useful, its competitor, the one reserved for topic (continuity) can be realized, and hence the accusative morphology.

This case naturally leads us to another type of restricted arbitrariness in language. Here the competition is between a more complicated, but fine-tuned form–function correlation and a simple, perfectly general rule, but one which creates redundancy sometimes, and is therefore less motivated. Split ergativity is not invariably the case. In some languages, despite the fact that it is less useful for the speech act participants, ergative case is obligatory for first and second persons. Durie (1995b) calls such cases functional overkill. Functional overkills are the inevitable result of grammaticization where a grammatical generalization replaces a carefully tailored form–function association (see also Givón, 1999, and chapter 6). Instead of marking ergativity only when absolutely necessary (third, but not first and second persons, where it is less useful), the marking applies to the whole paradigm, even when discoursally unnecessary (for first/second persons). Marking is unmotivated, but it is perfectly consistent. Another example is the use of "redundant" articles. Some languages (e.g. Greek) use a definite article with proper names, even though proper names are definite by definition. Other languages do not. They tailor the use of the definite article to the type of definite NP, using it only "nonredundantly." Some languages only sometimes use definite articles "redundantly." For example, Hebrew uses its definite article in conjunction with demonstrative noun phrases (but not with proper names). These are "redundant" markings, for demonstrative NPs are definite anyway. To conclude, functional overkills result from a competition between an external functional motivation (to indicate ergativity or definiteness when **necessary**) and a (possibly) internal grammatical motivation (to consistently and uniformly mark all definite/ ergative NPs; see Haspelmath, 1999a). Only one motivation can be satisfied. Examining the data with an expectation for the other motivation to manifest itself would lead to the conclusion that arbitrariness is involved.[17]

Diachronic analyses reveal another facet of the "what to code" competition. Should the language stick with its old motivated codes, or should it add on or simply switch to new ones at the expense of the old ones? In the following cases, the language initially chose one motivated path, but then, at a later point in time, chose another motivated path using the very same form. The result is at least partial arbitrariness. Some forms become arbitrarily ambiguous (English *keep*, Hebrew *kcat* 'a little'), an originally transparent meaning may become opaque (Hebrew *kcat*), or one well-motivated form–function correlation is simply

---

[17] We can perhaps view the competition here as a competition between favoring the addressee's interests (a preference for marking only when needed) and favoring the speaker's interests (an automatic marking system).

discarded for another (Hebrew first-person verbal agreement). Once again, whether some phenomenon is arbitrary or motivated depends on what aspects of it one considers, the synchronic state, or the diachronic state. Let's consider these cases one by one.

First, Heine (1997: 4–6) argues that the fact that English *keep* means both 'store' (e.g. *He kept some of them* – LSAC) and 'continue' (e.g. *he kept saying it* – LSAC) can be seen as either arbitrary or as motivated. Structurally, it seems arbitrary. Why should the same verb be both a main verb depicting a certain action and an auxiliary verb coding aspect? But the diachronic path leading from the main verb use to the auxiliary one is functionally motivated, hence, from this perspective, the polysemy is motivated. Similarly, the fact that the definite article is oblivious to the singular/plural distinction (*the child/children*), but the indefinite article is sensitive to it (*a child/*children*), is structurally arbitrary. But historically it is not, because the indefinite article (in many languages) developed out of the numeral 'one,' and hence can only modify singular count nouns.

Next, consider Hebrew *kcat* (Bardenstein, 2005). How can an expression originally meaning 'a little' now express 'some' (i.e. an indefinite partial amount, not necessarily a small amount) on some occasions and 'no(thing)'/'any' on other occasions (in negative polarity contexts)?

(7) a.
ani	maamin	she=im	ba=atid	yaxzor	ha=emun	ve=yisror
I	believe	that=if	in.the=future	will.return	the=trust	and=will.be
kcat	sheket	ve=bitaxon	hem	yaxzeru	la=asok	
some	quiet	and=security	they	will.return.PL	to=work.	

'I believe that if in the future trust will be restored and there will be some quiet and security, they will be back working.'   (Bardenstein, 2005: 13, ex. 16)

b.
ha-askan	ha-katan	haze,	kacav,	ma,	ein	lo
the-politican	the-small	this,	Katzav,	what,	there.is.not	to:him
kcat	kavod?					
any	respect?					

'This small-time politician, Katzav, doesn't he have any self respect?'
(www.haaretz.co.il/hasite/spages/768427.html?more=1)

As Bardenstein shows, each of these developments is motivated. When speakers use *kcat* 'a little' merely as a hedge, or when they contrast a part (denoted by *kcat*) with the whole, the quantity denoted is not necessarily small. Frequent uses of *kcat* in these functions must have altered its conventional meaning to that of 'some.' On the other hand, using *kcat* under negation, where the interpretation is 'not even a little' has paved the way for a reinterpretation of *kcat* as an emphatic 'no(thing).' The result is that, currently, *kcat* is used as 'some indefinite quantity,' as 'a little' (only with contextual support) and as 'nothing' (in negative polarity contexts). While it may seem to be anti-functional to have one expression denote three different degrees of quantity, each interpretation is well motivated (the literal one, a derivative of *kace* 'end/tip,' where only a small quantity can be found, is motivated too). Thus, here too, a well-motivated series of evolutionary steps have led to an unmotivated synchronic state.

Finally, in some cases, an originally motivated form has undergone change due to any number of reasons, and this change may have rendered opaque a motivated origin (see e.g. Givón, 1976; Haiman, 1985a; Mithun, 1991a, 1991b). These are cases where one motivation effectively drove another out. Here arbitrariness may seem unconstrained after all. For example, the natural evolution of verbal agreement morphemes in Hebrew past-tense paradigms (by reduction and merging of independent pronouns with the verb) is not transparent for the singular first person. Compare the transparent relation between the independent pronoun *ata* '2SG') and the counterpart second-person masculine singular agreement marker *-ta* (the latter derived by *a* reduction) with the nontransparent relation between the independent pronoun *ani* or *anoki* 'I' and the first-person agreement marker *-ti* (*a* reduction plus consonantal change):

(8)   S: **ani**   hitxal-**ti**   ita . . .
             I   started-1SG   with.her
         M: **ata**   hitxal-**ta**   ita . . .
             you   started-2SG   with.her . . .   (Lotan 1990: 3)

Can we somehow account for this opaqueness? It would seem so. The opaqueness was brought about because the first-person consonant (*k* of *anoki*) has changed to *t*. Now, although with this assumption we can "rescue" from arbitrariness the original grammatical formation (it is reconstructed to contain the original consonant of the first person), if language is truly motivated, one would expect that a change (to *t*) introducing opaqueness here should have never taken place, for it undermines a motivated correlation (but see below for why a loss of motivation poses no problem once the convention has been established). The point is that this change itself is in fact motivated. Most probably the change to *t* is a change to conform to the second-person agreement markers which have a *t* (in some Semitic languages it is the consonant of the second-person markers which changed to that of the first person – see Moscati *et al.*, 1964: 137–139). Such a change, which makes the first- and second-person agreement markers more similar to each other, supports the resonance between the most common reference shifts in natural conversation (between an 'I' and a 'you,' as John Du Bois, p.c. informs me). Resonance is highly valued in natural conversations, because it highlights both agreements and stance differences between speakers (Du Bois, 2004, 2007, and sections 5.2.1 and 6.4 below). Note that Hebrew past-tense forms are usually subjectless in fact:

(9)   S: rai-**ta**   rai-**ta**?
             saw-2SG   saw-2SG?
             'Did you see, did you see?'
         M: ba=siyur   rai-**ti**.   binyan   yafe.
             on.the=tour   saw-1SG   building   nice
             'On the tour I saw. Nice building.'   (Lotan 1990: 5)

The first-person agreement marker is obviously a limited good. We can either preserve the transparency of the first person (with a *k*), or resonate better with the second person (using a *t*). We can't have both. The Hebrew solution here was an arbitrary association between the first-person pronoun and the corresponding verbal agreement (i.e. the obliteration of an old motivated form–function correlation), but an explicit (transparent) association between first- and second-person agreement (the new motivated form–function correlation). The explanation for this case, as for all the other cases considered in section 4.3, is that language is motivated, but "you can't have it all," because of economy. There are many plausible motivations, and not enough linguistic forms to satisfy them all. Still, arbitrariness is heavily restricted. It's not the case that "anything goes."

4.4   Forms competing over motivations

In section 4.3 we examined cases where multiple functions (e.g. marking of ergativity and accusativity) compete over single forms (various morphological markers). We now examine cases where multiple forms are used for a single function. The argument will be the same, essentially. All we require is a motivated form–function correlation, not exclusivity. Choices among equally plausible linguistic expressions for one and the same function (the subject of section 4.4) are not so different from choices among competing motivations for some form (the subject of section 4.3). All arbitrary choices in grammar are heavily restricted to choices between motivated alternatives. The difference is that here, instead of choosing between two motivations (e.g. ergativity, accusativity) for some form (e.g. morphological case marking), the choice is between two forms, each equally suitable for **one and the same** function.

Consider the case of Maya, a devout chocolate lover. Maya was offered one of the following desserts on some family event: chocolate cake, chocolate mousse, pecan pie, cheese cake, fruit salad, vanilla ice-cream, apple pie, and lemon meringue pie. She chose the chocolate cake. Was that an unpredictable accidental (arbitrary) decision? Well, compared with the choice of chocolate mousse it certainly seems so. But compared with all the other choices, it was quite predictable and motivated. Chocolate cake and chocolate mousse have something in common which make them highly likely candidates for a dessert for Maya (although she may decide to skip dessert on some occasions, just as some languages may not have resumptive pronouns or LDs at all). Pecan pie, cheese cake, and all the other desserts do not share this feature, and are not as likely candidates. Some forms have a propensity to express certain functions, but others do not. Some functions have a propensity to be expressed by certain forms and not by others.[18] But these are merely propensities. The selection of form–function

---

[18] See Heine (1997) and especially Heine and Kuteva (2002) for such universal tendencies in grammaticization paths.

correlations resembles Maya's selection of desserts. It's restricted, but not inevitable. Researchers who want to see arbitrariness focus on the non-inevitability of the choice among equally plausible alternatives (between chocolate cake and chocolate mousse). Researchers who have argued for nonarbitrariness have focused on the restrictedness of the choices which are functionally motivated, contrasting this set with all other implausible alternatives (the chocolate desserts versus all the other desserts). If this is true, the general conclusion must be that language is highly motivated, although a limited degree of arbitrariness is not hard to find. Crucially, the conventionalization processes that have actually occurred in some language are motivated. The fact that so are others which the specific language did not undergo is immaterial. Recall that the argument is that linguistic evolution must be motivated. As long as the path of conventionalization is motivated, the thesis is confirmed, regardless of the existence of other potential motivated paths.

To see the pragmatically restricted nature of language variability let's consider resumptive pronouns again. This time, consider Keenan and Comrie's (1977) Noun Phrase Accessibility Hierarchy, which (also) outlines an implicational hierarchy as to where languages might employ resumptive pronouns in relative clauses:

(10)   Subject > Direct Object > Indirect Object > Oblique > Genitive > Object of Comparison

No attempt is made at predicting absolute distributions, nor whether some language may or may not employ a resumptive pronoun strategy. But, a rather strong prediction is made (and borne out by many diverse languages – see also Comrie and Kuteva, 2005a) that resumptive pronouns tend to be used in syntactic positions which are harder to relativize on. I have argued that the difficulty noted by Keenan and Comrie has to do with how activated the mental representation of the head is in the different cases.[19] Resumptive pronouns are associated with a relatively lower degree of activation than gaps are. Compare direct objects with indirect objects and other positions to its right. If a language allows/requires a resumptive pronoun for direct objects (associated with a relatively high degree of activation), argue Keenan and Comrie, it necessarily allows/requires a resumptive pronoun for indirect objects, obliques, genitives, and objects of comparison (associated with lower degrees of activation). The opposite is not true, however. A language may allow/prefer/impose resumptive pronouns for direct object positions, but not for subject position.

According to (10), if a language imposes resumptive pronouns for positions higher on the scale (left-hand positions), it necessarily does so for lower positions (on its right). If languages were arbitrary, any distribution of resumptive pronouns

---

[19] Unfortunately, Keenan and Comrie use the term accessibility and so too does Ariel, although differently defined. The former use it to refer to the ability to participate in some construction (a relative clause in this case). Ariel's Accessibility pertains to degrees of availability of mental representations. It so happens that there is a correlation between the two in this case.

would have been possible. It isn't. What varies among languages is where the cut-off point is for "low accessibility," what counts as a hard position to relativize on (or as a low mental activation) calling for the use of a resumptive pronoun rather than a gap. The point is that although all languages which have resumptive pronouns stipulate that relatively harder positions (affording low activation) prefer/require a resumptive pronoun, there is "competition" among grammatical roles on which ones should constitute the specific language translation of the cognitive concept of "hard to relativize" (or a low enough degree of activation). The hierarchy cannot motivate every finding. But once a cut-off point has been selected, all lower positions take resumptive pronouns. This is a clear example of a motivated grammatical pattern. The relation between the motivation and the grammatical pattern is not causal in the strong sense, but it explains its particular shape. Motivated choices are made from among a limited set of alternatives, each of them motivated. While the preference for one over another of these alternatives may be arbitrary because it is language-specific, this is a very diluted notion of arbitrariness. Just like Maya's choice of chocolate cake over chocolate mousse, a choice of indirect objects over obliques is a choice between two equally plausible grammatical correlates for a relatively hard position to relativize on (see Haiman, 1985a: 135). Motivations constrain form–function correlations, they do not narrow them down to one option.

Similarly, true (subject) zeros (where not only the subject slot is empty, but the verb does not encode person either, e.g. Chinese zeros), person verbal agreement markers (as in Italian and Hebrew, where the subject slot is empty, but verbs inflect for person), cliticized pronouns and independent pronouns, all part of the referential marking scale, compete on encoding the concept of very high mental activation. Here is the higher end of Ariel's Accessibility marking scale:

(11)   True zero < person verbal agreement < cliticized pronouns < pronouns

Each of these referring expressions is quite uninformative, nonrigid, and phonetically reduced (to varying extents), as compared with definite descriptions and proper names, so that the association between each of them and high activation is clearly motivated. This much is indeed both motivated and universal (see again section 2.2). Still, different languages translate extremely high accessibility into slightly different choices of referring expressions. Some languages lack pronouns (and use demonstrative pronouns instead), others lack verbal agreement altogether. As already mentioned above, a comparison between Chinese and Hebrew, for example, shows a much wider use of true zero in Chinese than in Hebrew, for Hebrew has person verbal agreement at its disposal (indeed, verbal paradigms lacking person agreement hardly ever take zero subjects in Hebrew). But, more interestingly, as mentioned in section 2.2, the activation slot assigned to each of these forms may vary even among languages which do have the same forms.

For example, Chinese translates a rather wide range of high activation into zero subject usage. English is quite restricted. It requires a higher degree of activation (as well as a restricted register) for an acceptable use of zero subjects. English pronouns are often used where Chinese and Hebrew might use zero subjects. What remains constant, however, is that no language allows or prefers zero subjects in contexts characterized by a lower degree of mental activation than those calling for the use of a pronoun in that same language. In other words, while pronouns and zeros compete over the encoding of very high activation, it's invariably the case that the latter specialize for relatively higher degrees of activation for each language. Languages care about relative degrees of activation, not about absolute translations of extralinguistic concepts such as degree of activation. This is why there is some variability as to which forms are used for the concept at hand, but the variability is highly restricted. Zero subjects in one language may routinely correspond to pronouns in another, but not to lexical NPs.

Finally, consider the grammaticization of topic marking. We here consider a competition between a grammatical subject category and morphological inflections not specifically geared to subject agreement. Mithun (1991b) argues that whether a particular language (e.g. Cayuga and Selayarese) evolves a subject category out of a topic category depends on grammatical features which are not even directly relevant to the category at hand. Cayuga morphology, for example, obligatorily marks each verb for person, human/nonhuman, and agent/patient. Considering that subjects evolve out of topics, and given that topics tend to be human and agentive, Mithun reasons that Cayuga does not need to further mark subjects, because the ingredients of prototypical topics are overtly marked obligatorily anyway (as agents, as humans). Addressees have no trouble identifying topics usually. In fact, a variety of additional markers assist addressees in figuring out those cases where some (human) agents are only peripheral, and do not therefore constitute topics, as well as cases where some noncanonical topics, such as patients, are nonetheless topical in specific instances, etc. Thus, while topics are functional in Cayuga just as they are in languages which have grammaticized them as subjects (their conversations normally exhibit topic continuity), Cayuga speakers don't need to grammaticize topics, for they are anyway identifiable for the most part. Morphological richness competes with grammatical status for subjects in this case. Both seem to be motivated forms for indicating topicality, but both do not have to be selected for.

To sum up, we have seen that some language-specific grammatical decisions are arbitrary to some extent in that different forms are selected in different languages for one and the same function. In the case of resumptive pronouns, a specific cut-off point on a cline is selected, although another could have been selected. The different choices adopted by different languages stem from the somewhat different translations they adopt for some extralinguistic concept (e.g. what counts as a low enough activation justifying the use of, say, a pronoun, how topics should be indicated). We have seen, however, that a continuous set of categories on marking clines are carved out for grammaticization. No positions on the cline may be "skipped." Each language, while possibly unique, is heavily restricted in that it does not associate forms with functions randomly. Although there is no absolute cut-off point justifying one specific low-activation marker for all languages, and while languages differ as to what referring expressions they have available, no language picks resumptive pronouns (for example) for higher- but not for lower-activation contexts, or zero subjects for lower- but not for higher-activation contexts. It's invariably the case that lower-activation contexts (the definition of which is language-specific) require or have a preference for lower-accessibility markers (the choice of which markers is again language-specific). But, invariably, arbitrariness is heavily restricted. Form–function correlations are motivated, even if they are not exclusive.

4.5   Unmotivated grammaticizations?

In sections 4.3 and 4.4, we have reviewed cases where competition between equally motivated form–function correlations forced one of the competitors out, so that if we examine the case from the point of view of the "rejected" form–function correlation it seems arbitrary. While the grammar is based on an arbitrary choice from that perspective, the choice made is motivated from a different perspective, that of the "winning" motivated form–function correlation. We now address products of change which seem totally unmotivated in that they go against speakers' best interests, and there is no way to see any reasonable gain in them. Note that if grammar is motivated, such changes are surprising. Moreover, if grammar has been motivated for a long time, one would have thought that natural language grammars should have perfected themselves by now, so that no "improvements" should be necessary anymore. Why do we then still observe semanticizations and grammaticizations? Why haven't grammars stabilized? It is such cases that underscore the claim that what must be motivated is the process of conventionalization, not convention itself. Section 4.5 demonstrates how linguistic change, an inherent part of speaking, is a motivated process, but its product, i.e. grammar, is not necessarily motivated.

We begin with a few puzzling facts. Why do speakers reinvent the wheel time and again, introducing, for example, *have to* when *must* is perfectly suitable, and then *have got to* and *gotta* for (almost) the same purpose? Note (12b–d) (see Bybee *et al.*, 1994: 22), where new form–function correlations have arisen even though the language already had a viable way for expressing the very function they indicate (an unnecessary duplication – see Heine, 1994b: 282 and references therein; Romaine 1999; Traugott and Dasher, 2002):

(12) a.   Every boy that is born,
             must be –
             . . . you **must** throw into the Nile.   (SBC: 030)
      b.   (H) . . you **have to** take this class.   (SBC: 001)
      c.   you**'ve gotta** do the two-handed style thing.   (LSAC)
      d.   (H) You #**gotta** #go downstairs,   (SBC: 006)

Of course, the first time around, language users often find the evolution of semantically encoded concepts quite useful, provided the conveyed meaning is worthy of lexicalization. But why repeat the process more than once?

Consider a few other cases of "unnecessary" conventionalizations. Why do we frequently evolve new expressions for bodily functions such as *using the toilet*? Why do speakers continually innovate intensifiers, e.g. *awfully, terribly, really, pretty, incredibly*, in addition to *very* (see Hopper and Traugott, 1993/2003: 121/ 122)? And why did English evolve *indeed, actually*, and *in fact*, rather similar expressions, within a relatively short period of time, when in addition it had *in truth* and *really* at the time as well (see Traugott and Dasher, 2002, and below)?[20] Note also that languages which have conventional connectives for concessive and causal meanings may nonetheless keep evolving new ones. These new expressions, crucially, show the very same path of grammaticization (out of temporal expressions). *While* and *at the same time* have quite similar paths of change, for example (see Traugott and König, 1991). Just like *while*, *at the same time* can be used in contexts where some contrast is involved, as in:

(13)   It's very funky and **at the same time** it's a little bit rock.   (LSAC)

Like other languages, Hebrew has quite a few causal connectives, which developed out of temporal adverbials (*ki, meaxar she, ekev*). Why did it evolve all of these, in addition to others of a nontemporal origin (*biglal/mipney she-*)?

Other forms actually defeat the motivations they are based on, or even their usability. This happens when changes, especially phonetic ones, create ambiguities. Most ambiguities are actually unproblematic, for context provides ample cues for selecting the appropriate meaning. But some ambiguities are harder to resolve than others, for contextual factors cannot easily resolve the ambiguity. For example, the current *t* deletion in *can't* seems highly counterproductive, for it's the *t* that indicates negation in this case, and opposites (*can* and *can't*) are very often equally plausible in the same context. Why is it deleted then? Why doesn't the need for clarity block it? Note the following:

(14)   As for "**can**" and "**can't**," when some American English speakers use these,
        I always have to interrupt and ask "do you mean 'can' or 'cannot'?"
        (Message from a British English speaker on Linguistlist, Sept. 30, 1993)

Hot is similarly ambiguous (between temperature hot and spicy hot) when predicated on food:

(15)   While having dinner with a group of friends, Paris Hilton recited her famous
        catch phrase, "That's Hot,". . . Tiffany Chambers, an acquaintance of Ms. Hilton,

---

[20] According to Traugott and Dasher (2002), both *indeed* and *in fact* start out as adverbials meaning something like 'in action' (*actually* first means 'effectively'). *Indeed* is used this way starting c. 1300 and *in fact* starting c. 1670. They then each become epistemic markers of adversative facts (c. 1450 for *indeed*, c. 1680 for *in fact*, c. 1750 for *actually*). Finally, they all become discourse markers, adding, rather than contrasting with the previous utterance(s) (c. 1670 for *indeed*, c. 1815 for *actually* and *in fact* – see below).

was under the impression she was speaking about the food. "**Hot hot or spicy hot?**" she asked Ms. Hilton, who was actually referring to her new handbag.
(http://www.underneathhollywood.com/seven.html)

Why did speakers initiate the use of *hot* for 'spicy' when *spicy* seems perfectly suitable, and why do they maintain it? We can also think of the opaque association between first-person singular verbal agreement (*-ti*) and the independent first-person pronoun in Hebrew (*anoki*) mentioned in section 4.3 in this connection. Why demolish one motivated form–function correlation (that between the independent pronoun and the corresponding verbal agreement) for another (an alignment between the speech participants)? Finally, current spoken French negation often takes the form in (16b) rather than in (16a):

(16) a. ~ Je ne bouge pas.
        I   not move   NEGATIVE PARTICLE
     b. ~ Je bouge pas.
        I   move   NEGATIVE PARTICLE
        'I don't move.'

French *pas*, originally 'step,' has come to denote negation in general (e.g. *pas mal* 'not bad') and has been driving the original negator *ne* out. The result seems to be a highly arbitrary form–function correlation where the negative marker is redundant, and 'step' denotes negation.

Why do languages create "superfluous" forms, or worse, defeat extant transparent motivated functions? Amazingly enough, this is true even for some form–function correlations which evolved directly out of the very use that speakers originally recruited them for (see below): some form–function correlations seem to self-destruct. Why should that be? After all, convention makes interpretation faster, and at least some of these semanticizations create linguistic expressions for concepts which seem worthy of lexicalization (e.g. causal and concessive connectives). Why aren't we happy with some newly created semantic meanings in the long run? More generally, how can we argue that language is motivated in view of the above cases where grammaticizations seem unjustified? The short answer for these puzzles is that the "unnecessary" form–function correlations did evolve in a motivated manner, despite the fact that they ended up seemingly or even truly detrimental to language use. Motivations are applicable to processes of grammaticizations. Not (necessarily) to their products.

Proposing that language is molded in response to extragrammatical or communicative pressures should not be confused with a belief in functional teleology (the belief that innovative forms/constructions are especially initiated to meet some felt communicative need – see Heine, 1994b; Heine *et al.*, 1991a, 1991b; Levinson, 1995). Bybee *et al.* (1994) are rightly opposed to such teleological explanations of grammaticization. As they point out, no functional need is universal, and, hence, absolutely necessary (see also Comrie and Kuteva, 2005b; Du Bois, 1985). For example, while grammatically marking future tense is very common among the languages of the world, it's not an absolute universal. The same is true for lexemes for *and* and *or*. Teleological accounts must be rejected even when the end result of the grammaticization process is a useful grammatical tool (e.g. encoding future tense). The initial change, even if intentionally and consciously introduced to serve the speaker's communicative goal, must be seen as a very local extension of use for the individual communicative act, not as an attempt to change or "improve" the grammar. For this reason Heine *et al.*'s (1991b) proposal that grammaticization results from problem solving is somewhat misleading, especially when we combine this proposal with their terms **source** and **target**. Speakers do not have set targets regarding grammatical categories, e.g. future tense, which they proceed to create out of grammatical sources (e.g. verbs of desire – Bybee *et al.*, 1994). While speakers may very well wish to **convey** some interpretation on some occasion (e.g. future event) in the absence of conventional means to do so, we cannot ascribe to them a wish to **conventionally encode** that interpretation in general, and not even on the specific occasion.

This is why many grammaticizations are not necessarily "success stories." In addition to the above "irrational" changes, consider Li and Thompson's (1974) analysis of the grammaticization of Chinese *bǎ*, originally a verb, 'take hold of', into an object marker. This grammaticization has not (yet?) been completed, even though the process was initiated in the eighth century already. As we also see in chapter 5, the key concepts here are local and short-term versus general and long-term goals (see *inter alia* Bybee and Scheibman, 1999; Bybee and Hopper, 2001b; Bybee *et al.*, 1994: 297–300; Keller, 1994). Speakers do have local goals, which they proceed to achieve by motivated means, but these only pertain to the specific utterance at hand. Speakers don't have long-term goals regarding their grammar, so they never deliberately set out on a grammaticization journey to evolve a certain form–function correlation for a communicative need which will be useful to them in the future, once the grammatical form has evolved. In this respect, grammaticization is not goal-directed (teleological). Still, its initiation is goal-directed in that the individual act of the speaker is always (locally) goal-directed, and is always subject to principles of use.

Bybee *et al.*'s (1994) conclusion from cases of this sort is a denial of the role of **functional** motivation for grammaticizations (see also Labov, 1994: part E). They see grammaticization as far more mechanistic in nature.[21] But what they mean by that is that grammaticization is not need-based, such that if a specific language does not have a means to express some function, it evolves an appropriate form for that function (a rejection of teleology). Very often, grammaticization processes are simply automatizations of high-frequency discourse patterns (see Mithun, 1989, 2003). Still, the initiation of grammaticization is motivated (in fact, governed) by language use (e.g. promoting phonetic reduction). Innovations are always motivated or they won't be shared with our interlocutors. Now, although in many cases the local goal may also be functional and motivated in the long run, as we saw above, this is not always true. The indefinite article in English is functional but no

---

[21] See also Labov (1990), Haiman (1994), Bybee (2003a, 2003b), and chapter 5.

longer motivated (why should it be restricted to single entities?). The inflated intensifiers may still be motivated, but no longer functional. *T* deletion in *can't* seems both unmotivated (from the perspective of negation marking) and dysfunctional. Uncontrolled automatic processes may be functional in highly supportive contexts, but not in others.[22] They may be functional for many, but not all expressions. This is the case of *can't*.

Let's now try to understand the motivations behind the puzzling cases above. We start with the cases of frequent renewals. Intensifiers are one case where automaticity causes an expression to self-destruct, and for regrammaticization to surface. As Hopper and Traugott (1993/2003: 121/122) argue, intensifiers often add an emotional facet. Haspelmath (1999b) and Dahl (2001) similarly talk of extravagance, an "inflationary" use of mostly evaluative expressions (e.g. calling all men *gentlemen*, saying that someone is 'very fast,' rather than just 'fast' – in Mandarin Chinese). In the local, short run, the result is an inflated, stronger meaning. In the long run, however, the result is the same as when there's inflation. While everybody has more money, the money is worth less than before. The very same (strong) evaluative expressions are not as strong once they become frequent expressions (e.g. the Mandarin Chinese intensifier is semi-obligatory now – Ansaldo, 1999, as cited in Dahl, 2001). Habituation (a lessened response to a frequent stimulus) is quite detrimental to the use of intensifiers. This is why some expressions gradually come to defeat the very purpose that triggered their initiation and, hence, we find a relatively high rate of renewal for such expressions. Intensifiers are one example where a perfectly motivated local change can lead to an "unjustified" duplicate (and so, unmotivated) convention (Meltzer, 2005 lists three quite recent cases from current spoken Hebrew).

Euphemisms, the modals, the concessive and causal connectives, and the discourse markers are somewhat different cases of renewal, where grammar "cuts the (communication) branch it's sitting on." Initially, frequent uses trigger automaticity, the result being that a previously contextually inferred interpretation (such as a conversational implicature) undergoes semanticization, namely, it becomes a conventional semantic meaning of some expression. Now, such conventionalizations constitute a productive source for many useful expressions in the language, e.g. causal and concessive adverbials, such as *since* and *while*. Still, the problem here is the very conventionality. Semanticization makes indirect, implicit meanings direct and explicit. But addressors do not always wish to

---

[22] The reason why I say that many processes are probably not controlled is that they seem to occur as a result of routinization (Haiman, 1994), and they are sometimes redundant, and even pointless. For example, Hare *et al.* (2001) convincingly argue that even regular past-tense verb forms in English (e.g. *allowed*) are represented in our mental lexicon, despite the fact that a regular rule exists to derive these from their lexical stems (see Bybee, 2001). Such an entry is then quite redundant. The following anecdotal example also testifies to how uncontrolled language production may be. As an adult, I was in close contact with a non-native speaker of Hebrew for a few years, who consistently mispronounced Hebrew *tuna* 'tuna' as *tona*. Although I was well aware of her speech error, after a while I found myself thinking twice before I pronounced the word, even mispronouncing it sometimes, against my better (conscious) judgment.

explicitly assert some interpretation they wish to convey. Some interpretations are intended to be inferred rather than encoded. Speakers care about the explicit–implicit distinction. Hence the repeated need for renewal. If so, such cases again show how long-range effects may defeat initial local and motivated goals.

Consider euphemistic expressions first. The reason why we periodically feel we need to innovate these expressions is that the euphemistic expression undergoes a semanticization of its contextual meaning. Thus, when *use the toilet* is felt to be too direct an expression, we feel we have to switch to a more roundabout expression, such as *go to the bathroom*, where 'toilet' is only inferred. However, since *bathroom* here is contextually interpreted as 'toilet,' automatization, which makes the inferred 'toilet' interpretation be the semantic meaning of *bathroom* in this idiom, causes the whole expression to lose its euphemistic, veiling character. No wonder we then need to devise a new euphemistic expression once again. The whole idea about euphemism is being indirect. Semanticization, on the other hand, makes the (unpleasant) meaning direct, and hence defeats the speaker's initial purpose.

Similarly, speakers sometimes prefer to convey a causal (or concessive) relation as conversational implicature, rather than explicitly:

(17)   The lawyers reported that **after** ((following – MA)) one of the suicide explosions in Jerusalem the criminal prisoners threw glasses into the Palestinian prisoners' cells, and threatened them with murder. **Following** the commotion that took place, policemen sprayed tear gas into the Palestinian prisoners' cells . . .   (Originally Hebrew, *Noga* 41 (2002), 4)

Note that in the report in (17) the Hebrew semanticized causal adverbials are not used, despite a causal connection between the two sets of earlier and the later events. Of course, recurrent uses of temporal connectives in contexts where a causal interpretation is generated (such as in (17)) may lead to the semanticization of the causal implicature. Once again, the long-range effect of automatization undercuts the initial motivated use, to implicate so as to not fully commit to some interpretation. Hence the repeated initiation of a "fresh" temporal adverb into the cycle, where at first, the causal relation will only be implicated. Intensifiers, euphemisms, and causal and concessive connectives are all cases where the local goal of the speaker (merely implicating some interpretation indirectly) clashes with the long-term consequence of such recurrent uses (semantically asserting that interpretation). The same applies to various modal innovations. Automatization may then be responsible for developments deemed dysfunctional in the long run (see also Dahl, 2001).

Next, consider a different set of cases, where an independently motivated linguistic change actually undermines a useful form–function correlation, the ambiguity created by *t* deletion in *can't*. *T/d* deletions occur for frequent words (in response to an economy pressure – Bybee, 2000; Jurafsky *et al.*, 2001). *Can't* is a very frequent phrase, and is in fact taken as a word (Bybee and Scheibman, 1999). If so, phonetic reduction processes apply to it quite mechanically, without speakers actively choosing to apply them in this case. Thus, the mechanistic phonetic process, economical and well motivated in many cases, produces a dysfunctional result in the case of *can't*. In a sense, examples such as *can't* belong in section 4.3, where we discussed competing motivations. Sound changes are well motivated, so we could say that we have a competition here between clarity and economy. But there is a difference. In the cases in section 4.3, the competitors were more or less equal. Shall we go accusative, or shall we go ergative? Some languages choose one option, others choose another. For *can't*, it seems that the loss of clarity by far outweighs the economy achieved by the phoneme deletion, and still reduction is selected. Even creating an exception to the phonetic reduction would seem "worthwhile" in the case of *can't*. But we don't find such solutions. Automaticity is not like any competing motivation. It plays a more absolute role in shaping language. It seems to have no equal rival, and hence invoking the competing motivation account is pointless in such cases. In cases such as *can't* we don't expect some languages or some expressions to go one way (conform to the sound change) but other languages, or other pieces of grammar, to select the other option (i.e. avoid the sound change in order to prevent a hard case of ambiguity). Automatic changes seem quite unavoidable, perhaps because they operate without any conscious attention. Phonetic rules are (almost) exceptionless indeed. They are automatically triggered, and they apply even when they undermine a perfectly useful form–function correlation.

Let's consider now the puzzling development of French negative forms. To understand how what looks like a puzzling or arbitrary connection may nevertheless be highly motivated on the local level, consider the following parallel nonlinguistic case. The Jewish Day of Atonement has been taking on a new, secular significance in Israel over the last few decades. It has basically become "Bicycle Day." Now, cycling is unequivocally incompatible with the spirit of the religious holiday. In fact, cycling is religiously forbidden on that day. How did Israelis evolve such an arbitrary correlation, then? Originally, secular Jews joined religious Jews in avoiding driving on this holiday, considered the holiest day of the year. Not driving is in conformity with the religious Jewish decree not to work on religious holidays (use of any means of transportation is considered work). The religious ban imposes a motivated correlation, then, between Day of Atonement and no driving. However, once cars were out of the way, the holiday was soon perceived as a once-a-year opportunity for cyclists, mostly young ones, to ride on safe, empty roads. The correlation between no driving and cycling is another motivated correlation. The fact that cycling is (religiously) forbidden on the Day of Atonement is now beside the point, because the holiday has been reinterpreted as 'the one day of the year when roads are empty' (because of the high correlation between the two events). And thus the motivated correlation between the holiday and not driving, on the one hand, and between not driving and cycling, on the other, have paved the way for an arbitrary connection between Day of Atonement and bike riding.

I suggest that a similar path of change accounts for the puzzling French negatives, and see Mithun (in press) for a fascinating, similar, but far more complex analysis of a seemingly arbitrary marking of syntactic relations in Northwest Coast North American Indian languages. (i) The original addition of *pas* 'step' in some contexts to create an emphatic negative is quite motivated. Note the following English example:

(18)   Get off my back at once, Rinkitink, or I wo**n't** budge **a step**.
                          (http://enelye.home.mindspring.com/pingaree.html)

(ii) The reduction of *ne* is phonologically motivated (frequent forms tend to be phonetically reduced, see chapter 5). (iii) By habituation, a frequent use of *pas* brought about a "devaluation" in its emphatic force, as well as a generalization of its negative effect, to the point where its meaning has been reanalyzed as a negative particle. This must have happened before *pas* started replacing *ne*, so it's not really the case that 'step' suddenly means 'not.' This is how a series of locally motivated steps ended up with an arbitrary form–function correlation between negation and 'step.'[23] The most important point for our purpose here is that the fact that *pas* and 'negative' are arbitrarily associated with each other poses no obstacle for speakers (just as secular Jews don't worry about the arbitrary association between the religious Day of Atonement and cycling). Arbitrary form–function correlations can be as strong and as functional as motivated form–function correlations are. It is only the local steps leading up to the change which must be motivated.

Different conditions are placed on grammaticization and on grammar. Change will not occur if not motivated. But a form–function correlation is either useful or not useful for speakers. Its arbitrariness is beside the point. In light of the conclusion that only linguistic change must be motivated, not its product, we can revisit our analysis of the Hebrew first-person verbal agreement as reflecting a competition between two motivations. Rather than view it as a competition between two motivations, where it just so happens that resonance won over transparency with the independent pronoun, we can see it as a two-stage change, which it must have been historically, each well motivated. The first, recall, must have turned *anoki* 'I' to *-ki* '1SG verbal agreement.' The second turned *-ki* into *-ti* for resonance with *-ta*. The fact that the result of the second change brought about an arbitrary connection between *anoki* and *-ti* actually poses no problem, for the agreement marker has already been conventionalized. Set conventions do not need to be motivated, for their conventionality guarantees mutual intelligibility by speaker and addressee. Original motivations for form–function correlations are

---

[23] English *never*, as in the following, may serve a similar purpose:

   (i) M: My mom's gonna give the kids Chanukah money tonight.
          I **never** gave them! (Dec. 22, 2006)

   Note that M means that she didn't give her kids Chanukah money this year, not that she never gave them. *Never* here serves as an emphatic negation marker.

probably not difficult to abandon, once they have served their purpose (establishing the convention), so that newer motivated changes can take place. The fact that he who laughs last laughs best is no hindrance to functional conventions.

But now, although grammatical conventions do not have to be motivated, they have to be functional. Arbitrariness is no obstacle to a functioning grammatical system, but dysfunctionality is. We have seen above a few such cases. It is important to note that language is not totally at the mercy of automatic processes pulling it to self-defeating form–function correlations. If dysfunctional, the products of semanticization may simply fall out of use, and disappear from the language (see Durie, 1995a; Hopper and Traugott, 1993/2003: 206–208; Keller, 1994). For example, Mishnaic Hebrew *beit kavod* 'honor house' has been lost, and similarly, Modern Hebrew *beit kise* 'chair house' has been disappearing (both are euphemistic terms for 'toilet'). Some self-defeating cases involve some kind of repair for the problem, either by renewal, reverting to a new "virgin" expression (e.g. a different euphemistic expression, a different temporal expression), or else, the addition of a reinforcing expression, as in French negation, where emphatic markers were added, and one of them, *pas* 'step,' became obligatory once the original negative marker was phonetically reduced.[24] Chinese, according to Li and Thompson (1981), underwent very many sound changes, resulting in massive homonymy. The remedy for that is a very high proportion of compounding (not too different from the English combination *spicy hot* in (15)). Thus, locally goal-oriented, recurrent uses may end up with self-defeating forms in the long run. While speakers cannot prevent these self-defeating forms, they can remedy such outcomes. Note that these "therapeutic" actions are not necessarily immediately initiated, however. There may be a period where some point of grammar is dysfunctional, despite the fact that it was evolved during goal-oriented discourse.

Moreover, some consequences are not as easy to remedy as others. Dysfunctional lexical items are easily enough not used and lost, but obligatory forms cannot fall out of use in the same way, precisely because they are obligatory/automatic. In such cases, language users can accept an arbitrary linguistic convention, or they can redefine the form–function correlation involved. This redefinition can only come about if preferred patterns of use already in existence may be reinterpreted as integral to the form rather than to the context. To anticipate chapter 6, English reflexives, which have evolved as marked coreference indicators, have later been mobilized for indicating co-argument coreference regardless of markedness.

All in all, the "arbitrary" form–function correlations exhibited by language are heavily restricted: options equally motivated cannot all be satisfied by a single form–function correlation. First, not all conceivable motivations can be encoded

---

[24] See also Deutscher's (2005: 167/168) brief historical survey of the different variants for French 'today,' which underwent phonetic reductions as well as emphatic strengthenings: *hoc die* 'this day' ultimately reduced to *hui*, then it was reinforced to *au jour d'hui*, which shortened to *aujourd'hui*, and finally renewed as *au jour d'aujourd'hui*.

by a single form/language because of economy. Hence, equivalent forms may have different functions. Second, more than one form can serve some function in a motivated way. Hence the use of different, although equally motivated forms for the same function in different languages (and occasionally within the same language). This is why very often what seems to be arbitrary for some form–function correlation is actually motivated, but for another, competing form–function correlation. In section 5.3 a possible explanation is outlined for such partial arbitrariness in language: the adoption of precedents and linguistic conservatism. In some cases, the counterproductive force is not a specific motivated form–function correlation, but, rather, another external motivation, e.g. the tendency to generalize or the tendency to automatize. Partially or even fully arbitrary linguistic conventions pose no problem. But, in some cases, the gap between the local goal and the long-range cumulative effects of many such local actions creates not just arbitrariness, but a dysfunctional form–function correlation. Only these are cases which may trigger remedial changes.

The general picture is that the synchronic grammar is at least partially motivated. However, the point is that this is actually a by-product of the emergence of grammar, not a condition on possible grammars as such. It is only the initiation of grammar (i.e. regular language use) which is motivated by definition. Conventions cannot be born arbitrary, but they can certainly be made arbitrary later. The only condition they must meet is functionality for speakers. Nonetheless, the fact that language is as (transparently) motivated as it is testifies to the central role of ongoing conventionalizations. Had the process of conventionalization not remained a constant force in language use (forever remolding grammar), motivated form–function correlations would have been hard to find. As we shall further see in chapter 5, they are not.

Once we recognize the central role of conventionalization in language, we can understand why language can be motivated and arbitrary at the same time. If grammar is a natural historical product, then explaining its precise shape should resemble the explanations we provide for other human conventional practices. We can motivate their initiation, but we cannot predict when or even if they will develop, nor their exact shape once they do develop. For linguists to conclude total unpredictability (arbitrariness) from lack of complete predictability (this is Prince's 1988, 1998 line of argument) would be equivalent to historians declaring human history chaotic and arbitrary, just because they are unable to predict historical developments. In fact, the linguistic case is much stronger (less arbitrary). While history hardly ever repeats itself, very similar paths of linguistic change are often observed in many unrelated languages. Extralinguistic motivations cross the grammar/pragmatics divide quite regularly, and in rather predictable ways. We see how in the next chapter.

5   All paths lead to the salient discourse pattern

Consider a simple example, provided by Langacker (2000). It is quite obvious, he argues, that the suddenly needed term for a 'computer device' *mouse* was derived from the word's literal 'rodent' meaning. It's equally uncontroversial that when first used for the new instantiation, it was through pragmatic inferencing that the new interpretation was derived. Of course, nowadays, *mouse* is already semantically ambiguous (polysemous) between the two meanings. The computer-device meaning is part of our conventional, grammatical knowledge of the lexeme *mouse*. Note that it has a different plural form (*mouses*), and it can serve as the basis for yet a new derived interpretation, as in (1), where *clitoris mouse* refers to the small, centrally located pointing stick used as a mouse on some laptop computers:

(1)   A: It's got a **clitoris mouse**.
         B: It's got a what.   (LSAC)

But when/where/how did the change in cognitive status happen for *mouse*? It did not come about by stipulation. All we can assume is that many speakers started using this innovation because they found it useful, not because they were seeking to change their lexicon. But when did the change actually take place? On the first uses it may not have been easy to even understand (witness B's difficulty in (1)). On the seventh use event of the metaphoric *mouse*, asks Langacker? We cannot determine a precise moment when the inference leading from 'rodent mouse' to 'computer mouse' gave way to a conventional, semantic meaning for *mouse* (see Deutscher, 2005: 152). Langacker concludes from cases of this sort that semantic meanings in general are indistinguishable from pragmatically induced interpretations (he does not require linguistic interpretations to be conventional). This is not a necessary conclusion, however. Intermediate cases, as *mouse* must have been a while ago, or as *clitoris mouse* is for many people currently, do not rule out the existence of other, sharply differentiated cases. But how do we get from pragmatics to grammar?

   Chapter 4 was devoted to arguing that to the extent that we can trace its origins, grammar is motivated by external forces, not because grammar needs to be motivated (arbitrary conventions are just as functional), but because the process of conventionalization must be motivated. As was emphasized, grammar is constantly in the making, and if so, it must somehow constantly be interfacing with external motivations. But what is the nature of these external forces? How do they come to affect grammatical convention? Where does the interface between external forces and grammar take place? These are the questions we address in chapter 5. In addition to the grammar/pragmatics interface at the very high cognitive level of the conveyed meaning, which is relatively conscious and controlled, we also have an interface between external forces and grammar at a very low, quite unconscious and uncontrolled cognitive level: one which is sensitive to salient discourse patterns. This is the level that enables the crossing of the extragrammatical into the grammatical.

What makes language (initially) potentially take the shape it does? Two radically different answers are simultaneously correct. On the one hand, we could say, just about any motivation can affect grammar. On the other hand, we could equally name just one factor: the salient, or privileged, discourse pattern. The choice of answer depends on how far we choose to go on the causal chain. While many factors are responsible for the shape of grammar, they cannot affect grammar directly. Only the salient discourse pattern does. As we shall see (section 5.1), researchers have persuasively argued that language is affected by the way the world is, our cognition, our human processing mechanisms, especially our memory limitations, our sociocultural norms, and our ability to draw on pragmatic inferences. In addition, our current grammar constrains our future grammar as well. We never start from "scratch." Finally, many discourse grammarians have emphasized the role of frequent discourse profiles. But how does the speaker juggle all of these? What's the relation between these factors? Recall that linguistic change is what happens when speakers are busy making other plans, namely using language to serve whatever local goals they have. All of the above sources are involved in molding grammar, but the picture is not as chaotic as it might seem. Discourse use is one major gate-keeper, regulating all the potentially competing influences on grammar (section 5.2). And then, there is a further, rather narrow funnel through which all influences must go – the salient discourse pattern (section 5.3). Probably all successful grammaticization paths had previously led to salient discourse patterns, themselves only necessary (but not sufficient) conditions for conventionalization.

Chapter 5 exemplifies some extralinguistic influences on our grammar, starting with the highest cognitive effect, the world and its conception, and ending with the narrowest, very low-level effect of the application of automatization. The argument is that if it doesn't make it into a salient discourse pattern, no factor can grammaticize, no matter how well motivated it is cognitively, socially, or what have you. Only "discourse profiles set the agenda for subsequent grammaticization" (Du Bois, 2003b: 44).

5.1   External forces behind grammar

We here examine a few cases where our cognition (section 5.1.1), our sociocultural norms (section 5.1.2) and our inferential practices (section 5.1.3) can affect the way our grammar is. These factors work in an additive manner, so that e.g. the creation of some grammatical code must not only be compatible with our cognitive make-up, it must also not clash with our sociocultural assumptions, etc.

5.1.1   Grammar and our cognition

One obvious potential source of influence on grammar is the world we live in. For example, according to Levinson (2000b and others; see also section 6.1), where Condition B of the original Binding Conditions (banning a sentence such as *She$_i$ saw her$_i$*) is obligatory, it is due to the grammaticization of a pragmatically induced interpretative pattern, based on reality. A pronoun cannot have its antecedent be a co-argument of the same predicate in the same clause, because the prototypical transitive activity is one where an agent is acting upon an entity which is **distinct** from itself. Such coreference is disallowed, argues Levinson, because "that is how the **world** stereotypically **is**" (2000b: 328, emphasis added).

Most researchers, of course, emphasize that it is not the "raw" world that is reflected in language. Rather, it's the way the world is, filtered by the human cognitive make-up. For example, Haiman (1980, 1983, 1985a, 1985b) is mostly associated with the suggestion that language is at least partly arranged according to an iconicity principle, but note how he formulates this principle: "linguistic structures are often similar to non-linguistic diagrams of **our thoughts**" (Haiman, 1985a: 8, emphasis added) and see also Givón (1984, 1990, 1993), the various articles in Haiman (1985b), Heine (1991a), and Duranti (1997: 205–207), who discusses the differences between the degree of iconicity manifested by different languages.[1] For example, Bybee (1985b) argues that the degree of semantic closeness (relevance) of various concepts related to the verb determines their (physical) closeness to the verb. And Bolinger (1985, 1989) argued that intonation is an iconic system, trading on metaphorical associations of the notions up and down. Hence, high or rising pitch, for example, universally marks some emotional arousal. Ladd (1990) has criticized this position, and in fact, more often than not, languages do not manifest such direct reflections of the outside world. For one thing, incompatible, seemingly arbitrary linguistic facts may derive from other, natural, extralinguistic motivations, such as simplicity and economy (competing motivations). The various articles in Haiman (1985b) support much the same ideas, and attest that it is not the objective world that we find reflected in grammar. For example, Wierzbicka (1985) proposes that the seemingly arbitrary decision to code some nominals as count nouns (e.g. *oat/oats*), but others as mass nouns (e.g. *wheat*), is motivated, after all, by reference to our **perception** and use of the specific referents.

Other discrepancies too can only be explained if it is the human conception of the world that is iconically reflected in grammar. The structure of the complex

---

[1] Historically, of course, the above linguists were not the first to propose that languages contain iconic aspects – see Peirce (1932/1965) and, following him, Jakobson (1971).

clause has also been argued to iconically reflect the relations between the clauses combined (Croft, 2000; Foley and Van Valin, 1984; Givón, 1984, 1990, 1993; Langacker, 1991; Silverstein, 1976): the tightness of the cohesion between the propositions is mirrored in the tightness of the structural relations between them. The stronger the semantic/pragmatic relation, the higher the syntactic fusion between them. Thus, many languages do not even express the most highly cohesive relations as clausal (e.g. possessive), but hardly any language exists that does not express two non-sequitur propositions as a sequence of two syntactically independent clauses.[2] Here and in between one can measure the syntactic (in)dependence of combined clauses by the (in)dependent choice of tenses, illocutionary forces, participants, etc. Thus, causative and modal relations are high on the cohesion hierarchy, representing one perceived event, temporal adverbials and conditionals are intermediate, and two unrelated events (propositions) end the cohesion hierarchy.[3] Corresponding to this semantic/pragmatic scale is a syntactic scale of bondedness, starting with verb serializations, e.g. *let go* (sharing arguments, illocutionary force and tense), gerunds, nominalizations and raising to object constructions, adverbial and *that* clauses, and, finally, coordination (not necessarily sharing tenses, participants, and illocutionary forces).

The argument is that a tight semantic/pragmatic connection is expressed by a tight syntactic structure (and vice versa for loose semantic/pragmatic connections). The same iconicity claim also predicts that *X and Y, X, and Y* (*and* following a break), *X. And Y* (initial sentence *and*), and *X. And then Y* (*then* joining *and*) – each conjoining the two units 'X' and 'Y' to a different phonological and physical extent – will imply different degrees of clause connectivity. Indeed, concentrating on the extremes, only 15 percent of the second conjuncts in (nonpunctuated) *and* conjunctions switched the subject of the previous clause, while all of the subjects were switched when . *And then* was used (Givón, 1993). While all of these reflect an iconic relation between cohesion and syntactic bondedness, cohesion is clearly not an objective fact about the world. Rather, it reflects our imposed order on the world.

Newmeyer (1991) has accused pragmatists of treating any consistent form–function correlation as iconic.[4] As Durie (1995b) convincingly argues, iconic motivations have been overrated in the literature, and many putative iconic form–function correlations are a linguist's construct more than a conventional interpretation speakers count on hearers to make (Durie notes the nasal consonant characteristic of very many words for *nose* in the languages of the world in this connection).[5] Often, the iconic representation is actually a historical product of a

---

[2] Non-sequitur propositions are ones not connected to each other.
[3] But see Kemmer and Verhagen (1994) for a graded view of the perceptual unity of the causing and caused events.
[4] Indeed, it is not clear to me in what sense Levinson's (1995: 103) Q2 heuristic, "minimal expressions invite stereotypical, rich interpretations," is iconic, as he claims it to be.
[5] See Haspelmath (to appear) for a thorough critique of many types of iconicity.

noniconic origin (this is Bybee's 1985a proposal regarding the ordering of tense, aspect, etc. within the verb – see below). We can often better motivate seemingly iconic linguistic facts by reference to other cognitive considerations (e.g. relevance for Bybee's findings regarding verbal morphology, processing ease for the match between linear ordering of verbs in serialization and the chronological ordering of the events depicted; see also Carston, 2002a: chapter 3). Note, however, that whereas Durie's criticisms of the overuse of iconicity in explaining linguistic form are well taken, the form–function correlations under discussion, while not world-grammar correlations, are still correlations between our cognition and linguistic forms, and thus constitute legitimate examples of external considerations involved in linguistic form.

The thesis that language reflects our cognition, rather than the "objective" world has recently been forcefully argued for by Cognitive Linguists (Lakoff, 1987; Lakoff and Johnson, 1980; Langacker, 1987; Sweetser, 1990; Talmy, 1985, 1988). Langacker and Lakoff have in fact been the chief advocates of a language–cognition blurring. Grammar is seen as reflecting, even encoding people's conventionalized conceptualizations of reality (see also Bowerman, 1996; Croft, 1991; Lakoff and Johnson, 1980; Talmy, 1983, 1985). Lakoff (1987: 91) moreover argues that since language is a major part of cognition, we can use language to learn about our cognition in general (note Lakoff's famous 1987 book title, *Women, Fire, and Dangerous Things: What Categories Reveal about the Mind* – emphasis added). One of the many examples he quotes is that of noun classifiers.[6] Lakoff argues that noun classifiers reflect categorization systems. Thus, according to the Dyirbal classifier system "the universe is divided up into four clearly defined mutually exclusive domains" (1987: 102). Within categories, classifiers distinguish between prototypical and less or nonprototypical members of a category, rather than between members and nonmembers, the organizing principle being family resemblances, not a set of properties shared by all members. For example, in the Dyirbal classifier system (from Dixon, 1982), the moon and men are in the same category, but men are central members of the category, while the moon is not. Fish equipment is classified with fish, although fish belongs in the category of animals. Animals and fish equipment do not share conceptual features, but they do share something with fish: "Complex categories are structured by chaining; central members are linked to other members, which are linked to other members, and so on" (Lakoff, 1987: 95). Last, categorization is subjective, so that metaphoric and metonymic links are at work, and myths and beliefs create links within a category, allowing, for example, for a view of birds as the spirits of dead women.[7] The idea is that our cognition operates metaphorically, and this is why language does too (see also Lakoff and Johnson, 1980; Sweetser, 1990).

---

[6] Noun classifiers mark the semantic category the nominal belongs to.
[7] But see Aronoff (1997) for the opposite, arbitrariness view of grammatical gender (he takes Dyirbal noun classes as manifesting genders rather than classifiers).

Deutscher (2005: chapter 4) presents ample evidence for the ubiquity of metaphor in language use, which drives semanticization.

In conformity with Cognitive Linguistics, many historical linguists have been arguing the basically traditional view of semantic change brought about by metaphorical extension (Bybee and Pagliuca, 1985; Claudi and Heine, 1986; Sweetser, 1988, 1990, *inter alia*), but see Bybee *et al.* (1994). Heine (1997: 10) stated: "I believe that much of what languages offer in terms of structural complexity and diversity can be . . . explained with reference to extralinguistic forces . . . **most of all with reference to cognition**" (emphasis added). "Language structure is the product of our interaction with the world around us" (Heine, 1997: 3). This is the source of the universal in language: "human beings . . . have the same intellectual, perceptual, and physical equipment; they are exposed to the same kinds of experiences; and have the same communicative needs" (Heine, 1997: 10–11). Heine (e.g. 1997) has been leading this type of research in grammaticization. For example, our minds are not objectively similar to our bodies, but we (universally) metaphorically conceive of our internal selves in terms of our external, physical selves (e.g. *You're getting **soft*** – LSAC). This is the source of polysemies, pragmatic ambiguities and semantic historical changes of lexemes referring to the body used also or exclusively for higher-level activities (e.g. *see* also meaning 'understand'). Heine (1997) is a detailed analysis of how languages extend mostly the human body parts for deictic orientations, ultimately deriving a variety of prepositions from them (e.g. *behind*). More generally, Sweetser (1990) argues that the fact that semantic change is unidirectional mirrors and proves the influence of cognitive processes on language. Just as metaphoric conceptualizations are unidirectional (i.e. perceiving of X as being similar to Y does not entail the perception of Y as being similar to X), so are their linguistic reflections. Hence, concrete objects may develop more abstract meanings but not vice versa.

Note, however, that there are very many ways we could grasp and classify world objects, events, etc. Indeed, different languages code the same human experience (e.g. feeling cold) differently (cold being predicated of the subject, or possessed by the subject). As Croft (1993a) argues, the reason for the differences is that the linguistic coding of some experience may highlight one of its aspects over others, or it may rely on its resemblance to one type of concept (coded in a certain way) rather than another concept (coded in a different way), even though conceptually speakers may well be aware that similarities to other experiences and hence other codings are quite feasible. Conceptions are often too complex for one type of construction to fully reflect all their facets. Hence, one language may opt to focus attention on one aspect, another on another aspect of it. For instance, in the Malay classifier system, 'table' is classified as 'three-dimensional,' which indeed it is, but in Mandarin it is classified with 'flat' objects, no doubt since it is the (flat) surface which is the prominent part of the table. Both classifications are cognitively plausible, yet they are different.

Jurafsky (1996) argues that female gender is connected with augmentative meanings in some languages but with diminutive meanings in others. As he reasons, neither of these is arbitrary. Languages where 'female' is associated with 'large/important' are ones where women (mothers, actually) are seen in comparison to children. They are then seen as salient, important family members. In languages where 'female' is associated with 'small/unimportant,' women are compared with men. Thus, while the two conceptualizations of females taken together seem contradictory, each by itself is cognitively coherent (see also his discussion of diminutives as approximators as well as exactness markers, and see Ariel, 1998c about deictics as sources for both Accessibility and Newness particles). Thus, of course the grammar that emerges out of discourse is in congruence with our cognitive structure. But the point is that it reflects a very intensive process of selection among many possible conceptualizations, in interaction with discoursal use, as well as other factors.

Another cognitive factor affecting grammars is the human processing mechanism. Psycholinguistic research may seem irrelevant to grammar, for it pertains to production and comprehension strategies adopted by speakers producing and processing their synchronic grammar in real time, presumably in order to optimize language processing. From this perspective these strategies may have developed in response to the nature of grammar, which is "independently" given. However, a number of researchers have proposed that such performance strategies may grammaticize, or at least constrain the evolution of grammar.[8] There is a feedback relationship between grammars and actual processing, which creates what Bates and MacWhinney (1989: 23) call the "processing determinism." To the extent that there is some convergence between sentence processing and/or production and actual grammars, and provided that it is the former that shapes the latter and not vice versa, we can argue that processing constraints mold or constrain natural language (change).

Hawkins (1990), for example, argues for an Early Immediate Constituents principle in natural languages, which ensures an early recognition of all immediate constituents of the node currently being processed (this is Hawkins' 2004 "Minimize Domains" principle). Such a constraint accounts for the tendency of heavy constituents to shift to the right. Hawkins (2003) proposes that placing short constituents before longer ones is the optimal arrangement for our short-term memory, both for the speaker (production) and for the addressee (comprehension), for it minimizes the amount of material needed to identify two adjacent categories.[9] As typological evidence for this preference Hawkins presents Greenberg's cross-category correlations. Let's examine the frequency of various orders of verbs and verb phrasal PPs in the languages of the world:

---

[8] See Hawkins (1990, 1994, 2003, 2004) and MacWhinney and Bates (1989).
[9] In fact, it's not always the case that production and comprehension call for the same pattern. Whereas previous research tended to hypothesize an addressee-based preference, current research shows that production may take precedence (see Arnold *et al.*, 2000, and references cited therein). And see Rosenbach (2005) about Saweru, which has a preference for long before short constituents.

(2) a. $[_{vp}V + [_{pp}P + NP]]$: 41.4% of languages

    b. $[_{vp}[_{pp}NP + P] + V]$: 52.4% of languages

    c. $[_{vp}V + [_{pp}NP + P]]$: 4.6% of languages

    d. $[_{vp} [_{pp}P + NP] + V]$: 1.5% of languages

Note that what the two frequent structures (2a, b) have in common is that the short preposition separates the two phrasal categories, thus minimizing the load imposed on working memory. The nonoptimal arrangements require placement of the heavier (possibly longer) NP in working memory. All in all, there is impressive evidence that grammar is shaped in accordance with human cognitive abilities.

5.1.2   Grammar and sociocultural norms

While grammar is no doubt a product constrained by our cognition, other external sources leave their imprint on it as well: culture, for example. Following Traugott (1982), Sweetser (1990) emphasizes the subjectivity involved in metaphorical processes leading to semanticization, where by subjectivity she means that the process is performed by people in a specific society and culture, rather than by strictly logical and objective inferential steps (see also Lichtenberk, 1991; Wierzbicka, 1985). For example, English *candid*, a derivative of Latin *candidus* 'white,' reflects a cultural, not an objective association between honesty and whiteness. Logically, there is no reason to assume that Latin *candidus* should have meant both 'white' and 'open, honest.' But if the specific culture is taken into account, the transfer from 'white' to 'honest' is not at all surprising.

Heine's (1997) fascinating study of how languages evolve deictic orientation expressions out of body parts indeed testifies to our anthropocentric conceptualization. We perceive other things in terms of our own bodies. But although the human body is essentially invariant, our conception of our body is a cultural construct.[10] It's not surprising then that languages differ in what body parts are mobilized for various deictic orientation expressions. Heine (1997: 14) claims that "The way people in Siberia or the Kalahari Desert experience the world around them can immediately be held responsible for the way they shape their grammars."[11] The fact that these differences span over specific geographic areas where different languages are spoken raises the possibility that cultural differences are at the basis of what body part is selected for what further use. This is what Heine (1997: 11–14) proposes. For example, in Africa, a great majority of the expressions for 'down' derive from 'buttocks,' and the rest derive from 'foot/leg.' But 'foot/leg' is the only body part relevant for the evolution of an expression for 'down' in Oceania. Another interesting difference pertains to whose body parts

---

[10] From a completely different point of view, this has also been the feminist position.

[11] This generalization, conveniently predicated on an "other" community, should be qualified. Grammar can at best reflect the world view of its speakers during the time in which grammaticization took place. It does not have to be an ever-present world view (think of the English *The sun sets in the west*).

are used for orientation. It's not invariably the human body (or not exclusively so). Some languages adopt an animal body (zoomorphic) model, and that's why in some languages 'back' has evolved to mean 'up,' 'head' is used for 'front,' and 'buttocks' for 'back' (Heine, 1997: 40). Interestingly, 'head' used for 'front' (the zoomophoric model) is only found in Africa. 'Belly' for 'front' (the human body model) is found almost only in Oceania.

Witkowski and Brown's (1983) study also argues for the role of culture in shaping grammar. Culturally central concepts are coded by relatively unmarked linguistic forms. Witkowski and Brown note the lexical changes induced in various American Indian languages with the introduction of an animal previously unknown in those cultures, the sheep. Their detailed historical survey reveals a clear tendency for languages to code culturally marked concepts by linguistically marked expressions, and unmarked/important cultural concepts by unmarked linguistic expressions. Thus, in Tenejapa Tzeltal, initially, sheep were referred to as *tunim chih* 'cotton deer,' i.e. by a complex, marked expression. However, once sheep became prevalent and more useful than deer, there was a marking reversal, and sheep have since been referred to by the short expression (*chih*), whereas deer are now *te?tikil chih* 'wild sheep.' Similarly, a cartoon in a supermarket newsletter (Trader Joe's, undated) shows a client pointing to his coffee mug, asking for another cup. The waiter then asks him, "Decaf or Non-decaf?", indicating that decaf coffee is now becoming the unmarked type of coffee, and hence should be represented by a shorter form.

Traugott and Dasher (2002: 284) note that cultural/ideological considerations may render the expression of objectivity and/or subjectivity and/or intersubjectivity more or less relevant/salient to speakers of different communities. For example, Myhill (1997) argues that *ought* is used for obligations which are socially based (more objective), whereas *should* indicates more individually based obligations (more subjective). Since social obligations are no longer culturally prominent, we find that SBC only has 6 occurrences of *ought*, but 68 occurrences of *should* (see also Verhagen's 2000 analysis of the use of Dutch causatives in light of changes in the concept of authority and gender). Hebrew *armumi* 'cunning' has not changed in denotation since Biblical times. It's our attitude to being cunning which has changed, and has rendered the word negative. This negativity is now part of its semantics. A similar change characterizes English *cunning* (Stern, 1931: 414). So, sociocultural forces render some concepts (and hence some linguistic expressions) more useful, and others as less, or not at all useful. This may have repercussions for the emerging grammar.

Note that we have so far referred to cultural factors in order to explain language diversity. Ochs (1996), however, rejects the cultural–universal opposition. She argues that universals may derive from extralinguistic propensities, or from a common adaptive capacity we all share. Culture, she argues, is also a derivative of our humanity, and it is not surprising therefore that similar linguistic codes are used for achieving similar (though not necessarily identical) communicative goals across communities. She offers the universal-cultural means–end principle to account for that. As examples she notes that often, expressions used to mark that the speaker is adopting the other's point of view will also be used to mark her own lower ranking, and similarly, respect forms may be used in an equal encounter to mark a request. For an interesting example, where universal/cognitive and cultural motivations intertwine, see the discussion of the linguistic coding of anger in various languages in Geeraerts (1995), Kövecses (1995) and Matsuki (1995).

Another cultural (near) universal is male bias, which is often reflected in language. In language after language, where there is a markedness distinction between forms denoting biological males and females, the masculine forms are unmarked, shorter and/or morphologically simpler than the feminine forms, which are often derived from them (e.g. Hebrew *talmid(-a)* for 'student' masculine versus feminine, *shatkan(-it)* for 'silent' masculine versus feminine, *halax(-a)* for 'walked' masculine versus feminine). Similarly, semantically, there is a bias for interpreting generic terms as masculine rather than feminine. Note how (the Hebrew counterpart of) *adults* must be interpreted as 'adult males' in (3):

(3)   Billy the kid: the first homosexual doll is targeted for **adults** and is very
         popular among **women too**.   (Originally Hebrew, *Haaretz*, Sept. 6, 1998)

Next, social factors have long been implicated in certain aspects of linguistic change. Croft (2000) distinguishes between actuation and propagation in language change. Actuation, the first, individual innovative use by the speaker, does not guarantee an actual historical change (see also Stern, 1931). It only has a potential for change. For change to actually occur, propagation, the spread of some linguistic innovation within the community, needs to take place. Weinreich *et al.* (1968) and Labov (1980, 2001) argue that innovations tend to spread if used by prestigious community members. Indeed, quite a few innovations in Hebrew originated with a famous Israeli comedy group ("Ha-gashash ha-chiver"), e.g. the expression *celex cavo*, a dialectal pronunciation of *telex tavo* 'go come,' now also meaning 'bureaucratic hassle' (see also Deutscher's (2005: 175–176) discussion of the innovative English *grotty* by Beatles singer George Harrison). Milroy and Milroy (1985), on the other hand, argue that sound changes they examined in Belfast were first adopted mostly by individuals with looser ties to the community, and only later by prestigious community members, who then helped the change spread quite rapidly. Croft (2000: chapter 7) prefers social identification as an explanation for propagation, with attention paid to covert prestige forms. Accommodating one's speech to that of the community one identifies with constitutes part of one's self-definition as a community member. Regardless of which of these factors is/are more important, no doubt social factors are mediators of linguistic change.

We have seen above how cultural norms select among equally feasible cognitive options. Let us now see how social factors weed out cognitively viable options. Note how social conventions and rules of politeness intervene to prevent us from expressing things "as they really are" (in reality or in our mind). For example, it seems only reasonable that we often think about ourselves and that we constantly indulge in self-love. Quite possibly we ourselves more often than others form the objects of our thoughts and love. Still, of the 1,807 occurrences of *think/thinking/thought about* in SBC and LSAC, only two showed coreference between the subject and the object. Of the very many *love x* cases, there was one case of coreference. In other words, despite "objective" truth, it is socially improper to report on our love for ourselves and thinking about ourselves. Hence, discoursally speaking, thinking about oneself and loving oneself are extremely marked, regardless of their high frequency in the real world. Next, consider socially "improper" bodily functions. Here it is perhaps easier to quantify the frequency of the activities "in reality." I think it's fairly uncontroversial to say that we use the bathroom more often than we eat, and more often than we wash ourselves. Still, there were only 187 verbal references to going to the bathroom in SBC and LSAC. There were almost twice as many references to self washing in the same corpora (345 cases), even though in reality, the former activity must be performed some eight times more often than the latter.[12] As against these two private bodily activities, there were 3,411 mentions of *eat* in the same two corpora (18.2 times more than going to the bathroom, this, when cases such as *have lunch/ an apple*, etc. were not even counted). This gap cannot possibly reflect mere "objective reality." Eating is a social event, or at least not a private event. Politeness norms therefore allow us to freely report such events. When we discuss the role of the frequent discourse pattern below, we will see what the grammatical repercussions of these facts are.

An interesting case for the influence of politeness is argued for by Stefanowitsch and Gries (2003) regarding imperatives. Whereas imperatives are used for requests, they are overwhelmingly used for requests imposing on the addressee for his own benefit (rather than the speaker's). They also often involve actions which don't produce results (e.g. *let, see, look, listen,* and *don't worry* head the list). In fact, they tend to call the addressee's attention to something. In other words, the discourse profile of imperatives is very different from the 'commanding' speech act style analysis of imperatives. Of course, politeness is responsible for why such direct impositions on the addressee are predominantly used for his benefit and for activities which are not highly demanding. Others are better off hedged. Social norms, then, suppress some contents, while promoting others. Discourse, as we experience it, and grammar derivatively, reflect this social filtering.

5.1.3   Grammar and pragmatic inferencing

Finally, we come to pragmatic enrichments as a source of linguistic change. A significant factor in the grammaticization of pragmatics is the fact that although we use the existing grammar to produce our utterances, grammar always

---

[12] The verbs checked were: *go to the bathroom, pee, urinate, (take a) piss/leak, shower, wash, bathe* + periphrastic expressions such as *take/have a shower/bath*.

leaves out (i.e. does not provide an obligatory code for) some of our intended meanings. We routinely rely on our addressees' ability and readiness to draw inferences, which they perform based on the semantic meanings we do provide them with. Some of these inferences are one-offs. Many are not. Often, the message conveyed by the code augmented by the inference is useful to other speakers as well. Moreover, even if the linguistic utterances are not underdetermined, the states of affairs about which utterances are predicated are far richer in detail, so addressees may associate an uncoded but concomitant interpretation with the meaning of the form (even truth-compatible inferences, see again chapter 3).

Traugott (1988, 1989, 1991, 2002) has argued for a very powerful mechanism for language change, via pragmatic inferences (see also Levinson, 1995, 2000b, and, as a precursor, Stern, 1931, e.g. p. 415). Traugott and Dasher (2002) emphasize that meaning is not only a cognitive phenomenon. For them, pragmatically induced inferences are the main driving force behind semantic change. Traugott bases her analysis on the neo-Gricean enrichment principle (she prefers Horn's 1984 more general R-based Principle over Levinson's I-Principle, which emphasizes enrichment to the stereotype). She argues, however, that Geis and Zwicky's (1971) term of invited inference is more appropriate than the term implicature, because it emphasizes the active role of the speaker in generating the inferred interpretation. The idea is that a very natural process may attribute to the (semantic) meaning of the utterance an interpretation which is actually only a contextual inference. As Hopper and Traugott (1993/2003: 76) note, the originally temporal *since* may have been used in contexts where a causal invited inference was generated long before it semanticized (see (17) in chapter 4 and (58) in chapter 7).

Let's examine the path taken by English *indeed*. Traugott and Dasher (2002: 159–165) argue that *indeed* starts out with *deed* (spelled *dede*) as a lexical (modifiable) noun meaning 'action' in Old English (I will quote the translations into Modern English, when provided by Traugott and Dasher, except for the *indeed* expression):

(4)   there is none of them that does not . . . sin greatly **in** foolish display or evil
        deed
        ('action,' c. 1225, *Sawles Warde*, p. 167, Traugott and Dasher, 2002: ex. 9)

In the first stage, *indeed* becomes an adverbial (occurring as a bare PP). At this stage, *in dede* specifies the respect in which some proposition holds (here, that the predicate *sin greatly* applies to 'action'). Under such uses, argue Traugott and Dasher, a reasonable contextual assumption is that the event was observable:

(5)   "Wolf," said Fox to him then, "All that you have done before this, in thought, in speech and **in dede** (('in action' – MA)), in evil of every other kind, I forgive you for it."
        (c. 1300, *Fox and Wolf*, p. 34, Traugott and Dasher, 2002: ex. 10)

Observable actions (unlike thoughts, intentions) are often considered "true" ("seeing is believing"). In other words, what is described as action is often also seen as true (via invited inference). Notice the current evidential use of *I saw it*:

(6)   Video <name> has it. **I saw it** the other day.   (LSAC)

Here is a relevant example with *in dede* indicating truth:

(7)   Often where matters of history are concerned, scripture repeats men's com-
           mon opinion, but does not affirm that it was so **in dede**
           ('in actuality,' c. 1388, Purvey, Wycliffe, 56, Traugott and Dasher, 2002: ex. 11)

Now, when does one need to explicitly state that one's words are true? After all, as
Grice's Quality maxim stipulates, we should always only say truthful things.
Indeed, we don't go around announcing the truth of our words most of the time.
One context that Traugott and Dasher find as calling for the use of *in dede* is
contrast, where the speaker might need to specifically indicate that her words are
true, despite the fact that it may seem or even be expected otherwise. This is the
case in (7). And compare with the use of *I swear* in:

(8)   A: When the line forms to get your mechanical brain, I, I suspect you
               wouldn't walk away from it.
           B: **I swear** to you on everything I can possibly swear on, I would be walking
               away from that line. **I swear** to you.   (LSAC)

When truthfulness is in doubt, for whatever reason (as is the case in (7) and (8)),
speakers may wish to indicate their commitment to the truth of their proposition.
Traugott and Dasher argue that marking the truth of the proposition is a marked step,
justified by Levinson's M-Principle, which states that speakers use marked expressions to express marked circumstances. This is why many uses of *indeed* invoke
adversativity, and were first accompanied by explicit adversatives such as *but*.

In its second stage, argue Traugott and Dasher, *indeed* has become a modal
adverbial, which **encodes** the speaker's commitment to the truth of her proposition. At this point, the invited inference has semanticized. At first, it retains an
adversative tone, as in (9):

(9) a.   The men of the town, being suspicious that their reports were lies (as it was **in
           dede** – 'in actuality'), rose.
               (1452, Capgrave Chronicle, p. 216, Traugott and Dasher, 2002: ex. 14b)
    b.   "It is not perfect by any means," Cheney said of the rescission bill, "it
           will create some difficulties . . .".. "We do **indeed** want to retain the
           capacity to produce nuclear submarines" . . .
           (May 22, 1992, United Press International, Traugott and Dasher, 2002: ex. 15)

Note that Defense Secretary Cheney (in (9b)) indicates his commitment to 'wanting to retain . . .' in spite of the problems he himself mentions, *indeed* thus
combining commitment to truth with adversativity.

The seeds for the next phase can be seen in uses such as in (10), where *indeed* is
clause-initial:

(10)   SHAL: I dare say my cousin William is become a good scholar. He is at Oxford
                 still, is he not?
           SIL: **Indeed**, sir, to my cost.   (1598, Shakespeare, *2 Henry IV*, III.ii.9,
                                                        Traugott and Dasher, 2002: ex. 20a)

The adversative tone is missing here, but *indeed* is still epistemic, confirming the truth in the assertion of the previous speaker. In the next stage, *indeed* becomes a discourse marker in utterance-initial position, where the epistemic meaning is marginal. *Indeed* is mainly used to signal an additive contribution, 'what's more.' The following is a transitional case:

(11)   a certaine repyning enuious man, being full gorged with a malicious ralying spirit . . . reported that the aforesaid plaister (De Ranis) was dangerous vnto the patient . . . and picked phrases, like as young children vse to doe, when (in mockery) they counterfeite a strange kinde of language . . . **Indeed** it is a most true saying: That fish which is bred in durt wil alwaies taste of the Mud.   (1602, Clowes, p. 16, Traugott and Dasher, 2002: ex. 21)

According to Traugott and Dasher, the primary interpretation of *indeed* here is the epistemic 'certainly,' but the initial positioning of *indeed* invites the inference that a culmination of the previous argument follows. This is already the additive meaning, which does not only agree with the preceding material, it supports it. This is the predominant modern use:

(12)   The idea of the Constitution as a living document, written so it can adapt to changing social and political times, is a major theme in U.S. judicial history. **Indeed**, it is the constitution itself that allows those dissatisfied with the Supreme Court rulings to turn to the amendment process.
(June 16, 1990, United Press International, Traugott and Dasher, 2002: ex. 23a)

Schematically, *indeed* starts out as meaning 'in the act' and used to implicate 'in truth.' Once this inferred interpretation has semanticized it is often used when the speaker is implicating 'in addition.' Later on this inference gets semanticized and *indeed* is now a discourse marker encoding 'what's more.' So a series of conventionalizations of contextually induced inferences has led to the semantics of *indeed* today.

Whereas *indeed* shows how informativity causes some forms to convey more than they originally did, the following shows how it is possible to reach a high meaning–form ratio by keeping meaning constant and reducing linguistic form. Trudgill (1995) traces a grammaticization path for East Anglian dialects which seem to have turned auxiliary *do* into a connective meaning 'otherwise,' as in *Don't take yours off, do you'll get rheumatism*. The origin of this construction is *Don't take yours off, ((because if you)) **do** you'll get rheumatism*, with the bracketed material now truncated. Now, we have no syntactic convention mandating such deletions. But sometimes, some material is highly predictable, to the point that mentioning it feels so redundant as to violate the Quantity maxim (see (21) in chapter 1). Moreover, the deleted material here is restricted to specific constructions, and hence quite predictable. Similar cases are the standard English *Clean your room or ((if you don't)) I'll be mad at you*; *Clean your room and ((if you do)) I'll be happy*, and Hebrew *im efshar xeshbon* 'if possible check,' i.e. 'Can I have the check?' originally from a full conditional sentence containing some thanking proposition as the consequent ('I'll be obliged if I can have the check').

In other words, we can explain the creation of a new connective (*do*) meaning 'otherwise' relying on the fact that the articulation of highly predictable material may be avoided. This is then a case of a linguistic change brought about by a different aspect of Quantity. Interestingly, initially, an ungrammatical sentence is produced. Such changes are far less common, but the next mechanism we examine also creates an initially ungrammatical utterance.

Another type of inference is metaphoric in nature. In a metaphoric transfer, the addressee is asked to derivatively understand one concept (the target, usually more abstract, less familiar, nonlexicalized) by reference to another from a different domain (the source, usually more concrete, familiar, lexicalized), relying on some perceived similarity between the two.[13] This is a clear case where speakers use "old means for novel functions" (Heine *et al.*, 1991a; Werner and Kaplan, 1963). For example, the change from body parts to spatial expressions is generally viewed as a change which is metaphorically induced. The difference between informativeness strengthening and metaphorical inferences is that in the former the semantic meaning which gives rise to the invited inference remains contextually relevant, the implicature merely added to it, whereas in the latter, the semantic meaning which triggers the metaphorical interpretation is irrelevant and must be suppressed. (In fact, this is probably the difference between implicated and explicated inferences – see chapter 7.)

This has two implications: first, it means that the initial metaphoric uses, but not the informativeness strengthening cases, may involve some grammatical violation (compare initial uses of e.g. *mouse* for conveying a computer device with the initial use of *following x, y* implicating 'because x, y'). Second, there is more of a discontinuity between the source and the target meanings in the metaphoric cases. Traugott (1989; Traugott and König, 1991; Traugott and Dasher, 2002) has discussed robust tendencies in linguistic change which seem to be metaphoric: from meanings based in the external world to meanings based in the internal (evaluative, perceptual) situation (e.g. spatial *after* – ultimately going back to body part 'back' changing to temporal *after*), from meanings based in external or internal situations to meanings pertaining to textual connectivity (e.g. prepositional *after* becoming a subordinate conjunction), meanings of any of the above bases becoming speaker-based, i.e. subjective, reflecting the speaker's perspective (e.g. the Hebrew causal *me=axar she=* 'because,' derived from *axar* 'after' – causal connections are subjective in that they crucially depend on speakers' assessments). Other common shifts involve meanings becoming intersubjective, nontruth-conditional and procedural (e.g. discourse markers such as *after all*).

Note that there has been some discussion in the literature on how important metaphorization is in grammaticization, and on whether it is metaphor that is at work in all of the above cases. At least some cases which seem to be metaphorical extensions of earlier meanings (e.g. 'ability' *may* developing into 'epistemic' *may* –

---

[13] See Sweetser (1990), Traugott and König (1991), Heine *et al.* (1991b), Heine (1993), and Bybee *et al.* (1994).

see Sweetser, 1990: chapter 3) are probably better analyzed diachronically as cases of informativeness enrichments or generalization. Bybee *et al.* (1994) and Traugott and Dasher (2002) observe that often a semantic change might look like a metaphorical shift, just because linguists compare original source meanings with derived endpoint meanings (see Heine *et al.*, 1991b), both taken out of context, skipping the piecemeal changes which can only be traced in real discourse, where collocates, as well as extralinguistic context, independently and redundantly express the meaning attested later, and thus support its emergence.[14] For example, Bybee (1988) found many cases of *may* used with its root possibility meaning, but probably **implicating** (in addition) an epistemic interpretation in Middle English:

(13)   You are so unwary a sleeper that someone may (=can) sneak in here.
                          (*Sir Gawain and the Green Knight*, Bybee, 1988: 258, ex. 18)

The root meaning of *may* in (13) is 'can,' but it implicates an epistemic possibility, indeed, rendered by Modern English *may*. If so, what seems like a metaphoric shift between root and epistemic possibility turns out to be a transfer to a conveyed meaning incorporating a strengthening implicature.[15]

Come and *go*, which may develop into future markers, also seem to be good candidates for a metaphorical transfer (see Heine *et al.*, 1991b: 46). But note that they undergo this change only in certain well-supported contexts, such as when the originally motion verbs are accompanied by a purpose clause. Consider the emerging Hebrew 'come' verb used as 'be going to' in the following telephone conversation:

(14)   (Context: MOTHER: Maya, where are you, why didn't you call me?)
         MAYA: bidiyuk   bati   le=calcel   elaix.
               exactly   came. 1SG   to=call   to:you
               'I was just about to call you.'   (Aug. 20, 2004)

To explain this new use we do not really need to appeal to the SPACE > TIME metaphoric path much discussed in the literature. Rather, verbs of motion often implicate intentional activity which is perforce imperfective. It was rather a long time after *be going to* was used to indicate intended action (as in the Hebrew (14)) that it started being used as a purely temporal expression (as in *It's going to be boring tonight* – LSAC). Indeed, the Hebrew 'come' construction cannot (yet?) be used for such pure temporal interpretations. Hebrew 'go,' however, can. So what ultimately looks like a metaphorical change (moving in space interpreted metaphorically as moving in time) did not (necessarily) arise via metaphoric inferencing, but, rather, via contextual strengthening inferences. In fact, what are currently clear cases of metaphoric associations (e.g. WHITE and INNOCENCE) may not be

---

[14] See *inter alia* Traugott and Dasher (2002: 117 and their chapter 4), Traugott (2004a). See also Stern (1931: 180), who argues against an "abrupt" change in the meaning of *beads* from 'prayers' to 'little balls.'

[15] Heine *et al.* (1991b: 75), on the other hand, suggest that the inference between the temporal and the causal interpretation of *since* involves a metaphoric step as well. I am not convinced, however.

diachronically metaphorically related. Rather, as Traugott and Dasher (2002: 81) imply, the opposite may be the case, namely, the gradual invited inferences brought about a (semantic) polysemy, whereby *white* implicates 'innocence,' which can retroactively be reinterpreted as metaphoric polysemy. Traugott and Dasher conclude that informativeness inferencing "rather than metaphorizing is the principal mechanism that drives semantic change" (2002: 282). Note that an extensive use of metaphorization entails a pervasive use of (mildly) ungrammatical strings. Traugott and Dasher's reinterpretation of researchers' findings is compatible with the only reasonable assumption that speakers don't often violate grammatical conventions.

As Bybee *et al.* (1994) demonstrate, we can actually distinguish between the two different processes, strengthening versus metaphorization. Note that the transfer from 'obligation' to 'probability' in *should* is quite general. The two senses are also compatible with each other. If *I should check it out* (SBC: 002) (obligation sense), then probably 'I will check it out' (probability sense). This is a case of informativeness enrichment, which is **added** to the original semantic meaning. This is not the case for *must*, where Bybee *et al.* have proposed a metaphorical change. The two interpretations are here mutually exclusive. *We must face our fears* (SBC: 021) only has the future-oriented obligation sense, not the probability sense, and *You must have good stereo* (SBC: 021) only has the present-oriented probability sense, not the obligation sense.[16] The two meanings are independent of each other. This is typical of metaphorization. The same is true for the metaphorical change involved in the new meaning of *mouse*. These two senses are mutually exclusive too. This is why if speakers use *mice* instead of *mouses* for the computer devices, the initial metaphorical transfer is revived. It therefore seems that speakers do use a variety of metaphors in order to convey more than the linguistic code allows, at least sometimes.

The literature about historical change in general and grammaticization in particular refers to many types of mechanisms of linguistic change, in addition to informativity-strengthening inferences (e.g. temporal > concessive *while*) and metaphoric inferences (e.g. 'body part' > spatial expression *back*).[17] Other mechanisms discussed are metonymy (e.g. a person > a painting by that person, as in *an O'Keeffe*), broadening and generalization (e.g. specific breed > general *dog*), narrowing (e.g. general > specific breed *hound*), pejoration (e.g. Hebrew 'the rich/important' *am ha=arec* literally 'the people of the land' > 'ignorant'), amelioration ('simple, ignorant' > 'pleasant' *nice*), and so on. Traugott (most recently in Traugott and Dasher, 2002) has also discussed the tendency for meaning to become text-based, subjective and inter-subjective (see above). Note that some of these changes are actually diametrically opposed, e.g. broadening and narrowing, pejoration and amelioration (and recall the contradicting semanticizations discussed by Jurafsky, 1996 – see again section 5.1.1). Croft (2000)

---

[16] In a different context this sentence might be interpreted with the obligation sense, but the point is that it doesn't implicate the probability sense then.

[17] See many of the articles in Joseph and Janda (2003), Bybee *et al.* (1994), Traugott (1982, 1989), Traugott and Dasher (2002), *inter alia*.

classifies various changes in form–function associations into several types: hyper-analysis (where a semantic property of form x is attributed to form y which cooccurs with it, so that x loses its original meaning), hypoanalysis (where a contextual interpretation is attributed to some form), metanalysis (which combines hyperanalysis with hypoanalysis, so contextual and semantic interpretations exchange their statuses), and cryptanalysis (where an implied interpretation is given overt coding despite the fact that it is anyway entailed).

Such detailed differences, as important as they are, need not concern us here. These are relevant to our discussion only as far as they pertain to the grammar–extralinguistic interface. As noted by Traugott and Dasher (2002: 29/30), different mechanisms, opposites included, we should add, can coexist, since speakers are never directly performing, e.g. broadening or narrowing per se, or adding (hypoanalysis) versus subtracting meaning (hyperanalysis). Speakers need not be consistent in applying these processes. As emphasized by Carston (2002a) and Wilson (2003), what speakers do consistently is use language in an optimal manner to serve their local goals. This cannot be achieved by codes alone very often, so speakers invite their addressees to infer various interpretations, based on their explicit utterances. Invited inferences can be of all the above types, because our inferential abilities allow for all these processes. What all of these have in common is that they (initially) arise as ad hoc inferences in supportive contexts. All that is relevant to us here is that contextually induced inferences can become grammatical facts. The precise nature of the inference, as well as significant correlations between inference type and type of grammaticization (see Traugott, 2004b), is not directly relevant.

So far, we have seen that many external factors contribute to the shape of our grammar. The way the world is is one such factor. But the reality outside language is reflected in grammar only through the mediation of our (human) cognition. Sociocultural norms further impose restrictions on possible messages. Another source for innovating grammar is pragmatic inferences accompanying linguistic strings. These constitute an integral part of communication, because the linguistic code is forever under-determinate. Indeed, language change is not only a function of external forces. The extant grammar is quite relevant, of course. Let us now see how we never start from scratch. Language users always make the best of the grammatical forms they already have available to them. Hence, external motivations must somehow be integrated into the current grammar. We here briefly discuss three relevant cases.[18] Consider washing. The literature abounds with what seems to be only common sense: People normally wash themselves rather than others. This is supposed to motivate the typologically well-known fact that *wash* and other verbs of grooming tend to take less-marked reflexive markings. Indeed, English *wash*, *shower*, and *bathe* are lexically reflexive verbs (according to Reinhart and Reuland, 1993). As such, they are zero marked, as compared with

---

[18] Section 6.2.1 is a more detailed description of how speakers use current grammars (ones lacking reflexive pronouns) to express functions not yet encoded in their grammar (the marking of a marked coreference).

the very marked reflexive pronoun used in *she talks to **herself*** (LSAC). Hebrew
***hit**raxec* 'washed himself' is a morphologically reflexive verb (the root is *raxac*),
where reflexivity is expressed with a less-marked form than in the Hebrew
counterpart of 'she talks to herself' – ***acma***). French *se laver* 'wash' takes *se*,
and does not usually take the emphatic *même* form in addition (as verbs denoting
activities we do not normally perform on ourselves do, such as 'make love' – see
chapter 6). These seem to be straightforward cases where linguistic coding reflects
the way the world is (see Levinson's 2000b: 328), or at least, our perception of
how the world is. But is that the whole story?

When we examine the distribution of the English monolexical washing verbs in
LSAC we face a bit of a surprise. Consider first the statistics for *shower* and *bathe*.
These verbs confirm our predictions: all 15 *bathe* cases involve self-bathing, and
all 25 (literal) *shower* cases involve self-showering. This is not what we find for
wash, however. 184/299 (61.5 percent) of its occurrences describe nonself-
washings (Haspelmath, 2004c has similar findings for the British National Corpus).
In fact, while 115 (38.5 percent) of the cases describe self-washings, the majority of
these are not reflexive, in fact, because the washee is a specific body part (hands,
hair, face), which is only partially identical in reference with the agent. It is not
hard to explain why *wash* actually tends to depict nonself-washings. Since English
has *(take a) shower/bath* and *bathe*, dedicated to self-washings (and there were
230 of those), *wash* can have a different distribution. Interestingly, even if we
focus on intransitive *wash* occurrences (30), the understood 'washee' is not
invariably the self: 11 of these (37 percent) are interpreted as 'wash' something
else (dishes, clothes). In other words, alienable objects can also be zero marked
with *wash*. We cannot then assume an automatic, transparent translation of a
cognitive fact ('people mostly wash themselves') into a linguistic fact (verbs of
washing will show this bias). Perhaps languages with just one 'washing' verb
might better conform to our expectations here, but languages with more than one
lexeme may show specialization, whereby different verbs have partially different
discourse distributions, despite the single cognitive concept behind them.[19] So,
"raw cognition" must interact with the existing grammar (lexicon in this case).

Another intriguing difference distinguishes *hide* and *conceal*. Smith (2004)
treats the event of 'hiding/concealing' as one concept, depicting a self-directed
activity (namely, an activity one usually performs on the self and not on others).
Now, if there is a transparent transfer from world/conceptual reality to grammar,
the two verbs should have the same grammatical structure, but this is not at all the
case. Only *hide* is (also) an intransitive verb (compare *She's hiding* (SBC: 023)

---

[19] Note that if we combine the counts for all three verbs, self-washings constitute close to half of the
total washings (155/339, 45.7 percent), which can explain the possibility for reflexive *wash*. The
numbers for Biblical Hebrew *raxac* 'wash' demonstrate an even higher rate of self-washings (47/
56, 83.9 percent). It is quite conceivable that reflexive *wash* evolved at a time when the discourse
frequency for English *wash* was more similar to the Biblical numbers than to the current numbers.
The current possibility for objectless *wash* to indicate washing some inalienable (mostly dishes
and clothes) testifies to the grammatical response to new discourse patterns, reflecting the
currently frequent (talking about) washings of such inalienables.

with *She's concealing*). Obviously, it cannot be the event in the world in itself which determines the status of verbs as self versus other-directed. Rather, it is the world as filtered not only by our conceptualizations, but also by the grammatical options available to speakers. Note that it's not the case that what we have are simply two verbs for two separate concepts, one for 'self-hiding' (say *hide*), another for 'other-hiding' (say *conceal*), because both verbs can be used for either function (compare *I hid x, I concealed myself*). Languages may have two lexical items which depict roughly the same event in the world, but have different grammatical statuses. External motivations must interact with the extant grammar.

An intriguing finding supporting the assumption that our current grammar plays an important role in possible innovations can be seen in Cifuentes-Férez and Gentner (2006). With respect to the encoding of motion by verbs, Talmy (1985) has distinguished between "path" languages, where the verb encodes the path (as in *enter, descend*), and "manner" languages, where the verb encodes the manner of motion, leaving it to other satellites (particles, prepositions) to express the path (as in *go in, go down*). Spanish is a typical path language, whereas English is a manner language.[20] Cifuentes-Férez and Gentner presented Spanish- and English-speaking subjects with passages describing unusual events using either novel verbs or novel nouns, and asked them to explain what those verbs and nouns meant. The results showed that the subjects tended to map the new verbs according to the dominant pattern in their language. Spanish speakers produced many more path verbs, English speakers produced many more manner verbs and many more satellites (for describing the path). These results must derive from the different verbal systems of the two languages, rather than from some general differences between the two languages, for no such differences were observed for the novel nouns. The current grammar has a constraining effect on innovative uses.

As we next see, discourse use introduces other sources of potential influence on grammar. But most importantly, discourse serves as the arena for making decisions by weighing all the relevant motivations, some of them potentially in conflict with each other. Many forces call for all kinds of grammatical forms/functions, but it is discourse which has the final word in selecting grammaticization paths.

5.2   External forces propose, discourse disposes

Discourse grammarians insist that discourse is the most important force shaping grammar.[21] Discourse does not always simply reflect cognition,

---

[20] Indeed, *enter* and *descend* are rather marked in English. For example, there were 20 different forms of *go in* in SBC as opposed to one *enter*.
[21] See especially Givón (1979a and onwards), Hopper and Thompson (1980, 1984, 1993), Du Bois (1985, 1987), *inter alia*.

nor any of the other external forces. "In natural language it is not enough to come up with separate solutions for the problems of semantic expression, of referential pragmatics, of cognitive processing and speech production. There must be one integrated solution for all of these problems at once" (Du Bois, 2003b: 48). Thus, although discourse reflects our communal decisions on how to mobilize our knowledge of the world, our cognitive abilities, our social norms, and our grammar and sensitivity to current discourse patterns, all in the service of our current, local communicative purpose, these don't amalgamate in a simple additive manner, as it might seem from the discussion in section 5.1. Discourse reflects the bottom line of all these resources pulled together in a complex process. Just as cognition does not directly reflect objective reality, so discourse does not directly reflect cognition. Crucially, grammar is directly affected only by discourse. In order to see that it is indeed discourse which has the last word, we need to examine cases where there is a potential discrepancy between the way the world is, or the way our cognition works, and the way discourse proceeds. This is the goal of section 5.2.

5.2.1   Discourse versus cognition

Cognitive Linguists have now joined discourse grammarians in their commitment to grammar being usage-based (see e.g. Kemmer and Barlow, 2000). They therefore need to connect the cognitive underpinning of grammar, on which they insist, with the use of grammar. Heine (1997: 14) is probably representative of the approach: "Although conceptualization strategies are perhaps the **main driving force** for linguistic categorization ... **Another, equally important**, force is communication" (emphases added). It might seem a trivial step to add discoursal use. Implicitly, Cognitive Linguists must make the following (quite reasonable) assumptions: people are naturally (psychologically) disposed to thinking, conceptualizing in certain ways. If that's the way we cognize, then it stands to reason that that's the way we would speak, and discourse will then reflect it. They seem to assume a direct and unproblematic link between our cognition and the products of language in discourse. Up till now we have only seen how our conceptualizations are less constrained than grammar is (e.g. the encoding of 'being cold'), and how we don't get a one-to-one relationship between cognitive concepts and grammatical categories ('washing,' 'hiding'). Grammar was seen to carve out concepts for encoding from among cognitively plausible candidates. We here examine harder cases, where there is actually a clash between a reasonable cognitive concept being behind the grammatical convention and a discourse-related factor determining the grammatical convention. In all these cases, we will see, discourse wins out, and the grammar goes the discourse, rather than the cognitive, way. Discourse is, then, not merely "another, equally important force." It is the most important factor in grammaticization. Haspelmath (to appear) makes a similar point when he argues against (certain types of) iconic (cognitive) explanations, offering to replace iconicity with a frequentist account.

Hopper and Thompson (1980, 1984) were the first to insist on the crucial role of discourse above other factors in creating grammar. As they forcefully argued, not all cognitively viable classifications would serve us equally well in communication. Consider their arguments for a discoursal, rather than semantic or cognitive, basis for the category of noun (Hopper and Thompson, 1984). Cognitively, it would stand to reason that prototypical nouns should denote "thing-like" entities, which have properties such as tangibility and visibility, and are highly time-stable. Such is most probably the category used by children first learning language (see Bates and MacWhinney, 1982). Nonetheless, this cognitive definition simply cannot be the driving force behind the natural language **grammatical category**, they argue (and see also Tomasello, 2003b: 5.2.2). Hopper and Thompson examine nominal markings, and show that to account for the **forms** that nouns actually take we must consider the discourse role played by the specific noun, more so than the cognitive concept behind it. Those nouns which may seem highly prototypical according to the cognitive definition above, e.g. *deer*, may not always be grammatically central exemplars of the noun category. And what is crucial is that grammatical shape is determined by the ad hoc **discourse function** of the noun, and not by its **cognitive/semantic** features. Consider the following (based on Hopper and Thompson, 1984: 708, ex. 3):

(15)   I went **deer** hunting one time.   (LSAC)

Although the concept associated with *deer* denotes an object which should be a prototypical noun (it's a concrete, visible entity), the noun is not prototypical in (15). Hopper and Thompson's point is that the behavior of nouns such as *deer* does not depend on the inherent properties of the real-world conceived objects they denote, but on their discourse function. In (15), *deer* is not used as a prototypical noun (it's not referential, it modifies another noun), and this is why it cannot receive noun trappings (determiners, modifiers, plural where applicable; compare *I went (*the) deer hunting*). The prototypical noun, which would receive the maximal morphosyntactic encoding of the category, is one which introduces a new participant into the discourse for later references. It is such nouns that are maximally distinct from other categories (e.g. verbs). Nouns which are not used to introduce trackable discourse participants (later to be referred to again, manipulable in Hopper and Thompson's terminology) may be only minimally distinguished from verbs, because they do not receive nominal trappings. Incorporated nouns (conflated with their verb), for example, are often nonreferential. They may then show vowel harmony with the verb, and may not even count as NPs, so that the verbs they are attached to count as intransitive (as in (16b); see also the *self* + verb in (52) in section 6.4). Such (non)markings apply to any noun fulfilling such a discourse function, regardless of its cognitive prototypicality. Note the following from Kosraean, where 'knife,' a cognitively basic type of noun, only manifests nominal morphosyntax in (16a), not in (16b):

(16) a.   ~ El   twem-lah   mitmit   sahfiht   sac.
            he   sharpen-ASPECT   knife   dull   ARTICLE
            'He sharpened the dull knife.'

b.　　~ El　　　　twetwe　　　　　　　mitmit-lac.
　　　　he　　　　sharpen-INTRANSITIVE　knife-ASPECT
　　　　'He has knife-sharpened.'　　(Hopper and Thompson, 1984: 712, exx. 15a, b)

As Mithun (1984) notes, in order to later refer to the entity first denoted by an incorporated noun, a full referential form must first be employed. In other words, the incorporated noun, lacking nominal trappings, does not count as a proper introduction for a discourse entity. Predicate nominals are another example of a noun serving a noncentral nominal discourse function. It may indeed be accompanied by less than maximal nominal morphosyntax. Note the two different uses of 'cadre' in the following Chinese examples. Only in (17b), used when the predicate nominal is going to be referred to later in the discourse, is a noun classifier used:

(17)　a.　　~ Tā　　　shi　　　gànbù.
　　　　　　s/he　　is　　　cadre
　　　　　　'S/he is a cadre.'
　　　b.　　~ Tā　　　shi　　　**yī-ge**　　　　gànbù.
　　　　　　s/he　　is　　　one-CLASSIFIER　cadre
　　　　　　'S/he is one of those cadres.'
　　　　　　　　　　　　　　　　(Hopper and Thompson, 1984: 716, exx. 29, 30)

French and Indonesian similarly use no determiner for predicate nominals, and Japanese uses no nominal particles with them. No classifier is used in Chinese negative sentences, since, usually, the negated noun will not be further discussed in the discourse. The numeral 'one' in Hebrew and Persian is sometimes used as an indefinite article with NPs, but only upon initial introduction into the discourse of entities to be mentioned again. In other words, the most highly categorial noun (with the most trappings) is not the prototypical one as defined by its inherent features in the abstract. It is the local discourse role which determines what the highly categorial noun is, and its markings accordingly.

Next, consider entities whose mental representations are highly activated. These are not highly categorial according to Hopper and Thompson, because they do not share the prominence and the autonomy of entities first introduced into the discourse. Pronouns, and even more clearly so, ellipses, are examples of de-categorialization. This can explain Mithun's (1984) curious finding that incorporated nouns are either nonreferential or else entities already mentioned in the discourse. Although the two types of entities are radically different in terms of referentiality and accessibility to the addressee (nonreferentials are not at all activated, whereas subsequent-mention entities are referential and highly activated), they are similar in being noncentral exemplars of the nominal category (see also Hopper and Thompson, 1993). What's crucial for our point is that although these activated entities are referential and definite, they receive the same encoding as nonreferential indefinites in some languages. The reason is that they don't serve the marked discourse function of nouns (entity introduction), and hence the fact that they are definite/referential need not be marked. Marking follows discourse function, not (necessarily) inherent semantic characteristics of entities.

Hopper and Thompson (1993) make similar points regarding other morpho-syntactic facts which are hard to account for on the basis of cognitive or semantic distinctions. For example, in many languages, generic NPs (general is the term they use) are differently marked from specific (particular) NPs only in object position, not in subject position. For example, in Eastern Armenian, both specific and generic subjects are marked as definite, but whereas specific objects are marked definite and accusative, generic objects are not so marked. Cognitively, there is no justification for such selective marking. However, once we take into account the differential discourse roles played by subjects and objects, the facts are no longer so puzzling. Virtually all subjects (97 percent) are used to track referents, but a majority of the objects (65 percent) are used as part of the predication (together with the verb) (as in *I watch bad TV* – LSAC). If so, it makes sense that it is in object position that we need to distinguish between specific entities (we track) and generic entities (used for predicating). Hopper and Thompson analyze a few other phenomena in a similar fashion, and conclude that "the primary source of explanations for grammatical observations is the set of discourse . . . motivations" (1993: 372). In fact, as in their 1980 and 1984 papers, they go on to propose that semantic concepts are derivative of discourse functions, rather than the other way round.

Another example showing how cognition only proposes, with discourse actu-ally disposing, is Bybee's (1985b) intriguing claims about which elements tend to form verbal affixes and which do not. Tense, mood, and aspect are often expressed by affixes attached to the verb (rather than as independent lexemes). The reason is that these have a fundamental effect on the interpretation of the event denoted by the verb. Bybee has argued that semantic categories highly relevant to a verb's interpretation are the ones that tend to morphologize with it. This is a cognitive-based motivation for grammatical distributions. Indeed, a high number of the languages examined by Bybee showed bound morphemes for tense, mood, and aspect. Moreover, Bybee also predicts differences between these three categories. For example, mood pertains to the speaker's assessment of the truth of the situation she is referring to, but tense pertains to the situation itself, grounding it in time. Given Bybee's (1985b) cognitive-style logic, the expectation is that the frequency of merging for these two should show tense as bound to the verb more often than mood, since tense is more inherent to the event described by the verb than mood is (mood indicates a speaker's subjective comment on the objective event referred to by the verb).

As Hopper and Traugott (1991: 144) note, however, findings did not complete-ly bear out this last prediction. More languages have bound forms for mood (68 percent) than for tense (50 percent). This goes against the cognitive-based prediction which states that the meaning element pertaining to the internal structure of the event (tense in this case) would be more fused with it. However, if one adopts a discourse perspective (which Bybee has in later writings, e.g. 2000 and onwards), one is less surprised by this finding. Although the coherence of the event depicted predicts a certain cohesion of morphology, social interactions impose quite a different demand on speakers. For interlocutors, the speaker's (degree of) commitment to her proposition (the function served by mood) may be far more crucial, hence more frequently indicated. Recent research has pointed to the thoroughly subjective nature of conversations, where speaker-stance markings abound (Engelbretson, 2007; Kärkkäinen, 2003; Ochs, 1996; Scheibman, 2002). Hence, the deeper grammaticization often shown by the "external" mood markers, which exceeds that of the "internal" verbal modifiers. Note, moreover, that discourse role here disrupts the coherent conceptual picture of internal event structure.

Another surprising finding comes out from a comparison between tense and person markers on the verb. As Bybee notes, the cognitive relevance principle predicts more morphologization for tense than for person (the tense modifies the action directly, the person indicates who the subject performing the action is – indeed, they belong to different syntactic constituents). Still, although an impressive set of the sample languages contained bound morphemes for tense (50 percent), equally as many (56 percent) had bound morphemes for person–number (agreeing with the subject). Why is the less relevant person verbal agreement equally prevalent as the more relevant tense as a bound morpheme on verbs? (i) Accessibility considerations operate to reduce the phonological size of independent pronouns, especially those referring to first and second persons (due to the consistently high activation of the speaker and addressee); (ii) reduced forms tend to cliticize (see Ariel, 2000, and references cited therein). In this case, then, two independently motivated processes, pronoun reduction and an automatic phonetic process of cliticization of reduced forms, combine to work against the perfectly sensible cognitive principle outlined by Bybee (1985b). Discourse use in this case does not reflect a pure/coherent cognitive unit. What it reflects is the output of a frequent discourse pattern whereby certain reduced pronouns repeatedly cooccur with verbs, and hence tend to cliticize with them, despite the lack of a corresponding unified cognitive concept. All in all, then, the verb unit often binds together distinct cognitive concepts. Discourse use creates formal hybrids, because it juggles a variety of motivations, which it may package together even in the absence of cognitive coherence behind the packaging.

Case marking is another case where cognitive considerations don't seem to motivate the complex grammatical picture we actually find. If all there was behind case marking were cognitively coherent concepts (As, Os, etc.), one would expect an 'all or none' situation, where either the language uses case markings or it doesn't. Durie (1995a) argues otherwise. Finnish case marking, for example, is not invariably used whenever the relevant categories occur. Durie reasons that the discrimination between grammatical functions (this is the function of case markers) is also indicated (with varying degrees of confidence) by other marking systems in Finnish: word order, focus particles, voice, class systems, cross-referencing verbal affixes, and a few other markers. Only by examining all of these, can he motivate the seemingly arbitrary grammatical conventions of Finnish specifying where to mark cases and where not to. The explanation lies in the interaction between the various factors which potentially code or indicate with more or with less certainty the role of the given NP. Durie thus explains inconsistent markings, such as why Finnish accusatives are marked in all contexts but two. Those two contexts are precisely where the accusatives couldn't possibly be interpreted as nominatives (e.g. the overt NP in an imperative, since the nominative is obligatorily a second-person inexplicit reference). Note that it is not just speakers in specific contexts who pragmatically suppress grammatical marking when redundant or less necessary (though this can sometimes be the case, as the variable frequency of the Samoan ergative case marker shows). It is the grammar itself in Finnish that dictates the limits to the functional overkill – see section 4.3 – by banning marking in certain contexts (in Fore and Achenese too, according to Durie). Such intervention of discourse-based considerations in an otherwise cognitively coherent marking system shows how grammar is the product of language in use, where a multiplicity of factors is at work, rather than just pure conceptualization.

Next, let us compare verbal versus nominal case-marking systems for both ergative and accusative languages. Recall that ergative languages classify Ss and Os together as absolutives, and accusative languages lump together As and Ss as nominatives. Dixon (1979: 79, 1994) notes a seemingly puzzling fact. Nominal absolutives (where absolutive case is indicated on the noun) are often zero marked, but verbal absolutives (where absolutive case is indicated on the verb) are sometimes overtly marked. Similarly, nominal nominatives are often zero marked, but verbal marking for nominatives is overt. Now, if absolutive is the unmarked case for ergative languages, it should be morphologically unmarked, just as if nominative case is unmarked for accusative languages, it should be morphologically unmarked. While these markedness expectations are fulfilled when nominal systems are considered, they are (sometimes) reversed for verbal systems. Thus, in the verbal systems, it is often the nominative (in accusative languages) and the absolutives (in ergative languages) which are morphologically marked. Why should this be the case? To phrase this in cognitive terms, if the absolutive role is cognitively unmarked (as shown by zero nominal marking), why is it (sometimes) marked on the verb? The same applies to nominatives. There is no cognitive basis for viewing nominatives and absolutives as unmarked in nominals but as marked in verbal agreement.

But there is a discourse basis for distinguishing between nominal and verbal case marking. As noted by Dixon, in the nominal system, case marking serves to directly identify grammatical function. Hence, the different markings for the typologically different languages. But in verbal case systems the marking actually participates in a reference tracking system. If it's a referential system, then we have different predictions for what should be overt and what should not be overt. Here it is Newness and activation which are crucial. We expect overt verbal agreement for highly activated referents, for these are the entities that speakers may wish to encode with reduced (cliticized) forms, rather than with overt lexical expressions (see section 2.2 again). If so, absolutives are not even expected to pattern uniformly. Third-person absolutives (even more than third-person nominatives) often denote New discourse entities, and hence there is no pressure to consistently reduce their form. They do not trigger a reduction of pronouns into verbal agreement markers, therefore. Hence, third-person absolutives are often zero marked on the verb. First- and second-person referents, on the other hand, regardless of whether they are nominative or absolutive, overwhelmingly denote highly activated discourse entities (these are the speaker and the addressee). Hence the tendency to reduce the referential form used. Overt verbal agreement markers are then suitable for first- and second- , but not for third-person absolutive. Thus, whereas in nominative markings it is the unmarked category (absolutive for ergative languages, nominative for accusative languages) which is formally unmarked, in verbal agreement systems, it is the higher activation category that tends to be marked on the verb (hence, first- and second-person absolutives and first-, second-, and sometimes third-person nominatives). Grammatical categories are not necessarily about our classifications of objects, as they are about categories which are functional to us in discourse. Since the discourse functions of nominal and verbal case markings are different, so are the ensuing grammatical facts about them.

Noordman and Vonk (1998) provide us with another opportunity to compare between the working of cognitive factors in the abstract and their realization in discourse, where they have to give way to discourse constraints. Noordman and Vonk have offered convincing evidence for the following, perfectly reasonable argument. Our experience of the world is such that states of affairs taken to be causes for other states of affairs temporally precede their effects. For example, in connection with (18) below, first Sharon 'had to do . . .' (line 3), and then, and because of that, she 'felt horrible . . .' (line 2). Noordman and Vonk argue that our conceptual representations of such relations are iconic to this perception, also putting causes before effects. If so, it would make sense for the linear ordering in which such relations are presented in discourse to mirror such conceptual ordering as well. An iconic linear order should help addressees map propositions related as causes and effects. Indeed, their findings are that subjects read mini discourses with causes preceding their effects faster than mini discourses where the linear order was effect-first, cause-second. Now, if our cognition is biased towards this ordering, one would expect to see a reflection of this bias in natural discourse too. Surprisingly perhaps, this prediction is not borne out. In Ariel (1985) I found that 90 percent of written Hebrew 'because' clauses followed, rather than preceded, the clause that they were related to as causes, explanations, justifications, etc. A quick look at English *because* and its more colloquial variant *cause* in SBC revealed that this cause-second pattern is even stronger in the spoken corpus.[22]

---

[22] Note that (*be*)*cause* explicitly marks reasons etc. Such marking was absent in the narratives tested by Noordman and Vonk, where (the strong) causality was left to inference. But appealing to cognitive factors, Noordman and Vonk's argument should hold in general.

I didn't find any examples where the *(be)cause* clause preceded the clause it was associated with (see also Ford, 1993; Schiffrin, 1985).[23] Here is a typical example:

(18)	SHARON:	And it was really awful,	1
		cause I felt horrible about it,	2
		cause I had to do shit like,	3
		(H) they have a conduct chart. (SBC: 004)	

As argued in Ariel, causes, justifications, and explanations very often become relevant in discourse only after their effect has been mentioned (see also Magliano *et al.*, 1993). It's the effect that is directly relevant to the discourse topic at hand. The cause is only relevant because it bears some relevance to the effect.[24] In fact, note that in (18), once Sharon states that *it was really awful* (her initial experience in teaching) in line 1, she mentions the cause for this in line 2. She then explains this cause itself (treating it as an effect) in line 3. Hence, despite the cognitive facilitation of the cause–effect order, coherent discourse structure often dictates that reasons follow rather than precede what it is that they explain or motivate. Once again, discourse requirements overcome cognitively motivated preferences.

Now, these findings are not restricted to discourse patterns. They have repercussions for grammar itself. While many 'because' expressions are free to precede or to follow their effects, not all are. Some, such as Hebrew *ki* 'because' and English *for*, both only when used as 'because,' can only occur following the clause they are associated with. The same is true for Hebrew *harey* 'after all,' often used to provide justification for a specifically previous proposition. And most intriguing is the marked acceptability difference between English *because* and its reduced version *cause* in the preceding position. Only *because* is perfectly acceptable in pre-effect position (cf. ~ *Because/??cause I had to punish my students, I felt horrible about teaching at first*). So, at least explicitly marked causes are sometimes restricted to post-effect position, which is quite the opposite of what we would expect given the human cognitive disposition identified by Noordman and Vonk. It is, however, quite compatible with the typical role that causes and reasons play in discourse.

Our final example is a striking case of the victory of discourse over cognition. We here touch upon an innovative use, which has probably not (yet?) grammaticized in English. Consider the expression *for the whole part* interpreted as 'totality' (i.e. not when it denotes 'the whole part of something larger than it'). How could it possibly mean a totality? Isn't the expression an oxymoron, *part*

---

[23] There were 354 *because* and 426 *cause* occurrences. I checked every eighth *because* and every tenth *cause*. None of the 45 *because*s and 43 *cause*s preceded the proposition they were related to.

[24] This is not the case for the narratives examined by Noordman and Vonk. In narratives the causing event is often relevant all by itself, which is why facilitation in reading the cause-first versions was observed. In other words, when discourse coherence and cognitive principles are not in conflict, speakers are expected to adopt the cognitively preferred strategy identified by Noordman and Vonk.

denoting the opposite of 'whole'? It would seem so, but note the use of this supposedly contradictory expression in the following examples:

(19) a.   The weather was nice for the most part and the people were nice **for the whole part**
           (ultragrrrl.blogspot.com/2004/03/these-bunnies-look-like-puppies-im.html)
     b.   For the most part, in fact **for the whole part**, the minister was not political,
           (www.hoa.gov.nl.ca/hoa/business/hansard/43rd,%203rd/98–05–29.htm)

In both examples the speaker wants to contrast partiality with a totality. They could have used the perfectly appropriate and noncontradictory *the whole time* instead, of course:

(20) a.   ~ The weather was nice for the most part and the people were nice **the whole time**.
     b.   ~ For the most part, in fact **the whole time**, the minister was not political.

But this was not what the speakers chose to say. They preferred the "illogical" expressions. Only conversational practices can account for these cognitively surprising innovations. Du Bois (2007, 2004) has proposed that Dialogic Syntax, according to which interlocutors "reuse" immediately preceding structures to construct their current utterances, may be responsible for such initiations of grammatical change. The idea is that speakers try to resonate with each other (and, as a derivative of this, with themselves). Resonance has a variety of pragmatic functions, among them, highlighting a (stance) differential. Differences stand out more conspicuously when the options compared are phrased in highly similar terms (see also section 4.3, (8) and (9)). Minimal differences among highly similar forms are not only aesthetically more pleasing, they also confer prominence on the contrast. This is the difference between the "illogical" (19) and the "logical" (20). The innovated *for the whole part* is especially patterned to resonate with *for the most part* while *the whole time* does not resonate with it (to the same extent). It stands to reason that it is the discourse function (emphatic difference through high resonance) which triggers the ad hoc creation of a cognitively unmotivated expression, then.[25]

Summing up, the examples in section 5.2.1 all support the claim that when in conflict, it is discoursal use, rather than pure cognition, that drives grammar.

5.2.2   Discourse as arbiter

Next, consider the findings regarding postverbal constituent ordering presented in Arnold *et al.* (2000). In general, NPs harder to process tend to be postposed, so Arnold *et al.* find that longer NPs tend to follow shorter NPs and that New NPs tend to follow accessible NPs (e.g. in ditransitive constructions). However, in order to account for 100 percent of the data, one must recognize a whole variety of factors (Rosenbach, 2005). First, the two just mentioned have to be weighted against each other, because they don't fully overlap. Arnold *et al.* propose

---

[25] Indeed, in the few cases where *for the whole part* is not juxtaposed with *for the most part*, it denotes a hedged totality, similar to *on the whole*, where the word *part* is simply redundant.

that when incompatible, speakers tend to go according to the stronger of the two principles in the given case. In other words, if there is a large gap in NP length, length will determine the order of the NPs, the short one preceding the longer one, possibly regardless of Newness. Or, if there is a large difference between the activation of the entities referred to, the one that's highly accessible will occur first, possibly regardless of length differences. But the competition between the factors involved in the decision does not end here. Consider the following:

(21)   Having given [much consideration and attention] to [it] ...

(Arnold *et al.*, 2000: 50, ex. 17)

This attested example violates both principles above: the first NP is both longer and Newer. Arnold *et al.* argue that other factors are involved in determining which constituent ordering will be preferred. One factor that has been found to affect constituent ordering is priming. Based on laboratory experiments, Bock (1986) has argued that speakers tend to preserve the ordering of a priming source in the target sentence. Thus, subjects tended to produce double object constructions (such as *I gave [him]$_1$ [a copy of all the gym schedule]$_2$* – LSAC) when the priming sentence was a double object construction, but a prepositional dative construction (*I gave [a copy]$_1$ [to him]$_2$* – LSAC) when such was the priming source.

Another factor which accounts for some violations is ambiguity avoidance (a weak parameter). Third, the specific verb may have a preference for one or the other construction (see Stefanowitsch and Gries, 2003). In addition, Arnold *et al.* suggest that idiomatic collocations, especially opaque ones, show a preference for the shifted construction. For example, *take ... into account* showed a clear preference for the shifted construction (*take into account X*), which preserves the idiom as one chunk. All in all, decisions regarding constituent ordering where the grammar allows more than one option must be discourse-based, just because they are too complex to be determined in the abstract. The speaker has to choose between options, based on which of the parameters she decides to apply to the case at hand (in this case Newness, length, idiomaticity), for different parameters may predict different choices. Discourse-based decisions weigh different pressures pushing towards different solutions.[26] It is ad hoc discourse-related considerations which prompt speakers to opt for one solution over another.

Next, Deane (1992) analyzes exceptional extractions from syntactic islands, in terms of attention states during processing. Extraction is a task which imposes a heavy load on the attentional resources available in working memory, because of the discontinuity between the head and the extraction site. He argues that for extraction to be successful, both the extracted NP and the extraction site should be Dominant in terms of processing, whereas the intervening material should be nondemanding in terms of processing. This is, of course, a processing constraint. Note, however, that which NPs and other material are considered (non)Dominant is for the most part

---

[26] See Gries (2003) for the predictability of double objects versus prepositional dative constructions, based on a range of parameters, including Arnold *et al.*'s.

discourse-based, rather than cognitively dictated: topics and New/Dominant information automatically attract more attention. It is then such extractions that are relatively freer. Thus, while what directly accounts for extraction is capacity to attract attention, this capacity depends on the discourse status of the constituents involved. Cognitive factors must combine with discourse factors in this case, then.

Finally, let's see how semantics is intertwined with discoursal factors. According to Goldberg (1995), the ditransitive construction's basic meaning is that the agent causes the recipient to receive the theme (e.g. *I gave him a red pepper* – SBC: 011). It is not surprising then that Stefanowitsch and Gries (2003) find that *give* is the verb most strongly associated with this construction. *Send, offer, lend,* and a few others are also strongly associated with ditransitives.[27] However, as Stefanowitsch and Gries note, the second verb strongly associated with the ditransitive is not at all a prototypical transaction verb. It is *tell*, and, in fact, many of the verbs strongly associated with the ditransitive instantiate one of the construction's extended, rather than basic, uses. In the case of *tell*, Goldberg proposes that we seem to imagine communication as a transfer of objects. In the case of *promise*, there is an implication that the agent will cause the transfer, etc. The relevant point for our discussion is that in terms of discoursal use, we very often find the idea of transfer more relevant for the nonprototypical acts of transfer, such as communicated messages, than for object transfers (e.g. *buy* is only number 22 on the list of verbs associated with ditransitives). Thus, while the basic meaning of the construction remains a transfer, what people find interesting to talk about as transfer is often not the cognitively prototypical, physical object transfer, but the discourse-relevant transfer of verbal messages.

The point of section 5.2 has been that discourse use, rather than various kinds of raw external forces, must be taken into account when we consider impact on grammar, because discourse serves as an arbiter between all the speaker's possibly conflicting pressures, not least among them the need for economy, which means that not all potentially viable categories/functions can be expressed. The main argument concerned the imperfect correlation between language and cognition. For the most part, our cognitive system is by far richer and more flexible than our grammar. There is a lot of selection to be done by language, therefore. First, concepts are imbued with much more meaning than grammar can express, if it is to be compact. More often than not, concepts have to be cut to fit the linguistic mold (recall the comparison between the experience of being cold and its encoding in various languages in section 5.1.1). Second, cognitive classifications can go very many ways. Discourse use, it is claimed, is responsible for the choices actually

---

[27] We should note that Stefanowitsch and Gries determine collostructional strength (the strength of the association between some target lexeme, *give* in our case, and some target construction – the ditransitive here) by measuring not only the frequency of the target item in the target construction (e.g. *give* in the ditransitive). They compute this frequency against the frequency of all nontarget lexemes in the target construction (other verbs in the ditransitive), as well as the frequency of the target lexical item in other constructions (e.g. the frequency of *give* in general) and the frequency of nontarget lexemes (all verbs other than *give* in all constructions other than the ditransitive). This is then a very reliable way to establish (non)associations.

made, which is why we find, for example, an inconsistent marking and/or use of noun classifiers, grammatical cases, the distinction between generic and specific NPs, all coherent cognitive categories. The reason is that these categories are more useful in some discoursal situations than others: it is discourse function which determines the usefulness of the particular cognitive distinction. Moreover, since discourse use is at the basis of our selection, we mix together general cognitive considerations and ad hoc discourse considerations (as we saw for extractions from islands, heavy NP shifting). We even create cognitively hybrid categories, such as the verb and its cliticized elements (mood, subject NPs).

It's through our participating in many discourses that we note and extract discourse patterns, which become our grammar, mainly by automatization. Only by locating the arena of grammaticization in discourse can we rely on habituation, for example (see Bybee and Hopper, 2001a; Haiman, 1994). Only by locating grammaticization in real discourse time can we show how it builds on expectations based on world knowledge on the one hand, and on a host of other knowledge bases, including specific linguistic expressions, on the other hand. We're left with three questions. First, what is the source of differences among languages? If discourse has such an important role in shaping language, and if it's the case that all languages more or less share communicative needs, shouldn't discourse, and following it, grammar, be quite similar across languages? For example, how come some communities opted for female as augmentative while others for female as diminutive? Could it have been the other way round? Second, if our cognition is so much richer than our language usually, how come we encounter cases such as *hide/conceal*, where the language seems richer than the concept behind the lexemes? Third, accepting that discourse is the arbiter between all the external forces as well as the current grammar, how does it transmit its "conclusion" to the grammar? Recall that we're here committed to a nonteleological view of grammar. In section 5.3 we discuss very low-level automatic processes, which are responsible for turning salient, often high-frequency discourse patterns into grammatical conventions. Thus, we've started chapter 5 with a host of external factors all involved in molding grammar: cognition, sociocultural norms, pragmatic inferences. In section 5.2 we have narrowed the path to grammar by subjecting all these influences to actual discourse and its goals. But that is not enough. Discourse is full of ad hoc phenomena, performance errors included. Obviously, we need one more filter, from discourse to grammar. We're finally zeroing in on the salient discourse pattern. The key to answering all three questions is the salient discourse pattern.

5.3   Discourse proposes, the salient discourse pattern disposes

Discourse for the point at hand, is above all a set of patterns, some of which are more privileged/salient than others, some of which are more frequent (and hence salient) than others. These salient and frequent patterns are determined by the aggregate of individual uses made by speakers, each act presenting its own unique solution based on the speaker's cognition, culture, ad hoc communicative goals, her current grammar, as well as extant discourse patterns, which she tends to follow.

> The changes of tomorrow are the consequences of our acts of communication today. A theory of language change is thus at one and the same time a theory of the functions and principles of communication.   (Keller, 1994: 14)

(See also Givón, 1979b; Stern, 1931.) The analyses presented in sections 5.1 and 5.2 demonstrate that there is an extralinguistic basis behind "our acts of today." Indeed, the mechanisms discussed in the literature on diachrony as mechanisms for linguistic change (briefly mentioned in section 5.1.3) are not necessarily about linguistic change as much as they are about (synchronic) processing and production. Strengthening inferences, broadening, narrowing, metaphorization, reduction, cliticization, etc., are all pragmatic processes implemented for effectively expressing (sometimes) innovative ad hoc synchronic indirect meanings, or for expressing old meanings by somewhat innovative means, all in fully supportive contexts. All of these mechanisms constitute synchronic interpretative and production strategies. Hence the insistence in section 5.2 that it is discourse, rather than the various external forces, which directly determines change. However, the occurrence of some inference or some innovative form in discourse does not guarantee linguistic change, whereby the innovative step becomes part of the grammar. In fact, most ad hoc forms and interpretations do not become entrenched, which accounts for the fact that for the most part grammar remains quite stable. So how do we get from our acts of today to our (different) acts of tomorrow?

Grammatical conventions often result from steps taken independently by speakers in their everyday communicative acts. Keller (1994) compares the emergent grammatical convention to the creation of a diagonal path through a lawn, leading from building A to B. The work of "an invisible hand" in creating the path is actually produced by many individuals, each deciding to make themselves a shortcut on the way from one building to another. Each individual may have come up with the shortcut idea on their own, or they could have seen somebody else do it. What is important is that it takes many individual footsteps along more or less the same track to create a long stretch that's lawn-free, a path (see also Haspelmath, 1999b). The same applies to the emergence of a linguistic form or a certain function. Often, individual speakers find a specific innovative form to be a successful means for expressing a specific communicative goal (regardless of whether they each come up with it independently, or they've heard another use it – see Stern, 1931: 176–177). If speakers start producing such a form intending the specific function with some frequency, that form–function correlation may crystallize into a grammatical convention. Hence, grammaticization is **the unintended** product of an aggregate of local, **intended** actions (see also Croft, 2000). Speakers do have local communicative intentions. What they don't have are intentions to create grammatical conventions. Just as people did not convene to agree on creating a shortcut path, speakers cannot convene to create conventionalized forms for "worthy" functions. But, by repeatedly making consistent choices for optimal expression of local goals of communication, the current discourse patterns also become potential paths of change, whereby origin-ally optional choices become conventional, sometimes even obligatory.

The only path leading a speaker from a **novel** meaning to linguistic expression, and the only path leading an addressee from some form to the speaker's intended **novel** meaning is a motivated, transparent association between form and function, made available by heavy reliance on a supportive context. The same is true for form–function correlations involving innovative forms. This is what pragmatics provides. Arbitrary conventionality can serve as an equally efficient form–function association, but natural languages can never start with (arbitrary) con-ventions (see Heine *et al.*, 1991b: 27).[28] We don't seek conventionality per se. It happens to us. To start with conventionality would require a much more conscious cooperative endeavor, such as we engage in when we lay out rules or terms of a legal agreement. Languages do not come about by stipulating rules. They gradu-ally evolve by small motivated steps (see Haspelmath, 1999b), even though they may eventually come to be arbitrary. There is a fundamental difference between arbitrariness in conventions (no hindrance to communication) and initial novel (and ultimately diachronic) arbitrariness. The latter involves an implausible assumption about speakers either convening and declaring allegiance to some form–function correlations, or else, some interlocutors stipulating such arbitrary associations and addressees somehow guessing what the innovative form–function correlation is. In other words, if an arbitrary association were to be invoked initially, it is unclear how interlocutors would be able to implement it (either as speakers or as addressees).

Recall the distinction between actuation (the initial innovative use) and propa-gation (the spread) of linguistic change. While the distinction seems appropriate for highly innovative changes, ones which initially constitute some violation of the current grammar (e.g. novel metaphors), for many grammaticization pro-cesses, it is actually hard to identify the first, "violating" occurrences of a change. What constitutes a change? Many potential changes are hard to pin down to a specific innovator, just because they involve mere conforming to the current grammar. Note that the current grammar does not totally account for language use, not only because it never encodes all the meanings that we wish to convey. Grammar underdetermines use in that it leaves many options for the speaker's choice. If the grammar at stage I does not specifically bar some combination between two elements, speakers may gradually turn these two elements into a new complex unit with its own specialized function at stage II, creating a change

---

[28] Attempts at initiating linguistic conventions are often made by nationalistic language academies, but more often than not, their decisions remain on paper.

without violating any current grammatical convention. Still, a new category has been created, which may involve new grammatically specified conventions. New constructions routinely arise by repeatedly combining grammatical elements allowed for by the current grammar in a statistically skewed fashion, such that a special function is assigned to this combination. Thus, language change often results from noninnovative use. "Grammars code best what speakers do most" (Du Bois, 1987: 851), or, more appropriately for our focus here, grammars **come** to code (best) what speakers do often enough.

Take the case of the creation of verbal person agreement out of independent personal pronouns (e.g. Hebrew *halax at* > *halax-t* 'you walked' > 'walked-you'). Does it make sense to claim that there must have been an innovative individual who came up with a phonologically reduced pronoun for the first time? Not necessarily. Many linguistic changes are so mundane, so minimal and so much in keeping with the synchronic grammar, that it's implausible to attribute them to a first initiator. It's more likely that many speakers were taking similar steps, possibly independently of each other (at least to some extent), until the new discourse pattern gained some degree of salience, at which point it may be followed not just because it's appropriate for the speaker's local goal, but because it presents itself as a salient strategy to adopt.[29] Thus, if up until a certain point in time several options were available for expressing some message, at a later point in time, one of them may become privileged, because it's more salient to speakers. High frequency then follows in a snowball effect. This seems to be the case for the development of the future *be going to* construction. Bybee (2005) points out that in Shakespeare's times *be going to* was one exemplar of a series of a general purpose construction (others being *be returning to*, *be journeying to*). There was then no violation involved in gradually using the more frequent exemplar of the construction, which later accrued strengthening implicatures until it became an independent construction of its own.

Explaining the process of conventionalization by reference to a salient discourse pattern has a few advantages to recommend it. It accounts for linguistic change (whether conformist or innovative – as we see below) through language use in discourse (in light of the conclusion in section 5.2); it is an invisible hand change, since no individual initiator is necessarily implicated and no conscious act is involved; it does not require us to attribute to interlocutors an intention to create a new piece of grammar; and it lends itself to an analysis of entrenchment whereby an optionally constructed pattern gradually receives its own independent status (representation).

Before we launch into a discussion of salient discourse patterns, I should like to reiterate the conclusions we reached in section 2.3, namely that it is no easy matter

---

[29] We shall examine the history of English reflexive pronouns in chapter 6, and see how at each point, grammatically viable options were used to consistently convey certain functions with the reflexive form, and these consistent uses led to their grammaticization from emphatic adjuncts to indicators of marked anaphora.

to decide whether a certain salient discourse pattern constitutes a piece of grammar or not, i.e., whether it is a discourse profile or a discourse function. While the picture seems quite clear when we compare the initial and the endpoint states of a historical change, the process of conventionalization is quite complex. The following two cases demonstrate the crucial role of the salient discourse pattern, but they also show the complex relation between salient discourse patterns and perfectly general grammatical conventions. The salient discourse patterns considered discriminate between seemingly identical contexts, so conventionalization is not as general as one would expect from grammatical change. Are these then cases of grammaticization? In other words, has a grammatical convention actually emerged?

Consider first the innovative Hebrew deletion of *tov* 'good' from some speakers' greetings such as *boker* 'morning' and *laila* 'night' for 'good morning/night.' Such practices show an in-between status. It's clear that the deletion is enabled due to contextual circumstances rendering the adjective redundant (recall the *do* > 'otherwise' shift). But then, other greetings, such as *erev* 'evening' and (*axar ha*) *cohoraim* '(after)noon,' do not license the deletion, although 'good' is as contextually predictable here as in the other greetings. There is no *tov* deletion in all greetings. No doubt the difference stems from frequency differences. The latter greetings are not as frequent in discourse, and have not therefore created salient enough discourse patterns to enable the omission. But the result is that what we have is a very limited convention of *tov* 'good' deletion. The following case from Bybee *et al.* (1994: 284) shows a more complex intermediate case. Some body parts, they note, can be used to express spatial relations, but they have not grammaticized, they claim. They are constrained to specific cases, and are not freely used with others. Compare *the foot of the bed/hill/*pot* with *the bottom of the bed/hill/pot*, or **the foot* with *the bottom* (meaning 'the bottom'). *Foot of* meaning 'bottom of' does form a salient discourse pattern with some nouns, but not generally so. Only four types of nouns account for 80 percent (44) of the first 55 occurrences of nonliteral *the foot of* on WebCorp: Mountains/hills, furniture, buildings, and statues.

There is a clear difference between (i) ad hoc inferences (needed e.g. for interpreting the innovative *the foot of the rainbow* – selfknowledge.com/349au.htm), (ii) salient discourse profiles (e.g. *the foot of a mountain*), and (iii) a perfectly general grammatical convention (stipulating that *foot of* lexically means 'bottom of,' in addition to its literal meaning). While it is clear that we are not (yet) at stage (iii) for *foot*, are the facts, as presented above, not grammatical? They are not if we expect grammatical conventions to be perfectly general. If we examine whether *foot of* is now a spatial preposition in English, then indeed, it is an intermediate case. However, if we allow for small-scale grammatical conventions, there is every reason to ascribe to *foot of*, when preceding any of the four categories of nouns listed above, a grammatical status of a preposition. Indeed, Macmillan (2002) lists *foot of* as 'bottom of.' It seems then that intermediate cases may actually be quite conventional, although not maximally general in application. Should *foot of* become a full-fledged preposition, our current state might retroactively be seen as intermediate, but, from a synchronic point of view, there is no reason not to consider small-scale regularities as grammatical conventions. We have devoted chapters 2 and 3 to the question of what constitutes grammatical status and what constitutes pragmatic status. We therefore here ignore this question, and focus on the precondition for conventionalization, the formation of salient discourse patterns. How do salient and frequent discourse patterns come about? Two main forces lie at the basis of salient discourse patterns: discourse communicative goals (section 5.3.2) and cognitive propensities (section 5.3.3). But first, we discuss the concept of the salient discourse pattern (section 5.3.1).

5.3.1   The salient discourse pattern

Here's the challenge: we need to explain how the crossing from the extragrammatical to the grammatical is motivated (since we saw that grammar is thus motivated in chapter 4 and section 5.1), but at the same time, we must avoid attributing any teleological intentions to interlocutors. In addition, the process must be discourse-dependent (section 5.2), but still discriminatory: obviously, not all innovations and not all discourse profiles attested in discourse constitute potential grammatical conventions. In fact, most probably the great majority of ad hoc innovations leave no mark on the grammar of the language. It is the salient discourse pattern which is the final gate-keeper for potential conventionalizations. Only the salient discourse pattern can guarantee that change is motivated, occurs in discourse, yet does not depend on interlocutors aiming at grammaticization, and is not open to just any discoursal phenomenon. Grammaticization must be seen as resulting from very local extensions of use, which later gradually get entrenched because unmarked/frequent contexts call for their employment, till they acquire a conventional status. Innovative components must first form a recurrent discourse pattern to qualify for a potential change. Only in this way can grammaticization be seen as brought about by small increments, many of them involving rather mechanistic and automatic processes (see Labov, 1990). Such processes can then explain the puzzling phenomenon of grammar being motivated on the one hand, and unintentionally stumbled upon, so to speak, on the other hand.

What triggers automaticity? According to Bybee *et al.* (1994), automaticity generally arises when some process is frequently or routinely performed. It increases production speed, it decreases error rate, and it is less costly in terms of processing, because it does not require conscious attention, which is then available for other tasks (Givón, 2002: 74). The active role of frequency in molding linguistic forms has long been noticed. Zipf (1929) is the one most often cited as pointing to the connection between frequency and word length (see additional earlier and later references in Jurafsky *et al.*, 2002). Frequent linguistic expressions tend to be short, which attests that frequent use contributes to phonetic reduction. This is true for function words (which is why they tend to be shorter than content words), but it also applies to content words.[30] Hooper (1976) argued that a potential reductive sound change applied to the original schwas in *every, artillery,* and *memory* according to their respective frequencies. The fact that *every* has no schwa preceding the /r/ now, but *artillery* does, is due to the fact that the former is a highly frequent word, whereas the latter is quite rare. In between in terms of frequency is *memory,* which is also phonetically intermediate, with a syllabic /r/. Speakers' goals dictate which linguistic forms are more frequent. Routinization and automatization lead to more efficient, but less careful execution in language production of frequent forms (as in other motor activities).

In order to arrive at the conventionalized three-way distinction above, out of a historical unified source where /r/was preceded by a schwa, we must assume that it's not just the case that sound change takes place in production (which, of course, it must). We must also assume that our mental representations are forever changing, in principle, being affected by each and every token used (Bybee, 2000; Langacker, 1987; MacDonald, 1999). This is the only way we can account for why *every* lost the vowel completely, *memory* underwent a partial loss, while *artillery* has not been affected. Note that a use-driven process (reduction of frequent forms) gradually creates a change in the phonological shape of linguistic items. Since *every* must have started with a full vowel, and passed through a stage of syllabic /r/ as well, the assumption is that intermediate pronunciations must be lexically represented as well (Pierrehumbert, 2001, 2003). The more frequently a word is used, the more opportunities speakers have of applying the sound reduction, and hence the more entrenched the change becomes for frequent words. Bybee (2000) similarly demonstrates that *t/d* deletion in English is gradual, and advances at different rates within the lexicon. Frequent target words undergo the change faster than infrequent target words. In general, final /t//d/ deletions are more inhibited when they constitute morphemic units (as in the regular past tense *-ed*).[31] However, we still find differences between high- and low-frequency verb forms in past tense. Bybee reports that frequent verbs show an *-ed* deletion more than twice as often as infrequent verbs. Similarly, the general findings for double-marked past-tense verbs, e.g. *told, left* (where past tense is indicated by both vowel change and *-ed*) is that they allow for more reduction than regular past-tense verbs. But again, Bybee finds that *told* (high frequency) was reduced in 68 percent of its occurrences, while *left* (much less frequent) was reduced in only 25 percent of the cases.

---

[30] Note, however, that frequency is not the sole factor involved in such reductions. Berkenfield (2001) finds that despite the fact that pronominal *that* is far more frequent than complementizer and relativizer *that* the latter are more reduced in pronunciation than the former. Indeed, according to the activation accounts for reference, pronominal *that* is an intermediate accessibility marker, so unlike personal pronouns, which encode a high degree of activation, it is not as subject to reduction as they are.

[31] While this difference seems to be in service of clarity, Bybee (2000) notes that it so happens that regular past-tense verbs are followed by a vowel (an inhibitor of consonant deletion) much more often than other words ending in either /d/ or /t/. If so, the selective /t//d/ deletion is not (directly, at least) to be accounted for by the need for clarity.

Krug (2000: 24) similarly finds a correlation between grammaticization and high frequency: between 40 and 50 percent of the thirty most frequent verbs in English are auxiliary verbs, but only 20 percent of the next twenty verbs function as auxiliary verbs (the idea is that auxiliary verbs emerge out of main verbs). Krug also proposes that the fact that *What are you . . .?*, *What do you . . .?*, and *What have you . . .?* all allow for the deletion of the auxiliary (resulting in the homophonous *What you . . .?*), but not other, syntactically similar combinations, points to a frequency driving conventionalization process (see Krug, 2000: 178/179). So frequency of use, no doubt itself a product of our communicative goals (see section 5.3.2), is an ever present factor in linguistic change and grammaticization. And frequent patterns are potential paths to grammaticization. This point is true for other sound changes as well. Bybee (2005) suggests that the lexical entry of words gets updated for their semantic content with each use. If so, we should expect salient/consistent inferences generated for fairly frequent lexical items to semanticize faster/more than salient/consistent inferences accompanying less frequent items.[32] Indeed, this is why bleaching (loss of semantic meaning) occurs mostly to frequent words, and why lexical items turned function words demonstrate at least some rise in frequency prior to, and not only during and following, grammaticization. (See Bybee, 2003b; Hopper and Traugott, 1993/2003; and many articles in Traugott and Heine, 1991.)

Elizabeth Traugott (p.c.) proposes, however, that a rise in frequency follows, rather than precedes grammaticization, so that the high-frequency characteristic of grammatical morphemes may be the result rather than the trigger for the conventionalization process. Heine *et al.* (1991b: 38/39) quote Bertoncini's (1973) research on Swahili, where it is frequent, but not the most frequent, words that undergo grammaticization. And Hundt (2001) shows that on the whole, the various grammaticizations of *get* are not correlated with a decrease in the use of its original, 'obtain' meaning, which remains by far the most frequent of its uses. I have no way of deciding between the two proposals regarding the ordering between high frequency and grammaticization. It is perhaps not necessary for the emerging grammatical function to take over, so to speak, as Hundt expects it to. Maybe all it takes to render some form–function a potential source for conventionalization is a noticeable rise in frequency, even if the increased frequency rate is not very high in absolute terms. It is also quite conceivable that different processes work differently. It may be the case that phonetic changes first become frequent and then conventionalize, but the creation of new grammatical constructions doesn't necessarily require prior absolutely high frequency.

In fact, Bybee (1985b, 1994) herself and Hare and Elman (1995) underscore the fact that language change does not necessarily follow the most frequent pattern. Smaller-scale patterns may sometimes be more salient than more frequent ones. In addition to token frequency and type frequency (of the category the expression

---

[32] Of course, there is also decay, so infrequent ad hoc contextual meanings have no long-term effect on the form's meaning, even if they are initially added on to the representation.

belongs to), Hare and Elman argue that the coherence of the category also matters, because it makes it more or less salient. Hare and Elman (1995) demonstrate how minor patterns (applying to a relatively small number of linguistic items) can be maintained, despite the existence of competing more general patterns (they discuss so-called strong verbs in English, where the past tense is formed by specific vowel modifications, e.g. *drink–drank*, rather than by the general pattern of adding *-ed*). The connectionist model which they created in order to simulate the history of English verbs distinguished not only between high and low token frequency (of individual verbs) and type frequency (of the verb class). It also distinguished between well-defined classes – based on their phonological make-up (e.g. *sing*) – versus less well-defined classes (e.g. *freeze*). Regularization, they show, is not restricted to shifting only towards the one general pattern. Verbs were actually sometimes recruited to the irregular paradigms, provided the exemplar of the irregular class was highly frequent and the class easily identified. Similarly, verbs resisted regularization, first, to the extent that they were frequent, but also to the extent that they formed part of a coherent class.

The most important conclusion they reach is that the same principle accounts for the change and for the maintenance of both regular and irregular verbs, namely, analogical formation, restricted by the above parameters, which are biased towards following frequent as well as consistent classes of forms. The fact that different verbs behaved differently although they seemed similar morphologically (either regular or irregular) is accounted for by reference to different rates of use, then, and differential analogical processes performed by speakers. The basic principle we seem to operate with is adopting some template based on its analogical attraction. Pattern and rate of change were different for individual verbs, indicating that inflection is not governed by a set of abstract automatic rules, but rather, by probabilistic tendencies of various templates one could adopt as exemplars. As corroborating evidence they cite an experiment which found that subjects made errors in producing past-tense forms of regular verbs such as *bake* just because of its phonological similarity to frequent irregular verbs such as *take*. Ernestus (2005) has similar findings for Dutch, where she moreover found that analogical formations increased, rather than decreased, with children's age (9- to 12-year-olds). What is relevant for our discussion is the importance of the salient discourse pattern, even if it's a very small-scale pattern, in prompting both change and stability.

Discourse patterns followed must be privileged. But not only frequency confers such a privileged status. Hence the choice of a more general term for discourse patterns which are candidates for conventionalization – salience (adapted from Traugott and Dasher's 2002 concept of salient innovations). Salient discourse patterns stand out either because they are frequent, or because of other reasons.[33] Such reasons may be that the form–function correlations are exceptional, or they

---

[33] The concept of a salient discourse pattern here discussed is also inspired by Giora's definition of the salient meaning, i.e. that which immediately comes to mind (see Giora, 2003).

may be especially useful because they are compact in expressing some complex message, or they may be used by the "right" set of speakers one wants to identify with. The most important feature of salience is that what is salient is highly accessible to us, foremost on our minds, and hence more easily available for use. Salient discourse patterns may lead to various conventionalizations. They may conventionalize contextually induced phonetic changes; they may render optional elements obligatory (e.g. reduced independent pronouns turning into person verbal agreement markers); they may create syntactic options not previously available (the creation of the *be going to* construction); and they may conventionalize contextually derived interpretations (semanticization, e.g. the additive meaning of *indeed*). We end this chapter by considering the possibility that **any** discourse pattern may bring about conventionalization, even in the absence of a motivating functional basis. This is important in that it shows how the extralinguistic–linguistic divide is crossed rather mechanically, and not due to communicative goals (or rather, not directly so). Given a salient pattern, a grammatical convention may emerge out of it.

As we have noted in sections 5.1 and 5.2, many factors contribute to grammaticization: grammar itself, and pragmatics and other extralinguistic factors. Below we see other factors as well, mainly conservatism, following precedents and structural priming. The point is, however, that linguistic change is mediated by discourse pattern, specifically, by the salient discourse pattern. Salient discourse patterns, **no matter what their source is**, are a prerequisite for grammaticization. We discuss salient discourse patterns formed due to recurrent communicative goals achieved by recurrent means in the next two sections. These salient discourse patterns may be functionally motivated (section 5.3.2), but they may be (partly) arbitrary (section 5.3.3).

5.3.2   Motivated salient discourse patterns

Some discourse patterns are more prevalent than others, because they contain recurrent encodings for recurrent message components. They reflect useful strategies for useful communicative goals. As we have emphasized in section 5.2, speakers' communicative goals are a most important impetus for the formation of discoursal patterns. These naturally create differences between more versus less useful forms and more versus less useful interpretations. This distinction is relevant for the conventionalization of innovative forms. The length/ complexity of codes is crucially tied to frequency for the most part. But the point of this section is that frequency seems to take effect regardless of the extralinguistic motivation behind it. To see this, we now go back to some of the external sources proposed above as potential pressures molding grammar. As we shall see, it is only by forming **a salient discourse pattern** that such pressures can have an effect on grammar. The salient discourse pattern is the last gate-keeper on the road to grammaticization. It alone must mediate all change, and since it can be prompted by rather low-level production and processing mechanisms, high-level cognitive and pragmatic motivations must be seen as only indirectly affecting grammar.

We have mentioned above Hawkins' (2003) proposal that memory limitations are responsible for prevalent constituent orders cross-linguistically. But, as Hawkins himself emphasizes, the path from processing preferences to grammatical ordering is not direct (nor teleological). It is mediated by discourse frequency. In support of his proposals regarding preferred constituent orderings, Hawkins quotes counts for sentences containing two PPs. In 85 percent of the cases a PP which is either shorter (67 percent) or equal in length (18 percent) precedes a longer PP.[34] Such an ordering of short before long constituents is easier to process, and his proposal is that it is such counts which form the basis of the cross-category correlations established by Greenberg, showing clear preferences for minimizing recognition lag of two adjacent categories (see section 5.1.1 above). In other words, his claim is that the reason why most languages end up with one of the two preferred constituent orderings is that these orderings are naturally opted for by individual speakers in discourse (the implicit assumption is that the previous stage of the grammar did not stipulate any particular ordering). A high frequency of a certain order, perceived as a salient discourse pattern, may have gradually led to a rigid constituent ordering. Presumably, other processing-sensitive constraints (those proposed in e.g. Deane, 1992; Frazier, 1985, 1990; Hawkins, 1994, 2004; MacWhinney and Bates, 1989) can be analyzed as having arisen in a similar fashion.

Next, recall the argument that it is not raw reality which is reflected in language. For example, speakers don't find bodily function descriptions attractive conversation materials, and hence such content is not very often selected, despite its high frequency in reality. Indeed, it is discoursal (in)frequency, and not real-world (in)frequency, which is relevant for (un)marked linguistic expressions. This is why a majority (117, 62.6 percent) of the "impolite" bodily activity verbs found in SBC and LSAC were quite long (mostly *go to the bathroom*). The thousands of mentions of eating of course used the verb *eat*, an unmarked, short expression. This is just as we would expect markedness to operate. Linguistic expressions used frequently are unmarked, and linguistic expressions used infrequently are marked. It is the frequency in discourse, and not in reality, which determines the degree of formal markedness (Croft, 2000: 75–76).[35] It is not surprising to find, then, that languages require rather marked expressions to express less acceptable self-activities (e.g. *love **oneself***) as compared with self-activities which are socially acceptable, frequently talked about, and hence encoded by less marked expressions (e.g. *dress*). Since they are impolite, bodily activity verbs are not

---

[34] Excluding the equal-length cases, close to 82 percent of the cases obey Hawkins' prediction, and just over 18 percent violate it.

[35] Haspelmath (2004c: 3) too argues that "structural (Zipfian) economy derives from **speech frequency**, not from **world frequency**" (original emphases). Haspelmath (2006a) proposes to do away with the concept of markedness altogether, replacing it with frequency, articulatory effort, etc.

frequent, they do not create a privileged discourse pattern which is then potentially subject to formal reduction.

Different words naturally have different frequency/salience rates, just because some words are more useful to speakers than others (compare *artillery* with *every*, mentioned above). But raw word or word-meaning frequencies are not the only relevant contexts leading to reduction due to repeated use. Other patterns may similarly be discoursally privileged, for example, high predictability (of occurrence) in context. Jurafsky *et al.* (2002) find that English *to* reduction affects infinitival *to* much more than prepositional *to*. An examination of the frequency of these uses of *to* showed that infinitival *to* is almost three times as frequent, but even that cannot alone account for the difference. Now, such a change, affecting one use of *to* but not another, may seem to be motivated by an attempt at creating a one form/one function association. Jurafsky *et al.* argue that this is not the case. As they emphasize, what is prompting phonetic reduction here is a high degree of contextual predictability.[36] Words which have a high probability given their neighboring words tend to trigger reduction more often. Now, what they found is that statistically, infinitival *to* is more predictable than prepositional *to*, and this is what accounts for the differential reduction rate. In other words, there is a "conspiracy" between a word's predictability and its phonetic reducibility, which may create a phonetic and later a phonological distinction along lines of different meanings (homonym splits).

This is no accident. Contextual distributions are derivative of words' functions. This is why the potential result of such automatically triggered processes is that different forms (pronunciations in this case) may specialize for different functions (infinitival versus prepositional *to*) without speakers ever aiming for such a distinction. What might seem like a motivated teleological change is then not in fact so motivated. The most salient discourse profile of infinitival *to* shows it to be predictable, and hence the potential change. But we should note that while potentially functional, this change is not (directly) functionally motivated. It is the mediating discourse pattern which is responsible for the change. Regarding *of*, the process seems even more advanced (this is my interpretation of Jurafsky *et al.*'s 2002 findings). The significant statistical differences in pronouncing the partitive (most frequent, more reductive) versus genitive and complement (less frequent, less reductive) *of* are only partially accounted for by considering their contextual probabilities. In this case, the different functions of *of* must (already) contribute directly and not just indirectly to the statistical differentiation between their pronunciations. Here, it seems, a connection has been initiated by speakers between the reduced pronunciation and partitive function directly.

Very often the relevant unit for the effect of high versus low frequencies is the string frequency. Grammaticization, it is now believed, often occurs within constructions, where, presumably, the component constituents are highly predictable.

---

[36] See Delong *et al.* (2005) for empirical evidence for the role of probabilities in anticipating upcoming linguistic material.

Such is the case with *gonna*, *wanna*, and *gotta*. These verbs are not only among the thirty most frequent verbs (Krug, 2001), they also repeatedly occur in specific linguistic contexts (with specific auxiliaries and subjects – see Bybee, 2002; Bybee *et al.*, 1994). Such frequent cooccurrences may lead to chunking as a single unit (Bybee, 2002), which explains why these expressions are currently undergoing a categorial change from main verbs (+auxiliaries) into (emerging) modal verbs (Krug, 2001). "Items that are used together fuse together" (Bybee, 2002: 112; Krug, 2003). This is Bybee's Linear Fusion Hypothesis. Such fusions are then expected for frequently cooccurring adjacent forms, and, one would expect, for intra-constituent elements more than for cross-constituent elements. Indeed, as Bybee (2001) argues, French Liaison (the occurrence of a consonant at the end of a word preceding another which begins with a vowel, even though no consonant is pronounced in other phonetic environments) seems to be tied to specific constructions. This explains why *l'un* only shows Liaison when in the construction of *l'un avec l'autre* 'with one another,' and why numbers which did not end with a /z/ originally now trigger a /z/ Liaison before nouns beginning with a vowel (e.g. *quatre* 'four'). Presumably, a /z/ Liaison is now widespread in the number construction (in general).

But note that constituency is not a necessary condition (Bybee, 2001, 2002). Instead, Bybee proposes sheer string frequency as the determining factor, which accounts for why *nous (z) avons* 'we have' manifests Liaison, despite the constituent boundary between the subject and the verb. The same goes for the extremely high proportion of Liaison (98.7 percent) for *est un* 'is a.' This string forms a construction according to Bybee (*est* is followed by *un* in almost half of its occurrences). Bybee (2002) demonstrates how fusion occurs for subject–verb combinations rather than for VP-internal constituents (*I'll go* rather than **I ll'go*).[37] She cites research on African languages where prepositions are suffixed to verbs rather than to the nouns they form a PP with, suggesting that frequency of cooccurrence with specific tokens accounts for these cases. Crucially, it's not the case that subject–verb combinations have a preference for fusion in general. It all depends on how frequently the specific subject and the specific verb cooccur. This is why the combination of *I don't*, which is more frequent than that of *they don't*, shows a higher degree of phonetic fusion. All in all, some strings are more useful to speakers than others. They then more often become a production (and processing) chunk, which then prompts their formal integration into one unit. Most intriguing are findings by Bod (2006) in this connection. Bod reports that subjects responded faster to high-frequency sentences (based on the BNC, e.g. *I like it*) than to less frequent sentences, although the component words in the pairs of sentences compared were equally frequent and complex, the sentences were

---

[37] But as John Du Bois (p.c.) notes, these are all cases where cliticization has a phonological rationale, even if not a syntactic or morphological one. Cf. *I'll* (creating a VC phonological word) with **ll'go* (an impossible CCV phonological word in English).

syntactically identical and equally plausible. He concludes that we may even store whole sentences, if they are frequent enough.

As Traugott (2004a; Traugott and Dasher, 2002 *inter alia*) has emphasized, pragmatically induced invited inferences must first become salient before they entrench into encoded meanings. Different degrees of salience for specific inferences accompanying the use of the same forms may then account for different semanticizations across languages (Traugott and Dasher, 2002: 35). Thus, whereas Middle English and Modern English (as in (22)) (see Traugott and König, 1991) both show cases where *while* is used with a causal interpretation, such cases must have not acquired salience and therefore did not become semanticized:[38]

(22)   Patty: (H) And there would never be a Jacky Bast.
                ... **While** she ... is ... uh the head of .. of that h– .. household.
                                                                                        (SBC: 023)

Presumably, this is what happened in German, however. The difference between English *while* and German *weil* may well have been a different degree of salience for the concessive and the causal inferences respectively in the two languages. Each of the forms could have potentially semanticized differently. Thus, the mere availability of an inferential chain from some semantic meaning to another conveyed meaning via some invited inference/implicature is far from accounting for semanticization. A salient, very often high-frequency discourse pattern is the only path potentially leading to semanticization and grammaticization.

But we're still left with some puzzles. We can explain the German discourse pattern of *weil*, and we can explain the English discourse pattern of *while*. We can also explain each of the preferred word orders analyzed by Hawkins (1994) and onwards. But why did some languages opt for one pattern and others for a different one? How can we account for the partially arbitrary grammars? Section 5.3.3 makes an attempt to explain such differences between languages.

5.3.3   Relatively arbitrary salient discourse patterns

At any point in time, discourse is rife with consistent patterns which are actually only partially motivated by speakers' communicative goals. For example, the discourse profile of the verb *happen* shows it to be associated with unpleasant events (Sinclair, 1991: 112). But not so the nominal *happening*. Each of these has a different discourse profile. Similarly, Cohen (2005) notes that while Hebrew *taxun* 'ground, minced' implies a finer grinding than *garus* 'ground, crushed, pounded' (so we can have pepper and cinnamon either *taxun* or *garus*), many nouns take just one or the other, regardless of how fine the grinding is. Thus, meat and coffee take *taxun*, even though coffee at least can be ground coarsely or finely, and meat is only ground coarsely. Wheat only takes *garus*, so some bread lists as two of its ingredients *xita* **grusa daka**, *xita* **grusa ave** '**finely pounded**

---
[38] See section 5.3.3 on the role of precedents too.

wheat, **coarsely pounded** wheat' (Tushiya bread, Feb. 2, 2005), rather than *xita txuna ve-xita grusa* 'ground wheat and coarsely ground wheat.' Why should this be so?

Section 5.3.3 examines the motivation behind the formation of salient discourse patterns, whose ultimately high frequency cannot be explained by the communicative functionality of the specific pattern. We have so far reviewed cases where mainly speakers' local communicative goals either directly or more indirectly render some (strings of) forms or some inferred interpretations more useful. Naturally, they are more frequent and more salient, paving the way for salient discourse patterns, some of which may conventionalize. We have also seen that communicative goals are not always the direct force behind new conventions. Other external motivations commonly create discourse patterns, even though they do not directly serve immediate communicative goals. Since it is the salient discourse pattern which is a potential source for grammaticization, these patterns too may grammaticize. In fact, just because it is the salient discourse pattern which provides a potential grammaticization path, even partially arbitrary paths may grammaticize, provided we can account for their creation. This is what we do in section 5.3.3. We will mention conservatism, following precedents and priming. These can account for the partially arbitrary conventions discussed in chapter 4. The idea is that although more than one motivated form–function could serve speakers, the one which first reached salience is the one to conventionalize, not because it's superior in serving interlocutors' communicative goals, but because it is the one that conservative uses, which follow precedents, happened to promote. Once a salient discourse pattern has formed, the way to potential grammaticization has been paved, regardless of the basis behind the pattern.

Recent research, most notably Hopper (1987) and Sinclair (1991), has emphasized the massive role that collocation plays in natural language. Sinclair (1991 and onwards) proposed that discourse is governed by two principles. One is the open-choice principle, enabling the freedom of choice we have in language, a freedom constrained only by grammatical conventions. The more important (default) principle according to Sinclair, however, is the idiom principle, according to which choice is rather limited and not completely motivated. Much like Hopper (1987; see also, Hopper and Thompson, 2001; Thompson, 2002), Sinclair (1991: 110) finds that we have "a large number of **semi-preconstructed** phrases that constitute **single choices**, even though they might appear to be analyzable into segments" (emphases added).[39] Thus, *of course*, and even *set eyes on, set fire to, hard work, hard evidence, hard facts* constitute single choices despite their obvious syntactic and semantic components. This principle explains why it is that highly frequent words (open-class included) contribute only minimal semantic content on their own (e.g. *take, make*), as opposed to their occurrence with their collocates (e.g. *take a look, make up one's mind*). The pervasiveness of

---

[39] Erman and Warren (2000) found that such uses constitute over half of our spoken as well as written language.

collocations proves the pervasive reality of salient discourse profiles. Now, if these preconstructed phrases were totally motivated by speakers' communicative goals, we would have seen a significant cross-linguistic convergence on such collocations. This is not the case, however. The collocates above are specific to English. How did they come about? What is the motivation behind the idiom principle?

Languages contain a large repertoire of what I proposed to call "ugly facts" (Ariel, 1999b; Goldberg, 2006). "Ugly facts" are those which seem (to native speakers – Clancy, 1989) to be perfectly natural compositional meanings (derived by combining the semantic meaning with contextual assumptions guided by pragmatic principles), but, in fact, are idiomatic collocates (what Morgan, 1978 called short-circuited implicatures). When I first heard the English *Do bears shit in the woods?* I was completely baffled. I shouldn't have been. I should have used my pragmatic abilities to reason as follows: since facts about bears are irrelevant to the conversation at hand, the speaker must intend for me to draw some implicature from her utterance. Moreover, the question is rhetorical because the positive answer is obvious. One way to render the utterance relevant is to conclude that just as the response to the irrelevant question is self-evident, so is the proposition on which the "bear question" is commenting. In other words, what the speaker is conveying is that the proposition commented on is trivially true, and need not have been uttered. As a speaker of Hebrew, I might have instead used the counterpart of 'You're discovering America' under similar circumstances, implicating, 'you're informing me of something that is well-known,' by breaching Quantity, as well as Relevance. I imagine that a non-native speaker of Hebrew might have the same reaction to this expression, as I initially had to the "bear question."

Other differences are not hard to find, including similar uses of opposite meanings. When we want to convey that some proposition is outrageous we might rhetorically ask in Hebrew 'Are you normal?' An English speaker would probably use *Are you out of your mind?* When Hebrew speakers want to convey that something is amazing we say the counterpart of 'What are you saying!' But English speakers might instead say *You don't say.* Such non-native difficulties show the entrenchment and partial arbitrariness that conveyed meanings manifest in different languages. Note that interlocutors' goals cannot explain these language differences, for in both languages the same speaker goals are involved. Moreover, the means used by both languages transparently point addressees to the proper inferred interpretations.

A possible source for the curious facts above is our conservatism. Conservatism is one cognitive source pushing for the creation of salient discourse patterns. Keller (1994: 100) argues for a strategy whereby we try to "talk like the others talk."[40] Assuming such a speaker strategy, homogeneity can spread within a

---

[40] Kasher (1982) argued for a similar principle on the basis of Grice's Manner, but Kasher refers to preference for conventionalized expressions. Conservatism here pertains to not yet conventional uses as well.

community over time, even if the starting point is divergence (and see Wedel, 2004 for a computer simulation for such a change). Some linguistic choices are made simply because we have a propensity to closely "follow the crowd." Research on child language learning has recently emphasized how closely children's grammar follows the output of their care givers. Verbs heard in some grammatical frame are first learnt in that frame alone, and are so used, argued Tomasello (1992, 2000, 2003a) (see also Berman and Armon-Lotem, 1996; Clancy, 1989). If so, verbs are learnt one by one (an item-based learning), so that what are considered syntactically similar verbs (e.g. transitive verbs) initially occur in different syntactic structures very often. For one child, *cut* was restricted to only taking a direct object, but at the same time, *draw* had five different syntactic frames (e.g. *Draw __*, *__ draw*, *Draw __ on __*, *Draw __ for __*, *__ draw __*). Why was this variety of constructions not available for the grammatically similar *cut*? Past-tense morphology was also quite inconsistently used across verbs, but remarkably consistently within verbs. There seems to be no pattern of use which crosses verb paradigms for children, a surprising finding for a rule-based system. Tomasello observed no generalization of structure from one verb to another, so for a while at least, each verb formed its own organizational island. It is at a later age that children develop the ability to generalize from one verb paradigm to another, once they have noticed the salient patterns of use in their language.

Adults are not all that different from children. They too tend to use linguistic expressions quite conservatively most of the time.[41] Recent research has brought forth evidence for quite detailed memorizations which subjects retain for later use, and these are not restricted to the ephemeral short-term memory (Johnson, 1997). Bod (2005) proposes that all linguistic tokens are registered in memory, even by adults (although not all are remembered, of course). Romaine (1999) found that in Tok Pisin *like*, used as a proximative ('almost,' 'be about to'), is heavily restricted to a few change of state verbs (e.g. *die*). Croft (2000: 117) maintains that "individual members have internalized knowledge of a partial history of the form, namely, its contexts of use that they have heard or used themselves." In fact, the meaning of some form is the history of its uses according to Croft. Language users do operate with high-level generalizations, but also with low-level, local patterns at the same time (see Goldberg, 2006: chapter 3; Langacker, 1987; Tomasello, 2003a).

We have mentioned above priming phenomena, where speakers choose specific forms just because they have heard them recently. Often this is done in order to create resonance with another in order to engage with him (Du Bois, 2004 and see section 5.2.1 above). Consider S's uses of preposed objects in the first four pages of Lotan 1990. Object preposing is quite a marked word order pattern in Hebrew, so S only had six of them (as compared with fifty nonpreposed clauses containing objects). Two of these six are clearly pragmatically justified (the preposed object is

---

[41] See Bresnan and Hay (to appear) for subtle but consistent differences between American and New Zealand use of the dative alternations (with regard to the factor of animacy of the recipient role).

used contrastively). Interestingly, however, three of the four remaining cases are no doubt prompted by a previous utterance. Most intriguing of these is (23), where S chooses the marked object preposing in order to secure the same initial position for the same absolutive referent. Dialogic syntax does not only explain S's preposed object construction, it also explains why he's repeating what is actually a performance error, Ch's failure to use the definite article although a specific 'parking lot' is referred to (see Bock, 1986):

(23)   CH: ve=xenyon   lo   shelaxem?
             and=parking.lot   not   yours.PL
             'And (the) parking lot is not yours?'
         S: xenyon   yesh   lanu   xelek.
              parking.lot   there.is   to:us   part
              'We have a part of (the) parking lot.'   (Lotan 1990: 3)

So adults too have good (interactional) reasons to use outputs similar to the inputs they just processed. And these are not necessarily dictated by communicative goals. The example in (23) demonstrates how priming/resonance may initiate an innovative form (see also the discussion around (9) in chapter 4 and (50) in chapter 6). The following discussion suggests that discoursal resonance may in addition constitute a driving force in entrenchment processes of grammaticization.[42] Priming can explain the mechanism whereby a discourse profile is created, becomes salient, and sometimes grammaticizes.

Priming explains why imitative patterning is observed even when the linguistic pattern selected is not particularly motivated (pragmatically). Thus, Levelt and Kelter (1982) found that Dutch subjects who were asked questions (e.g. merchants asked about the closing time of their shops) tended to use the same syntactic option selected by the question (+ or – overt preposition). Similarly, Weiner and Labov (1983) found increased frequency of the use of the passive construction in English when another passive construction has been used within the last five sentences. Interestingly, they emphasize that this factor better explains the choice of passive than maintaining the Givenness of the syntactic subject (a pragmatic motivation). Bock (1986; Bock and Loebell, 1990) found priming for both ditransitives and prepositional datives, as well as for actives and passives. In these last cases there was no relevance even between the priming and the primed sentences. Gries (2005) found syntactic priming for both ditransitive/prepositional datives and for particle placement (adjacent to the verb versus following the NP, cf. *pick up X, pick X up*) in both written and spoken data. Finally, based on laboratory experiments, Garrod and Anderson (1987) have argued that pairs of interlocutors faced with a coordination task (the interlocutors, seated in different rooms, needed to inform their partners of their location in a maze) tended to zero in on some strategy which they used consistently (the researchers identified four such strategies). They found that partners' descriptions became more alike the

---

[42] And see Clancy (in press) for the role of priming and dialogic syntax in language acquisition.

longer they were engaged with each other. Thus, whereas in the first game, half of the pairs selected a predominant strategy, by the second game, 95 percent of the pairs were using one strategy predominantly. The principle that speakers work with, they propose, is "output/input coordination": "formulating your output according to the same principles of interpretation . . . as those needed to interpret the most recent relevant input" (1987: 207).

Now, such discoursal priming may have an effect on grammar in that it promotes similarity among speakers, contributing to the creation and maintenance of salient discoursal patterns. Recent research has argued that syntactic priming is not just a matter of temporary increased activation (which it also is, of course). It seems to be effective long after short-term memory activation must have decayed.[43] Bock has suggested that we view syntactic priming as implicit learning (Bock and Griffin, 2000; Chang *et al.*, 2000).[44] "For better or worse, the nervous system stores traces of actions . . . Sometimes this retention leads to efficacy with practice; sometimes it leads to blunders with preservation. Whether good or bad, there need be no specific linguistic motivation for the existence of structural priming" (Bock and Griffin, 2000: 189). In fact, although semantic priming (where accessing the meaning of some word, e.g. *teacher*, facilitates the accessing of the meaning of another, following related word, e.g. *school*) disappears very rapidly, the fact is that frequent words are recognized faster than nonfrequent words, and a word's frequent meanings are accessed faster than its nonfrequent meanings. There is then some learnt residue from repeated use. Bock suggests that the learning involved is procedural, where the processing operations are (very slightly) modified, and the change is restricted to performance of the same task.

Gries' (2005) findings regarding syntactic priming demonstrate how priming can contribute to the creation of mini distributional patterns. Gries finds that priming distinguishes between different verbs, such that although some verbs can get primed for both the ditransitive and the prepositional dative (e.g. *send* and *lend*), some verbs tend to prime more for one construction but not for another, which they resist more easily. Thus, *give, show*, and *offer* show a higher priming effect for the ditransitive construction, but *sell* and *hand* show a preference for prepositional dative priming. Indeed, he finds that different verbs favor different constructions: *send* and *lend* are not strongly associated with either construction; *give, show*, and *offer* are strongly associated with the ditransitive; and *sell* and *hand* are strongly associated with the prepositional dative. In fact, lexical differences were already noted in Levelt and Ketler's study (where one preposition was primed in 98 percent of the cases, but another only in 64 percent of the cases). It's quite possible that the salient discourse patterns for each verb constitute default strategies (akin to Comrie's 1994b discourse strategies) for constructing speakers'

[43] See Bock and Kroch (1989), Bock and Griffin (2000), Boyland and Anderson (1998) and Branigan *et al.* (2000).

[44] Rosenbach and Jäger (2006) similarly propose that asymmetrical ("unidirectional") priming effects (e.g. as demonstrated by Boroditsky, 2000) explain the unidirectionality of linguistic change.

messages. Findings show that priming promotes reuse of the same structure in the absence of a privileged discoursal pattern, and when there is one, it tends to strengthen it (more often than it promotes the nonprivileged pattern).

Sticking to a frequent discourse pattern is not the only reason we follow in others' footsteps (when our communicative goals could have been served differently). After all, how did the emulated pattern come about in the first place (in cases where it wasn't specifically motivated)? Croft (2000: 195) notes that "It is possible that an innovation is particularly salient in some respects and may thus become part of the linguistic system quite rapidly." Such was the case with President Clinton's farewell words at Prime Minister Rabin's funeral (Nov. 1995), which included a very old-fashioned Hebrew address term (*xaver*, which had fallen out of use): *Shalom, xaver* 'Good bye, friend.' The pattern immediately caught on, as attested by numerous different bumper-stickers pro and even against the late Rabin (e.g. *xaver, ani zoxer* 'friend, I remember,' *ha-kol biglalxa, xaver* 'it's all because of you, friend').[45] On the other hand, while Hebrew has had the doubling option for intensification for quite some time (*tov tov* literally 'well well,' in effect 'VERY well'), not till very recently has this option become productive and in fact quite frequent among young people (e.g. *mashu mashu* 'something something,' i.e. 'something special'). It seems that only recently has the pattern become salient for some reason. Finally, note the following joke, where a single interpretative event is sufficient to set up a later inferred interpretation (note also the consistent use of *the neighbour* to refer to just one of the two neighbors):

(24)   A cat-owner on holiday is phoned by his neighbour back home with the sad news that his cat has fallen to its death from the roof of the house. The cat-owner reprimands the neighbour for breaking the news so abruptly. "What else could I have done?" demands the neighbour. "Well," says the cat-owner, "you could have led up to it gradually. One day you could have phoned to say you have seen the cat poking around on the roof among the chimneys. Then you could say it was straying near the edge, and so on." A week passed. Then the neighbour phoned again. "Hi, it's me. I'm phoning to say I've seen your father poking around on the roof among the chimneys."   (Adapted from Sigmund Freud, *The Joke and its Relation to the Unconscious*, 2002, p. ix)

---

[45] Here's a similar case. In the 1970s a famous advertisement declared that with a certain bra, it's 'walking with – feeling without' (the Hebrew slogan roughly means 'you wear the bra but you feel as if you're not'). On this background consider the following:

(i)   A: Tell me, does she go with or without?
           B: How can you talk like this! It's my mother!
           A: It's not what you're thinking. Does she go with or without a hearing aid?
           B: Uh, of course she goes with!
                 (Originally Hebrew ad for hearing aids, Reshet Bet radio, May 18, 2005)

It is clear that the phrase has conventionalized to such an extent, that the inferred completions (what she walks with and feels without) required for the original ad automatically come to mind.

The spreading of buzz words shows that we tend to follow salient precedents, even if they are not particularly frequent (initially). Consider first the current Hebrew buzz word *hitnahalut*, roughly 'management, handling,' mostly used when discussing mismanagement. Up until a few years ago, it was one of a variety of synonyms available for describing the way things are run. By 2005, practically every news broadcast contains a mention of this word. Note that it's not the case that a new concept has been introduced into Israeli discourse, which required a new word. Rather, for some reason (unclear to me), it has recently gained in salience, which then accounts for its high frequency as compared with its competitors. For example, a (rather short) night news broadcast contained two occurrences of *hitnahalut*, one of them quite redundant (note that *hitnahalut* and *nihul* are two nominalizations of the same root):

(25)   INTERVIEWEE: I have a very hard feeling about the whole ***hitnahalut***
(management) of this ***nihul*** (managing).
(Israeli TV Channel 1, Nov. 9, 2004)

Another expression which is "in the air" these days even more in Hebrew than in English is the Hebrew counterpart of 'upgrade.' We now have 'upgraded schnitzels' (YD, June 3, 2004), whereas we used to have 'improved schnitzels' etc. A reporter recently used 'upgrade' to mean 'political advance' (either as a verb or as a noun) six times within a three-minute political commentary on the radio (Reshet Bet, Nov. 21, 2004). While one could say that 'upgraded' has a different connotation from 'improved,' it isn't any different from a similar metaphorical Hebrew expression, 'promote to the next (school) grade,' which is now disappearing. The point is that speakers these days are not (necessarily) after the different connotation so much. More likely they are unconsciously following a well-trodden fashionable discourse pattern, which renders the expression 'upgrade' highly salient and hence highly accessible for use.

But not all (initial) uses stand out so much that they immediately attract our attention. It seems that we often simply follow precedents, just because they were there first (the principle of the 'survival of the first' – Michod (1999), and see also Mufwene (2001: chapter 2) regarding the Founder Principle in explaining the development in Creoles). Following Lewis (1968) and Schiffer (1972), Clark (1996: 81) discusses the role of precedent in guiding nonconventional use of language. As an example he cites Garrod and Anderson's (1987) experiment which we have already alluded to. Once one partner chose the term *row* (rather than *line* or *column* or *path*, which could have served her purpose equally well), a precedent was set, and both speakers tended to stick to that term. A partially arbitrary convention can be created quite rapidly due to our tendency to adhere to precedents. Such experiments (see also Branigan, Pickering and Cleland, 2000; Clark and Wilkes-Gibbs, 1986) are important in demonstrating how people naturally and rather quickly reach conventionality of use through priming of precedent form–function correlations. Garrod and Anderson emphasize that there were very few explicit discussions on the conventions to be adopted. Moreover, such discussions were not particularly effective, in fact.

It is this tendency to produce conservative outputs closely resembling hitherto encountered patterns of speech which may account for the variability among languages (dialects, genres) we discussed in chapter 4. Recall that it was emphasized that conventionalizations must be motivated, and since there is more than one way to encode some message in a motivated way, languages may vary, although each can be seen to have evolved a motivated form–function correlation. If we now add to the account the idea that interlocutors tend to adopt precedents, we can account at least for some differences between languages: it so happened that a certain motivated pattern was first to gain salience rather than another in some language but not in another, and this is why conventionalization took this shape rather than that shape. Following Traugott and Dasher (2002: 35) this is a reasonable explanation for the difference between English and German 'while' mentioned in section 5.3.2.

Next, note the following examples from English, Spanish, and Hebrew:

(26) a.   English: Rickie: .. well (*the) **my** (*the) **name** is Regina,   (SBC: 008)

   b.   Spanish: ***mi** libro*   ***el mi** libro*   ***mi el** libro*
               my book   the my book   my the book
                                                               (Haspelmath, 1999a: ex. 2)

   c.   Hebrew: S: naxon   mar   marvani   (*ha=)**shim-xa**
               S: right,   Mr.   Marvani   (*the=)name-2sg
               'Right, Mr. Marvani is your name?'   (Lotan 1990: 2)

Even though Rickie's name (26a), the book (26b), and Marvani's name (26c) are all identifiable, specific entities, the NPs referring to them cannot be modified by a definite article in English, Spanish, and Hebrew. This complementary distribution between the possessive and the definite markers repeats itself in many languages (see Haspelmath, 1999a; Lyons, 1999). Haspelmath explains this restriction by reference to economy (akin to the I-Principle). Since, overwhelmingly, possessed NPs are understood as definite (between 94 and 96 percent of possessive NPs in English, Italian, and Greek in the data he cites), no definiteness marking is necessary. It is superfluous to explicitly code (by a definite article) what is anyway "freely" inferred (definiteness).

Given economy, no variability between languages is expected. Provided that the definiteness interpretation is a default interpretation of possessed NPs, any language which demonstrates this default interpretation is expected to follow the same pattern. This is not the case, however. In some languages the occurrence of the definite article with the possessive is optional (Brazilian Portuguese), and in others it is actually obligatory. Some languages have more than one way of expressing possession, and these different expressions may pattern differently. Note the following (and Bernard Comrie (p.c.) notes that Spanish too has *el libro mío* 'the book mine,' 'my book'):

(27)   **ha=bat**   **sheli**   ve=**ha=xatan**   **sheli**   lamdu   sinit.
               the=daughter   my   and=the=son-in-law   my   studied:PL   Chinese
               'My daughter and my son-in-law studied Chinese.'   (Lotan 1990: 17)

Whereas the Hebrew possessive pattern in (26c) cannot cooccur with the definite article, the pattern in (27) obligatorily does if the possessed NP is definite. Why doesn't the anti-redundancy force, appealed to above, apply here to preclude the unnecessary definite article? This cooccurrence of the definite marker with the possessive is observed in Italian, Modern Greek, Basque, and Samoan, for example, according to Haspelmath (1999a).[46] Haspelmath therefore addresses the question of why economy (=anti-redundancy) does not always apply.

The answer he supplies is diachronically motivated. Haspelmath argues that languages where the (specific) possessive construction had evolved before the definite article did demonstrate the economic/blocking effect. But languages in which the definite article had been in use before the development of the (specific) possessive construction do not demonstrate this restriction. The reason is that the spread of the definite article to nominals which are semantically definite was gradual. Where possessive marking preceded definite marking, possessive NPs were skipped in this process of definiteness spreading, for there was no reason to explicitly code their definiteness, which, as we saw above, was inferred in the majority of the cases anyway. However, in the other chronological development, where the definite article preceded the development of the possessive construction, the definite article was well established, and speakers did not stop using it once they added on a possessive construction, even though the former was equally redundant in this case. In other words, the "newcomer" may be blocked by redundancy, but not the entrenched form (note that unlike the newly introduced definiteness marker, a newly introduced possessive is not informationally redundant). Indeed, in Hebrew, for example, the inflected possessive in (26c) preceded the development of the definite marker, whereas the initiation of the analytic possessive construction in (27) followed the rise of the definite marker. Once the language was set in its way regarding definiteness, the possessive form was added on, despite the redundancy. Set precedents tend to persevere, even in the absence of a communicative rationale. Once a privileged discourse pattern has been established, it is so salient for interlocutors that they tend not to abandon it.

Next, note that closely following precedent discourse profiles does not only create privileged cooccurrences for messages that could just as easily have been conveyed differently, potentially leading to their conventionalization. It may also trigger semantic change, which is then not necessarily motivated by speakers' communicative goals. A word's meaning and its discourse pattern are intimately related, even if not in a one-to-one association. This is especially clear in the case of polysemous words (Sinclair, 1991), see e.g. Sinclair's analysis of *yield*. Firth's (1957: 11) "You shall know a word by the company it keeps" can be taken to mean not only that words naturally occur in contexts compatible with their meanings, which is why "the company" can **testify** to the meaning of the word (this is the motivated way to create a pattern). In addition,

---

[46] Note that the formal solution proposed for this patterning is untenable. Haspelmath provides counterexamples to the proposal that prenominal possessives preclude the definite article but postnominal possessives do not because only in the former is the slot where the definite marker would occur already occupied (by the possessor).

words may actually accrue new meanings from their contexts, even in the absence of speaker intention, in which case "the company" **initiates** a meaning change, brought about by entrenchment of meanings not necessarily even intended by the speaker, just because of adjacency. In other words, in some cases, all the speaker actually does is be conservative/idiomatic, namely maintain the same restricted distribution (discourse profile) for linguistic expressions as others do. This may in turn create distinct patterns (even for synonyms). And a distinction in meaning between them may come later, as a derivative of the use, through abstraction from distribution.

Abstraction (even if not conscious) must be a precondition to grammaticization. Not only children engage in abstracting generalizations (see Akhtar, 1998; Tomasello, 2003a). Adults do it too (see Aronoff, 1976; Clark and Clark, 1979); see e.g. Deutscher (2005: 175–176) regarding the creation of English *grot* on the basis of *grotty* by analogy with pairs such as *blood–bloody*. Thus, different niches we tend to carve out for words, using frozen, or more often semi-frozen combinations, may have an effect on their semantics. Anecdotal evidence for the constant pattern generation adults are engaged in is provided by two mistaken (conscious) generalizations from salient discourse patterns. One is the suggestion that Hebrew *raayato*, a formal variant for *ishto* 'his wife,' is restricted to VIPs' wives (proposed on a radio program in the late 1970s – Alexander Grosu, p.c.), but incorrect in fact. Although *raayato* is restricted to formal contexts, where VIPs' are often discussed, *raayato* is not (yet?) thus restricted. The other one is a (failed) attempt (by kindergarten teachers in the 1970s) to distinguish between Hebrew *ec* and *ilan*, both meaning 'tree.' The idea was that *ilan* is specifically a 'young tree,' no doubt because *ilan* is mostly associated with a certain holiday when Israeli children plant young trees. We are constantly driven to extract generalizations from (discourse) patterns (see the experiments described in Goldberg, 2006: 4.4, 4.5). As Deutscher (2005) suggests, we are forever craving for order.

On the basis of Google searches, Cohen (2005) notes that *prohibit* and *forbid* have quite different distributions: there are 26.5 *prohibits smoking* occurrences for each occurrence of *forbids smoking*. However there are 19.4 occurrences of *forbidden sex* for each occurrence of *prohibited sex*. Now, it seems that *prohibit* means 'disallow by formal power,' whereas *forbid* means 'disallow by moralistic justification.' But then, the question is, is it the different meanings that led to the different distributions? In which case the different discourse profiles are motivated. Or is it the other way round, namely, speakers first adhered to the same contexts the verbs were encountered by them, whereby for the most part *smoking* cooccurred with *prohibit* and *sex* with *forbid*, and only then, due to the moralistic undertones in one and the legal restrictions in the other, a generalization was derived?[47] The latter interpretation receives support from the fact that the same pair of words have different, but still distinct distributions in spoken English. There were 13 *forbid* occurrences in LSAC + SBC. In 12 of them God (or Heaven)

---

[47] As Labov (1994: 580) emphasizes, even fish and ducks can replicate an observed pattern by performing probability matching. Humans do it too, and this process is in fact blind to communicative needs according to Labov. At least sometimes, then, there is no particular functional

is the subject of the verb in the idiomatic expression *God forbid*. *Prohibit* only occurred 3 times, all in formal, legal contexts.

Here's a similar example, which can shed light on the process which may be responsible for creating meaning differences out of privileged distributional cooccurrences. Hebrew has a variety of synonyms for 'gift,' *shai* and *matana* among them. They are listed as synonyms in current dictionaries, but the first is a gift in formal circumstances (an institutional gift), whereas the second is personal (between individuals). The Biblical concordance (Mandelkern, 1937) revealed only 3 occurrences of *shai*, all of them gifts to God. *Matana*, on the other hand, occurred 15 times, 9 of which concern gifts to regular people, 4 to God and 1 to a priest (1 was not clear). Since *matana* is biased but not absolutely restricted to personal gifts, it's quite possible that rather than start out with a meaning distinction between the two words, we can hypothesize that because we tend to be conservative and use words in the same contexts we heard them in, the first stage is enhancing the skewing in the use of *matana*. Then, because we automatically (subconsciously) generalize from patterns of use, a new prototypical use of *matana* may have been extracted, different from *shai*. Speakers may have concluded that *shai* specializes for institutionalized gifts and *matana* specializes for personal gifts. Entrenchment may have then created the semantic differentiation between these two originally synonymous words. If this is the case, then a low-level mechanism (following privileged patterns) may bring about a higher-level semantic change, regardless of communicative goals.

An alternative but similar explanation would hypothesize that the specialization of contexts was triggered by relegating *shai* to formal registers and *matana* to everyday use (again by conservative maintenance of discourse pattern), and then a generalization about institutional versus personal gift was extracted, because formal contexts tend to discuss institutionalized gifts and informal contexts tend to discuss personal gifts. But note that this explanation too assumes that the distinct discourse pattern becomes salient prior to the new distinct meaning. A relevant case in point is the Hebrew *mi she* . . . literally 'who that . . .' appositive, which, when adjacent to a proper name, is restricted to prestigious position holders (Ariel, 1983), a restriction which does not apply to other appositives:

(28)   anastas mikoyan,   **mi   she-** haya   nesi   brit hamoacot
        Anastas Mikoyan   who   that-was   the.president.of   the Soviet Union
        bein   ha-shanim   1964   le   1965,...   met   emesh   be-moskva.
        between   the-years   1964   to   1965 ...   died   last.night   in-Moscow
        'Anastas Mikoyan, who was the president of the Soviet Union between 1964
        and 1965, ... died in Moscow last night.'   (*Maariv*, Oct. 22, 1978)

A reasonable evolutionary path for this construction is the specialization of this appositive to journalistic style (it is restricted to this register), where famous

motivation behind this step, and this is why many collocations are quite language-specific (and why variability may last very long – Labov, 1994: 583).

personalities are often discussed. A conservative tendency will maintain the same context for the appositive even if its semantics allows for other contexts as well. Eventually, a salient discourse pattern must have emerged, where the prototypical use of *mi she* ... became associated with VIPs. A reanalysis may then be performed, leading to an absolute restriction, as is the case today. Note that the restriction to VIPs only applies to the appositive *mi she* ... construction, not to the free relative *mi she* ..., where the referent is not necessarily a VIP. This testifies again to how conservative (i.e. local) our generalizations may be, whereby the restriction applies only to one sub-construction *mi she* ... participates in.

Finally, recall our discussion of *hide* and *conceal*, where only the former is also intransitive. It is because the language has two lexical items for roughly the same concept that it can develop different discourse profiles for each, which create and maintain different expectations regarding their themes.[48] Indeed, note the following facts about the distributions of these two verbs: 48 of the first 50 occurrences of *conceal* on the web (LSAC had only one example of *conceal*) were other-directed (i.e. conceal another, 96 percent); only 2/50 (4 percent) showed a self-directed action (conceal oneself). The findings for *hide* (based on SBC and LSAC) show it to be an intermediate case: 72/156 (46.2 percent) denote a self-directed activity, and 84/156 (53.8 percent) show an other-directed activity. It seems then that despite the potentially single cognitive concept behind the two verbs, they are not similarly used in **discourse** for self- versus other-directed activities. Given these discourse findings, we can better understand why intransitive *conceal* is impossible (compare *I hid* with **I concealed*). Grammaticization (the fact that *conceal* but not *hide* is only a transitive verb, which then **requires** a reflexive pronoun for depicting a self-directed situation) follows the salient discourse patterns of the two verbs. And a functional differentiation between the two verbs is not a necessary prerequisite for their differential discourse profiles.

5.3.4 A possible mechanism for crossing the grammar/pragmatics divide

Now, if, as argued at length in part I, there is a sharp dividing line between encoded and inferred meanings, and in general between the grammatical and the extragrammatical, how can the robust findings supporting the emergence of grammar out of discoursal use be compatible with a grammar/pragmatics divide? While a grammatical/extragrammatical division of labor can and should be drawn, this dividing line is historically often only gradually arrived at. Potentially, any grammar/extragrammatical borderline can be crossed. Indeed, at least for a certain period of time, the borderline between the grammatical and extragrammatical status of the new meaning of (computer) *mouse* was probably

---

[48] It is not surprising, then, that Smith (2004) finds that different languages, or even the same language in different periods, treat the "same" verbs differently regarding self- versus other-directedness.

not sharp. But the fact that some interpretations (a minority) are in between inferential and grammatical, a status they may maintain for long periods even, does not mean that we routinely do not draw clear boundaries between codes and inferences, grammar and use in other cases (as we've seen in chapter 3 for *most*, for example). How can we understand these intermediate statuses, which are neither purely inferential nor purely conventional? In what way are they intermediate?

As we have seen, grammaticization often occurs when speakers try to conform to their grammar. In fact, grammaticization of pragmatic/semantic functions can be seen as a rather mechanistic and automatic process (see Bybee *et al.*, 1994; Labov, 1990, 1994). This automaticity may explain why languages sometimes form grammatical categories where functionally equivalent categories already exist in the language, a seemingly dysfunctional step (see Ariel, 1998b; Heine, 1994b: 282 and references therein; Lord, 1976), or worse even, why grammatical changes sometimes "defeat themselves" (see section 4.5).

(High) salience has a key role to play here. A higher salience of the use of some form with some interpretation – a salient discourse pattern – leads to stronger connections between the form and its interpretation. Once there's an automatic and **necessary** triggering of a certain interpretation for a certain form we have a change in grammar. Grammaticization on this view is in many ways "more of the same" mechanism at work in synchronic production and interpretation, then: a weak connection gradually turning stronger and stronger until it becomes not only fast and automatic but also necessary and hard to cancel. Once entrenched, frequency has less of an effect on form–meaning connections.[49] But, as is expected on this view, frequency effects do not totally disappear once some meaning has been entrenched into a lexical meaning for some form. Numerous psycholinguistic experiments testify that frequency contributes to what Giora (1997 and onwards) has called the salience of some meaning for some form. High frequency contributes to higher salience, which, in turn, affects accessing rate (see Giora, 2003; Howes and Solomon, 1951; *inter alia*).[50] What is crucial for the grammar/pragmatics interface is that connections between forms and meanings constantly need to be maintained (see Croft, 2000; Langacker, 1987). Just as frequent form–function associations increase conventionality, form–function connections which are rarely used lead to weakened connections, which may

---

[49]   See Swinney (1979), Onifer and Swinney (1981), Seidenberg *et al.* (1982), and Giora (2003), who find that infrequent meanings of words are often accessed along with frequent ones.

[50]   In addition to a growing number of experimental results demonstrating that frequency is something we pay attention to even for grammaticized items (see MacDonald, 1999 for arguments and references) the phenomenon is also attested to by numerous anecdotal examples. At a linguistics colloquium (Tel Aviv University, Dec. 13, 2001) CK, a professor commenting on the speaker's lecture, used the idiom *you can have your cake and eat it too*. He then hastened to comment on his use of the idiom, "This seems to be my favorite phrase today. I've used it in class today." The speaker obviously felt that he "violated" the expected (low) frequency of the idiom. Similarly, in response to my using 'Anglo-Saxon' (in Hebrew) recently (Nov. 28, 2004), my daughter commented that it was the third time someone used that word with her that day.

ultimately be neutralized, at which point a (semantic) meaning or function has been lost.

Given this picture, the most accommodating models for understanding the intimate connection between synchrony and diachrony, performance and competence, and pragmatics becoming grammar are neural networking and statistical models, such as Parallel Distributed Processing models (McClelland and Rumelhart, 1986),[51] and exemplar-based and probabilistic models of grammar (Bod, 1998, 2003b; Bresnan, 2006; Bresnan *et al.*, 2007). According to Bod (2003a), "probabilities permeate the linguistic system." And Gahl and Garnsey (2004) argue that probabilities actually form part and parcel of grammar. If we view meanings as connected to forms via neural signals firing between memory units (or, alternatively, as related to each other with a certain statistical probability), and we assume that the connections between them differ in excitation strengths (probabilities), we can account both for extreme and for borderline cases. A sharp dividing line distinguishes between entrenched, automatic, fast (very strong, high-probability) grammatical forms/function associations, and nonentrenched, nonautomatic, time-consuming interpretations, generated in ad hoc cases due to contextual support triggering certain inferences. The latter are characteristic of extragrammatically derived interpretations, where neural/statistical connections are weak. A high frequency of the employment of such inferences can, however, render an originally extragrammatical/slow connection between some form and some interpretation gradually stronger, relatively more and more entrenched and ultimately grammatical (uncancelable). Similarly, a high frequency of two adjacent forms may lead to their chunking as one unit, so that accessing one triggers the accessing of the other. Borderline cases are then seen as ones with intermediate strength/probability connection. They may show a very high frequency, but the interpretations are still cancelable (the hallmark of pragmatic inferences).

The advantage of these models is that they are compatible with current findings regarding grammar. They allow us to distinguish grammatical conventions from pragmatic inferences on the one hand: networks and probability models can operate categorically (see Elman, 2001; Pierrehumbert, 2003; and see Wedel, 2004 for a simulation of pattern formation). On the other hand, such models can accommodate intermediate cases and, more generally, the fact that grammar emerges by very small, usually unfelt increments, so there are no abrupt leaps from inference to code, from nonconstruction to construction (see Zuraw, 2003). Even if these current models turn out to be wrong, the ultimate model will have to account for a continuum of entrenchment. We must assume some representation of frequency of use, because our linguistic behavior demonstrates frequency effects. "The language-processing system tracks, records, and exploits frequencies of various kinds of events" (Bod *et al.*, 2003a: 3).

---

[51] See MacWhinney (2000, 2001) for other models.

At the same time, such a view does not commit us to an assumption that grammar is merely a collection of statistically strong or fast form–function associations. As we have seen in section 2.3, there can be a qualitative difference between a very strong neural/statistical form–function association and grammatical convention (see also Moore and Polinsky, 2003 about the compatibility rather than reducibility of grammar to frequent discoursal patterns). Thus, the same strong (high-probability) form–function correlation may be grammatical, or it may be statistical, lacking grammatical status. Preferred Argument Structure (PAS) correlations (Du Bois, 1987, 2003a and see 2003b: 2.3.3) are statistically extremely high, not so different from grammatical conventions. Still, they maintain quite a different cognitive status. There is a difference between violating even a very strong discourse tendency ("no harm done") and violating a grammatical convention (if they are aware of it, speakers would classify it as an error). Although discourse patterns may be highly salient, and hence potential grammaticization paths, they differ from grammatical conventions.[52] Furthermore, as we saw above, Du Bois (1987) finds that ergative languages (Sakapultek) manifest accusative discourse patterns, and accusative languages (English) equally manifest the ergative discourse pattern. Nonetheless, their grammars are quite different. There is then a difference between discourse profiles (nongrammatical) and discourse functions (grammatical). Grammatical conventions are automatic and uncancelable; salient discourse patterns may be as automatic, but they are still cancelable.

An intriguing experiment by Clausner et al. (1996) clearly brings out the difference between high frequency and lexicalization. Clausner et al. asked native speakers of Chinese to determine as fast as possible whether the combination of a pair of words was meaningful. Some of the combinations were compounds bearing a noncompositional meaning (e.g. 'white vegetable' = 'cabbage'), others were phrases interpreted compositionally (e.g. 'white paint'), and yet others were nonsense (e.g. 'loyal foot'). The compounds and the compositional phrases were matched for frequency, not only for each element by itself (e.g. 'vegetable' with 'paint'), but also for the cooccurrence of the pair (e.g. 'white paint' and 'white vegetable'). Now, frequency is certainly relevant for such a task: low-frequency combinations took longer to respond to in both types of expressions. However, if frequency alone were responsible for entrenchment and lexicalization, there should not have been any difference between the two types of word combinations. This is not what Clausner et al. found. The compounds (e.g. 'white vegetable' = 'cabbage') were responded to faster and more accurately than the compositional phrases (e.g. 'white paint'), despite the equal frequency rates. Such findings suggest that although frequent nonlexicalized combinations too have some entrenched cognitive status (hence the difference between high- and

---

[52] Langacker (1987) defines entrenchment as the status whereby some linguistic pattern is salient and relatively easily recognized by hearers. As far as I can tell, he does not attempt to draw the grammatical–discoursal distinction here drawn (based on conventionality).

low-frequency compositional phrases), conventionalization is not reducible to high frequency. There is more to grammar than a set of salient discourse patterns.

Summing up, section 5.3 has been devoted to the importance of the salient discourse pattern in the creation of grammar out of extralinguistic pressures. Salient discourse patterns probably most often emerge out of recurrent choices interlocutors make in order to meet their local communicative goals, which accounts for the fact that grammar is as functionally motivated as it is. But there are other extralinguistic incentives which drive speakers to create and maintain privileged discoursal patterns (conservatism, sensitivity to priming, adoption of precedent strategies, as well as abstraction of generalizations). A paradoxical result from our **conservative** following in the footsteps of others is the initiation of **new** grammatical conventions. Thus, a slight discoursal preference for a certain construction (e.g. the ditransitive) for some verb may eventually lead via conservatism to the obligatory (and innovative) occurrence of that verb in that construction only. Or a salient pattern of cooccurrence of certain linguistic items may lead to a change in their meaning due to contextual influence. Indeed, innovating our grammar is very often the result of our conservatism, rather than our innovativeness. But the main idea is that although discourse patterns are often created by recurrent strategies successfully employed in the service of our communicative intentions, conventionalization itself seems oblivious to the motivation behind the salient discourse pattern. Conventionalization, which stipulates an association either between forms or between forms and functions, may emerge for any salient discourse pattern. The fact that the pattern may only reflect our conservative tendencies, or the effect of high frequency on the production of forms, rather than an inherent motivation, is not necessarily relevant.[53]

Going back to our initial question at the outset of chapter 5, namely, what is it that is responsible for grammatical change, and ultimately for grammar? We have seen that while the way the world is is reflected in grammar, it's not raw objective facts that we find traces of in language. The first filter we considered was human cognition. Instead of reality, what we can expect to see mirrored in language is our conception of the world. But even these conceptions don't show up in language as is. Not all raw facts that we can conceive of affect us and our grammar in the same way. Our cultural biases intervene, rendering some conceptions more salient or relevant to us, relegating to oblivion many others. And even that is not all. We're all social creatures as well. Our social norms play a role in shaping our grammar too. They dictate that we do not discuss certain topics, even if they are "real," cognized, and culturally central (e.g. sex). Suppose, then, that our message has passed all of these checkpoints. It's made it into a potential discourse message. The road to grammar is still not obstacle-free.

Once we are in the realm of discourse, a whole new set of factors come into play. Some of them compete with each other, as well as with the above factors over

---

[53] But see Ariel (2007c) where I discuss discourse profiles which are less likely to undergo grammaticization.

the limited good here, the speaker's utterance. Production has to be factored in. Our short-term memory affects our processing abilities, which are said to mold grammar for optimal processing. In addition, we have to be cooperative speakers, as Grice taught us. We should do our best to facilitate communication, or we might not be listened to. We have to have a good discoursal reason to utter our messages (it's not enough that they represent real concepts, culturally and socially accep-table, etc.). They have to be discourse appropriate, that is, relevant, interesting, etc. In short, various extralinguistic factors can propose, but it is discourse which disposes. Whereas researchers have rightly pointed to connections between grammar and cognition/culture, etc., there is no direct link between any of these extralinguistic factors and grammar. Discourse is where the speaker juggles all of these factors. And more.

Discourse doesn't start from scratch. First, a fundamental characteristic of human languages is that they are underdeterminate (Carston, 2002a; Clark, 1996; Sperber and Wilson, 1986/1995; Traugott and Dasher, 2002). They trade on a pervasive mechanism of inference generation to supplement the code they provide, a mechanism enabled by our higher cognitive capacities (accounted for by inferential pragmatic theories). This means that not every interpretation we intend to convey must be expressed explicitly. It's been widely acknowledged, ever since Grice (1975), that pragmatic implicatures can make their way into grammar. In fact, in view of the distinction between implicatures and explicated pragmatic inferences, we should extend Grice's suggestion to any pragmatic inference, not just conversational implicatures (see chapter 7). In addition, fea-tures of the specific grammar also play a role. Each language has its own grammar, which must be complied with by each utterance. This is partly the reason why different languages develop differently (we are here concerned only with gram-maticization, not with the ultimate, initial evolution of human language). What syntactic constructions are available, what word orders the syntax dictates or allows, what lexical items one can choose from, etc., matter. Hence, grammar too opens up some (but not other) new possibilities for its future shape. Using all of these creates discourse patterns, and it is these patterns, provided they are salient to speakers, which serve as raw material for the future grammar. Only salient, often frequent, discourse patterns may become entrenched. Messages and their forms can then impact grammar only by fitting into some salient discourse profile.

So, what does it take for a new grammatical convention to emerge? Ultimately, just one of these factors matters, the salient discourse pattern, which potentially develops into a new grammatical convention. But of course, the attested salient discourse patterns are the complex product of any and all of the external factors we discussed. Some of these form a filtering chain (e.g. our subjective cognition colors our perception of reality, it is later filtered by our cultural and social norms, which are then filtered by relevance considerations pertaining to the immediate discourse). Other factors compete with each other (e.g. encoding of pure semantic or cognitive categories versus encoding of information status for nouns, for example), conforming to current discourse profiles versus innovating. The grand picture is then that very many factors, including many extralinguistic ones, propose paths of grammaticization, but only the salient discourse pattern, which depends on the aggregate of speakers' use, can dispose.

This is why grammar is extralinguistically motivated to a significant extent, although no teleology need be assumed. Speakers don't develop a motivated grammar as such. They use their grammar for their local communicative goals as best they can. At the same time, they can't but also behave (linguistically) in accordance with their general cognitive abilities, propensities and limitations, as well as their production practices. The aggregate of all these factors results in a huge web of discoursal patterns, some of them more salient than others. Only a small subset of the salient discourse patterns undergoes conventionalization. Although salient discourse patterns are a product of very many extralinguistic factors, there is no direct link between any of the extralinguistic forces and grammar. Salient discourse patterns must always mediate. The grammar/pragmatics interface shows an abundance of boundary crossings. But the mechanism responsible for such changes in the cognitive status of linguistic expressions is only indirectly motivated by our conceptions, culture, and communicative functions.

Finally, note that whereas we have here outlined potential paths for some salient nonconventional language pattern to become grammatical, no account was offered as to why or which salient discourse patterns actually do turn grammatical (e.g. the use of reflexive pronouns – see chapter 6), and which do not (e.g. Preferred Argument Structure constraints – see section 2.3). Constituting a salient discourse pattern is only a necessary condition for conventionalization. It's not a sufficient condition. Indeed, Romaine (1999) describes a grammaticization process which got aborted. What chapter 5 shows is that, at best, our theory can lead the grammar horse to the extralinguistic water, but it cannot make it drink. In chapter 6 we turn to a detailed examination of the grammaticization of one form in English – reflexive forms. The extralinguistically motivated grammaticizations briefly surveyed here, supported by the case more extensively studied in the next chapter, should hopefully convince the reader that possibly all grammatical codes ultimately derived from such extralinguistic patterns. Distinct cognitive statuses for grammar and pragmatics do not preclude the evolution of the grammatical out of the extragrammatical, and the evolution of grammar out of discourse patterns does not preclude a dichotomous division of labor between the two. We should bear in mind that at any point in time, the great majority of the cases where speakers follow salient discourse patterns leaves the linguistic/extralinguistc (and specifically, grammar/pragmatics) divide in place. Only a minority of the vast number of discourse patterns is actually in the process of crossing the extragrammatical/grammatical divide, and at least some such intermediate stages (recall *foot of*) can be analyzed as having as rigid a grammar/pragmatics divide as any expression.

6   The rise (and potential fall) of reflexive pronouns

Keenan (2003) compares the history of reflexive pronouns to the history of the Eiffel Tower. Built for an international fair towards the end of the nineteenth century, the plan was to destroy the building once the fair was over. However, it just so happened that radio became popular in those days, and the Eiffel Tower was found useful for housing a radio antenna. It is its function in radio transmission, a totally new and unrelated function, which is (partly) responsible for the survival of the building. The story of reflexive pronouns is the story of a construction evolved for the encoding of emphatic reference, which now serves for quite different functions. We discuss this history firstly in order to exemplify the theoretical points made in chapters 4 and 5.[1] In line with chapter 4, the process of conventionalization is argued to be motivated, although the ultimate conventions are not completely motivated. In line with chapter 5, we see how linguistic change is part and parcel of language use, how recurrent discourse patterns lie behind grammatical conventions. Next, given that reflexive pronouns were initiated by a pragmatic process, we need to determine whether reflexive pronouns are by now fully grammaticized. What is the grammar/pragmatics divide for the use and interpretation of reflexive pronouns if they are constantly evolving? The conclusion we will reach is that it is not just grammar, but pragmatics too, that governs the current distribution of reflexive pronouns. Neither one is sufficient by itself. In other words, despite the grammaticization process, pragmatics still plays a role in how we use reflexive pronouns.

Note that the approach here adopted is that of discourse analysis, rather than of historical linguistics per se. Our point is that by examining Modern English conversations we can see how salient discourse patterns may have been potential grammaticization paths in the past. Modern English can be used to explain the grammaticization process English underwent in the fifteenth century, because the discourse patterns which drove the grammar then are still with us now.[2] The relevant pragmatic motivation here is the inference that entities we tend to refer to as engaged with each other in some event which is encoded within a linguistic

---

[1] I thank Tanya Reinhart, Makoto Shimizu, Tal Siloni, and Sandra A. Thompson for comments on various sections of chapter 6.

[2] Throughout this chapter, pragmatically skewed synchronic statistics are presented, in order to motivate not just potential future grammaticizations, but also long-completed grammaticizations. This is in line with Lass' (1997: 26) uniformitarian assumption, according to which "the general distribution of likelihood in a given domain was always the same in the past as it is now."

clause tend to be distinct. This interpretation must have been a recurrent pragmatic inference in the past, just as it is in the present. If so, speakers were prompted to indicate cases where this inference was not appropriate. It is this indication that initiated the grammaticization of what are now known as reflexive pronouns.

Levinson (1991, 2000b) suggests that the English grammatical pattern of anaphora responsible for the distribution of personal and reflexive pronouns, as we know it today, is actually a (slightly imperfect) freezing of such pragmatic tendencies.[3] Reflexive pronouns have evolved in an attempt to indicate a marked coreference relationship with a central antecedent within the clause. The analysis presented below is based on Levinson (1991, 2000b), Comrie (1998), König and Siemund (2000), Haspelmath (2004c) and others.[4] Note that, as Levinson rightly points out, the first remarkable fact about reflexive pronouns is that their distribution, considered a core part of universal (supposedly innate) grammar, is a historical product, one which is not in fact shared by all languages, and certainly not to the same extent.

We will mainly examine the English case, where reflexive pronouns have reached a rather grammatical phase. However, the point is that current English reflects both vestiges of the initial pragmatic stages, which set the whole process in motion, and preliminary steps towards newer functions. We end by pointing to the potential loss of the original markedness function of reflexive pronouns, and with it the grammatical conventions associated with the reflexive pronouns. This is what Hopper (1991) termed layering. The idea is that earlier grammaticizations do not preclude newer ones, and newer ones do not always cancel out old ones. Instead, the language simultaneously displays various grammaticization layers which coexist with each other, even when they potentially clash (see also Romaine, 1999).[5]

We shall see older patterns next to newer ones (e.g. reflexive pronouns as emphatic adjuncts, as marked coreferential NPs). Each grammaticized phase is at once the end-product of grammaticization, as well as a potential starting point for the next stage on the grammaticization path. Indeed, while English reflexive pronouns are to a large extent anaphors obeying Binding Conditions currently, they are gradually taking on a new grammatical function, that of detransitivizing (see Ariel, 2006a). This again is not too different from the case of the Eiffel Tower, which now has an additional, new function, again quite unrelated to its function in radio transmission: the tower currently symbolizes France, and attracts hordes of tourists to Paris every year.

---

[3] See also Ariel (1985: 115, 1987, 1990: chapter 5).

[4] In fact, Haspelmath (2004c) and this chapter were written more or less at the same time without either knowing about the other.

[5] Hopper discusses a variety of forms which arose in different language phases, simultaneously serving one and the same grammatical function (e.g. past-tense forms in English). We here focus on a parallel phenomenon, where one form (reflexives) currently signals a variety of functions, which evolved at different times.

We begin by introducing a structural synchronic account of reflexives in section 6.1, which we motivate pragmatically in section 6.2. Section 6.3 is then devoted to the question whether we need both a structural and a pragmatic account for reflexive pronouns. We end with the possibility that reflexive pronouns may lose their evolved pragmatic (markedness) function (section 6.4).

6.1   A structural account of reflexive pronouns

Let us start by presenting English reflexives as they are analyzed in structural terms. Reinhart and Reuland (1993) offer a reformulation of the original, highly hierarchical Binding Conditions A and B. Both conditions now pertain to reflexivity, and the crucial domain for reflexivity is taken to be the predicate and its arguments, rather than the minimal syntactic domain (NP or S): a coreferential co-argument must be a reflexive.[6] We will here simplify Reinhart and Reuland's proposal as follows:

(1)   Condition A: A reflexive-marked predicate (e.g. if one of its arguments is a reflexive pronoun) must be reflexive (i.e. two of its arguments must be co-indexed).

Condition A would rule out the following example if *she* and *herself* were not co-indexed:

(2)   But **she** wasn't blaming **herself** or anything?   (LSAC)

Since the direct object here is a reflexive pronoun, its predicate (*blame*) is reflexive-marked. Hence, it must co-index two co-arguments (*she* and *herself*). This is similar to the original Condition A, which ensured that anaphors be bound within a minimal governing category, except that now reflexives must be "bound" only if they occur in argument positions. This is why the reformulated Condition A does not rule out nonbound logophoric reflexives: these do not occur in argument positions. If so, they don't reflexive-mark any predicate, which means that no co-indexation with a co-argument is required for the acceptability of the reflexive pronoun:

(3)   JIM: and I wanted him to talk with Matt,
                (H) Vivian,
                myself,
                . . and,
                . . sometime during the day to the two of you.   (SBC: 014)

Myself in (3) is not (by itself) a co-argument of *talk* (*Vivian, myself and . . . the two of you* is). Hence, *talk* is not reflexive-marked, and is not required to have two co-indexed arguments (indeed, it doesn't).

---

[6] The fact that Binding Conditions are now both defined over reflexivity is compatible with the view that it is the development and grammaticization of reflexive pronouns which created the grammaticization of pronouns as disjoint from their clause mate NPs, as a by-product, in effect (see Levinson, 2000b).

Condition B also concerns reflexivity, and seems to complement Condition A:

(4)   Condition B: A reflexive predicate (i.e. where two of its co-arguments are
           co-indexed) must be reflexive-marked (e.g. by a reflexive pronoun).

This condition ensures that the following will be ruled out should the two pronouns
be co-indexed:

(5)   DANNY: .. (H) **he** buried **him**,   (SBC: 030)

Were *he* and *him* to be co-indexed in (5), *buried* would be a reflexive predicate,
which then requires reflexive marking according to Condition B. Since there is no
reflexive pronoun here, this derivation would be ruled out, which is exactly right.
This is of course reminiscent of the original Condition B, which specified that a
pronoun (*him* in (5)) must be free (i.e. not co-indexed with an antecedent within
some minimal domain). But note that it now only needs to be "free" from its
co-arguments, rather than from all the arguments in the sentence.[7]

To see the different predictions made by the two versions of the Binding
Conditions, consider (6), where we certainly interpret *Tom* and *him* as disjoint:

(6)   **Tom** works with **him**, see?   (LSAC)

According to the original Binding Conditions, since the pronoun must be free in
the S domain (in this case), it cannot be co-indexed with *Tom*. This seems to be the
correct result for this sentence. The revised Condition B, however, does not rule
out co-indexation here, because the two NPs are not co-arguments. Hence,
coreference is allowed, which seems to sharply contrast with our interpretation.
Note, however, that Reinhart and Reuland can here rely on the pragmatic tendency
outlined in section 6.1.1 below, namely, addressees' presumption that co-participants in an event are normally distinct entities. Coreference between *Tom* and *him*
would then be pragmatically ruled out.[8] Reliance on pragmatic factors, on the
other hand, cannot rescue the original Binding Conditions by providing an
account for the following findings for *near* objects. A Web Corp search showed
a majority of reflexive forms here. When we remove from consideration all the
high-rank antecedents of *himself* (a vestige of the old use of reflexives – see
below), there's an equal number of reflexive and nonreflexive forms (12 vs. 13
respectively), some of them virtual minimal pairs, as in:

(7) a.   He$_i$ wouldn't let anyone **near himself**$_i$ (Web Corp)
    b.   He$_i$ won't let anyone **near him**$_i$ (Web Corp)

Such findings are impossible to reconcile with the original Binding Conditions,
where there must be complementary distribution between pronouns and

---

[7] The new formulation therefore correctly predicts that outside a single predicate, pronouns and
reflexives are not in complementary distribution.
[8] *I'm having it* ((dinner – MA)) **with myself** (LSAC), as well as *I want to talk about how director
works* **with himself. Or herself** (direct.vtheatre.net/intro.html – 63k) show that it's not impossible
to have anaphora here. It's just very marked.

reflexives. (7a) and (7b) cannot both be grammatical. If the whole S is here the relevant domain, then (7a) is predicted to be grammatical, but (7b) should not be. If the relevant domain is smaller (a small clause containing *anybody near him/himself*), then (7b) is predicted to be grammatical, but (a) should not be.[9] Since pragmatics cannot resurrect options precluded by the grammar, there is no way that the classical Binding Conditions can handle the free variation in (7). But it is compatible with Reinhart and Reuland's analysis, which leaves open the choice of either form in nonargument positions. Let us now try to motivate such conventions pragmatically.

6.1.1   Motivating the structural pattern

According to the grammaticization approach to language here advocated, what lies behind the Binding Conditions is a pattern of expectations, based on our assumptions about discourse entities. It is a nonlinguistic pattern which sets our story in motion. Simply put, interlocutors tend to describe activities/situations in which a participant engages in some activity with other participants, rather than with herself. We should reiterate that such events/states are the ones that human beings actively choose to talk about, regardless of whether this is true of reality. One of the reasons why multi-argument verbs usually involve distinct discourse entities is that we have a strong tendency to code activities we routinely perform on ourselves by what is traditionally termed middle voice (indicating a rather low degree of transitivity) or intransitive verbs, where there is a low degree of elaboration of events, as Kemmer (1993) suggests.[10] We thus downgrade the fact that we are actually acting upon ourselves. This is a clear speaker choice not really dictated by reality (cf. the alternatives in parentheses below):

(8) a.   I'll **shower** later.   (LSAC) (cf. I'll shower/wash myself later.)
   b.   I **ate** a little bit.   (LSAC) (cf. I fed myself a little bit.)
   c.   FRANK: you **put on** a jacket,
                                 (SBC: 019) (cf. you put on a jacket on yourself)

And note the following, where the same "objective reality" is alternatively described as a transitive activity involving an agent (*it*) and a patient (*the radio*) and as a middle (intransitive) activity involving one participant (*the radio*):

(9)   We didn't have it in sync and **it was burning up the radio. The radio would self destruct**.   (LSAC)

Are the intransitives in (8) conceptualized as a person acting upon herself? Does reality here pertain to two participant roles which happen to be realized by one discourse entity, or is it a truly single participant activity? The linguistic choice (of an intransitive) points to a one-participant conceptualization of the events, even

---

[9] Chomsky's (1981) attempt to argue that (7a) does not, but (7b) does, contain a small clause is ad hoc, and has also been argued against on syntactic and semantic grounds.

[10] Note that some linguists (e.g. Reinhart and Siloni, 2005) use middle in a much more restricted way. We here follow Kemmer (1993) in the traditional use of the term middle.

though we can rather easily take them to "objectively" involve an initiator (an agent) affecting an endpoint (a patient – this is Kemmer's 1993 terminology), which happen to be an identical entity (or part of the same entity – say, one's body, belly, shoulders respectively for (8a–c)). Profiling choices (choices pertaining to event elaboration, and especially to the number of distinct participant roles) follow speakers' choices, then. As argued in chapter 5, social conventions and rules of politeness may also intervene to prevent us from expressing things "as they really are" (in reality or on our mind).[11] This explains why many activities we do perform on the self are not ones we tend to talk about (e.g. *think/love ourselves*). The idea is then that regardless of how the world is, human discourse is such that most events referred to involve distinct entities. If so, interlocutors would tend to assume that this is the case, and where not clearly indicated by the speaker, they would pragmatically infer it.

Even though this generalization is extralinguistic, pragmatic tendencies often take a more defined, in fact, grammatical shape in due course. It is quite conceivable that the presumption of distinct participants got narrowed down to exactly the terms that Reinhart and Reuland use. In other words, from a generalization about co-participants in general to participants encoded by specific grammatical roles (co-arguments of a predicate). Indeed, many have proposed that co-arguments of a predicate tend to be disjoint in reference; see Faltz (1977/1985: 242/243), Farmer (1980, 1984), Harnish (1984), and Levinson (1991, 2000b) following them. It should not be surprising if we have firmer expectations (here, of disjointness) about co-arguments than about nonarguments. After all, co-arguments are those arguments which obligatorily (and hence frequently) cooccur with the predicate. They form a natural locus for grammaticization. Nonetheless, as we will see, repercussions for grammar are not necessarily limited to syntactically defined co-arguments (see Comrie, 1998 for different patterns of grammaticization cross-linguistically).

This discussion is restricted to the question of coreference/disjointness with the clause subject. Such (non)coreference is the most relevant issue for reflexives.[12] Let us start by examining whether it is reasonable for interlocutors to develop expectations regarding potential coreference/disjointness among participants mentioned within a clause.[13] As mentioned above, the claim is that we expect entities referred to within a clause to be distinct. Note the following findings for one conversation from SBC (006). Only cases where objects were coded by either a pronoun or a reflexive were examined, to see whether they were coreferential or disjoint in reference from the subject of the clause. Of course, had lexical NP objects been included, the findings would have been even more dramatic. Still, 101/134 of the pronominal objects (75.4 percent) were not coreferential with the

---

[11] Clark (1998) makes the same point.
[12] See Stirling and Huddleston (2002). Biber *et al.* (1999) find that subject coreference is by far the most frequent pattern for reflexives.
[13] The figures presented below pertain to event participants rather than specifically to co-arguments (the relevant count for Reinhart and Reuland), since the point about disjointness is broader.

subjects of their clauses. Most examples are then similar to the following. The relevant clause appears in square brackets (note that the subject sometimes only appears overtly in a separate clause). All the participants are here marked in bold, even though only the pronominal ones were included in the count:

(10) a.   ALINA: And Mom said,
                   .. n– **you**$_i$ know,
                   don't bring it up to Linda,
                   [don't tell **her**$_j$ about **Mike**$_k$].   (SBC: 006)
     b.   ALINA: [**she**$_i$ never calls **her**$_j$],   (SBC: 006)
     c.   ALINA: so **Liza and Antonio**$_{i+j}$ followed them over there,
                   to pick up Cassandra,
                   [and take **her**$_k$ for **a day**$_l$ in the **park**$_m$].   (SBC: 006)

Still, almost a quarter of the objects were coreferential with the subject. While 75.4 percent is a significant statistical skewing, it does not justify an automatic presumption of disjointness by inference. Indeed, we need to qualify the extra-linguistic expectation as stated so far. Not every discourse participant is equally presumed distinct. Clausal coreference in the above conversation is overwhel-mingly due to possessor NPs, as in (11):

(11)   ALINA: .. Would you move,
                 so **I** can come park **my** car.   (SBC: 006)

It turns out that of the 33 coreferential cases, 31 are possessors as in (11). We then conclude that the extralinguistic generalization concerns participants to the exclu-sion of possessors (which, of course, are not co-arguments). When we eliminate possessors from the count, 101/103 (98.1 percent) of the pronominal objects are disjoint in reference from their subjects in this conversation. Such a percentage certainly justifies a speakers' strategy to assume disjointness among (nonposses-sor) clause-mate arguments, even when pronouns are involved.

Here are some additional discourse patterns in support of the disjointness inference. In 562/589 cases of *with him/himself* in LSAC (96.6 percent), the object was disjoint in reference from the subject, as in (12):

(12) a.   [**I** just really disagree with **him**].   (LSAC)
     b.   [**Mr. <name>** didn't have the meeting with **him** last week].   (LSAC)

Similarly, *look/ed at* first person are virtually always disjoint cases (154/158, 97.5 percent). No doubt, once again, had lexical NPs been included, the percen-tages would have been even higher. Similarly high rates of disjointness between subjects and objects characterize the transitive occurrences of the following verbs in SBC and LSAC, where nonpronominal objects were also included in the count: *check out, blame, forgive, judge,* and *be okay with* (296/308, 96.1 percent). Finally, zeroing in on direct objects in a completely different text, from a com-pletely different era, there were absolutely no direct objects coreferential with their subjects in all of the book of Genesis in Hebrew (1,534 verses, with an estimated

4,500 clauses). The general picture is quite clear. Our utterances consist of clauses where nonpossessor arguments refer to distinct participants almost invariably. It's safe to assume that interlocutors would draw this interpretation as a pragmatic inference, then.

6.2   The grammaticization path of indicating marked coreference

The grammaticization path we here concentrate on shows how a referential form suitable for cases of marked coreference often leads to the creation of reflexive pronouns. Briefly, the combination of formal complexity (pointing to a marked interpretation) with a bias towards coreference (very often due to the use of certain possessed body parts) actually defines the essence of the grammaticized reflexive marker: indicating unexpected coreference.

6.2.1   Before grammaticization: indicating marked coreference with old means

We have thus far seen that in an overwhelming majority of the cases, arguments within the same clause (with the exception of possessors) are disjoint. But then, what should speakers do if it is the minority case that they want to talk about, where a participant engages in an activity with herself? Should we simply avoid it, as seems to be the case in Genesis (re direct objects)? It seems that speakers can find various ways to express reflexivity even without having a dedicated grammatical means for expressing it. As we emphasized in chapters 4 and 5, speakers often find ways to conform to the current grammar, using old forms for new functions, when they are engaging in what we later call grammaticization. Some (but not all) of these strategies may eventually lead to the creation of reflexive markers.

Some languages simply ignore the markedness issue, employing their old means, regular personal pronouns, for co-argument coreferential cases. The decision between coreferential vs. disjoint readings is then left to pragmatic inferencing. In such languages, we expect the majority of nonsubject pronouns to be interpreted as disjoint from the subjects of their clauses, but if coreference seems to be the speaker's intention, then it will be read in anyway (by inference, we may conjecture that such interpretations might take longer to process). Old English is an example of a language which lacked reflexive forms:[14]

(13)   swa hwa swa   eadmedaþ   **hine**
        whoever   humiliate-PRS **him**
        'Whoever humiliates him/himself.'   (from Faltz, 1977/1985: 19, ex. 53)

---

[14] Levinson (2000b: 304) discusses another solution to the problem: an antipassive construction, which can (but need not) be interpreted reflexively, is used in Guugu Yimithirr.

According to Keenan (2002, 2003), 80 percent of the locally bound anaphors in Old English were pronouns, rather than reflexives, and even in Middle English only a minority of these showed -*self* forms. However, most of these were nonarguments, mostly pleonastic pronouns (such as *The king went him to London*). Like Old English, Biblical Hebrew too lacked a reflexive form. Though rarely so, personal pronouns could be used for coreference of an object with the subject of its clause, as in:

(14) a.   va=yave   ota   **elav**   el   ha=teva.
          and=brought   ACC: it.F to.**him**   to   the=ark
          'And he₁ brought it to **himself**₁ to the ark.'   (Genesis 8: 10)

   b.   ad   egva   lo   asir   tumat-i   mi=**meni**.
         till   I.will.die not I.will.remove   integrity-my   from=me
         'Till I die I will not remove mine integrity from me.'   (Job 27: 5)

   c.   va=ir?u   shotrey   bney   israel   **otam** be=raʕ.
         and=saw.pl [the.officers.of the.children.of Israel]₁ **them**₁ in=evil
         'And the officers of the children of Israel did see that they were in evil case.'
                                                                       (Exodus 5: 19)

Another strategy which lets speakers use their old means to indicate coreference when disjointness is the norm is for speakers to tailor their utterances in such a way that the coreferential entity will be coded by an argument which is rather commonly interpreted coreferentially. They thus, in effect, turn a marked coreference relation into an unmarked one. As we have mentioned above, possessors are quite often coreferential with the subjects of their clauses. Out of 51 object possessor NPs in SBC: 006, 31 (61 percent) showed coreference with the subject of the clause. This ratio quite sharply contrasts with the very strong tendency towards disjointness among participants noted above for the same conversation (less than 2 percent coreferential arguments).[15] So, one can construct the predication in such a way that it would include a reference to a possessor in object position. (Heine and Kuteva, 2002 note that 'owner + pronoun' is a potential source for reflexive forms.) Possessors of inalienable possessions are possibly even more often interpreted as coreferential with the clause subject.[16] Out of 653 possessive pronoun + *head*/*heart*/*body* occurrences in LSAC, 417 (63.9 percent) were cases of possessors coreferential with their clausal subjects. Biblical Hebrew objective *libbo* 'his heart' and *nafsho*, 'his soul/life' are also mostly used coreferentially with their subject (68/91, 74.7 percent).

The following examples from Biblical Hebrew (15a–c), collected by Bendavid (1971: 880), illustrate the point about taking advantage of extant grammatical conventions. The writer here constructs the predication in such a way that reference is made to a possessor of an inalienable possession. This is how coreference is more easily conveyed, despite the lack of a reflexive marker. Note the parallel (later)

---

[15] This large discrepancy (31.3 times more coreference with possessors than with other arguments) justifies our previous decision to separate out possessors from other participants.
[16] Some of these expressions are even restricted to coreferential readings: *lose one's way/mind*, *hold one's breath* (see Farmer, 1980, 1984).

Mishnaic Hebrew examples (15a'–c') he quotes, where a conventional reflexive is already employed:

(15)   **Biblical Hebrew**   **Mishnaic Hebrew**

a.   manaʕ   **raglo**   me ...   a'. manaʕ   ʕacmo   mi=lelex ...
        prevented his:leg from ...   prevented himself from=to.go
        'Avoided going to . . .'   'Avoided going.'

b.   kissa   et   **besaro**   b'. kissa   et   **ʕacmo**
        covered ACC   his:flesh   covered ACC   himself
        'Covered himself'.

c.   haya shafel be=ʕenav   c'. roʔe ʕacmo   ke=ʔilu ...
        was   meek   in=his:eyes   sees himself as=if ...
        'Saw himself as meek.'   'Sees himself as . . .'

Now, of course, 'the leg'/'flesh'/'eyes' are used literally here. As Bendavid argues, however, the synonymous Mishnaic versions (15a'–c') suggest that the Biblical style is actually a strategy due to the lack of reflexive pronouns. Interestingly, although Japanese does have anaphoric expressions which are also equivalent to reflexive pronouns, Shimizu and Murata (2004) find that one translation equivalent of English reflexive pronouns is precisely such body parts (e.g. *brace myself* was translated literally as 'brace (my) heart,' *transforms itself* as 'change (its) body'[17]).

At this stage, where a possessed body part is used to overcome the lack of a reflexive form, there may be some ambiguity in interpreting the possessed body part, which can either be interpreted literally or as a reflexive (Heine, 1994a, as cited in Schladt, 2000). Here is a case in point:

(16)   wa=yyiqqaḥ ʔavraham$_i$ et   ʕacei   ha=ʕola   wa=yyasem ʕal yichaq$_j$
        and=took   Abraham ACC the.woods.of the=sacrifice and=put   on Isaac
        bno   wa=yyiqqaḥ be=yado$_i$ et   ha=esh
        his:son and=took   in=**his:hand** ACC the=fire
        'And Abraham took the wood for sacrifice and laid it upon Isaac his son; and he took the
        fire in his hand'   (Genesis 22: 6)

Is it the case that Abraham took the fire in his hand, or that Abraham himself took the fire (after all, how else can one hold anything)? Ælfric's translation of the verse (c. 1000 – as quoted in Keenan, 1996) is the emphatic *he self*. The King James version is literal, as in the gloss.

Finally, we can also mobilize marked referring expressions available in the language system to describe a marked (coreferential) state of affairs. Whereas the pronouns in the Biblical (14) and (15) corefer with the subject, coreference in itself is not unexpected for the activities at hand (except for (14c)). Where it is marked,

---

[17] It is noteworthy that unlike the subject of *brace*, that of 'change (its) body' is the Deutsche Bank,
      which, of course, does not really have a (physical) body.

and addressees may need more encouragement to interpret coreference, Biblical Hebrew had (a very limited) use of emphatic personal pronouns:

(17)   va=irʕu   ha=roʕim$_i$ **OTAM$_i$** ve=et   coni   lo   raʕu.
        and=herded   the=shepherds **THEM**   and=ACC my:flock not herded
        'But the shepherds fed themselves and fed not my flock.'   (Ezekiel 34: 8)

According to Kautzsch (1898), the pronoun in (17) was stressed (the more common Biblical style for anaphoric direct objects is suffixed inflections on the verb). An accusative free pronoun is used "rarely, and only when marked emphasis is intended" (1898: 461). So, the free pronoun in Biblical Hebrew is much more marked than its Old English counterpart.[18] It codes a lower degree of accessibility (i.e. an antecedent thus referred is not as highly accessible to the addressee), and is appropriate for more marked antecedents (a similar pattern seems to characterize Fijian – Dixon, 1988: 255/256).[19] Faltz (1977/1985) notes that Igbo, Lakhota, and Yoruba developed their reflexive forms out of stressed pronouns.

   In sum, even in the absence of a specialized grammatical form working against the pragmatic inference of distinct entities, reflexive readings can be conveyed. Some languages use their regular pronouns, leaving coreference to be inferred due to special contextual factors. Other languages construct the predicate in such a way that reference is made to a possessor so that coreference is unmarked and hence facilitated. Still other languages facilitate the marked coreference interpretation by employing marked pronouns.

6.2.2   The grammaticization of emphatics into reflexives

   If we are correct in assuming that reflexive pronouns indicate a marked coreference, then the development of reflexives involves the emergence of a (grammaticized) marked referring expression. Indeed, since the English pronouns were unmarked expressions, Old English speakers at some point started adjoining an independent emphatic form (*self*) to their pronouns in order to counteract the default pragmatic inference to disjointness. Once these combinations lost their obligatory contrastive interpretation (this is Keenan's 2003 proposal, which dates this change to the 1400s), the path was paved for the (eventual) creation of a complex referring expression suitable for marked (but not necessarily emphatic) references. Gradually, these became the reflexive pronouns as we know them

---

[18] If this is overwhelmingly the case, the unstressed pronoun in (14c) may represent a special strategy too.
[19] The similarity between stressed referring expressions and emphatic reflexives regarding markedness (noted by Levinson, 2000b: 334) can be seen in the following, originally Hebrew example, quoted by Borochovsky Bar-Abba (2006), as an example of the difference between spoken and written language. (i) Was the spoken version, (ii) is its rendering into writing:

(i)   I am not sure if the **INSTIGATORS** understood . . .
                                            (Elik Ron, testimony, Sept. 3, 2001)
(ii)   I am not sure if the instigators **themselves** understood . . .
                                            (*Yediot Achronot*, Sept. 4, 2001)

today.[20] A similar motivation lies behind the following noncanonical, doubly emphatic form *my own + self*. Just as pronouns were not marked enough for marked references in Old English, so are *one's own* and *-self* forms (each by itself) not emphatic enough today (see section 6.4):

(18)   Frankly, I'm torn **my own self** as to which way to raise hell.
                    (Clark Reed, quoted in *International Herald Tribune*, Jan. 2–3, 1999)

Whereas *my own self* sounds innovative in current English, the following must have similarly sounded innovative at some point:

(19)   **Him self** he hynge
            'He hanged himself.'   (Faltz, 1977/1985: 19, ex. 56 from Middle English)

Reflexive pronouns have time and again emerged out of adjunct emphatic expressions. Emphatics start out as optional adjuncts, but often enough, they gradually grammaticize and become obligatory in certain contexts (to various degrees). It is only at this point, once grammaticization has taken place, that the extra-linguistic pattern we started with, namely the markedness of coreference among co-participants, has repercussions for the grammar. König and Siemund (2000) mention Turkic, Finno-Ugric, Caucasian, Indic, Semitic languages, Persian, Japanese, English, and many other European languages, as languages where emphatics and reflexives are identical in form, which points to the historical source of the reflexive pronouns. König *et al.* (2005) identify this pattern for 56 percent of the 168 languages they surveyed.

A very common route to reflexives via emphatic expressions involves reference to body parts (König and Siemund, 2000). Note the following (Modern) Hebrew innovative emphatics, where the conventional emphatic (i.e. the reflexive) is avoided. The ad hoc emphatic reference is created by mobilizing as an oblique a body part possessive NP:

(20) a.   We with **our very hands** should punish him and not let the disease kill him.
                        (Originally Hebrew, *Haaretz*, Oct. 10, 2003)
    b.   Jacob with **his hands** gave me money. Not Ofer. Jacob.
                        (Originally Hebrew, *Hair*, April 26, 1996)[21]

Still, it is not common for expressions for 'one's hands' to grammaticize into reflexive markers. It is no accident that ʕ*ecem+* possessive 'one's bone' has conventionalized as the Hebrew reflexive pronoun (the same is attested for Bantu languages – see Haiman, 1998: 74). The body part or possessed item must stand for the essence of the person for the form to grammaticize as a conventional emphatic pronoun (Heine, 1994b). While possessed body parts

---

[20] Similarly, Levinson (2000b: 304) notes that the addition of an emphatic to the semantically general antipassive construction in Guugu Yimithirr encourages the reflexive (and reciprocal) interpretation.

[21] Note that *with one's hands* in the above (and in similar other cases) occurs adjacent to the modified NP, rather than in the more natural position for prepositional objects (postverbally).

can help us express coreference (as in (15)), when conventional means are lacking, or when the existing means are not sufficiently emphatic (as in (20)), most of them can only achieve this pragmatically, in ad hoc cases, where if one's leg doesn't step somewhere, then the whole person doesn't (15a), and if one's flesh is covered, then one's whole body is (15b), etc. The same body parts, however, cannot so easily perform the reflexive function in direct object positions, such as x_i *hurt her$_i$ leg*, because in this case, the leg is not automatically inferred to stand for the whole person. Thus, although body parts are a common source for reflexive markers, only a small subset routinely gives rise to conventional emphatics, later turned reflexive pronouns: *body, head,* and *soul* head the list, no doubt because they can stand for the whole person more easily than one's leg or elbow can.[22]

Indeed, the use of 'one's bone' as a reflexive form from Mishnaic Hebrew and onwards is motivated, once we examine how Biblical singular possessed 'bone' is already used to symbolically represent the person possessing the bone, as in (21), where 'thy bone/flesh' definitely carry their literal meanings, which, in turn, give rise to the figurative interpretation (the whole person) by inference:

(21)   hinnenu   ʕacmexa   u=vsarxa   anaħnu
        are1PL   thy:bone   and=thy:flesh   we
        'We are thy bone and thy flesh' ('flesh and blood')   (2 Samuel 5: 1)

One more step required for a reflexive pronoun to develop out of an "essential" body part is its use as an emphatic marker (König and Siemund, 2000). In fact, Biblical singular ʕecem 'bone' is already ambiguous, used as an emphatic adjunct in addition to its literal argument use:

(22)   ʕad   ʕecem   ha=yom   ha=ze
        until   the.bone.of   this=day   the=this
        'Until this very day'   (Joshua 10: 27)

Such emphatic uses must have paved the way for the later use we find in Mishnaic Hebrew of possessed ʕecem 'one's bone' as a reflexive marker.

But what is it about emphatic markers that makes them so readily available for grammaticizing into reflexive markers? Cohen (2004) convincingly argues that current English emphatic reflexives indicate to the addressee that a highly accessible entity is being referred to, and, moreover, that he is to compare this entity to a set of alternatives. This comparison yields a variety of context-based conversational implicatures, among them, interpretations previously considered polysemous uses of emphatic reflexives in the literature: contrast, remarkability, prominence. Whereas Cohen's analysis can cover a wider range of data, the analyses of Baker (1995), Kemmer (1995), and Kemmer and Barlow (1996), Zribi-Hertz (1995) and König and Siemund (2000) of emphatic reflexives (as in *the marriage itself* in (23)) can be seen as describing the common discourse

---

[22] See Heine and Reh (1984: 272), Heine (1994b), Heine and Kuteva (2002), König (2005).

profiles and ad hoc interpretations of these expressions. It is generalizing over these that gave rise to reflexive pronouns.

The entities referred to by emphatics commonly constitute prominent discourse entities, more prominent than other contenders for the antecedent role. Prominence can result from an inherent characteristic of the entity, such as high rank: following Farr (1905), Keenan (2003) mentions that English reflexives were very often used for references to God and kings in the early stages (some languages have special forms reserved for such entities – see König and Siemund regarding German *höchstselbst*). But more often, prominence is a discourse-based concept (today). Kemmer (1995) argues that the prototypical use of emphatic reflexives is to access a discourse topic (clearly discoursally prominent), following a preceding shift to an entity associated with that topic (discoursally more peripheral). While prominent, the antecedent of an emphatic cannot be maximally accessible at the point when reference to it is made. Consider the following:

(23)   PAMELA: I used to have this,
                        .. sort of,
                        .. standard line,
                        that,
                        there were two things I got out of .. my marriage$_i$.
                        One was a name that was easy to spell,
                        and one was a ,
                        .. (H) a child.
                        (Hx) .. . . . That,
                        . . . really got me grounded.
                        But,
                        (H) the fact of the matter is,
                        . . . (H) that **the marriage itself**$_i$,   (SBC: 005)

Pamela here uses an emphatic reflexive to resume talking about her marriage, because even though it has been the discourse topic (the center, to use König and Siemund's terminology), other subtopics (the things Pamela got out of her marriage, the periphery) have been discussed since the announcement of the topic in the first line. 'The marriage' is therefore prominent, but no longer maximally accessible.

Now, the prevalent view is that reflexives, just like emphatics, refer to unexpected referents.[23] However, Baker (1995) and König and Siemund (2000) demonstrate that emphatics do not invariably refer to unexpected entities.[24] Indeed, there is nothing unexpected about referring to the marriage again in (23). König and Siemund then propose that just like the emphatic, the reflexive pronoun points to a center (the subject referent). A somewhat different formulation for this explanation is here preferred. As proposed by Kemmer (1995), what

---

[23] See Faltz (1977/1985), Levinson (1991, 2000b), Kemmer (1995), Haiman (1983, 1998: 73).
[24] But note that actually, grammaticization can follow a salient discourse pattern, even if it is not an absolute one.

an emphatic is in the discourse, a reflexive is in the clause. We can then say that both emphatics and reflexives select entities one would have expected to have a maximal degree of accessibility, even though they in fact do not.[25]

Indeed, the reflexive pronoun refers to an entity which should theoretically be central and prominent, because it is the clause subject. But this antecedent is nonetheless not highly accessible when we consider candidates for the antecedent of the reflexive, because we tend to rule out coreference for arguments standing for same-event participants (see section 6.1.1). Similarly, the emphatic often refers to a central entity (one which should be maximally accessible), which happens not to be highly accessible, most commonly because the speaker has shifted to talk about an associated topic (or else, the entity is only an implied discourse entity – see Kemmer, 1995). What emphatics and reflexive pronouns have in common, then, is reference to a prominent entity which nonetheless is not maximally accessible.[26] Seen in this way, we can understand why unmarked reflexive events (as in self-washings – see below) do not invariably/initially get coded by reflexive pronouns. Even though the antecedent in these cases is equally central (it is the subject), its accessibility is not lowered, because there is no disjointness expectation. Hence, the subject is here a natural antecedent for the coreferential argument.

In conclusion, emphatics naturally turn into reflexive pronouns because both prototypically refer to central entities whose high accessibility has (temporarily) been reduced. The accessibility lowering results from different discoursal factors for the two cases. Crucially, for reflexive pronouns, it is the expectation for disjointness among event participants which lowers the subject's accessibility and renders it a marked antecedent.

6.2.3   The nonunitary nature of the grammaticization of reflexives

Grammaticization is optional, gradual, and nonunitary. As we emphasized in chapter 5, speakers never engage in an endeavor to create a new grammar. We thus expect a gradual shift from the functional principle 'encode marked coreference by marked means, such as a reflexive marker' to the English

---

[25] This position is different from Kemmer's and Cohen's, who actually follow my own earlier work (Ariel, 1990), where I argued that the reflexive indicates a very high degree of accessibility. In Ariel (2001), I argue that reflexives encode a nonmaximally high degree of accessibility.

[26] Incidentally, the gradual evolution of reflexives to indicate a marked antecedent when competing with another, rather highly accessible antecedent is not unique to reflexives. Many have noted that stressed pronouns (e.g. in English) or demonstrative pronouns (e.g. in Russian, German, Afrikaans, Dutch, Hebrew) pick a dispreferred antecedent (see Ariel, 1990; Comrie, 1997; Solan, 1983). In these cases a more highly accessible antecedent (the subject or the topic, depending on the language – see Comrie, 1997) is rejected in favor of a slightly less accessible antecedent (usually a nontopical recently mentioned entity). In other words, both reflexives and demonstratives instruct the addressee to pick a less expected antecedent. For the demonstrative pronoun, a peripheral one is chosen over a central one, whereas for the reflexive, a central one is chosen over a peripheral one.

grammatical convention, as represented by the current Binding Conditions. Indeed, different languages manifest different degrees of grammaticization of reflexivity. Some languages have no special reflexive markers, and use their regular pronouns for local coreference, e.g. Frisian, Haitian, Bamako Bambara, Malagasy, the majority of Australian languages, and English-based Pidgins and Creoles (see Huang, 2000: 222–223; Levinson, 2000b: 335; Siemund, 2003; Zribi-Hertz, 1995). It is then important to note that grammaticization of reflexives is not inevitable.

Next, even if grammaticization is initiated, it is not (immediately) total. For one thing, old functions don't just gracefully disappear into oblivion. They often linger on. Carden and Stewart (1988) note that pronouns coreferential with clause-mate arguments continued to be used for hundreds of years after a reflexive had been created in some dialects of Haitian Creole. LSAC contains a few pleonastic pronouns, such as *I have me a new home*. English reflexive pronouns have also not lost their function as emphatics: 15/79 reflexives (19 percent) in SBC were nonargument emphatics. Another curious fact that can perhaps be explained as a vestige of an old use is the fact that over half of the reflexives governed by *near* on the Web (14/26, 53.8 percent) refer to high-rank entities (such as God, king etc. – compare only 2/15 *near him* on the Web – 13.3 percent – refer to high-rank figures). Some association of the reflexive with high-rank figures seems to have survived in written Modern English, then. Other skewed distributions too point to the origin of the modern English reflexive.

Even where reflexive pronouns are available, they don't necessarily obey the Binding Conditions in (1) and (4) (Comrie, 1998). It's quite clear that the structural account in section 6.1 is specific to English, rather than universal, as the claim has been. The distribution of reflexives in the languages of the world follows a cline of syntactic contexts, argues Comrie, where reflexive expressions are obligatory, optional and/or banned in a variety of contexts (in addition to the co-argument position). More importantly for our discussion here, his findings corroborate the assumption that extralinguistic expectations regarding the likelihood of coreference lie behind the universal cline. We expect the use of reflexives to develop (earlier) where needed most, i.e. in contexts especially prone to triggering the pragmatic inference to disjointness. Speakers would employ them more often in such cases, because an extra effort is required to block the default pragmatic inference. What are such contexts? Third- versus first-person references, contexts where referential continuity is not expected versus contexts where it is, and other-directed versus self-directed actions/predicates. Let's briefly consider each of these contexts.

According to Faltz (1977/1985: 120/121), it is most important to code reflexivity for third persons, and least so for first persons, since, unlike third persons, no ambiguity results for first persons (see also Comrie, 1998, 2003). The pragmatic inference to disjointness is in fact blocked for first persons (*me* cannot be disjoint from *I* in the same sentence). This is why Faltz finds some languages which only have specialized reflexive forms for third persons (e.g. German, Swedish, Latin;

Siemund, 2003 adds the English-based creole Sranan), but no language with reflexive marking only for first (or second) person.[27] Similarly, Keenan (2002, 2003) reports that the use of third person reflexive anaphors in English historically preceded that of first/second persons. Heine (2005) observes that creoles which use pronouns as reflexives more often add an emphatic in third person cases. Even in current English, *about* objects show a person gradation in the use of a reflexive versus a pronoun. While all third-person objects were coded by a reflexive (see below), this was true for only 65.5 percent (36/55) of the first/second person cases in LSAC.

Comrie (1998) provides support for the second contrast, that between referential continuity contexts and contexts where referential continuity is less or not at all expected. The relevant question here pertains to the potential coreference between some subject and a discourse entity mentioned later, whether within the same clause or even outside that clause. Where coreference is less expected we expect to find more/earlier uses of reflexive pronouns to indicate the nonapplicability of the disjointness inference. Where coreference is expected, there is no need to counteract the disjointness inference, and hence reflexive pronouns should be less prevalent. Comrie translates these contexts of varying coreference expectations to different syntactic contexts. Consider the following English examples, each expressing coreference in a different syntactic context (examples in (24) are based on Comrie's exx. 19–23):

(24) a.　　I$_i$ **saw myself**$_i$ in the mirror.　　(LSAC) (co-argument)
　　b.　　She$_i$'s saying this to a voice **behind her**$_i$.　　(LSAC) (adjunct)
　　c.　　He$_i$ saw **his**$_i$ **cardiologist**.　　(LSAC) (possessive)
　　d.　　He$_i$ likes for me **to stay with him**$_i$.　　(LSAC) (nonfinite clause)
　　e.　　FRED: .. and he$_i$ said,
　　　　　　that the lady told him$_i$,
　　　　　　that it usually takes ... a week,　　(SBC: 014) (finite clause)

Predictably, (24) shows that English restricts the use of reflexive pronouns to the most local domain, where coreference is most marked. It sometimes allows reflexives in (24b) contexts (see below), but not beyond that. If we were to compare the equivalent structures in Russian, however, we would find obligatorily reflexives in (24a–c), and optionally in (24d). Danish shows a similar distributional pattern to Russian, except that the reflexive slots are divided between two types of reflexive expressions (more on such cases later). Japanese too has more than one reflexive form, and it can stretch the use of reflexives all the way, in (24a–e).

As Comrie explains, the contexts (24a–e) are not randomly ordered. They are associated with gradually decreasing expectations for disjointness among participants. Whereas we definitely expect disjointness in (24a) (recall the findings in section 6.1.1), we actually have an expectation for coreference in (24d) and (24e)

---

[27] As Comrie (1998) points out, French first- and second- person "reflexive pronouns" (*me/te*) are actually the regular French pronouns. Only third person has a special reflexive form (*se* versus *lui*).

(we expect referential continuity between clauses, especially with the preceding subject). Languages differ as to where the cut-off point is for the use of their reflexive pronoun, but the prediction is that no language will use a reflexive in e.g. contexts (24d) and (24e), but not in (24a–c). Such typological findings support the nonunitary grammaticization of reflexives, which predicts a selective discrimination between more versus less likely contexts for reflexivization, in accordance with our expectations for disjointness among participants. The distributional patterns of English, Russian, Danish, and Japanese, although distinct, are perfectly compatible with the assumption that grammaticization is pragmatically motivated. What is important for our discussion is that the different grammaticization patterns are not random. Invariably, the more marked coreference is, the more likely the use of a reflexive.

Next, self- versus other-directed actions also matter to the grammaticizations of reflexives.[28] Not all events typically involve distinct entities. Some activities would encourage the disjointness inference more strongly than others. These would be predicates which depict actions we tend to perform on others (other-directed). If so, coreference under such circumstances is more marked. The more marked it is, the higher the chances for the use of reflexives. Other activities are not necessarily only performed on others (non-other-directed). Some are even preferably performed on the self (self-directed). Such predicates may not trigger the disjointness inference so strongly or automatically, so addressees don't need so much help in suppressing the disjointness inference. A regular pronoun may be appropriate to indicate coreference in such cases. We expect the grammaticization of reflexive pronouns to be earlier and more obligatory in other-directed contexts, since it is in such contexts that a marked coreference indicator is most needed.

Indeed, this is what we find. The (obligatory) use of reflexive pronouns is more prevalent in (more) marked coreference contexts, and the "ban" against anaphoric pronouns between co-arguments is more prevalent in such contexts. But in unmarked coreference contexts, the use of reflexives is not necessarily obligatory, and a pronoun can be used. The French pronoun *lui* 'him' is a good example for these points. *Lui* shows only a partial grammaticization of Condition B (see (4) above). Zribi-Hertz (1995, 2003) argues that, unlike English *him*, French *lui* is not grammaticized for disjoint reference with a local antecedent. However, although it can sometimes be coreferential with a co-argument subject, this is not invariably so. Thus, 'himself' in the counterpart of 'Pierre is jealous of/dependent on/happy with himself' cannot be rendered by *lui*, but it can in the counterpart of 'Pierre is proud of himself.' As is pointed out in König and Siemund (2000), it is quite rare that one is jealous of oneself. Not so for being proud of oneself. So, *lui* is not allowed to be co-indexed with a subject where coreference is marked (with *jealous*, an other-directed predicate). A more marked means of coreference is then required. But *lui* is acceptable where coreference is less marked (with *proud*,

---

[28] The terms are Kiparsky's (1990), as cited in König and Siemund (2000).

a non-other-directed predicate).[29] All in all, the functional principle regarding markedness and reflexives predicts that grammaticization does not necessarily apply uniformly to structurally defined cases (such as Conditions A or B). In the case of *lui*, Condition B (banning coreferential pronouns) seems to apply to marked coreference cases, but not to unmarked coreference cases. It is precisely such nonuniformity that is predicted by the functional account.

French also distinguishes between self- and other-directed actions for the optional *lui-même* 'him himself.' Indeed, whereas the preferred way of expressing reflexive 'wash' (a self-directed activity) is with the unmarked reflexive form *se* (*se laver*), for some other-directed action verbs where coreference is especially remarkable, speakers prefer to add the emphatic *même* to the *se*. For example, suppose the following appears as a summary of a newspaper article about friendly fire, in which the artillery bombarded the infantry of some army:[30]

(25)   Notre armée s'était   attaquée (elle-même).
        our   army SE=is.imperfect attacked (it itself)
        'Our army has attacked itself.'

Many delicate distinctions can be observed, even within one language, then. Whereas the overwhelmingly skewed frequencies cited in section 6.1.1 above show that event participants, especially co-arguments, tend to be disjoint in reference from the subject participant of the clause, this is not equally true of every type of co-argument. Probabilities vary quite a bit, in fact. It should therefore be interesting to examine actual distributions of pronouns and reflexives for different predicates. The idea is that the use of reflexive pronouns is more regular (obligatory, prevalent) between entities which are expected to be disjoint in reference (other-directed cases). They should not be used (or less often so) between co-arguments where coreference is not marked (non-other-directed and self-directed). Let us now see whether these distinctions apply to current English data. We examine below the hypothesis that co-argument reflexives occur (diachronically earlier, more frequently, more obligatorily) in contexts where coreference is marked, because the predicates are conventionally other-directed (i.e. disjointness is expected), but not (or less so) in contexts where coreference is not marked, because the predicate does not depict a conventionally other-directed situation. Recall that markedness is predicted purely on extralinguistic statistical grounds, based on salient discourse patterns.

We start with marked coreference cases where we expect a consistent (grammaticized/frequent) use of reflexive pronouns. One context where coreference is quite marked, and thus, if the language has reflexive pronouns, this is where they

---

[29] Note that these claims should not be difficult to refute. A language where partial grammaticization affected less marked coreference cases (e.g. *proud*) but not marked cases (e.g. *jealous*) would pose a counterexample to the account.

[30] I thank Jean Lowenstamm (p.c.) for providing the example and the judgments from nine French speakers. All chose *se + elle-même* in the above, but they all preferred *elle se lave*... 'she SE-washes...' over *elle se lave elle-même*... 'she SE-washes herself').

are predicted to occur, is when the activity depicted is bodily harm inflicted by a participant upon herself. We do not usually expect people to talk about causing bodily harm to themselves. A search in LSAC reveals the basis for this expectation. Out of 110 cases of *hit/hits/hitting* a singular first- or a third-person masculine pronoun in LSAC, 109 (99.1 percent) cases depicted a distinct entity hitting the speaker or the third person, as in:[31]

(26)   And twice Chris saw **her hitting him**.   (LSAC)

Not surprisingly, one of the first contexts for the grammaticization of reflexive forms in English was objects of verbs of bodily harm (see Keenan, 2002, 2003): an emphatic *self* was added to indicate the contrastive reference in Old English. In LSAC, only one example (0.9 percent) had a coreferential subject. Since there was only one coreference case with *hit* in LSAC, there was exactly one reflexive form (*himself*) here:

(27)   **He** <laughing> accidentally **hit himself**.   (LSAC)

The marked referring expression (*himself*) was used to indicate the marked coreference case. Similarly, there were nineteen verbal forms of *fight with*. Only one of them showed coreference, and was, accordingly, marked by a reflexive pronoun:

(28)   when they got to court, they started **fighting with themselves**   (LSAC)[32]

A comparison between *kill* and *hurt* (bodily harm verbs) and *help* and *find* in LSAC is interesting for the point at hand. All 4 verbs are among the 9 most frequent verbs in LSAC to appear immediately preceding a reflexive form, probably governing the reflexive.[33] However, proportionately (i.e. relative to its general frequency), *kill* is accompanied by a reflexive pronoun 3 times more often than *help* and 6.6 times more often than *find*.[34] Similarly, *hurt* cooccurs with a reflexive 2.2 times more often than *help* does, and 4.8 times more than *find* does.

Inflicting physical harm is not the only context where we have high expectations for disjoint co-arguments. Other activities, inherently social ones, are also typically conducted between distinct individuals. A search for *with himself* in LSAC revealed only 7 such coreference cases. Here are two of them:

(29) a.   He's **bonding with** himself.   (LSAC)
     b.   You say a monologue where somebody is **speaking with** himself.   (LSAC)

---

[31] The search was conducted for *hit/hits/hitting me/myself/him/himself*. Again, had lexical objects been included in the search, the ratio of disjoint objects would have been even higher.

[32] But note that the reading of the reflexive in (28) is actually reciprocal.

[33] The hedge ("probably governing") is due to the fact that emphatic reflexives were not excluded here. But chances are that emphatics have a more or less constant frequency with different verbs, so it shouldn't matter.

[34] Haspelmath (2004c) finds that only 5/109 (4.6 percent) of the *kill* occurrences in the BNC were self-killings. Checking the first 40 occurrences of *kill* in SBC + LSAC also showed that only a minority were self-directed (8, 20 percent).

Social activities, such as bonding and speaking, are typically conducted between distinct entities. Coreference here is therefore marked. For example, there were 46 cases of an entity speaking with some entity.[35] (29b) was the only one showing coreference, and indeed, a reflexive pronoun was used.[36] Similarly, all 39 cases of *have lunch/sex/a meeting/a talk/fun*, etc. *with her/him(self)* in LSAC (all inter- active activities) had disjoint pronominal referents, as in (30a, b). No coreferential *with* objects were found for such activities. On the Web, however, I managed to find one case where an activity usually involving two distinct referents happened to involve the same individual in two roles. As expected, a reflexive pronoun was used in (30c):

(30) a.   I just **had sex with her**.   (LSAC)
     b.   We **had two dinners with her**.   (LSAC)
     c.   The woman who **had an affair with herself**.   (Web)

Note, however, that current use is not necessarily limited to initial patterns. New predicates where coreference is marked routinely take reflexive pronouns. Causative reflexives seem the most frequent reflexives now (*get* and *make* head the list of verbs cooccurring with reflexive pronouns), and cognitive verbs are very frequent too (*see, find, consider*). All of these indicate what Haiman (1998) calls a "divided self," where one and the same referent is profiled by two discourse roles (often, a more conscious self versus a more emotional self). This is an important function of reflexive clauses nowadays (see section 6.4 and Ariel, 2006a).

   Now, contrast these other-directed activities, where coreference is marked and reflexives are routinely used, with activities which are commonly self-directed, where coreference is not marked. Here the prediction is that grammaticization should be slow and not as consistent. Hence, reflexive pronouns should not occur so commonly. Verbs of grooming depict actions which we normally perform on ourselves (see Faltz, 1977/1985; Keenan, 2002, 2003; Kemmer, 1995; König and Siemund, 2000). Indeed, we presented statistics on 'washing' verbs in chapter 5, which showed that no overt reflexive was used. Similarly, out of 64 examples with *(get/got) dressed (up)* in LSAC, 60 were performed on the self, and only 4 had a disjoint object (as in (31)):

(31)   Plus you have to **get them dressed** and out of the house at certain times.

                                                                                        (LSAC)

Finally, 40/55 (72.7 percent) of the shaving activities in LSAC depict self-shavings. Now, as expected, virtually none of the cases of Biblical *raxac* 'bathe' and English *shower, bathe, (get) dressed (up)*, and *shave* showed overt reflexives. These are reserved for marked coreference cases. Instead, intransitive verbs were used (see below).

---

[35] The search included *speak, speaks, speaking, spoke*, and *spoken*.
[36] Haspelmath (2004c) has similar counts for German and Czech verbs for 'hear.'

So, all in all, coreference with marked antecedents (for bodily harm and social predicates) is indicated by a marked reflexive. For unmarked coreference, on the other hand, a marked reflexive may be avoided, and other strategies are preferred. For verbs of grooming it is mostly the intransitive strategy (verbal reflexive marking). In other cases we will later examine, pronouns may be used for clausal coreference. The findings clearly support a nonunitary grammaticization process for reflexive pronouns along the pragmatic lines we considered. So the path which led to the development of reflexive pronouns as we know them today in English is very clearly pragmatic in nature. Does that mean that reflexive pronouns today are still pragmatically governed, or have they become completely grammatical? We address this question in section 6.3.

6.3   Reflexives: grammar or pragmatics?

We have now reviewed a synchronic structural account for English reflexives (section 6.1) and a functional account for the grammaticization process which lies behind the synchronic facts (section 6.2). According to the former, the Binding Conditions account for the use of reflexives. According to the functional principle, reflexives are used to indicate a marked coreference with a central antecedent. We must now ask whether we need both principles synchronically. It is possible that while the functional principle has been responsible for the creation of the current (sometimes structurally idiosyncratic) distribution of reflexive pronouns, it is no longer productive, and hence need not form part of the current grammar. It is equally possible that the opposite is true, namely, that the structural principle is actually an epiphenomenon, because the functional principle can account not only for the diachronic data, but also for the synchronic data. In other words, are reflexives governed by grammar or by pragmatics?

Let's compare the structural and functional accounts. The first point we should note is that Reinhart and Reuland's (1993) formulation of the Binding Conditions is highly compatible with the pragmatic motivation attributed to the use of reflexives. Looked at functionally, the motivation behind the Binding Conditions is to help addressees interpret marked cases, where coreference is intended despite the fact that other things being equal disjointness is expected.[37] A reasonable site to have such expectations is the argument structure of the predicate, of course. As Du Bois (2003a, b) argues, "from a cognitive point of view, an argument structure is nothing more than a structure of expectations triggered by a verb" (Du Bois, 2003b: 55). He goes on to distinguish core arguments (subject, direct and indirect objects) from noncore arguments (obliques), noting that core arguments tend to be more grammaticized than noncore ones, just because there is a structure of expectations for the occurrence of core but not of noncore arguments.

---

[37] This is not quite right. Not all reflexive markers indicate a marked coreference. Only marked ones do. We will briefly address this question below.

Indeed, it may very well be the case that grammaticization takes place in a restricted grammatical environment. It would not be surprising if the grammaticization of reflexives were restricted to co-arguments, because if a predicate obligatorily occurs with specific arguments consistently, expectations regarding coreference/disjointness may be quite robust, given the high frequency of the cooccurrence of the predicate with the same type of arguments. We might even distinguish between direct objects and indirect objects. While there are co-argument coreferential PP pronouns in the Old Testament (see again (14b)), there are only a handful of such direct object pronouns. Similarly, in the history of English, reflexives became obligatory in direct object position first (Keenan, 2002, 2003; König and Siemund, 2000; Siemund, 2003). In fact, much in the spirit of Comrie (1998), König and Siemund (2000: 58–59) propose that "if a language has any locally bound anaphors at all . . . these occur in non-subject argument positions. Only later may this use also spread to adjuncts." Synchronic data supports this claim. For example, there were 1.5 more direct objects than PP reflexives in SBC. Note, however, that the pragmatic motivation refers to the disjointness of participants in certain depicted events/situations, and the discourse counts quoted in section 6.1.1 support it for clause-mate arguments in general (Gast, 2006 calls such cases "co-participant reflexives"). While the difference in status between core and noncore arguments is upheld in general, prepositional objects are sometimes recurrent enough to form structures of expectations (re coreference) with their verbs, as we see below (and recall Comrie's 1998 proposals above).[38] In fact, drawing the argument/adjunct distinction is not an easy task.[39]

Let us now compare the predictions of the two accounts. Both actually make the same predictions in the majority of the cases. Both the structural and the functional explanations can account for the facts when a marked coreference between co-arguments is involved. According to Reinhart and Reuland, a reflexive is mandated because of the co-indexation of two co-arguments. According to the functional explanation, coreference is marked where there exists a structure of expectations for **other**-directed activities, and a reflexive is then called for. But what about unmarked coreference between co-arguments? Here the two principles make opposite predictions. The structural principle predicts a reflexive because co-arguments are involved, whereas the functional principle predicts a pronoun, because unmarked coreference is involved. There are different predictions regarding non-co-argument coreference as well. Conditions A and B actually make no predictions regarding pronoun/reflexive preferences here (both should be acceptable), but the functional principle predicts that should there be a structure of expectations according to which coreference is marked, a

---

[38] This is why Smith's (2004) claim that self-directed verbs never take reflexive PPs is an over-statement of the facts. See the statistics regarding *near* + reflexives in section 6.1.

[39] Manning (2003) argues that it is gradient, and Dowty (2003) proposes a dual representation for adjuncts and complements.

reflexive will be used. Should there be a structure of expectations for coreference to be unmarked, a pronoun will be used.

So, is it the case that grammaticization is restricted to co-arguments in English? It is not. Should we find consistent patterns of choices for either pronouns or reflexives, and should these conform to the functional principle, we would have an indication that the functional principle has a wider application than Conditions A and B. Should findings moreover reveal an absolutely consistent pattern, we may consider the possibility that the definition of argument structure be modified to structure of expectations à la Du Bois, thereby including some syntactic non-arguments under the definition as well. Note, however, that such cases, should they be found, do not actually constitute counterexamples for Reinhart and Reuland's analysis, for their rules make no predictions about nonarguments. They would demonstrate, though, that the structural principle is not as general as one could have (section 6.3.1). What would constitute direct counterexamples for Conditions A and B are cases where pronouns, rather than reflexives, are consistently (or even obligatorily) selected for co-arguments. Should these happen only for those predicates where coreference is expected or unmarked, we would have some evidence that the functional principle is to be preferred, because it correctly produces a pronoun in a syntactic environment claimed to require a reflexive. However, if we find co-arguments marked by reflexive pronouns in contexts where coreference is unmarked, we will have to conclude that the functional analysis is no longer applicable, and the structural principle by itself explains the data (section 6.3.2). We also compare how the two analyses fare with respect to differences among reflexive markers (section 6.3.3). Our conclusion will be that we need both the structural and the functional accounts (section 6.3.4).

6.3.1   Reflexives and coreference between non-co-arguments

Reinhart and Reuland have no predictions about whether non-co-arguments which are coreferential with the subject should be coded as pronouns or as reflexives. The functional principle predicts that where there are solid expectations for disjointness, coreference should be marked by a reflexive, and where there are strong expectations for coreference, pronouns should be used to indicate coreference. First, note that Reinhart and Reuland themselves point out that some non-co-arguments behave as if they were co-arguments, as in:

(32)   ~The queen$_i$ invited both Max and **herself$_i$/*her$_i$** to our party.

Herself/her is not a syntactic co-argument of *the queen* (by itself), but it is semantically so. Thus, semantic co-arguments may require reflexive forms even when they do not constitute syntactic co-arguments, which means that indeed, structures of expectations are not necessarily restricted to syntactic co-arguments. One such case is *except for* pronoun/reflexive. Syntactically, such prepositional objects are not co-arguments of the clause subject. Semantically, however, Reinhart (1991) has argued that the *except* constituent does form a constituent with its correlate at LF.[40] If so, the *except* object may be a co-argument of the subject semantically, and the prediction would be that a reflexive must be used. This is precisely what we find. A search of the Web for *me, myself, her*, and *herself* as objects of *except for* showed no cases where coreference with the subject was coded by a pronoun. All contained reflexives, instead, as in the following:

(33) a.   I'm not blaming anyone here, **except for myself**.
     b.   In fact, she saw no one else in the class **except for herself**.

Now, these findings are of course precisely what the functional principle predicts, since they confirm that structures of expectations are not always only syntactically defined. Note that the majority of the examples showed disjointness between the *except for* object and the subject. Thus, coreference is marked for such prepositional objects, and in the few cases where they were coreferential with the subject, a reflexive is predicted to occur.[41] A similar pattern was observed for *picture of him/himself* and for *jokes about him/himself* on the Web. Although *him/himself* are not syntactically co-arguments of the subject, a reflexive is chosen for the most part, because coreference is here marked, as is attested by the low percentage of coreference cases.

Now, consider example (6) again:

(34)   **Tom** works with **him**, see?   (LSAC)

In this context too, although *him* is not an argument of *work* it cannot be interpreted as coreferential with *Tom*. Since what we have here is a marked coreference (*work with* is an other-directed predicate), in order to create that reading a reflexive must be used. This is another case where a reflexive is obligatory rather than optional where non-co-arguments are involved (see the examples in note 8). In fact, Zribi-Hertz (2003) notes that coreferential NPs in constructions like *talk among, rehearse within, laugh despite* require a reflexive object, even though the PPs here are both syntactically and semantically optional, which should mean that they are not co-arguments of the subject. (35) presents relevant examples:

(35) a.   And we, we refer to him **among ourselves** as the killer guy.   (LSAC)
     b.   They develop these little, stupid, little routines **among themselves**.
                                                                              (LSAC)
     c.   Eventually she did make the rank of journeyman, **despite herself**,
                                                                              (Web Corp)

Indeed, all first 36 *despite herself* cases on the Web (search conducted by Web Corp) contained a sentential non-co-argument antecedent (as in (35c)). In other words, this is a 'disjointness' context, which explains the use of a reflexive to indicate coreference. Interestingly, among the first 75 occurrences of *despite him*, not one case involved an intra-sentential antecedent. It thus seems that the

---

[40] LF (Logical Form) is the linguistic semantic representation of the utterance.
[41] An alternative explanation is Keenan's (2003). Keenan argues that the contrast interpretation was never lost for inherently contrastive expressions, such as *except for*, which would account for the reflexive form.

reflexive is here obligatory for sentential scope, and the pronoun obligatorily banned within this scope.

Next, consider *about* + third-person objects. According to Reinhart and Reuland, either regular or reflexive pronouns are here grammatical. Still, excluding a consistent set of apparent exceptions (to be discussed below), 100 percent of the coreferential *about* third-person objects (52/52 occurrences) in LSAC showed a reflexive pronoun, rather than a personal pronoun.[42] This is quite reasonable given the working of the functional principle, since the prototypical case for *about* third-person human object is disjointness rather than coreference (as originally noted by Faltz, 1977/1985: 242). Cases of coreference are then marked, so even though they do not constitute co-arguments with their subjects, they are marked by a reflexive.[43] An examination of the coreferential *about* PPs (of all three persons) with *talk* revealed that 21/25 (84 percent) received reflexives rather than pronouns. In fact, the four coreferential pronouns all have a special meaning, distinct from the one they would have with a reflexive (see below).

So far, we have seen that coreferring non-co-arguments where disjointness is expected tend to receive reflexive pronouns. Let's see whether coreferential non-co-arguments where coreference is expected receive pronouns or reflexives. Consider *z* in *x put y on z*. Following Marantz (1984: 31), Reinhart and Reuland would probably not consider *z* a co-argument of the subject.[44] Reinhart and Reuland's prediction is, therefore, that should there be co-indexation between *x* and *z*, either a reflexive or a pronoun can be used. The facts are that in 2/7 cases a reflexive was used, but in the majority 5 cases a regular pronoun was used.[45] Why is that so? Because in such cases coreference is not marked. If so, a reflexive is not needed so much. In fact, in one of the reflexive cases (*put limits on yourself*), this is what we would expect under the functional approach as well: limits are not

---

[42] I am ignoring this set of "exceptional" examples here because we will see below that they are not actually exceptional at all for the functional account.

[43] Since argument structure is a dynamic phenomenon, with new arguments emerging out of adjuncts (Thompson and Hopper, 2001), it is far from trivial to determine the status of PPs in general, and of *about* PPs specifically as arguments versus adjuncts. It seems that at least the overwhelming majority of the cases counted above are nonarguments. In order to establish that I followed Thompson and Hopper's (2001) frequency criterion, and extracted all the verbs which cooccurred with any reflexive *about* PP in SBC and LSAC (125 cases with 21 different verbs). I then checked whether *about* PPs cooccurred with the most frequent of these verbs, *say, feel, tell, talk*, which constituted 65 percent of the tokens (each of the other verbs had at most 3 occurrences), by checking the first 50 occurrences of each of these verbs when they were not intransitive and did not take complements, infinitives, free relatives, or direct quotes. Results showed that the frequency of *about* PPs varied quite a bit, but never reached obligatoriness (varying between 8 percent for *say* and 64 percent for *talk*). In fact, Hopper and Thompson conclude that the distinction is meaningless for such cases.

[44] The rationale for such an analysis is that although locative PPs which are not co-arguments may be obligatory sometimes, crucially, their specific shape is not determined per verb. Indeed, one could use a variety of locative expressions instead of *on* for *put* (e.g. *under the table*).

[45] Data were collected from SBC, the London–Lund Corpus (LLC), LSAC, and the Web in this case. While the search on the spoken corpora was conducted on *put* +0–3 words + *on*, the Web search was restricted to *put (the) stuff/it on* + all pronouns and reflexives. The reason is that the Web Corp search engine is not sophisticated enough.

something we expect to put on ourselves. When one puts something on oneself which we expect to put on others a reflexive must be used. So eliminating the marked coreference case, 5/6 cases where we expect coreference indeed had a pronoun rather than a reflexive. We return to the sixth case below.

Is this the only adjunct that behaves like this? Consider cases, already noted by Faltz (1977/1985: 101), who argued that locative PPs with verbs of perception and certain verbs of motion take pronouns, rather than reflexives, in English:

(36) a.   He$_i$ felt something **near him$_i$/?*himself$_i$ ...**

                            (www.netcentral.co.uk/geoffana/unicorns/stories/helinth1.html)

      b.   Can you$_i$ reach the pepper **behind you$_i$/?*yourself$_i$?**   (LSAC)

There were 9 cases of coreference between the subject and *behind* second-person singular objects in LSAC, where the predicate allowed such coreference.[46] All but one showed a pronoun, as in (36b). Note that the only reflexive occurred with a predicate which literally is an other-directed verb:

(37)   You were a little **behind yourself**.   (LSAC)

So, in fact, 8/8 unmarked coreference cases showed a pronoun, rather than a reflexive. Similarly, there were no reflexive pronouns for coreferential *around* objects. Only pronouns were here used. It is clear that the nature of the main verb is crucial in such cases. One cannot (literally) be behind/around oneself. Coreference is then marked for *be behind/near*, etc., and a reflexive must be mobilized.[47] All in all, where coreference is unmarked, a pronoun is used, and where it is marked, a reflexive is used. Such findings are fully predicted by the functional principle. While they are compatible with Reinhart and Reuland's account, they are not predicted by it, which is a disadvantage of that theory.

6.3.2   Reflexives and coreference between co-arguments

Let's begin by considering recipients and beneficiaries, which at least sometimes approach argument status. Kemmer (1993), discussing indirect reflexives, i.e. cases of coreference between an agent and a recipient or beneficiary, notes that these are very close to the basic, direct reflexive. Still, there are exceptions (e.g. some German dialects), where a pronoun is used. Note that some American dialects too allow for pronominal coreference in the following:

(38) a.   I **got me** a new alternator.   (LSAC)
      b.   I bought **me** a packet of cigarettes.   (LSAC)

---

[46] These 9 coreferential cases constitute a majority (69.2 percent) of the total number of cases (13) where coreference was potentially available.

[47] Smith (2004) also points out that whether an action is or is not other-directed depends on the action depicted by the whole clause. In addition, he notes the following from French (his ex. 59), which is a counterexample for the above. Perhaps collocations sometimes preserve older patterns:

(i)   Elle$_i$ était hors   d'elle/*elle-même$_i$.
            She   was   beside (of) her/herself

The special use here involves a verb of acquisition which is actually associated with coreferential beneficiaries (see Croft *et al.*, 1987).[48] A search for *I bought/got* + 0–3 words + *me/myself* showed 4 *myself*s and 8 *me*s. Now, what is the status of the *buy* beneficiary? Huddleston and Pullum (2002) suggest that beneficiaries are in between arguments and adjuncts. The fact that they can occur in the double object (ditransitive) construction (as in (38)) testifies that they are closer to being arguments. Still, a reflexive is not absolutely obligatory, at least in some dialects. Note, further, that the beneficiary of *sell* (the buyer) behaves differently, so substituting *sold* for *got* and *bought* is impossible in (38) (the same facts hold for Hebrew). Instead, *myself* must be used.

The difference between *buy* and *sell* must derive from the fact that while one often buys for oneself, one sells things to others.[49] We should expect the same to hold for *send*, another other-directed ditransitive verb. So, *buy* and *sell* have different structures of expectations regarding coreference with the beneficiary, and accordingly, different ratios of reflexive/regular pronouns for indicating coreference. Now, one could counter that a reflexive is mandated in (38) with *sell* because the buyer role is an argument of *sell*, while for *buy* the beneficiary is only an adjunct. Indeed, an examination of the first 40 occurrences of active transitive *sold* and *bought* in SBC + LSAC showed that the beneficiary for *buy* was not very often explicitly mentioned (9/40, 22.5 percent), which supports a nonargument analysis for it. However, the supposedly argument role of the buyer for *sell* was explicitly mentioned just as infrequently (8/40, 20 percent). So, it's not so clear which roles are arguments and which are optional adjuncts here. In fact, the seller role, considered an argument for *buy*, was only mentioned in 2.5 percent of the *bought* occurrences (1/40). This would seem to support a nonargument status for it, but still, a reflexive seems mandatory:

(39)   ~I bought a new alternator from **??me/myself**

It must be the different structures of expectations of these two verbs which are responsible for the selection of a reflexive or a pronoun. If the buyer and seller roles here are not arguments, then the examples above make the same point as section 6.3.1. If they are arguments, they constitute counterexamples to Reinhart and Reuland's account, which predicts a reflexive when coreference is intended.

Next, we come to a clearer set of potential counterexamples to Reinhart and Reuland's analysis, cases where what is a co-indexed co-argument is consistently coded by a pronoun rather than by a reflexive, just because coreference is unmarked in these cases. Verbs of possession (most notably *have*, *got*), accompanied by certain prepositional phrases (e.g. *with*, *on*, *about*, *around*), also form lexically specified structures of expectations, this time with an obligatory

---

[48] Indeed, of the first 35 occurrences of *I bought* in SBC + LSAC, 30 had an (implicit) coreferential recipient.
[49] All 16 *I sold* and all 15 *x sold* + 0–5 words + *me* cases in SBC and LSAC had disjoint beneficiaries, whether implicitly or explicitly mentioned.

coreference reading imposed. The reason for considering these prepositional objects co-arguments is precisely the obligatory co-indexation imposed: note the ungrammaticality of the disjoint variants on the examples in (40) (see also Smith, 2004). In the following, coreference is not just presumed to be the default case, it is in fact the only option.[50] Hence, the functional principle predicts that despite the fact that the prepositional object is a co-argument, a pronoun, rather than a reflexive, is to be used:

(40) a.   He$_i$'s just **got** that kind of air **about him**$_i$/*us.   (LLC)[51]
     b.   He$_i$ didn't **have** many spots **on him**$_i$/*her.   (LLC)
     c.   He$_i$ didn't **have** any **with him**$_i$/*you.   (LSAC)
     d.   Who's Bob$_i$ **bringing with him**$_i$/*me?   (LLC)

While this is precisely what the functional principle predicts, recall that Reinhart and Reuland predict that a predicate whose co-arguments are co-indexed must be reflexive-marked. One might then expect (41), but there were no such examples in the data:[52]

(41) a.   ~?He$_i$'s just got that kind of air about **himself**$_i$.
     b.   ~?He$_i$ didn't have many spots on **himself**$_i$.
     c.   ~?He$_i$ didn't have any with **himself**$_i$.
     d.   ~?Who's Bob$_i$ bringing with **himself**$_i$?

Similarly, in *keep x with y*, 6/6 of the relevant occurrences in SBC and LSAC were coreferential. Indeed, since coreference is unmarked in this construction, all the PPs contained a pronoun rather than a reflexive:

(42) a.   So I keep my purse with **me**.   (LSAC)
     b.   Do you keep a dictionary with **you** when you read, uh?   (LSAC)
     c.   ... Reagan had a plan ... which he always kept with **him**.   (LSAC)

Another case where a co-indexed pronoun seems to be lexically specified is the Hebrew counterpart of 'imagine.' One way to say 'imagine' is to (literally) say 'describe to one,' where the object of 'to' must be a pronoun co-indexed with the subject (*tearti li* 'I described to me,' 'I imagined'). Should the pronoun not be co-indexed, the meaning of the verb is perforce 'describe' (*tearti lexa* 'I described/ *imagined to you'). Note that here, a pronoun is used for a co-argument, because coreference is unmarked.

---

[50] See also Quirk *et al.* (1985) and Stirling and Huddleston (2002: 1489), who consider *keep x next to* and *direct x away from* as taking an argument rather than an adjunct.

[51] It is such *about* uses which were excluded from the count of *about* prepositional objects above. As can now be seen, these are not really counterexamples to the self- versus other-directed thesis. These cases are merely a subset which has an obligatory expectation for coreference. The other (majority) cases of *about* prepositional objects carry the opposite expectation regarding coreference.

[52] Alternatively, if for some reason we don't see the prepositional objects in (40) as co-arguments of the possessive verbs, it is still a mystery why a reflexive is barred from such nonargument positions.

Summing up section 6.3.2, there are (a few) cases where, contra the Binding Conditions, co-arguments must be coded by pronouns in English. Moreover, since in these cases coreference is consistently unmarked (obligatory in fact), the findings support the functional principle. We have in addition noted above that Reinhart and Reuland's analysis does not touch upon coreference among non-co-arguments, but the functional analysis can shed light on it (section 6.3.1). All in all, the findings show that there is no real free variation here. Rather, reflexive pronouns are preferred where coreference is marked, pronouns are preferred where coreference is unmarked. The structural conditions seem epiphenomenal, and the functional principle seems to account for the data better (but see section 6.3.4 below).

6.3.3   Markedness differences among reflexive forms

Another issue we should compare the two analyses for is the form of reflexive marking. Whereas Reinhart and Reuland predict reflexive marking in certain contexts, their formulation is silent about which reflexive marking it might be. To some extent this is justified, in view of the typologically variable ways available for expressing reflexivity: verbally or nominally, overtly or covertly, by a marked (morphologically complex and long) form or by an unmarked (monomorphemic, short) form (see König and Siemund, 2000). A related question is, how can we account for the connection of reflexive markers to both emphatic markers, which are clearly marked forms, and to middle markers (as the French *se* in e.g. *s'asseoir* 'sit down'), which are quite unmarked?

The structural principle does not attempt an account for such facts. For example, for why it is that in some (other-directed) activities performed on the self, the self acted upon is routinely expressed overtly, often with a marked reflexive (e.g. 'kill,' 'hurt,' 'talk with'), whereas other (non-other-directed) activities (e.g. 'be proud of') and self-directed ones (e.g. 'bring x with,' 'shower') are often coded by unmarked reflexive markings. The encoding of self-directed activities varies too. They are sometimes coded as intransitives (e.g. English *shower*), by an unmarked reflexive (e.g. French *se*), and in yet other cases they are coded by personal pronouns (e.g. idiomatic formulas such as *hold one's breath, have x about y*). The presence or absence of stress on the same form (a feature of markedness) is also mobilized in the service of this distinction: Zribi-Hertz (2003) notes that whereas *himself* can optionally be stressed when it is the object of *proud* (non-other-directed), it is obligatorily stressed when it is the object of *jealous* (other-directed). What needs explaining is, given the objective identity between an agent or experiencer and another participant, how does language code such relations? When do languages (tend to) opt for an intransitive verb (and if so, will the verb be zero marked, or will it be marked morphologically?), when will a personal pronoun be selected, and when will a reflexive serve for that function, and which type of reflexive? Kemmer (1993) has classified reflexives into light versus heavy forms, and Haiman (1998: 73) similarly proposes a distinction between unmarked reflexives (intransitive verbs, the middle voice, verbal inflection, clitic object pronouns) versus marked reflexives (reflexive pronouns). Huang (2000) even distinguishes between duplicated reflexives (less marked) and reflexives attached to pronouns (more marked), in addition to zero marking and simplex reflexives.

While we cannot fully predict the form–function correlation here, it is quite clear that the correlations are far from accidental. Comrie (1998) proposes that the more marked forms are reserved for the more local domains, i.e. where coreference is least expected. König and Siemund (2000: 62) similarly formulate the relevant generalization: "The more complex strategy tends to be used for the more remarkable (i.e. other-directed) situation; the less complex strategy tends to be used for inherently reflexive verbs and for non-other directed situations" (see also Huang, 2000). Basic self-directed activities tend to be expressed by unmarked/ short forms, whereas prototypically other-directed activities involving coreference tend to be expressed by marked/long forms. In other words, while there certainly is linguistic variation among languages, once again, it's not the case that "anything goes." Some patterns persist. The most general principle seems to be that no language uses a more marked strategy which it has for a less marked coreference situation. In terms of markedness of coreference/disjointness, we have referred to various syntactic domains following Comrie (1998) (see (24) above), and within the finite clause we have distinguished the following cases, arranged from least to most marked coreference:

(43)   Obligatory coreference (possession verbs + certain prepositions) > strong expectation for coreference (grooming verbs) > unmarked coreference (possessors, especially of inalienable possessions) > strong expectation for disjointness (verbs of bodily harm, interaction verbs).[53]

The functional principle predicts that if a language has more than one type of reflexive marking, the division of labor between them will follow the markedness of coreference here outlined. The less marked forms should be reserved for those cases where coreference is less marked, the more marked forms should be reserved for those cases where coreference is more marked. Historically, we expect the grammaticization of (emphatic) reflexive forms to proceed from more marked to less marked cases of coreference. Indeed, Kemmer (1993: 154) notes that reflexive *se* forms were rare and late to appear for the grooming verbs in Latin, presumably because coreference is strongly expected. The process was completed by the time of Old French. As for the connection of reflexive markers to both marked (emphatic) and unmarked (middle) forms, Kemmer (1993) finds that it is usually not an emphatic reflexive form which develops into a middle marker. Marked reflexive forms are related to emphatics (e.g. English -*self* forms), while unmarked reflexive forms are related to middle markers, e.g. German, Norwegian, French *se*- forms (see also König and Siemund, 2000). But, once the degree of

---

[53] There are also cases of obligatory disjointness, such as *cramp one's style* – see Farmer (1980, 1984), but these are irrelevant here.

markedness of some reflexive form decreases, as is the case in current English, a formerly emphatic reflexive may come to indicate a middle voice event (see Ariel, 2006a).

Synchronic findings in support of this functional–typological generalization include Russian *sebja* 'self,' which alternates with the shorter *sja*, a verbal suffix, for self-directed actions (Faltz, 1977/1985; Haiman, 1983). Similarly, Dutch has a variation between a relatively unmarked *zich* and a more marked *zichzelf* form. As Haiman (1998: 79) notes, whereas self-directed verbs may take either form, other-directed verbs must take the marked form. He also quotes data from Thai and Alamblak and Amele (Papuan languages) in this connection (see also Siemund, 2003 regarding Swedish). In general, it's never the case that grooming verbs employ a more marked reflexive form than verbs of bodily harm within the same language (in Russian and in other languages, see also Comrie, 1998 re Danish). Kemmer (1993) notes that any language which has middle markers (marking verbs as intransitive) uses them for the grooming verbs.

Next, English *bathe* is zero marked on the (intransitive) verb, whereas the counterpart (Modern) Hebrew is morphologically marked on the verb ***hit-raxec***. But each of the 'bathe' forms is less marked than the reflexive marker for bodily harm verbs (*he hit **himself**, hu hika et **acmo***), where both languages employ their complex reflexive. Lordrup (1999) finds parallels between the predicates taking the Norwegian unmarked reflexive (*seg*) in a local context and those taking inalienables with external possessors. Thus, *dry* takes both *seg* and an inalienable such as 'the face' (rather than 'one's face'), but *admire* must take the marked reflexive, and cannot take 'the face.' No doubt, what predicates of this former type have in common is a high expectation for coreference. Note that in other languages the same contexts might call for the use of a pronoun, but what Norwegian has in common with these languages (e.g. English, Hebrew) is the avoidance of the marked reflexive in such self-directed contexts. Another constraining universal is that languages which obligatorily select reflexives and not pronouns for prepositional phrases tend to show simplex, unmarked reflexives (e.g. Hindi, German, Latin), but languages which allow either option (e.g. English, Hebrew) tend to have complex reflexives (Faltz, 1977/1985: 99–107). This is in line with Comrie (1998).

We have presented above discourse counts for verbs of grooming, which depict actions we normally perform on ourselves. Indeed, the Biblical *rxc* 'bathe/wash' root is regularly used for self-washings, although for the most part, this marking is not overt. Only one occurrence of self-washing had a verbal overt marking in the Old Testament (***hit-raxec***). While this has changed in Modern Hebrew, where speakers invariably use the morphologically marked verbal form now, it is still the case that the nominal overt reflexive form is not usually used here (~??*raxaca et **acma*** 'washed herself'). If a reflexive pronoun indicates marked coreference, we expect languages to not code self-directed activities with their reflexive markers, especially those we are here concentrating on, namely, reflexives originating from emphatics. English *bathe* is similarly zero marked for reflexivity.[54] All the occurrences of *shower* were coded by intransitive verbs (see again example (8a)). So no reflexive pronouns occurred for this activity, which we expect people to perform on themselves. Similarly, 59/60 of the (*get/got*) *dressed* (*up*) cases (stereotypically self-directed actions) were coded by an intransitive verb, as in (44a). Only 1 used a reflexive, as in (44b):

(44) a.   That's the way I **dressed**.
     b.   I take off my clothes and I look at myself in the mirror and I check myself out
            and I wait until I'm okay with myself. I **get myself dressed**.

Of course, once we examine the context of the reflexive in (44b), it is not so surprising that the speaker used a reflexive, rather than an intransitive verb. The dressing activity here described is very different from the unmarked activity of dressing we usually think of. Finally, all shaving activities in LSAC which depict self-shaving without mentioning the body part shaved used intransitives rather than verbs + reflexive pronouns. While Reinhart and Reuland (1993) can argue that where the language offers two alternatives for reflexive marking, speakers would naturally opt for the shorter one, they cannot account for the consistent selection of unmarked reflexive marking for certain but not other activities cross-linguistically. Such an economy principle cannot explain the preference for a double marking (*se* + *lui même*) to mark the reflexivity of other-directed verbs, but not of self-directed verbs.

Here are a few other examples demonstrating the correlation between the (non) markedness of the coreference involved and the reflexive marking selected. Lyutikova (2000) distinguishes between a single and a double reflexive in Tsaxur. The more marked double reflexive is reserved for the more marked coreference cases (e.g. 'know' but not 'wash'; co-arguments, but not obliques). Dutch uses a reflexive in the *near* object case (where coreference is unmarked), but it is the less marked reflexive, *zich*, not *zichzelf* (Faltz, 1977/1985). Swedish 'attack' (proto-typically other-directed) requires a complex reflexive, but 'defend' (not necessarily other-directed) can take the simplex one (König and Siemund, 2000).

All in all, both co-arguments and non-co-arguments seem to pattern according to the functional principle involved, namely, when there is a structure of expecta-tions such that coreference with the subject is marked, a reflexive pronoun (tends to) be used, and when there is a structure of expectations such that coreference with the subject is unmarked, a pronoun (tends to) be used. In addition, while reflexive marking varies from one language to another, what remains constant is the relative markedness of the reflexive marker per situation type. Self-directed activities pick relatively less marked forms, whereas other-directed activities pick relatively more marked forms. Reinhart and Reuland's Binding Conditions can only account for some of the English data, where coreference is marked

---

[54] The 3/15 bathe + -*self* in LSAC are all attempts to translate (literally) Spanish *lavarse* 'wash (oneself),' where Spanish seems to have an overt reflexive form (*se*, a nonemphatic reflexive form).

among co-arguments. They leave open questions about other distributional facts, namely, consistent preferences for either pronouns or reflexives among non-co-arguments (section 6.3.1), and consistent preferences for either marked or unmarked reflexive marking for different predicates where the language has different reflexive forms (section 6.3.3). Finally, the cases where co-arguments obligatorily take pronouns rather than reflexives demonstrate that the Binding Conditions A and B do not only not cover the whole range of attested data, they are actually violated (when coreference is expected among co-arguments – section 6.3.2).

6.3.4 Grammar, and pragmatics too

Thus far, we have seen that the (non-)use of reflexive pronouns can be motivated by pragmatic expectations regarding coreference/disjointness. Conditions A and B seem both too weak, in that they can't predict all the relevant (English) data (consistent preferences for either reflexives or pronouns in non-argument positions – section 6.3.1), and too strong, in that they predict the occurrence of reflexives where they are impossible (unmarked coreference between co-arguments – section 6.3.2). In addition, they cannot account for consistent differences between reflexives of different degrees of markedness (section 6.3.3). Should we then conclude that reflexives are (still) governed by pragmatic principles, where there is no role for purely grammatical conventions? As we see below, the answer here is negative.

First, consider the following from Kemmer (1993: 54/55): "Certain actions which are performed on body parts such as trimming or combing hair, clipping nails and so forth are marked similarly to other grooming verbs involving whole-body actions in some languages." For example, Hungarian *fésül-köd-*, French *se peigner* literally mean 'comb oneself,' while in other languages these same activities are treated as transitive actions involving the specific body part as object (e.g. English 'I combed my hair'). Dutch and German use the same etymologically simplex reflexive marker. In German, however, the emphatic *selbst* is added to the reflexive rather rarely, to indicate contrast. In Dutch, on the other hand, the emphatic addition is rather common, only a handful of verbs making do with the simplex reflexive alone (Kemmer, 1993). Hebrew 'comb one's hair' is expressed by a morphologically reflexive verb (*histarek*), but 'brush one's hair' requires the explicit mention of the hair in a transitive construction. As Huddleston (2002) notes, while English *dress* is a lexical reflexive, *clothe* is not. Similarly, *change* is (also) a reflexive grooming verb, but, although it is also a transitive verb, one cannot say **I need to change myself for dinner*. These are clear cases where there is grammatical stipulation, the details of which cannot be accounted for by the functional principle.

But it is not just these small-scale differences that justify positing a role for grammar in dictating reflexive pronoun use. And it is not even deeper differences between languages (some languages do, others do not have reflexive markers; in some they are optional in others they are obligatory;[55] in some languages reflexive marked coreference is obligatorily to the subject, in others it is not so restricted; in some languages the reflexive can function as a subject, in others it cannot; in some it occurs for possessors, in others it does not; some languages extend the use of their reflexives beyond the finite clause, etc.). These (and the previous) differences all stem from the fact that when an extralinguistic principle gets grammaticized, it applies in those cases that seem to speakers to reflect that principle. Since a translation of a functional principle into a grammatical practice is involved, and since there is never a one-to-one relationship between pragmatic and grammatical categories, variation is inevitable. Naturally, how widely the functional principle is applied, namely, where the cut-off point is for its application, is language-specific (as we have mentioned above, and see Comrie, 1998).

To take a concrete example from reflexive marking: will the intermediate case of nonmarked coreference (e.g. as in the case of possessors – 61 percent show coreference) be treated like expected coreference (e.g. as in the case of *have x about* – 100 percent coreference), or like unmarked disjointness (e.g. as in the case of *have lunch with* – 100 percent disjointness[56])? If they are paired off with the former, coreference will employ a pronoun; if with the latter, coreference will be indicated by a reflexive pronoun. Indeed, some languages use regular pronouns (e.g. English, Hebrew), others use reflexive pronouns for the role of possessor (Russian, Latvian, Swedish, Turkish, Hindi, Japanese according to Faltz, and Icelandic according to Maling, 1984). The functional principle can only account for the limited extent and nature of linguistic variation (the markedness generalization offered by Comrie, 1998, König and Siemund, 2000).

While these differences point to the relevance of arbitrary grammatical conventions in the use of reflexives, they do not directly motivate Conditions A and B, of course. A more crucial argument for the need for grammatical specification in general and for the Binding Conditions specifically is that once a grammatical convention sets in, the motivation behind it may become less or even not relevant at all, automatic processes (such as the Binding Conditions) taking place regardless, and even in spite of the original motivation. Thus, while it is quite plausible that markedness of coreference is the driving force behind reflexive pronouns for direct objects of verbs of bodily harm such as *hit* and *kill*, once the pattern has been rigidly established that coreference in such cases is indicated by a reflexive, special circumstances in which self-hitting/killing is unmarked, or even expected, cannot block the use of a reflexive. The structural rule takes over. Indeed, the following, pulled out of a long psychological analysis of masochists, uses a reflexive, not a pronoun, although coreference is expected:

(45)   So he learns, in effect, to beat **himself** /~?? **him** to obtain relief.

(www.orgonomy.org/article_085.html)

---

[55] E.g. in Gumbaynggir (New South Wales) a reflexive suffix is optional (Levinson, 2000b: 336).
[56] 15/15 *have/has/had lunch with* in LSAC occur with a disjoint prepositional object.

And even in societies where certain people are expected to commit suicide (because they are too old, too ashamed, or they lost their spouse), we do not expect to find *~*She$_i$ had to kill her$_i$, because she reached the killing age*. Similarly, even though a human direct object of *express* must be coreferential (note: *I express myself /*~you better around here*, LSAC) – see Stirling and Huddleston (2002: 1488), a reflexive, rather than a pronoun is required (compare *I expressed *me/ myself*). Once convention sets in, distributional patterns often rigidify, and variation (according to the markedness of coreference) may be blocked.[57]

This rigidity results from redefining the pragmatic terms in structural terms. A reanalysis comes about when the linguistic output is abstracted to yield a different grammar from the original grammar that initially served as the source for the output (Hopper and Traugott, 1993/2003). Of course, in turn, the new grammar may very well produce a partially different linguistic output. In our case, whereas the original grammar may have contained the functional principle, the reanalyzed grammar could be the structural principle, with consequences for linguistic outputs (specifically, for unmarked coreference among co-arguments). Such reinterpretations followed by conventional change are not in fact unique to language (see the Korean marriage ban mentioned in section 4.3 and the concluding remarks in section 6.4). Moreover, the more structure-oriented the choice of reflexives becomes, the more obliterated the original pragmatic motivation becomes, because, increasingly, cases of unmarked coreference are coded by a reflexive. This is how an arbitrary rule may be created out of a well-motivated extralinguistic strategy.

In addition to the examples cited above, note that one can no longer say *~*She$_i$ bathed her$_i$* in current English. Rather, one must use a reflexive, if one is to overtly mention the direct object. Now, this is not because self-bathing has recently become a marked activity (as opposed to bathing others). It's just that since English has intransitive *bathe* for self-bathing, any overt mention of the bathee patterns according to the currently productive grammatical rule (Condition B), namely that if a predicate is reflexive, it must be reflexive marked. The fact that coreference here is unmarked is then irrelevant. The same applies to predicates such as *be proud/ashamed*, *hide*, which require reflexive forms, if an overt prepositional object is to occur. Even some collocations with obligatory coreference (middles) require reflexive forms, such as *think/wonder to oneself, can't help oneself* (see again note 57).

In fact, since the synchronic situation reflects both the structural and the functional principles, there is some conflict between them, where they make different predictions. This is a classical case of what Du Bois (1985) has called competing motivations (even though here, the principles were not initially in conflict with each other). The result is that the variation is sometimes arbitrary.

---

[57] Alternatively, *express* takes a reflexive because *express oneself* is semantically a middle, meaning 'talk in a way that other people can understand' (Macmillan, 2002: 486). See Ariel (2006a) for an analysis of present-day English reflexives as middle markers.

Such is the case for Hebrew *tearti le=acmi*, which can either mean the literal 'I described to myself' or (more often) the derived 'I imagined,'[58] even though the functional principle predicts the occurrence of a pronoun here for the 'imagine' meaning and a reflexive for the 'describe to oneself' meaning. To account for the possibility of the 'imagine' meaning with a reflexive, we can hypothesize that since the prepositional object here is an argument, reflexive marking is required by Condition B, and the productive rule for this marking is a reflexive pronoun. The same explanation could be applied to the one example (out of six) where *put stuff on* received a reflexive, rather than a pronoun in English. The structural convention is encroaching on the functional territory.

The conclusion we must draw is that both the functional and the structural principles are currently operative. The former is not only relevant for the history of the language, it is responsible for many of its synchronic patterns, especially for adjuncts (e.g. for *about* objects). But the grammaticized version of the functional principle (Conditions A and B) seems to be more productive than the functional principle when co-arguments are concerned. Conditions A and B increasingly apply in contexts which resisted them in the past because the coreference involved is unmarked. The functional principle seems to be receding for co-arguments. I have not been able to find a new coinage where the two principles clash, and the functional principle wins out. The opposite can be found. Quite a few cases where we expect pronouns are gradually being taken over by reflexives.

Take upon one/oneself is a relevant case in point. This is an idiomatic collocation with obligatory coreference (one cannot 'take upon another' to do something), and hence a pronoun is expected according to the functional principle. The structural principle predicts a reflexive, however, because the *upon* object is a co-argument. We should then see competition and therefore oscillation between the two forms. If, however, the structural principle is taking over, the distribution between the two forms may not be equal. This is exactly what we find on the Web: 59/243 (24.3 percent) cases contained a pronoun (as in (46a)), but the majority (183/243, 75.3 percent, as in (46b)) contained a reflexive (the Web search was conducted for *took upon her/herself*):

(46) a.   She **took upon her** the yoke of Christ.
     b.   She **took upon herself** the yoke of Jewish law.

Most interestingly, one example showed a modern editorial modification of the original *her* into *herself*, testifying that the modern ear has a preference for *herself* here:[59]

---

[58] Recall that *tearti li* (with a pronoun) can only mean 'I imagined.' Since there is no corpus for spoken Hebrew, there are no statistical data on speakers' preferences for pronouns vs. reflexives in the 'imagine' meaning.

[59] Similarly, the examples for the counterpart Hebrew expression (*kibel al acmo* 'received upon himself') in one dictionary (Even Shoshan, 1982: 1160) has pronouns for older periods of Hebrew and a reflexive for Modern Hebrew. The modern verbal form used in the definition (*natal al acmo*, 'took upon himself') shows a reflexive, rather than a pronoun (in two separate lexical entries). A more

(47)   "Herodias **took upon her(self)** to confound the laws of our country" says
              Josephus

Indeed, all 5 occurrences of *take upon* in the spoken SBC and LSAC contained a
reflexive pronoun.

Consider now the case of *near* objects. There were 4 cases of *near* + a second-
person coreferential with the subject in LLC and LSAC. All showed a pronoun,
rather than a reflexive, which is compatible with Reinhart and Reuland's predictions
(*you* is not a co-argument here), and predicted by the functional principle (coreference is here unmarked). However, recall that the Web contained an equal number of
reflexive and pronominal objects for *near* (even after we have eliminated the high
rank antecedents). It may be that written English is in this case leading the spread of
reflexive forms. What is interesting about this change (if indeed it proves to be one) is
that it doesn't only contradict the functional principle. It also goes beyond Reinhart
and Reuland's generalization. It seems that the reflexive may be reanalyzed as coding
coreference among event participants, regardless of their status as co-arguments and
even regardless of their status as marked coreference cases, provided they are coded
as clause-mate arguments. There are languages where a reflexive (albeit the simplex
reflexive type) is used in these contexts, as well as for possessors. In Russian,
reflexives are regularly used for prepositional objects (Comrie, 1997; and see
Comrie, 1998). Such uses point to the possibility of grammaticization going not
only beyond its initial pragmatic motivation, but also beyond the initial grammatical
translation of the functional principle (Conditions A and B).

Especially when we take into consideration cases such as *near* objects, where
reflexives are used in non-co-argument positions where coreference is unmarked,
we can speculate that the structural specification for the use of reflexives has been
extended. It now optionally, but increasingly, applies to cases which violate both
the Binding Conditions and the functional principle. It is possible that the appropriate characterization of the use of reflexives is increasingly a new structural
characterization, namely, a reflexive is to be used (or, rather, can be used) whenever there is clause-mate coreference. Since such contexts are far more numerous
than those of marked coreference among co-arguments of the same predicate, it
may well be this extension which contributed to what Haiman (1998) calls the
routinization of the English reflexive, which is leading to the potential "fall" of the
reflexive pronoun as a distinct marked referring expression (see below). The more
the reflexive is used according to the structural configuration, the more it may be
reanalyzed as a nonmarked coreference indicator. If so, the structural rule is
gradually less blocked when coreference is unmarked. There is, then, mutual
reinforcement between the structural patterning and the loss of markedness in
reflexives. The more the structural pattern is applied, the less the markedness
associated with reflexives. The less marked they are, the more readily useful
reflexive pronouns are in contexts previously blocked, just because coreference

modern dictionary (Choueka, 1997) only lists the reflexive, but mentions two older collocations with
a pronoun.

is not marked. We now turn to a further development of reflexive pronouns, where they show signs of becoming regular, deictic pronouns.

6.4   The potential demise of reflexive pronouns

We have thus far seen how an emphatic adjunct can develop into a grammaticized reflexive pronoun, where its distribution is for the most part governed by structural conventions. One might think that this grammatical development is where our story of reflexives should come to an end. But it doesn't. Linguistic forms which have reached a well-defined grammatical phase don't necessarily live happily ever after in their grammatical niches. The synchronic grammar, while necessarily a functioning system, is at the same time only the raw material for a potentially new grammar in the making, due to further functional pressures (Givón, 1993, vol. 1: 9). To conclude this chapter, let's look at some evidence that English reflexives may be headed towards a markedness reversal with pronouns.

Haiman (1998: 78) suggests that the modern English reflexive pronouns have been routinized, frequency causing an erosion in their meaning (through habituation), so they no longer indicate a marked coreference. One indication for this status is the fact that reflexive pronouns are not usually stressed. We have here reviewed one factor driving in this direction of markedness loss: the taking over of the structural conditions, which created contexts where reflexive pronouns are used even in the absence of marked coreference (provided they meet the structural specifications). Another factor, not here discussed, is the gradual evolution of a reflexive construction devoted to middle interpretations, which has also detracted from the markedness signaled by the reflexive pronoun. In middle situations, such as those encoded by grooming verbs, it is unmarked coreference that is encoded by reflexive pronouns (see Ariel, 2006a for analysis). Relevant examples are *behave/express/ask/think to/wonder to oneself*, and *express oneself*, which we have already mentioned.

One result is that reflexive pronouns no longer constitute a marked enough strategy for what Haiman calls "distinct representations" of a divided self, a major motivation for choosing a reflexive construction (see again section 6.2.3 and examples (29), (30c), (33), (35c)). Speakers then sometimes resort to pronouns instead of reflexives, in order to highlight that the self is here divided into two separate identities. Note the following, which Reinhart (1983 and onwards) has dubbed accidental coreference cases:

(48) a.   if it breaks I ca I can just blame **me**.   (LSAC)

      b.   If I were my boss,

          I'm not sure I would trust **me**

                        (Brian Wilson, announcer, *Fox News*, Feb. 15, 2004)

Blame myself, if used in (48a), would have been more of a (one-participant) internal activity of self-blaming, a possible paraphrase for which is the intransitive *feel guilty*. In *blame me*, on the other hand, there are two participant roles, both the blamer and the blamee being profiled. While the reflexive form tends to indicate an internal cognitive activity, the pronominal form probably involves some public, more objective act of blaming. Likewise, in (48b), there is a difference between 'self-trusting' (a middle, internal type of activity) and 'trusting me' a transitive event profiling two participants where 'me' is chosen as the object of trusting from among other potential entities, unrelated to the self. In fact, the speaker is here adopting his boss's identity for the truster's role, a clear case of self-alienation. Here's an example demonstrating that when a non-alienated divided-self reading is sought, a reflexive will be chosen:

(49)   Some people had doubts about me, but I never had doubts about **myself**.
                 (Misty May, *International Herald Tribune*, Aug. 26, 2004)

Accidental coreference is an attempt by the speaker to convey that the coreference at hand is neither what might be expected from a transitive reflexive (namely, that it is marked), nor from a middle reflexive (namely, that it is intrinsic, expected and subjective). In fact, coreference is presented here as incidental to the event. The speaker is conveying that there is nothing special about the coreference relation. It is, as Reinhart suggested, (presented as) accidental.

   Next, the example in (50) shows that if the reflexive doesn't necessarily indicate a marked coreference, there's less of a reason to select it over a regular pronoun. This is so sometimes even in cases where coreference is marked, i.e. in the very cases which initially gave rise to the development of reflexive pronouns. Now, it's not the case that speakers routinely use a pronoun instead of a reflexive in co-argument positions in English where coreference is marked. But if the speaker has a competing motivation to avoid such a reflexive, she might use a pronoun, as in the following:

(50)   A: so then Jamie said to David well David   1
             why **didn't you introduce me to your mother**.   2
         B: Logical question.   3
         A: Logical question.   4
         C: Hey, **I introduced me to her mother**. What's she talking about,   5
             she **never introduced me to her mother either**.   (LSAC)   6

Note that *introduce me* is perfectly grammatical in A's line 2. Not so in C's *I introduced me* (line 5). As mentioned in section 5.2.1, Du Bois (2004, 2007) proposes that speakers resonate with each other, the juxtaposition of similar structures triggering special pragmatic effects. Dialogic Syntax, combined with the general loss of markedness of reflexive forms (in favor of middle interpretations), can explain the tolerance for *me* instead of the grammatically mandated *myself* in (50) line 5. As Du Bois argues, such grammatical divergences, motivated by Dialogic Syntax, may play a role in promoting grammatical change. While C might not have chosen *me* in the absence of the supporting line 2 preceding it and his own line 6 following it, the fact that such creative violations happen for local reasons in specific contexts may pave the way for their becoming the generally accepted forms at some future stage. They introduce innovative forms/general-izations into the repertoire of possible combinations, and should these forms gain in frequency, they may become the norm (see again chapter 4).[60] But the reason why speakers are now being innovative about using pronouns where reflexives are expected is, we can hypothesize, the routinization of the reflexive pronoun, which eroded its markedness, and even its referentiality (see Ariel, 2006a).

Finally, while (50) shows the avoidance of a reflexive because it is not so different from a pronoun, the gradual loss of markedness attached to reflexives may also be responsible for innovations in the opposite direction: an increasing use of mainly first- and second-person reflexives instead of unmarked, regular pronouns in positions formerly reserved for regular personal pronouns. These reflexives often (but not always) occur in adjunct, nonmiddle roles, and they may lack a proper linguistic antecedent (see Stirling and Huddleston, 2002) for pre-ferred contexts:

(51) a.   A: Alright. . . . How are you doing?
           B: Alright, how about **yourself**?   (LSAC)
     b.   And we need more than, than **yourself**.   (LSAC)
     c.   She said then Robin X and **herself** uh <unclear> were all going to work together on the video.   (LSAC)[61]
     d.   It's still a close race between **himself** and John Kerry.
                                              (CNN interview, May 10, 2004)
     e.   Looks like detective Conklin shot **himself** the wrong nigger.
                                              (The movie *Crash*)

As Haiman (1998) argues, an interesting result of these developments is a seemingly anomalous situation where in some cases a formally unmarked form (the regular pronoun) now indicates a relatively more marked coreference rela-tionship than the formally marked reflexive pronoun does. Recall that originally, reflexive pronouns were introduced where the expectation was for disjointness of reference, and coreference was therefore marked. Thus, since we normally report about blaming others, when the object of our blaming is coreferential to the subject, a reflexive pronoun is used (see (2), (33a)). However, once reflexives tend to lose their markedness feel, speakers may start reverting to the nonreflexive form (regular pronouns) for the more marked cases (as in (48)). We may then end up with a relatively marked form (the English reflexive) indicating a relatively

---

[60] Consider the following innovative (ungrammatical) nominative use of a reflexive in Hebrew, no doubt triggered by considerations of resonance:

(i)   SI: Where have I seen this person? Where have I seen this person?
          shalosh peamim shaalti et **acmi**. ve=az **acmi** ana li . . .
          three   times   I.asked ACC myself. and=then myself answered to:me . . .
                                                    (Hebrew, IDF radio, May 27, 2005)

[61] This reflexive seems to be a case where a reflexive is used when speakers are not sure whether to use nominative or accusative pronouns (see Biber *et al.*, 1999: 339; Quirk *et al.*, 1985: 339).

unmarked interpretation (coreference due to middle voice), and a relatively unmarked form (the pronoun) used when a relatively marked coreference is involved (accidental coreference). This is a complete reversal in the distribution of regular and reflexive pronouns. In (51), however, we only witness half of this markedness reversal. Contra their original function, the reflexives in these examples do not indicate marked coreferences. But it's not the case that had regular pronouns been used instead, the readings would have been different, specifically more marked. Note, however, that there are some preliminary signs pointing to a countershift, which might result in the re-establishment of a match between formal and interpreted markedness. The following indicates a middle semantics by an unmarked reflexive form (the reduced *self*):

(52)   Wish my dream **self behaved** with a bit more decorum.
                        (www.ghost2138.org/phorum/read.php?f=3&i=431&t=431 – 94k)

Summing up, we have seen that the English reflexive pronoun, which we are used to thinking of as a type of referring expression, is historically tied to two quite distinct grammatical categories. It evolved out of an originally emphatic adjunct, which acquired argument status. As such, it became a marked form, used for marked interpretations. This is not invariably the case in current English, however. In fact, it is not inconceivable that in the future the English reflexive will follow in the footsteps of French *se* 'self,' in which case it will encode intransitivity, so the reflexive pronoun will lose not only its interpretative markedness, but also its argument status (once again).

While we can see a gradual historical path leading from emphatic adjuncts to reflexive pronouns and ultimately (possibly) to intransitivizers, it is important to note that as is very often the case, newer developments overlap with historically older processes (recall Hopper's 1991 concept of layering mentioned above; and see Fischer, 2003). Specifically, the establishment of the grammatical (rather than pragmatic) characterization of reflexive pronouns as referring expressions overlaps with the later development of reflexives into middle markers. This means that we have more than one grammaticization process taking place at the same time for the very same linguistic form. The picture that emerges is that current English simultaneously reflects various historical stages, competing motivations, and potential directions for future changes. The conflicting patterns are then (i) the functional principle, which stipulates that reflexives are marked referring expressions, (ii) the two competing structural patterns (Conditions A and B versus clause-mate coreferential arguments to be reflexive-marked), where reflexives are not necessarily indicative of a marked coreference, and (iii) the middle construction use, whereby reflexives indicate unmarked coreference. We have here seen how complex the distribution of reflexive pronouns is. Such complexity is no doubt characteristic of many other linguistic phenomena.

Language seems to operate with contradicting forces simultaneously, which accounts for the variation, and sometimes contradicting patterns of use we have observed above. For example, on the one hand, current uses of reflexive pronouns still show them to be more marked than pronouns, which accounts for why unmarked coreference cases may sometimes be indicated by pronouns rather than by reflexive pronouns despite the structural requirement for a reflexive (see again (40)). At the same time, reflexives are no longer felt to be as marked as in previous periods perhaps. This is why new, more complex emphatics are occasionally innovated by speakers, which better reflect the markedness involved (see again (18), (20)), and why reflexives are spreading into slots previously reserved for the unmarked pronouns (as in (46)). As Heine *et al.* (1991b) propose, grammar is to a large extent panchronic, rather than either synchronic or diachronic. Many grammatical forms are hybrids between old and new forms, reflecting both synchronic and diachronic processes.

A striking example for this point is provided by Heine *et al.* from the African language So, where *sú* 'back' may be case marked as a nominal (this is the old morphological pattern), even when it functions as a locative preposition 'behind' (this is the innovative semantic pattern, as in 'S/he is behind the mountain'). Alternative forms coexist with this pattern, where both *sú* and the relevant noun (e.g. 'mountain') are case marked, as well as cases where only the nominal receives case marking. The three formal alternatives respectively represent the old pattern (where *sú* was a noun), a hybrid stage (where both the newly created preposition and the noun are case marked), and the evolving (future) pattern (where only the nominal receives case marking).[62] We have seen similar facts for reflexive pronouns as well, where the synchronic grammar involves both change in progress (diachrony) and variation (which can be treated as purely synchronic) (and see Li, 1975 about the double function of verbs as prepositions in Chinese).

There seem to be quite a few surprising facts, and even apparent paradoxes in the history of reflexive forms. Why should an adjunct become an argument? Why should an argument lose its argument status? Why should a form reserved for marked coreference come to indicate unmarked coreference? Why should a form initially used in contexts of high transitivity come to indicate low transitivity (in middle situations)? How can both the rise and the (potential) fall of reflexive pronouns be functionally motivated? Why should language users give up a motivated principle (the functional principle) for an apparently arbitrary one (the structural convention)? And then, once grammaticized, why start the whole process again where a new functionally motivated change may ultimately lead to the replacement of one grammatical system (governing the distribution of

---

[62] Moreover, a So sentence such as:

(i)   néke cúc sú-o   im
         be   fly back-ablative   girl

is ambiguous between the original 'There is a fly on the girl's back' and 'There is a fly behind the girl.' It is precisely because various grammaticization stages overlap with each other that we get this ambiguity.

reflexive pronouns) with another (governing the encoding of intermediate transitivity or even syntactic intransitivity)?

We cannot address all these questions here, but we can try to understand at least some of the puzzling developments. Recall (chapter 4) that what must be motivated is each single step in grammaticization, not the complete shift seen in retrospect. As Heine *et al.* (1991b) emphasize, categories on grammaticization chains (in our case: emphatics > reflexive pronouns > intransitivizers) are linked by family resemblances. While each pair of adjacent items have something in common, not all items share a single feature. Recall the analogy we drew between the development of French negation and the shift in the meaning of the Jewish Day of Atonement. Now, the original impetus behind the use of a reflexive to indicate marked coreference (motivated) was given up in favor of a convention to use a reflexive when certain syntactic conditions obtain regardless of markedness – an arbitrary convention. In our case, the high correlation between cases where a reflexive is used because coreference is marked and the syntactic configuration in which the reflexive and its antecedent are co-arguments may have led to the automatic choice of a reflexive once the structural condition holds, regardless of whether the pragmatic condition holds. Thus, (i) just as the Day of Atonement correlates with not driving in a motivated way, so there is a motivated correlation between the marked reflexive expressions and marked coreference; (ii) just as there is a motivated correlation between no driving/empty roads and cycling, the correlation between marked coreference and coreference between co-arguments is far from accidental. Still, once we apply a chain of reinterpretations, the result is arbitrariness: (iii) just as the correlation between the Day of Atonement and cycling is arbitrary, so is the correlation between reflexives and (any) co-argument coreference. The developments very briefly outlined in section 6.4 can be equally shown to be locally motivated, even if in the long run they lead to a synchronically rather arbitrary connection between the formally marked reflexive pronouns and lack of interpretative markedness (and transitivity).

As emphasized in chapter 4, language users think and act locally and opportunistically (see Lass, 1997; Traugott, 2004b). Recruiting an emphatic seems to be a good solution for reference resolution. Later on, redefining the functional principle in structural terms was simply an automatization of the decisions about reflexive use, the structural rule approximating the products of the functional principle. Whereas the structural and the functional principles are at times quite incompatible with each other (for unmarked coreference between co-arguments, and to some extent for marked coreference between non-co-arguments), we must remember that structural, even if partially arbitrary rules are functional too. Substituting the functional principle with a structural principle is a motivated step, since it replaces a relatively harder/costlier decision (is the coreference at hand closer to being unmarked or marked?) with an automatic decision, where no choice is allowed (the speaker must only check whether the structural configuration is met or not – see Givón, 1999; Mithun, 1989). In fact, automatization may very well be an uncontrolled process. But then, once automaticity made reflexive pronouns rather prevalent, they could not maintain their high degree of markedness (a self-defeating process). Thus, the changes we have surveyed above are perfectly motivated when taken one step at a time (see Traugott, 2004b against discontinuity of linguistic change). They are opportunistic in that each change made others available, and speakers responded, rather than initiated change. Had it not been for the first development (e.g. the loss of markedness for reflexives), the newer functions (deictic pronouns, intermediate transitivity for middle situations) would probably not have developed.

The seemingly paradoxical conclusion is therefore that both the rise and the potential fall of marked reflexive forms are pragmatically motivated. In both cases, recurrent, contextually supported inferences (emphatics point to marked referents, frequent obligatory forms lose their markedness) set interpretative patterns, which gradually brought about changes to the grammar. Furthermore, the evolution of reflexive pronouns offers an opportunity for us to see how motivated language use and the grammar shaped by it are, even when the grammar seems partially arbitrary synchronically. Finally, we can now better understand why it is such a challenge to draw the grammar/pragmatics divide (recall part I). If grammar evolves out of pragmatic motivations (among other extralinguistic motivations), then we should only expect that it would be hard to disentangle the two, at least in some cases. Reflexive pronouns, we have seen, require both grammatical and pragmatic accounts.

PART III

Bringing grammar and pragmatics back together

Introduction

Part I was devoted to drawing the grammar/pragmatics divide, whereby grammar and pragmatics were seen as distinct and complementary. Grammar was defined as conventional code, pragmatics as extragrammatical inference. The distinction is not, however, absolute, and in more than one respect. First, the grammar/pragmatics division of labor is not topic-oriented. There are no exclusively "pragmatic" topics per se: all linguistic expressions involve both grammatical and inferred aspects (see Ariel, forthcoming: chapters 6–8). One case discussed in this book is presupposition (see again section 2.1): it is not either semantic or pragmatic. It is both. Another is reflexive pronouns. Second, as we saw in chapters 2 and 3, it is not always an easy matter to determine whether a given language use is coded or inferred, and different researchers have therefore proposed different grammar/pragmatics divisions of labor. But these difficulties do not challenge the very assumption of a division of labor between grammar and pragmatics. They only point to the difficulties in applying it to specific cases.

More challenging to the viability of a grammar/pragmatics divide are the diachronic analyses in part II, which testify that pragmatic inferences can and do cross the line to become codes. How can this be so, if grammar and pragmatics are so clearly distinct according to the code/inference proposal? The answer is that grammatical and pragmatic aspects of interpretations do interface. As Du Bois (2003b) put it, there is no discourse without grammar, and no grammar without discourse. Synchronically, speakers intend addressees to pay attention to all meaning aspects, and this is what addressees do. Despite the fact that they have two quite distinct cognitive sources (codes and inferences), consciously available utterance interpretations tend to constitute unanalyzed wholes. What interlocutors care about is recovering the speakers' intended meanings, be their source grammatical or pragmatic. No wonder that numerous psycholinguistic experiments have found that subjects sometimes mistake (some) pragmatically inferred interpretations for linguistically encoded aspects of the speaker's message (e.g. they sometimes think that inferences they drew from speakers' utterances were actually 'said' by the speaker, they recognize words related to an inference as fast as they recognize a word explicitly mentioned in the text).[1]

If so, both diachronic processes and synchronic interpretations attest to the existence of a meaning level which combines, even integrates into a single representation, grammatical and pragmatic aspects. Chapters 4–6 argued for the salient discourse pattern as the mediator enabling the change from inference to code. But what is the code/inference hybrid interpretation which is relevant for discourse patterns? Is there just one such "hybrid" meaning level which explains all the uses we make of representations where codes are supplemented by inference? In other words, where do(es) the grammar/pragmatics interface(s) take place? There is consensus in the field about at least one integrative meaning level, Grice's conveyed meaning. The conveyed meaning is the total intended meaning communicated by the speaker, composed of the semantic meaning plus all the speaker-intended pragmatic inferences, most notably various types of implicatures. Assuming such a level, the mere simultaneous occurrence of a semantic and a pragmatic interpretation for a single form may blur the distinction between them, allowing the inferred to be taken as coded. Grice (1975), Levinson (2000b), and most notably Traugott and Dasher (2002) set out from such an assumption in explaining semanticizations.

Recanati (2004), however, has argued that it's not the case that semantic meaning and implicatures are actually merged into a single meaning level. The simultaneity of the two types of interpretations does not entail integration between them. Instead, he treats the conveyed meaning as a mere cover term for two separate types of distinct meaning levels, which interlocutors are aware of and keep apart: the explicit and the implicit. It is a different interface level, that of 'what is said,' which shows a true merger of the inferred with the coded, according to Recanati (1989 and onwards). Indeed, in addition to a

---

[1] See Johnson *et al.* (1973), Singer (1979, 1980), Singer and Ferreira (1983), Potts *et al.* (1988), Jung-Beeman (2006).

level of total meaning (the conveyed meaning) and to a bare (nonhy-
brid) linguistic meaning, researchers have felt a need to define an
intermediate 'what is said' level of representation. 'What is said' is a
basic-level meaning, which is supposed to capture the minimal
descriptive content of the utterance. This would be a literal meaning,
which specifies the truth conditions of the utterance, and is therefore
binding for the speaker, perhaps as attested by legal interpretations –
see Katz (1972). 'What is said' is not as minimal as the purely
linguistic meaning, since the latter is missing quite basic information
for determining truth conditions (such as the referential identity of
entities mentioned). But how minimal/maximal should it be? Could it
be the relevant representation responsible for grammaticization and
semanticization as well? We address these questions in chapter 7.

7 Grammar/pragmatics interfaces

Our main goal in chapter 7 is to present various concepts of the semantic/
pragmatic interface level of 'what is said.' We first introduce the problems in
defining such a basic-level meaning representation (section 7.1), and then discuss
four proposals as to how to define the concept (sections 7.2–7.6). We reiterate the
main conclusions of the book in section 7.7, briefly considering the possibility that
'what is said' is not only important for grammar/pragmatics interfaces during
interaction, but also in processes in which pragmatics crosses over to become
grammar.

7.1 The widening gap between 'what is said' and a basic-level meaning

Ideally, as a basic meaning level, 'what is said' should stand for (i) a
complete truth-evaluable proposition, the speaker's basic intended meaning,
which is, moreover, (ii) expressed **explicitly**.[1] Conventional implicatures,
although conventional, do not constitute part of 'what is said,' because they are
neither explicit nor truth-conditional (but see section 7.5 below). Even Grice,
however, realized that as rudimentary as his 'what is said' was, it could not be
equated with pure linguistic meaning. This is why he proposed that 'what is said'
is "**closely related** to the conventional meaning of the words (the sentence)"
(Grice, 1989: 25, emphasis added). The gap between the bare semantic meaning
and 'what is said' was thought to be quite minimal at the time, caused by two types
of expressions requiring contextual support: (i) nonliteral expressions (e.g. metaphors and ironies, where the speaker intends something quite different from the
literal, semantic meaning), and (ii) referring expressions whose referents need to
be fixed in context, and ambiguous expressions, where a choice must be made as
to the contextually appropriate sense intended in the specific case. In principle,
whenever there's a gap between the explicit linguistic meaning and the intended
meaning, one can opt for either including or excluding the 'meant' from the 'said.'
In other words, the definition of the concept may be extended to reflect 'meant'
aspects at the cost of being unfaithful to the purely 'grammatically expressed', or it

---

[1] We should actually talk about propositional content instead of propositions, to include nonasserted
utterances.

may adhere to the 'explicitly said,' ignoring some aspects of the 'meant.' Thus, either the 'said' includes implicit content, or it excludes some 'meant' aspects.

Regarding figurative language, Grice chose the excluding line, so the intended meaning is not included in 'what is said' in this case. Consider the following hyperbole:

(1)   (Context: M: Seven hundred and thirty sheqels per couple)

> A: **bli**   **kesef**.
>   without   money
>   'They're giving it away.'   (Hebrew, Izre'el, 2002)[2]

It's not as if A is saying that 730 sheqels equals 'zero money.' She does not mean 'no money' literally. What she wants to convey is that paying 730 sheqels per couple (for four days at a hotel) is very inexpensive. She is exaggerating her reaction in order to communicate how great the hotel deal is. Inferred nonliteral interpretations have been taken to involve conversational implicatures, and thus, not included in 'what is said.'[3] Thus, with respect to the first issue (nonliterality), Grice opted for an excluding solution: what is meant in such cases (the nonliteral interpretation) is excluded from 'what is said,' because it is not explicit.

But with respect to the second issue (contextual reliance for reference and ambiguity resolutions) Grice chose the inclusive strategy, preserving the assumption that a semantic representation should provide the intended truth conditions for the proposition expressed. Grice's definition of 'what is said' therefore allowed it to diverge from the bare semantic meaning and include reference and ambiguity resolutions, based on the extralinguistic context. However, the assumption was that the context required is quite narrowly defined, the number of expressions requiring such contextual fixing is rather small, and the processing involved quite mechanistic (algorithmic). Most importantly, there is no need to refer to speakers' intentions for these completions. Bach (1994 and onwards) proposed the "Syntactic Correlation Constraint" which determines which contextually derived information can be added to the linguistic semantic meaning and still count as Grice's 'what is said.' The guiding principle is that any completions mandated by the grammar are to be added to 'what is said,' because they are restricted to a direct correspondence between explicit elements (and their grammatical characteristics) and inferred elements added on. Recanati (1989) similarly defines such a set of completions under the concept of saturation. Here are two relevant examples (some of the needed completions are provided in the double parentheses in (2)):

---

[2] Izre'el (2002) provides a few transcriptions from the pre-pilot of CoSIH, spoken Hebrew corpus under construction.

[3] At the same time, since Grice did intend 'what is said' to also be speaker-meant (Grice, 1989: 87–88), the unintended semantic meaning here was not quite incorporated into 'what is said.' After all, the speaker couldn't possibly intend to communicate the literal meaning of a hyperbole, or an ironical statement, for example. A variant, 'as if to say' concept was introduced by Grice, so that the literal meaning of e.g. an ironic or hyperbolic statement is an 'as if to say' instead of a 'what is said.'

(2) a. ALINA: (Hx) She ((**Lisabeth**)) just goes,

I ((**Lisabeth**)) feel like you've ((**Mar**)) got a whole other world outside of us ((**Lisabeth + others**)),

like you ((**Mar**)) don't even need us Mar,

and that you ((**Mar**)) have a whole other life.

LENORE: (H)

ALINA: Mom ((**Mar**)) said I ((**Mar**)) do ((**have a whole other life**)).   (SBC: 006)

b.

paam	xashavti	alayx	dvarim	raim.		
once	I.thought	about:you	things	bad		
hayom	((**ani xoshev**	**alayx**	**dvarim**))	harbe	yoter	raim.
today	((**I think**	**about:you**	**things**))	much	more	bad

'In the past I thought bad things about you. Today ((I think)) much worse ((things about you)).'   (Hebrew, Izre'el, 2002)

The idea is that pronouns, such as *she, I,* and *you* require identification, *I do* requires the recovery of a VP, and the gapped clause in (2b) requires the recovery of a few arguments.

Note that such contextual completions follow the so-called linguistic direction principle definition of 'what is said' (see Carston, 1988, Recanati, 1993: chapter 13), whereby pragmatic inferences are included in 'what is said' provided they are triggered by the grammar. This is why, despite the contextual enrichments included, the justification usually cited for the 'what is said' is that it represents not only a basic meaning, but specifically a **linguistic** (or semantic) meaning (see e.g. Bach, 1994, 2001; Berg, 2002; Horn, 2004; Saul, 2002). Here are two typical statements on this issue "there is a theoretical need for such a notion ['what is said' – MA] to account for the **semantic** content of an utterance that is **independent of the fact that the utterance is actually made**," "what is said is determined **linguistically**" (Bach, 2001: 28). In other words, 'what is said' attempts to meet two criteria: it should be a purely **linguistic** meaning, but at the same time, it should constitute a basic interpretative level, which provides at least some **truth conditions** for the proposition expressed. The problem is that it has recently become clear that these two requirements cannot simultaneously be satisfied by one and the same meaning level in many and not just in a few cases. Many researchers have reached the conclusion that such a basic-level meaning must necessarily be (also) pragmatic (Carston, 2004b; Recanati, 2001; Travis, 1991).

Many pragmatists and philosophers, most notably Relevance theoreticians (Carston, 1988 and onwards, especially, 2002a; Sperber and Wilson, 1986/1995), have pointed to the very wide gap between linguistic semantic meaning, or even the slightly richer, classical 'what is said' and a truth-evaluable proposition. Even if reference fixing and disambiguation have successfully been performed, conventional meaning falls short of providing the descriptive content of the utterance, as it is intuitively viewed by the interlocutors. And this gap is unavoidable, because of the fundamentally underdetermined nature of the linguistic code. The linguistic code is very often too schematic to encode a full

proposition. The assumption that linguistic semantic meaning radically underdetermines actual utterance interpretations in general, and truth conditions in
particular, is now shared by researchers in the field, regardless of their radically
different solutions for how to bridge this gap.[4] Note the following, where the
contextual material needed for completing the utterances is indicated in
parentheses:

(3) a.   A: ... That's what I was coming to talk to you about. I hadn't heard
                 anything from Liz so I didn't know
           B: but evidently she is better **((than she was))**
           A: Uh huh.   (LSAC)
     b.   Would you like some cheese and crackers or something. Have you
           eaten anything **((recently today))**.   (LSAC)
     c.   oh Michelle you know um . . . tt uh . . . I'm gonna be coming in . . . to some
           ((substantial amounts of)) money.   (LSAC)
     d.   I just spent a thousand dollars when I got this job, or more, on clothing
           because I had nothing **((=no appropriate clothes))**, I had jeans and tee
           shirts because I worked in a warehouse.   (LSAC)

In (3a), the comparative construction requires that the addressee retrieve some
object of comparison. But note that the implicit comparison in this case is to how
Liz was doing in the past, rather than, for example, to how someone else is doing,
although the specific comparison is not mentioned explicitly prior to or following
B's utterance. The inference is then far from trivial, even though it is grammatically mandated. Next, the bare, linguistic semantic meaning of the present perfect
tense (*have eaten* in (3b)) is assumed to be that the eating event took place at some
point in time in the past. This would mean that (3b) grammatically means something like 'have you ever eaten anything in your life?'[5] (3c) grammatically means
that 'the speaker has come into a nonzero amount of money,' in principle,
including insignificant amounts of money. Obviously, this is not the speaker's
intended meaning here. In (3d) the speaker means she has no appropriate clothes,
not that she has no belongings whatsoever (although this is the linguistic semantic
meaning of *nothing*).

   In order to verify what the states of affairs must be for satisfying the propositions in (3), one must enrich the semantic meaning with some version of the
completions provided in (3). Crucially, examples (3b–d) do not impose the above
completions grammatically. Moreover, the nonenriched versions (e.g. 'I had
nothing whatsoever') are perfectly truth-evaluable. In other words, the utterances

---

[4] See e.g. Recanati (1989, 1993 and onwards), Travis (1991), Berg (1993), Bach (1994, 2000),
    Stainton (1994), Levinson (2000b), and Stanley (2000).
[5] Here's an example where the present perfect is so intended:

             (i) The Governor of Virginia **has spoken up** for impeachment, saying "Guilt wherever
             found ought to be punished." Sadly, that was Governor Edmund Randolph in 1787
             (March 6, 2006 www.truthout.org/docs_2006/030306R.shtml).

    In this case, the relevant time frame begins in the eighteenth century, rather than at some point in the
    immediate past (i.e. when the current Governor of Virginia took office).

do not even require the completions provided for them in order to satisfy a second potential definition for a minimalist 'what is said,' namely the 'minimal truth-evaluability principle,' which states that pragmatic inferences are included in 'what is said,' if they are required for arriving at a minimal truth-evaluable proposition (Carston, 1988; Recanati, 1993: chapter 13). (3b–d) show that minimal propositions may be truth-evaluable, although they are not the propositions expressed by the utterances (i.e. they are not speaker-intended).

According to Carston (2002a: chapter 1, and see references therein), it is not merely out of convenience (production efficiency) that the linguistic code underdetermines 'what is meant.' Underdeterminacy is an inherent characteristic of human language, since no natural language sentence can encode interlocutors' intended statements fully. Each sentence is routinely used to express very many different propositions, with different truth conditions, as the following attest:

(4) a.   yesh   anashim   she=ohavim   **kubiyot ba=beten**   ve=yesh
           there.are people   who=like.PL   cubes   in.the=stomach and=there.are
           anashim   she=ohavim **kubiyot ba=beten**.
           people   who=like.PL cubes   in.the=stomach
           'There are people who like squares ((six-pack muscles)) on their stomach,
           and there are people who like squares ((of wafers)) inside their stomach.'
                                   (Hebrew, ad for wafers, *Haaretz*, March 25, 2004)

    b.   ha=manhiga ha=yexida im   **kubiyot ba=beten**.   hacba para
          the=leader.F the=single.F with cubes   in.the=stomach. Vote   cow
          Ad for a chocolate whose symbol is a cow, which figures on its wrapping,
          just before Israeli elections: 'The only ((political)) leader with ((chocolate))
          squares ((stored)) in her stomach. Vote cow.' (Spotted March 2006)

    c.   CUSTOMER: I'd like **another cup**.
          ((Server at the coffee stand hands the customer an empty paper cup.))
          CUSTOMER: No, another cup of chocolate milk.
                                   (Originally Hebrew, Oct. 29, 2002)

Although *kubiyot ba-beten* 'cubes in the stomach' are understood in three different ways in (4a, b), it's not the case that Hebrew *kubiyot* 'cubes,' *ba-* 'in the,' or *beten* 'stomach' are ambiguous. Rather, as Recanati (2001) argues, language presents us with many cases of constructional indeterminacies (the example he uses is *red pen*: is the red on the outside, or is it the color of the ink?). *Another cup* is similarly not ambiguous between 'another empty cup' and 'another cup with chocolate milk in it.' Rather, the customer's first utterance in (4c) can be used to express either proposition. Carston argues that natural languages evolved on the basis of very powerful "mind-reading" inferential abilities (which she accounts for by reference to Relevance theory), and hence did not need to develop an explicit code for each message. Of course, even if we did have such a code, it wouldn't solve the problem, for we constantly have new messages to communicate, which, as we have seen in part II, we have no choice but to express with the grammatical means already at our disposal.

The basic problem is this: 'what is said' cannot be minimal in that it requires only minimal, trivial context enrichments, which are, moreover, grammatically mandated (in line with the linguistic direction principle), and at the same time reflect the intuitive truth-conditional content of the utterance as intended by the speaker, because the latter requires more than what the minimal truth-evaluability criterion calls for. The intuitive truth conditions of the intended proposition may require a nonminimal representation. Thus, if it's minimal, it can't constitute the "official," intuitive content of the speaker's utterance on the given occasion. If, on the other hand, it's contextually enriched so as to faithfully reflect specifically the speaker's truth-evaluable proposition, it invariably relies heavily on ad hoc contextual assumptions, which render it maximal. We seem to be in a bind.

Moreover, as Levinson (2000b: chapter 3) has argued, the fact that 'what is said' is partly derived pragmatically gives rise to what he called "Grice's circle." If, as Grice thought, we first determine 'what is said,' and only then can we derive the additional pragmatic inferences (implicatures), based on that semantic meaning, then we're caught in a vicious circle. On the one hand, we need 'what is said' in order to determine the pragmatic inferences, but on the other hand, we need pragmatic inferences in order to determine 'what is said' (see again examples (2)–(4)). So, which of these comes first?

Levinson (2000b) is quite "Gricean" in his (partial) solution to the problem. He adds one more family of pragmatic interpretations to the list of those allowed to constitute 'what is said.' In addition to the recoverability of grammatically deleted constituents, and reference and ambiguity resolutions, he allows certain, but not other implicatures to form part of 'what is said.' Only generalized conversational implicatures can determine the truth conditions of the proposition expressed. Consider the examples in (44) in chapter 3, as well as the following:

(5)   Many of them know it [the Koran – MA], **most or all** of it, by heart . . .
        (Originally Hebrew, The Islamic Museum, Jerusalem, Dec. 2003)

Since *most* means 'more than half' for Levinson, the 'not all' generalized conversational implicature must be incorporated into 'what is said' here, or else there won't be two separate alternatives in the disjunction in (5). The logic behind privileging only generalized conversational implicatures in contributing to 'what is said' is that these inferences are default inferences, which go through without any context consultation (although they may be canceled by the ad hoc context). In this sense they are qualitatively different from other pragmatic inferences (particularized conversational implicatures).

This proposal, although on the face of it reasonable and attractive, cannot actually solve the problem, however. First, Levinson himself offers examples where particularized conversational implicatures, and not only generalized conversational implicatures, contribute truth-conditional aspects to utterance interpretations (see his 3.511). Second, as Carston (2004a) has argued, not all generalized conversational implicatures make truth-conditional contributions. So it seems that restricting the pragmatic "intrusions" into 'what is said' to generalized conversational implicatures is too restrictive on the one hand, and not restrictive enough on the other hand. We are then left with the problem of how liberal we should be in admitting pragmatic inferences into our concept of 'what is said.'

There are four types of resolutions for the problem of the widening gap between linguistic semantic meaning and 'what is said.' According to the predominant views in the literature, 'what is said' can either be defined minimally or maximally. It can't be both. Most researchers have then chosen either some minimalist concept of 'what is said' (e.g. Berg, 1993, 2002; Borg, 2005a; see section 7.2), or some maximalist concept of 'what is said' (Recanati, 1989 and onwards, and most notably Relevance theoreticians – Sperber and Wilson, 1986/1995 and onwards; see section 7.3). Many formal semanticists (e.g. Barwise and Perry, 1983; Kadmon, 2001; Kamp, 1995; Landman, 2000) have also adopted this position in effect, for they see semantics as responsible for providing **all** truth conditions, pragmatically derived ones included.[6] A third approach (Stanley, 2000) actually denies that there is such a conflict between a minimalist and an intuitive maximalist concept of 'what is said', insisting that 'what is said' can be minimalist and maximalist at the same time (section 7.4). Section 7.5 presents the dilemma of cases where even a minimalist 'what is said' is too maximalist. A fourth type of option out of this bind is to give up on the assumption that there is only a single 'basic-level meaning' (Ariel, 2002a, 2002b; Bach, 1994; see section 7.6). Under syncretic views (as Recanati, 2001 has called them) we can simultaneously hold separate minimalist and maximalist concepts of 'what is said,' each with its own different function(s).

We briefly survey below various positions regarding the optimal way to define 'what is said,' each representing some version of one of the four resolutions outlined above for the minimalist–maximalist conflict. Each meaning level defined should be evaluated not only according to how plausible, internally coherent it is, etc., but also according to how it fares as a potential arena for a grammar/pragmatics interface. As such, any proposed concept is justified to the extent that it can explain interlocutors' real-time interpretations when engaged in natural discourse, as well as attested paths of grammaticization. Recall that linguistic change often renders pragmatic inferences grammatical, so a grammar/pragmatics interface level must be involved in such processes.

---

[6] These formal semanticists will not, however, be discussed here, for they do not adopt an explicit stance on 'what is said' versus implicatures. Their take on the topic is that any pragmatic aspect which contributes to the determination of the truth conditions for some proposition should receive semantic representation. In other words, they do not problematize the 'what is said' and 'what is implicated' distinction. Most of the researchers here discussed acknowledge that truth conditions for specific cases may be determined in this indiscriminatory manner, but they are interested in explaining the different statuses that some of these pragmatic aspects have. For example, why some but not other pragmatically supplied values which are relevant for truth evaluability can be canceled more easily than others.

7.2   A minimalist 'what is said'

We start with a minimalist concept of 'what is said.' Salmon (1991), Berg (1993, 2002), Bach (1994), and Borg (2005a) are among those who argue for a strict adherence to a minimalist position regarding 'what is said' (Berg views it as 'strict semantics').[7] The minimal meaning level may only be enriched by contextual inferences provided these are (i) grammatically mandated, (ii) their content is straightforwardly provided by the application of grammatical rules to the context, and (iii) the relevant context consists of permanent contextual parameters, such as participants' identity, time and place of interaction, etc. In fact, Berg (p.c.) is quite restrictive: grammatically induced completions count as part of the strict semantic meaning only if they have a uniquely and grammatically determined interpretation (as in deletions under identity). So, even the completion in (3a) cannot form part of 'what is said' for him. These researchers are therefore content with a 'what is said' which is only saturated with grammatically specified elements, disambiguated, and (some of) its references determined (only those few which don't require reference to the speaker's intentions).[8] Such a restrictive concept is in fact even more excluding than Grice's original 'what is said,' which included all reference resolutions. For some (most prominently, Bach, 1994) 'what is said' need not be a complete proposition, and hence it does not (always) provide a truth-evaluable proposition.

The researchers here mentioned are willing to "pay the price" for their opting for such a minimalist definition. They fully acknowledge that this 'what is said' is not the representation which usually plays an active role in actual discourse: it need not be communicated, actually. For example, what if A's addressee finds out that there's only a little puddle of milk on the bottom shelf of the fridge?:

(6)   A: Um, I've got tea here, and there's sugar in that uh Indian looking thing,
           and **there's milk in the fridge** for   (LSAC)

According to Berg's analysis, A's utterance is taken as 'strictly' semantically true, although pragmatically it is, of course, misleading. Berg is explicitly not committed to a 'what is said' reflecting our intuitive truth evaluations (according to which what A said may be taken as false). In fact, Berg proposes that speakers have no intuitions about the technical 'what is said': "competent speakers do not always know what they are saying" (2002: 354). Bach (2002) too thinks that our intuitions are not about 'what is said.'

---

[7] See also Levinson (2000b: 3.271).

[8] Unlike many philosophers, most notably Recanati (1989), Berg cautions that we mustn't impose on the grammar endless cases of ambiguity and indexicality, just in order to enrich our representation to meet the truth-evaluability criterion on 'what is said.' Bach (1994) too is less radical than Recanati in declaring certain enrichments as grammatically triggered. Bach does not see such completions as applicable to just any conceptually missing constituents.

Note the following case, where there is a clear difference between the truth conditions of the minimalist 'what is said' and the intuitive truth conditions of the expressed proposition:

(7) Mom: Do you need money?

Iddo: No, I have money.

Mom: Where from?

Iddo: Dad gave me money to eat lunch at the Weitzman Center, and **I didn't go** in the end.

Mom: ((Laughing)) You did go, but you didn't pay.

(Originally Hebrew, Dec. 19, 2003)

(7) presents a gap between the truth conditions of 'what is said$_{min}$' and the intuitive truth conditions of the utterance ('what is said$_{max}$'). Literally, Iddo's *I didn't go in the end*, is false. The truth is that although he didn't go with his friends to have lunch at the Weitzman Center, he went and ate there with his family. Naturally, he didn't have to pay for his lunch then, which is why he still has money. In other words, Iddo told the truth when he said *I didn't go in the end* if what we take as truth evaluable is the intuitively enriched proposition: 'Dad gave me money to eat lunch at the Weitzman Center ((**with my friends**)), and I didn't go ((to eat lunch at the Weitzman Center with my friends)) in the end.'[9] Note that the mother is laughing when she corrects her son, saying he did go. She certainly doesn't consider his previous statement as false, because what counts is the enriched, rather than the minimalist, 'what is said.' Still, the fact that she does correct him attests that the minimalist 'what is said' has some interactional status (more on this in section 7.6). The following similarly shows the crucial role of 'what is said$_{min}$' to establishing the truth conditions of the utterance:

(8) MS: There is a God!

Mom: What happened?

MS: The scout's mother who is supposed to get her check back asked me where it was a few days ago, and I told her that **Y had it**. And now, I was corresponding with Y by SMS and she's got the check!

Mom: So, **it came out** that you didn't lie, **sort of**?

(Originally Hebrew, Dec. 16, 2003)

The background for (8) is that MS, a scout leader, had told her mother that she had lost the relevant check, but thought maybe she could still find it somewhere in her very messy room. Thus, for MS and her mother, MS's telling the scout's mother that Y (MS's leader) had the check was a lie (used to gain time to look for the check). However, miraculously, it turned out that MS's proposition was objectively true (she must have forgotten that she handed over the check to Y, or the scout's mother may have directly given the check to Y). Note that although both interlocutors felt that MS did lie, since, objectively, there was a perfect match between her statement and reality, the mother hedgingly says that MS did not lie

---

[9] Note that the completion of 'with my friends' is not grammatically mandated, since *eat* does not require such an argument.

after all. This seems to corroborate the point about 'what is said$_{min}$', devoid of speaker intentions, providing the truth conditions for the proposition expressed. Horn (2007) makes much the same point.

Borg (2005b) similarly argues that it is simply out of place to demand from semantics (which is supposed to provide sentence meaning) a representation which is the intuitively proper understanding of the sentence (a speaker meaning): the proposition expressed is naturally distinct from the thought entertained. It has a set of truth conditions, although these are perhaps not the intuitively suitable ones for the context at hand (the latter are a matter for pragmatics). In fact, argues Borg, we can never be sure how specific we need to render the speaker's utterance in order to make it truth-evaluable. We should also distinguish between grasping the truth conditions of some sentence (a semantic assignment) and knowing how to apply these truth conditions in order to verify whether they are satisfied or not on any given occasion. The latter is clearly beyond semantics. According to Borg, semantics only requires **some** truth conditional analysis for the sentence, not necessarily the one which is relevant for sentence verification. Thus, when a speaker says *I will go to the store* (Borg, 2005b: 249), but fails to go at a reasonable later point in time, saying that she never specified when she would go, we don't see her contradicting herself. Here's a relevant attested example:

(9)   A: You can call me **later**.
        B: Wait a minute, what's the time difference?
        A: . . . It's 10:30 p.m. here.
        B: So, I can't call you later.
        A: Well, **I didn't say later today**. You can call me tomorrow.

(March 5, 2005)

Since in most if not in all utterances there is a gap between the literal 'what is said' and what is meant (Carston, 2002a: chapter 2; Recanati, 2002a), Borg's proposal in effect turns most utterances into nonliteral utterances (see Bach, 1994 originally). With Grice's exclusive line adopted, very often it is the unintended semantic meaning that counts as 'what is said' for her, rather than the intended inferred meaning.

There are two questions regarding this minimalist meaning level. The first one is whether we can actually delineate it. In other words, are the highly restricted contextual inferences allowed to derive 'what is said$_{min}$' actually able to deliver the representation the minimalists define it to be, including the functions it is supposed to perform (produce a set of truth conditions for the sentence relative to its specific context)? Second, supposing we can somehow construct such a 'what is said$_{min}$', is it reasonable to assume that interlocutors undertake the generation of such a grammar/pragmatics interface? In other words, is this level psychologically real? The answer to the first question seems to be positive. But it comes with a very high price for the second question. The concept thus defined is almost always devoid of any justification.

We begin with the first question. Carston (2002a) does not see how the defined 'what is said$_{min}$' can actually be delineated, since the contextual completions for the product sought are not different in character from those required for creating a 'what is said$_{max}$'. Similarly, according to Recanati (1989 and onwards), 'what is said$_{min}$' cannot provide a full set of truth conditions, which defeats its purpose: "I claim that there is no such thing . . . as a complete proposition autonomously determined by the rules of the language with respect to the context but independent of speaker's meaning" (Recanati, 2004: 56). Both argue that the distinction between a narrow ("intentionless") and a wide context is untenable, and that even enrichments unequivocally included in the most restricted 'what is said' (saturations) must rely on speaker intentions. To see that disambiguation, which is viewed as a 'what is said$_{min}$' assignment, may require reference to speakers' intentions (Carston, 2002a: chapter 2; originally, Walker, 1975), consider the following (and see again the example in chapter 5, note 45, where the missing NPs of Hebrew 'walking with – feeling without' – require reference to the speaker's intentions):

(10)   M: S sounds AWFUL
         W: What do you mean –
                AWFUL,
                to YOU?
                or AWFUL to you.   (April 24, 2005)

What W is not clear about is whether M meant that S was being awful to M, or whether S sounded to M to be in an awful state. In other words, W could not decide on the correct syntactic parsing, precisely because M's intention was not clear to him. Disambiguation is not always the trivial task it's made out to be by minimalists. Another example of saturation requiring reference to the speaker's intentions is the following:

(11)   Nurse: Have you drunk?
         Patient: Yes.   (Originally Hebrew, June 21, 2005)

Following the patient's response the nurse proceeded to give her a blood test, but, as it turned out, the nurse meant 'have you drunk glucose for a glucose intolerance test,' whereas the patient took her to mean 'have you drunk anything this morning?' Since she had drunk some water the patient answered positively, although she hadn't yet taken the glucose. Now, *drink* requires the completion of an object, but the patient's failure to identify the nurse's intention cost her an additional unnecessary blood test.

If it is true that we need to mobilize speakers' intentions for such contextual completions, there is no way we can define a 'what is said$_{min}$' as 'what the sentence (rather than the speaker) says with respect to the narrow (but not wide) context at hand.' Note that even indexicals require a wide context (Recanati, 2001, 2002a, 2004). Consider the following, where *here*, a classical indexical, must refer to a copresent desk in (12a), to the whole situation in (12b), to the region in (12c) and to earth in (12d):

(12) a.   PHIL: (H) . . . I would like to . . talk to you about these three items.
                  I have **here**,   (SBC: 027)

   b.   J: I'm being incredibly lazy **here**.
                 I have the box as my excuse.

        W: The box?
                 Oh, you mean as an excuse for taking the elevator. (July 2, 2001)

   c.   FRED: (H) you know he's looking at that as his retirement income,
                 ((3 LINES OMITTED))
                 like some of the people do **here**.   (SBC: 014)

   d.   PAMELA: . . . (H) I look down at my body?
                 . . . And I feel like I'm in a spaceship.
                 ((7 LINES OMITTED))
                 I just think it's so damn weird we're **here**.   (SBC: 005)

In order to establish what *here* refers to in each example in (12), we must rely on our assumptions about the speaker's intentions. In fact, this is why W didn't quite understand J at first (another interlocutor present did get it right away). We cannot therefore attribute the interpretation of *here* in these examples to a trivial process of contextual reference fixing. The same applies to most indexicals (for a misunderstanding of *that*, see again example (15) in chapter 4). Recanati and Bach (2004b) think the narrow context assumption might work for *I*, but see Ariel (1998a) for the role of inference in determining even who the speaker is, and see (2) above where the two *I*s do not refer to Alina, the actual, current speaker. Referring expressions present much the same problem. As we have seen in chapter 2, the way speakers guide their addressees in retrieving referents for referring expressions is by encoding the degree of activation with which they expect addressees to entertain various mental representations. But the degree of accessibility with which some mental representation is available to the addressee is crucially determined by the speaker's topics, goals, etc. (see e.g. Ariel, 1990 and onwards). Here's an example (already quoted as (29) in section 2.2), which shows that identifying what the topic is is necessary for determining anaphoric interpretations:

(13)   mitbarer   she=la=uvda   she=**arafat**$_i$ noad   peamim mispar im
       turns.out   that=to.the=fact   that=Arafat$_i$ met   times   number with
       ha=melex   xusen$_j$ hayta   xashivut   raba.   **arafat**$_i$
       the=King   Hussein$_j$ was   significance   great.   Arafat$_i$
       hitdayen   im   **ha=melex**$_j$ be=et   **shehiyato**$_i$ be=rabat
       carried.discussions with   the=king$_j$ at=the.time.of   his$_i$:stay   in=Rabat
       amon,   ve=nire   she=**ze**$_j$ hicbia   **be=fanav**$_i$ al   ha=dimyon . . .
       Amon,   and=seems   that=this.one$_j$ pointed   to=him$_i$ on   the=similarity . . .
       'It turns out that the fact that Arafat met with King Hussein a number of
       times had great significance. Arafat carried on discussions with the king when
       visiting Rabat Amon, and it seems that the king pointed out to him the
       similarity . . .'   (Hebrew, *Yediot Ahronot*, Oct. 18, 1984)

Both Arafat and Hussein are legitimate antecedents for Hebrew *ze* 'this one,' as well as for the two third-person possessive pronouns. But since *ze* encodes a less than maximal degree of mental accessibility, it is the nontopic *King Hussein* which is selected as its antecedent, and since pronouns encode a high degree of accessibility, it is the topical *Arafat* which is seen as the pronominal antecedent. Reference resolutions, whether indexical or anaphoric, are not at all the automatic contextual completions minimalists take them to be, then.

Next, consider the following, where, as Recanati (2001) argues, the nature of the relation between the two NPs in bold is necessary for determining the truth conditions of the proposition expressed, yet it requires reference to speaker's intentions:

(14) a.   Maya: Can I use **the girl's colors**?   (Originally Hebrew, Sept. 17, 1996)
    b.   J: I'd like **MY parmesan**.
        M: This IS your parmesan.
        Iddo: Is this all for YOU?   (July 28, 2001)

The colors Maya (then 8 years old) is referring to in (14a) are the colors given to her by some girl as a birthday present a few days earlier. They certainly don't belong to the girl. The parmesan J is referring to is the one he himself bought (and not some parmesan which is only his to eat, as Iddo, 11 years old, takes him to mean). It's hard to see how reference determination in these cases can be performed without reference to the speaker's intentions (this is Iddo's problem). The same is true for the examples in (4) (the interpretation of 'squares in the stomach,' and of 'another cup,' where attributing to the speaker the wrong intention made the addressee misinterpret her reference). Finally, note the following conversation from a cartoon, where Calvin (the addressee) fails to take into account the teacher's intentions in reference determination:

(15)   In class:
      Teacher: Calvin, are you chewing **gum** in class?
      Calvin: Yeth.
      Teacher: Do you have **enough** to share with everybody?
      Calvin: ((Spits out a large wad of gum)) Probably. But do you really think
               they'd want it?
      In the principal's office:
      Calvin: It was HER idea . . .
               (Cartoon, *International Herald Tribune*, May 6, 2005)[10]

Enough needs to be saturated from context, and Calvin correctly interprets it to refer to his gum. Of course, the teacher meant fresh gum, whereas he took it to be the very gum in his mouth. Note that such an interpretation would have been perfectly reasonable had Calvin been baking a cake, and the teacher asked him whether he had enough to share with everyone. In this case, it's the very cake he

---

[10] I thank Gabriel Adelman for drawing my attention to this example.

was baking that he would have been asked to share with the other students. So saturations too may require reference to speaker intentions.

Now, in principle, the prevalence of such cases does not argue against a minimalist 'what is said,' for while it shows that 'what is said$_{min}$' is often not the intended message, it does not at all prove that it cannot be constructed. Still, it makes the second question we posed even more pertinent. Does such a concept, which is obviously too impoverished to represent speakers' intended meanings so very often, serve any other purpose? The rationale given for a 'what is said$_{min}$' concept is that (i) it accounts for our ability to produce and comprehend new words and sentences, in other words, for our linguistic competence, and that (ii) it expresses our beliefs about the world (see Berg, 2002). But surely, (i) is better served by assuming a bare semantic meaning level (i.e. 'what is said' minus any extralinguistic contextual inferences), which is anyway assumed by all research- ers. In other words, it's not clear how motivation (i) motivates a 'what is said' level in addition to a bare linguistic semantic level (see Ariel, 2002a; Recanati, 2004).

Next, consider Borg's argument that 'what is said$_{min}$' must express the most minimal, even if not the intended truth-evaluable proposition. If so, why should 'what is said$_{min}$' include reference resolution even? Truth conditions can be determined for sentences whose referents have not been fixed even (e.g. *She ran* is true if 'some female ran'), so there is again no need for the minimalist 'what is said' over and above a grammatical level of meaning. The same objection applies to Cappelen and Lepore's (2005: 185) justification of a minimal 'what is said' as "the proposition semantically expressed in our minimal defense against confu- sion, mistakes, and it is that which guarantees communication across contexts of utterance." In fact, it's hard to see any role which is unique to this minimalist 'what is said,' which is not fulfilled by either the bare semantic meaning or one of the richer maximalist concepts (see section 7.6 below). As Carston (1988 and onwards) adds, all inferred elements are cancelable, elements of a minimalist 'what is said' included, so once again there is no justification for privileging some pragmatic inferences (narrow context completions) over others.

It is also doubtful that the examples we have considered justify the extremely minimalist level assumed by Berg. Recall that for Berg the justification for 'what is said$_{min}$' is that it expresses our beliefs about the world. Berg's concept only provides a very general content for the utterance, but when A says that there is milk in the fridge, most probably her belief is quite specific, namely, that the milk comes in some specific form (e.g. contained in a milk carton, in a puddle, inside a coconut), etc. If so, the minimalist 'what is said' does not actually reflect that belief, as Berg claims it should. In addition, Carston (2004a) demonstrates how interpretations based (also) on clearly pragmatic processes must be allowed to form part of the proposition expressed when the latter serves as a premise in an argument (see again section 3.1). Thus, if Berg is right, on the basis of A telling B that there is milk in the fridge B cannot reason that he doesn't need to go buy milk at the supermarket (with some additional premises irrelevant to our discussion), for recall that there may only be a puddle of milk on the bottom shelf. In other words, 'what is said$_{min}$' is insufficient as a premise for drawing inferences. The only way to determine what the premise can be taken to be is by considering the derived interpretation from A's utterance, in this case, that 'there is ((usable)) milk ((in some container)) in the fridge.'

Recanati (1989 and onwards) has in addition argued that 'what is said$_{min}$' lacks psychological reality (recall our discussion of the "Availability Principle" in chapter 3). Meanings are holistic, and we can't ignore the very tight connection between the concept of 'what is said' and the speaker's intentions made publicly available by her utterance. What interlocutors have intuitions about are enriched linguistic meanings, and not bare semantic meanings, nor the minimalist 'what is said.' On this basis, Recanati set out against the assumption at the time that the semantic meaning of the numbers is only lower-bounded (e.g. *four* lexically means 'at least four'), while their actual interpretation (e.g. 'exactly four') is only a conveyed meaning, which routinely relies on a (generalized) conversational implicature ('at most four'). Recanati argued that what is available to interlocutors is just the 'exactly four' interpretation (see e.g. Recanati, 2004). Although 'at least four' is 'what is said$_{min}$' in such cases (according to the prevalent view at the time), interlocutors are not at all aware of such a meaning level, Recanati argued. Such a 'what is said$_{min}$' is then unjustified.

Similarly, Noveck and Chevaux (2002) had subjects verify whether 'p and q' is true (e.g. 'Laurent went to the hospital and broke his ankle?'), when the story the subjects had heard made it clear that the chronological order of events was, e.g. Laurent first broke his ankle and only then went to the hospital. According to minimalist approaches, the chronological interpretation is a pragmatic inference, hence excluded from 'what is said$_{min}$'. Nonetheless, as already mentioned in section 3.1.2.1, most subjects (71 percent) responded "no" to the above question posed to them. In other words, the majority of the subjects thought that the inferred chronological interpretation contributed to the truth conditions of the proposition. They must have ignored 'what is said$_{min}$', or they would have confirmed that 'p and q' was the case. Now, Borg could retort that the experiment only testifies to the verification of the proposition, rather than to its truth conditions, but then we need independent evidence that this is not so in all cases where researchers, Borg included, have attributed a truth-conditional status to some interpretation. It should be pointed out that A in (9) (the example which seemed to support Borg's position) actually added that he immediately felt funny about excusing himself in such a manner, and the mother hedges quite strongly when she says that MS did not lie in (8) (see section 7.6 for 'wise-guy' interpretations). Thus, speakers don't seem to find 'what is said$_{min}$' interactionally useful. This is because that meaning level is not psychologically real for them.[11]

---

[11] In addition, as Recanati (1989) argued, extending the concept of nonliterality in this manner is inconsistent with our understanding of the sentences at hand (consider again examples (3)–(14), which are quite literal, that is, nonfigurative).

One context where one would think that a minimalist 'what is said' might be functional is court rulings. Courts of law would seem to be prime candidates for adopting such a minimalist interpretation, since they are bound to consider the law, contracts, and people's testimonies in the strictest possible way. But they actually don't. Here are two cases first reported on in Ariel (2002b). In one case, an Israeli judge ruled that *a proven **three year** experience* specified as a requirement in a bid refers to 'the three years **((immediately preceding the bidding time))**,' rather than to just 'any three years of experience' – the 'said$_{min}$' meaning of the expression (originally Hebrew, *Haaretz*, Nov. 30, 1998). In a second case, a judge ruled that a certain Samuel Sheinbein be extradited to the US where he should stand trial, although by law Israelis are not extraditable, and the defendant's lawyer proved that legally Sheinbein was an Israeli citizen, to the judge's satisfaction. The judge explained that his 'linguistic intuition' (*Haaretz*, Sept. 11, 1998) told him that the defendant should be extradited nonetheless, because although legally he is an Israeli, he was born and raised in the US, he is a US citizen, he does not speak Hebrew, and when he visited Israel he used an American (rather than an Israeli) passport. The defendant therefore did not have 'sufficient linkage' to the state of Israel in the judge's opinion. In other words, although Sheinbein was proven Israeli (in the minimalist sense of the word), he was deemed a non-prototypical Israeli (this is my interpretation of the judge's notion of not having 'sufficient linkage'). The law according to this judge applies to a narrowed-down set of "relevant" Israelis, not to just any Israeli.[12] Once again, it was not the 'said$_{min}$' meaning which was applied by the judge, but rather, a pragmatically adapted 'what is said$_{max}$'. Thus, even court decisions don't necessarily see themselves bound by a minimalist 'what is said.'[13] We therefore conclude that while it is not absolutely the case that constructing 'what is said$_{min}$' is impossible, there seems to be no psychological or interactional justification for assuming this minimalist level of a grammar/pragmatics interface. The reason is that in order to comply with the minimalist criteria, the concept is deprived of any rationale.

7.3   A maximalist 'what is said' (truth-conditional pragmatics)

The important difference between minimalists and maximalists pertains to what is to be done with 'what is speaker meant' when it is not explicitly expressed. As we have seen, minimalists adopt Grice's exclusive stand quite consistently. They are content to simply enlarge the gap between the 'said' and the 'meant' under such circumstances, adhering quite strictly to the explicitly

---

[12] The rationale being that criminals should be tried and, if applicable, serve their prison term within their home community, and for Sheinbein, the US, and not Israel, is his home community.

[13] See Ariel (2002b), where I cite legal authorities advocating relying on intentions in legal interpretations.

expressed. Maximalists, most notably Relevance theoreticians (see Sperber and Wilson, 1986/1995) and Recanati (1989), have instead opted for Grice's inclusive line, consistently minimizing the gap, the assumption being that 'what is said' should represent the "intuitive" truth conditions speakers are taken to commit themselves to. Over the years, Relevance theoreticians have incorporated more and more of the 'meant (although not expressed)' into their explicature, a representation close to 'what is said' (see again section 1.4).[14] We thus have a truth-conditional pragmatics, rather than semantics.

7.3.1   Defining 'what is said$_{max}$'

Since a minimalist 'what is said' cannot be (usefully, nonarbitrarily) defined, and since it is, moreover, pointless according to Recanati and Relevance theoreticians (see above), they have instead argued for a 'what is said$_{max}$' (an explicature for Relevance theoreticians). According to the maximalist approach, 'what is said' must be meant/communicated (Carston, 2002a: chapter 2; Recanati, 2002b). Hence, where there is a discrepancy between the linguistic semantic meaning and the intended, fully propositional meaning, 'what is said$_{max}$' follows the 'meant' concept.[15] 'What is said$_{max}$' "corresponds to the intuitive truth conditions of the utterance, that is to the content of the statement as the participants in the conversation would gloss it" (Recanati, 2001: 79–80). According to Recanati, 'what is said$_{max}$' must therefore be sufficiently determinate, so that the truth conditions it represents are detailed enough to enable interlocutors to assess the proposition for its truth value (contra Borg, 2005a – see above).[16] This is a "Truth-conditional pragmatic," rather than a "truth-conditional semantic" view. Since

---

[14] The attempt to identify 'what is said' with the 'meant' explains Relevance theory's gradual extension over the years of what the minimal proposition must be. The first extensions were applied to the chronological interpretations associated with conjunctions (Carston, 1988 and onwards). Later, nonliteral uses of language were incorporated into explicatures (a decade later – see Wilson, 1995), and finally, Carston (2002a) has proposed that ad hoc concept adaptations constitute aspects of explicatures as well.

[15] There are, however, 'meant' aspects of interpretation which are not conveyed, and hence are not included even in 'what is said$_{max}$' (see Carston, 2002a; Recanati, 2002b). These are background assumptions (originally discussed by Searle, 1992: 180), which are taken for granted, e.g. for (i), that 'the pepper will be used in a stereotypical way in preparing some dish.' Such assumptions are not represented, although they are assumed to hold true:

(i)   Roy: . . . In that case I will use a yellow pepper for this evening.   (SBC: 003)

An example discussed by Johanna Rubba (Funknet list, Nov. 7, 1995) underscores the importance of such background assumptions. Rubba considers the case of *use a gun while committing a crime* (which increases one's penalty). She cites a court case where the judge ruled that the criminal indeed 'used a gun,' although the gun was kept in the trunk of the car, and not even shown to the victim at all. The judge justified this decision by saying that knowing that the gun was available to them gave the criminal reassurance in committing the crime.

[16] It is not so clear, however, how determinate the proposition must be made in order to be evaluated for its truth. Borg (2005a) rightly insists on a distinction between identifying the set of truth conditions associated with some proposition and verifying that proposition (see also chapter 3). She argues that maximalist approaches confuse the two, and impose on semantics ('what is said') the goal of enabling verification, which then pushes them to assume many (semantically)

'what is said$_{max}$' is a full-fledged pragmatic construction, there may be any number of 'what is said$_{max}$' per utterance form, according to the maximalists. Thus, each of the utterances in (4) has (at least) two potential explicatures (e.g. 'cubes in the stomach' can be explicated as 'six-pack on the stomach' or as 'squares of wafers/chocolate inside the stomach'). This is in contrast with the minimalists, for whom there is only one 'what is said$_{min}$' per utterance form (excluding differences due to different reference and ambiguity resolutions).

The contextual enrichments incorporated are not restricted to ones which are bottom-up and rule-governed. They may be fully pragmatic, i.e. top-bottom (Recanati, 2002b, 2007), 'free enrichments' (Recanati, 1993), expansions for Bach (1994), i.e. completions which are not grammatically triggered (e.g. (7) above, (16) below). 'Free enrichments' form the basis for Carston's (2002a: chapter 2) rejection of the "Minimal truth-evaluability principle." As she convincingly argues, although completions guided by such a principle do create a complete proposition, it may not be the one intended by the speaker. In some cases the latter may be a rather different utterance from the one overtly expressed, or even from its 'what is said$_{min}$'. Finally, 'what is said$_{max}$' must be consciously available to the participants in the conversation as a single-meaning representation, regardless of the resources drawn on (semantic meaning, contextually supported inferences). This is in line with Recanati's (1989) "Availability Principle."

Recanati (p.c.) remains agnostic about specific cases (e.g. (3b)) requiring saturation versus enrichment. Relevance theoreticians are more definite. Many of the cases potentially considered cases of saturation (grammatically mandated completions) by others are considered 'free enrichments' by Relevance theoreticians. (16) is a case quite similar to (3c), except that there is no quantifier here, so that the enrichment called for is less controversially a free (i.e. nongrammatically induced) enrichment:

(16)   DIANE: because he has no money,
                  no family money,
                  but she has ((**a substantial amount of**)) money,   (SBC: 023)

Note that whereas both Recanati and Relevance theoreticians agree on the need for a 'what is said$_{max}$', the grammar/pragmatics distinction can be differently drawn. The completions in examples (3c, d) above are considered fully pragmatic by both approaches in that they are inferred based on a "wide context." But Recanati does not rule out the possibility that they are grammatically triggered. According to Relevance theoreticians, 'free enrichments' are not grammatical. They are fully pragmatic, not automatically inferred, but rather, added on only

unnecessary enrichments. Carston (2002a; chapter 1) and Recanati (2002b), however, distinguish between inferred aspects which are actually conveyed (and should therefore form part of 'what is said') and inferred aspects which are not conveyed (see again note 16). The location in *Mary danced* plays a different role than it does in *It's raining*. Although both the dancing and the raining necessarily take place at some location, only in the latter case is the speaker conveying that it is raining at some specific place which the addressee must identify and include in the truth-evaluable proposition (Perry, 1993).

when Relevant to the conversation at hand. This is the case in (16), but not so in (17), where the amount of money involved is immaterial:

(17)   A: John actually bought one of these at the art fair.
          B: [<laughing> Oh no. </laughing>]
          A: I mean for all the things for him to spend his hard-earned **money**
                on.   (LSAC)

In (17), *his . . . money* is not necessarily enriched into a more specific amount of money. While some completions viewed as 'free enrichments' by Relevance theoreticians are potentially taken as saturations by Recanati, he too argues that 'what is said' completions must include 'free enrichments' as well. The following have been considered 'free enrichments' at least by some researchers. Recall that 'free enrichments' are fully pragmatic in that they are not grammatically triggered, and they access speaker intentions. They therefore also allow the substitution of some linguistic constituent with a pragmatically adjusted concept (Carston, 2002b: 8). They may introduce conceptual components into the linguistic representation, even in the absence of ready-made linguistic slots. (Additional examples are (3b–d) and (4a–c) above.) What I estimate to be the relevant 'free enrichments' are specified in double parentheses:

(18) a.   You might be walking across the street and a car might come and a guardian
           angel will stop the car. **((in a supernatural manner))**   (LSAC)

   b.   **Row 22a** has changed her mind. She wants tea, not coffee.
                            (Originally Hebrew, Flight attendant, July 14, 2003)

   c.   He threw a Frisbee off a cliff and the dog jumped ((**over the cliff**)) for it and
         got it.   (LSAC, inspired by Carston, 1988)

   d.   When was the last time ((**you had sex**)) you felt like the first time ((**you had
         sex**))?   (Originally Hebrew ad, spotted 1996)

   e.   ani   mecaref takcir . . . le=kenes   ilash . . . ode   lax
         I   attach   abstract . . . for=the.conference.of Ilash . . . I.will.thank to:you.F
         im   tuxli   le=histakel   ((al   ha=takcir)).
         if   you.will.be.able to=look   ((at   the=abstract)).
         'I'm attaching an Ilash abstract. I'll be obliged if you could look at it.'
                            (Hebrew, private message, April 22, 2006)

   f.   A: I wouldn't worry about it too much. I can look it over if you want me to.
         B: Yeah, yeah.
         A: I'll have a look ((**at it**)), put it in your box then.   (LSAC)

The guardian angel in (18a) will not stop the car in the stereotypical manner that a car driver stops her car, but rather, in some supernatural way, by somehow causing the actual driver to stop perhaps. In (18b), the adapted concept and referent of *row 22a* is derived via the seat concept linguistically mentioned, but is quite distinct from it (the traveler occupying seat 22a on the plane). Note the use of feminine pronoun, which follows the intended referent's gender.[17] The dog in (18c) must have

---

[17] While Hebrew *shura* 'row' is feminine too, the pronoun would have still been feminine even if masculine *moshav* 'seat' had been used instead of *shura*. It's not clear how minimalists could explain a choice of grammatical form (the pronoun) according to an implicature.

jumped over the cliff, rather than somewhere else (this is a bridged coreference case). In (18d), we must enrich the semantic meaning of 'the last/first time' so as to create representations of more definite events than the highly uninformative 'what is said$_{min}$' would predict. (18e) and (18f) contain intransitive verbs, which, as such, require no complements. But we do add these on. These are all cases of free (extragrammatical) completions, which are necessary for deriving the intended proposition.

Finally, note the following, where it takes M three turns to get the waitress to correctly interpret her use of the very mundane word *coffee*:

(19)   M: Which **coffee** do you have decaffeinated?
        WAITRESS: Colombian, I think.
        M: Yes, but how do you make it?
        WAITRESS: We grind it here.
        M: Yes, but what kind of coffee do you make from it?
                   Espresso, and such?
        WAITRESS: Oh, any kind. What would you like?

                                              (Originally Hebrew, Dec. 20, 2002)

Obviously, M has the 'coffee drinks' concept in mind, whereas the waitress has the 'coffee beans' concept in mind. Each finds her concept so obvious that it takes them a while to coordinate their concepts. The example demonstrates how natural and inevitable concept adaptations seem to us. As Recanati has emphasized, it is hard to sever the link between the purely semantic meaning and the developed 'what is said$_{max}$' concept (Recanati, 2001, 2007). This is why it takes so long for M and the waitress to agree on the interpretation of *coffee*.[18] The following cartoon demonstrates what happens when one is not able to adapt the concept (of niceness):

(20)   WOMAN: I've got a big date, Francis . . . Do I look nice??
        FRANCIS: Depends. How nice are you supposed to look?

                                              (*Los Angeles Times*, June 3, 2000)

Most intriguing is Carston's (2002a: chapter 5) suggestion that loosening, and not just narrowing, of semantic meanings also forms part of the explicature (see also Recanati, 2004, Wilson, 2003). Loosening cases are ones where lexically specified meaning components are actually pragmatically canceled. Note that such interpretations go against the accepted assumption that semantic features cannot be canceled by pragmatic factors. Still, it seems that even nonvague terms, such as *square*, *rectangle*, *bachelor*, all determinate lexical items, may nonetheless get used in a loose way (Carston, 2002a: chapter 5), as in:

(21) a.   There's this guy it was like bald and gray totally bald it is like on the front
           of his forehead I swear to God it is a **triangle** patch of hair. That he had parted
           in the middle.   (LSAC)

---

[18] Similarly, when a colleague commenting on a grant proposal asked me: "Why did you change the justification in the following?" it took the two of us a while to see what we each meant by *justification*. Whereas she meant margin justification, I took it to mean 'motivation.' Since we each adapted the concept, the (ambiguous) lexical meaning of *justification* was not available to either of us.

b.   A: I think he's trying to make it a nice little family place you know since
          you're here
      B: I know
      A: and when you're not here he's more like a **bachelor**, it's really
          funny.   (LSAC)

Most probably, the patch of hair (in (21a)) does not quite form a triangle, and
bachelor (in (21b)) refers to a certain life-style, rather than to marital status. One of
Carston's arguments in support of unifying loosening with narrowing is the observation that, in fact, concept adaptations often require both adjustments at the same
time. For example, whereas the triangle sides (in (21a)) need not be perfectly
straight (a loosening of the strict definition of a triangle), the size of the triangle
discussed is drastically narrowed down to small triangles which would fit the head
hair described, and its proportions are also not completely free. We expect it to be
prototypical, i.e. not a right triangle, not a very acute or obtuse one, etc.

   Note that in all of the examples here considered the adapted concepts
are created out of run of the mill lexical items. It seems unreasonable that they
are grammatically marked as requiring contextual completion. Indeed, utterance
interpretation involves constant constructions of ad hoc concepts. Note a few more
examples, (22) taken from one conversation in SBC and (23) from Lotan 1990:

(22) a.   LENORE: #Jan talked the whole time,
                     in a voice like this.
                     ((7 LINES OMITTED))
           ALINA: (H) God,
                     .. (H) **turn the volume down** @> @@,
                     .. (H) <VOX @let me out of here VOX>.
     b.   ALINA: She was taking the silverware,
                     and digging it into the table.
                     ((7 LINES OMITTED))
           LENORE: Th– .. those tables are museums,
                     could you please,
                     .. @@ @chill @out @in @the @uh @art @k@–
                     .. **art work** here.
     c.   ALINA: .. So I have this pair of suede pants that I got,
                     you've seen them probably **ninety million times**.
     d.   ALINA: (H) the one that told me I was **shoveling my food**,
                     and I didn't need a fork,
(23) a.   R: What's the value?
           S: When we went out to the stock exchange the company was worth
                8 million. In peak times it went up to 15–20 million it was once it
                tickled it ...   (Lotan 1990: 4)
     b.   S: Rubinstein is building ...
           R: He too made such **windowless cells**
                He too made such cubby-holes.   (Lotan 1990: 6)
     c.   S: If they ((workers – MA)) don't come then the building site **stands** on that
                day what can you do

M: What?

S: then the building site stands on that day in their subject.   (Lotan 1990: 7)

In (22a), *turn the volume down* is loosened, since no knob or anything like that need be turned for Jan to speak less loudly. But the resulting effect (less loudness) is maintained. The *art work* in (22b) ironically refers to the gouges made by someone digging silverware into the table. *Ninety million* in (22c) is loosened to 'very many'. For the person quoted by Alina as telling her that she was *shoveling* her food, *shovel* retains its 'lifting and moving bulk substances.' But the tool used is not a literal *shovel*, the substance moved is not soil or snow, but food, and the place it's moved to, is the mouth. Of course, the idea is that we adapt the 'shovel' idea just enough to allow for the real event to be depicted, but we are still supposed to compare the manner in which Alina eats to the manner in which one shovels snow or soil. 'Tickled' in (23a) is loosened to mean 'barely, or rather, rarely, touched/reached.' *Kuxim* 'windowless cells' in (23b) is interpreted as small uncharming rooms, but not necessarily windowless, and the Hebrew counterpart of *stand* in (23c) is loosened to 'is stopped/undergoes no progress.' These types of adaptations are routinely required in natural conversation in order to create 'what is said$_{max}$'.

On the maximalist view here discussed there is much more contact between grammar and pragmatics than on the minimalist approach. The two combine to create the most basic-level meaning, 'what is said,' and not only the total conveyed meaning. Moreover, explicated inferences merge with the linguistic semantic meaning to form one, inseparable meaning representation.

7.3.2   Distinguishing explicated and implicated inferences

Since maximalist approaches allow "wide context" inferences into their definition of the proposition expressed, as well as cancelability and some degree of indeterminacy, they must distinguish the latter inferences from conversational implicatures, and conveyed meanings from 'what is said$_{max}$'/explicatures, because all of these features are of course characteristic of conversational implicatures too. In other words, unlike proponents of 'what is said$_{min}$', proponents of 'what is said$_{max}$' need to justify why they do not view all communicated pragmatic inferences as having one and the same status, within one pragmatic layer, which is added onto the linguistic semantic meaning to create the conveyed meaning. Recall that the original Gricean picture only distinguished between a semantic 'what is said' and a pragmatic set of inferences (implicatures). We have seen why the researchers here discussed reject the minimalist 'what is said.' But they could replace it with the bare semantic meaning, which is to be enriched up to the conveyed meaning. Instead, they insist on a third intermediate meaning level, 'what is said$_{max}$'. They then need to motivate their distinction between two types of pragmatic inferences, those which enter 'what is said$_{max}$' and those which don't, namely, conversational implicatures. We have already justified treating some pragmatic inferences (*and*-associated inferences) as explicated in section 3.1.2. We have seen that at least sometimes, *and*-associated inferences are truth-conditional, and even Dominant. We here make the arguments more generally.

The idea is as follows. Carston's "Functional Independence" criterion and Recanati's "Availability Principle" constitute two sides of the same coin. Carston's "Functional Independence" principle states that inferences which are **external** to the linguistic semantic meaning and independent of it are conversational implicatures.[19] Recanati's principle states that inferences which speakers cannot see as external constitute **part and parcel** of 'what is said.' According to Recanati, speakers are not aware of lower-level representations, i.e. neither of the purely semantic level, nor of 'what is said$_{min}$'. Only 'what is said$_{max}$' is consciously available to them. The inferences included within this representation are inseparable from the semantic meaning, and are not implicatures, therefore. They are explicated inferences. Now, we can develop tests from these two principles, since they predict two distinct patterns for pragmatic inferences. Those inferences which partly pattern with semantic meanings are explicated, and those which do not are implicated.

One way to decide whether some inference is implicated or not is to see whether we have an expressed proposition, independent of the putative inference. If there is, it is an implicature, if there isn't, it's (part of) the explicature. The proposition expressed, insists Carston, must contribute an independent assumption. Consider (24a), already cited in chapter 3, which communicates (24b):

(24) a.   ~ LENORE: So that's put you off traveling down there?
          KEN: (H) So I eat the local food,
                  and get deathly ill.
     b.   I eat the local food, **and as a result** I get deathly ill.

The question concerns the status of the causal inference. If (24b) is implicated, rather than explicated (this is the minimalist view), then 'what is said' ('I eat the local food and I get deathly ill') is not functionally independent of what is implicated, argues Carston, for it is entailed by the implicature in (24b): if it's true that 'I eat and as a result I get deathly ill' then it must be true that 'I eat and get deathly ill.'[20] In order to view the proposition expressed as functionally independent, we should view the causal inference as explicated, then.

Moreover, it is explicatures which typically serve as premises for further inferences, the Gricean implicatures included (Carston, 2002a: 190). In (24), Ken confirms that he's put off traveling to Mexico. But he does so indirectly, by implicature, rather than directly. Crucially, this implicature is based on the causal

---

[19] However, Carston actually views this criterion as a practical heuristic rather than as an exceptionless principle. Ultimately, she suggests, it is interlocutors' intuitions which determine the status of some putative inference. See section 7.6 below.

[20] Recanati (1989: note 11), however, rightly argues that whether or not 'what is said' is entailed by a putative implicature depends on how one formulates the implicature. For example, for the chronological ordering interpretation from a sentence of the form *P and Q*, instead of assuming that the implicature is 'P and then Q,' which indeed entails 'P and Q,' we can assume it to be 'if P occurred at time t and Q occurred at time t', then t' is later than t.' It is then only the conveyed meaning ('what is said' plus the implicature), rather than the implicature itself, which entails 'what is said.' It remains to be seen whether this formulation of the implicature is psychologically reasonable, however.

inference between eating the local food and getting deathly ill. If we view Ken's utterance in (24) as implicating, rather than explicating (24b), then the proposition expressed has no independent role to play in the interaction. Hence, once again, the causal inference is explicated here.

The same argument regarding the independent status reserved for explicatures can be made for many other cases. Note the following, where we analyze the explicature of $(25A_2)$ as in (26a), and its implicature as in (26b), in order to ensure an independent role in discourse (and cognition) for the explicature:

(25) A_1: Are you hungry?
            B: Yo a bit, not much.
            A_2: **I ate a** <unclear> **house turkey sandwich**   (LSAC)

(26) a.   I ate a house turkey sandwich **recently today**.
     b.   I'm not hungry.

We don't here use as assumption the implausible unenriched semantic meaning ('There has been a house turkey sandwich eating occasion in my life'), and combine it with other contextual assumptions to derive (26b). Rather, it is (26a) which is the basis for (26b). Since the semantic meaning without the inference in (26a) has no discourse role, the inference must be explicated. The same is true for:

(27)   Well if you can don't break **a finger nail**   (LSAC)

Recanati's point is that while interlocutors take explicated inferences into account (*a finger nail* here refers to 'one of your fingernails'), they are not aware of their inferred status. These inferences feel like part and parcel of the proposition expressed. In (27), interlocutors are not even aware of the purely semantic meaning of *a finger nail*, i.e. 'anybody's finger nail.' They are only aware of the enriched interpretation, 'your finger nail.'[21] Similarly, all they are aware of in (16) is that 'she has a substantial amount of money,' the explicature, and in $(25A_2)$, the explicature (26a) is what we entertain consciously. According to Recanati, we have access to the premise(s) on which implicatures are based (explicatures), but not to the semantic representation without the explicated inferences added onto it. This is why we cannot reconstruct the transfer from semantic meaning to 'what is said$_{max}$', but we can consciously justify the inferential steps which led us (as addressees) from the explicature to the implicated conclusion via auxiliary implicated assumptions, according to Recanati. Although we must draw the required inferences in order to create the explicature, these inferences are not available to us as such, except as part and parcel of the finished product, the explicature. We only have access to post-enrichment (and pre-implicature) representations. Thus, Recanati predicts that for $(25A_2)$, the addressee can reconstruct the derivation of 'A is not hungry' from 'A ate a house turkey sandwich **recently today**,' but not the

[21] As mentioned above, minimalists too, such as Berg (1993), Bach (1994), and Soames (2002: 68), agree with Recanati's claim about speakers' intuitions not corresponding to 'what is said$_{min}$'. They differ as to what conclusion must be drawn from this observation, however.

derivation of 'A ate a house turkey sandwich **recently today**' from 'A ate a house turkey sandwich.'

Gibbs and Moise's (1997) experimental results seem to corroborate Recanati's claim (but see section 7.6 below). Their subjects, asked about what the speaker 'said,' overwhelmingly selected enriched semantic meanings (explicatures) over bare semantic meanings. This was not due to some automatic preference for pragmatically enriched interpretations, for where appropriate, subjects chose nonenriched semantic meanings, and they also refrained from selecting conveyed meanings as appropriate paraphrases for 'what is said.' Rather, it must be because semantic meanings and explicated inferences cannot be (easily) teased apart by naive speakers. Incidentally, subjects insisted on explicatures over semantic meanings (or rather, 'what is said$_{min}$') even after they were taught the Gricean 'said'/'implicated' distinction. Since they were asked to choose according to their own intuitions, they seemed unaffected by the Gricean minimalist concept, although they were sensitive to the explicature/implicature distinction.

Not only the explicature must have an independent status. If explicatures and implicatures must be functionally independent of each other, the implicature too must have an independent status. Indeed, (26a), the explicature, and (26b), the implicature, are clearly functionally independent of each other. They have different truth-conditional contents: the truth of 'I ate a house turkey sandwich' is independent of the truth of 'I'm not hungry.' Of course, the truth of the implicature does not depend on the truth of the proposition expressed. More crucial to the debate in the field, implicatures must not affect the truth conditions of the proposition expressed. As expected, even if it's false that 'I'm not hungry,' (26a) could be true. This is why although the implicatures from (28a), listed in (28b), are false (it is definitely harder to be admitted to the university than to the specific college), interlocutors don't regard the ad as stating anything false:

(28) a.   If you were not admitted by us – try the university.
                    (Originally Hebrew, ad for a teachers' college, spotted March 2003)
     b.   It is harder to be accepted to the college than to the university; the college is
           more selective; studies at the college are at a higher academic level, etc.

And similarly, note the following:

(29)   MA: Do you want to bring **things and Sandy**?
           ET: **Yes**. Not in this order.   (Originally Hebrew, Sept. 8, 2005)

In (29), when MA asked ET whether he wanted to bring over things and Sandy (the dog), ET disagrees with MA's choice of ordering (of importance), saying that the dog should have been listed before the things. This rejection of an implicature, however, does not stop him from giving an affirmative answer to the question (note his *yes*). Thus, the rejection of the implicature is irrelevant to the explicated content of the question.

In fact, the irrelevance to the truth of the proposition expressed is often the very motivation behind the use of implicatures. Implicating rather than explicating some assumption exempts the speaker from committing to information she may not wish to assume full responsibility for. This is clear in Josh's (30):

(30)   JS: Can I use my old Marker M48 or Tyrolia 590 racing bindings on new skis?
        JOSH: ... My personal recommendation? Well, I could tell you what to do, but
               then you'd go out and bust your leg up like a ceramic mermaid
               figurine in an anvil-testing machine and sue me. No way I'm telling,
               because *Skiing Magazine* doesn't indemnify me.
                                ("Ask Josh" column, *Skiing Magazine*, Dec. 2001)

The writer (Josh) here refrains from explicating an affirmative answer, 'yes, you can use your old Marker M48 or Tyrolia 590 racing bindings on new skis,' for fear of legal consequences.

So, implicatures are functionally independent from the semantic meaning and from the proposition expressed. What about explicatures vis-à-vis the semantic meaning? Explicatures are not functionally independent of the semantic meaning. They may entail the semantic meaning: 'I ate a house turkey sandwich recently today' entails 'I ate a house turkey sandwich' (and see (16) again, where the explicated 'she has a substantial amount of money' entails the encoded 'she has some nonzero amount of money').[22] Explicatures are (for the most part) merely developments of the incomplete conceptual representations provided by our linguistic semantic analyses.[23] They are built up from explicitly encoded material, typically by enrichments which render the utterance more specific. This is why (26a), the explicature, feels like the intuitive meaning of (25A₂), despite the fact that it contains some inferred aspects.

Here are additional examples for how explicated inferences combine with semantic meanings to form a holistic representation (the explicature), the explicated inferences contributing to the truth conditions of the proposition expressed.

(31) a.   There is a difference between **taking fire** and **taking fire**.
                           (Originally Hebrew, Israeli TV, Channel 10, March 23, 2007)
     b.   But most Israelis are happy to see that **the bulldozer**$_i$ ((Ariel Sharon – MA))
           has done the ((dirty/hard)) **work** for them. They are willing to **close their eyes**
           ((pretend not to see)) if he/it$_i$ **goes through a red light** ((commits an illegal
           action)), or **tramples on** ((brutally ignores)) the decisions of the party that
           elected him.   (*Haaretz* English edition, April 1, 2005)

What the soldier interviewed in (31a) means is that some degree of enemy fire is more difficult to take than some other degree of enemy fire. Obviously, we need to interpret the two events of 'taking fire' as different from each other, say 'taking fire$_{light}$' versus 'taking fire $_{heavy}$.' The inferred type of fire is an integral part of the proposition expressed and the truth conditions of that proposition here expressed must make reference to the inferred nature of the fire.

---

[22] Such entailment cases are called strengthenings. But not all explicatures entail the semantic meaning associated with them. Although *nothing* is explicated as 'no appropriate clothes' in (3d), the latter does not entail the former. And although *bachelor* is explicated as 'a person leading a free life style' in (21b), there is no entailment from 'leading a free life-style' to 'bachelor.'

[23] See Bach (1994), Carston (1988, 2002a), Recanati (1989, 1993: chapter 14).

Just as the explicated inferences in (31a) contribute to the very proposition which we assess for truth value, so do the inferences in (31b). In other words, a person who thinks Sharon does not take illegal actions (the explicature of *goes through a red light*), or that he did not brutally ignore (this is the explicature of *tramples*) his party's decision, is most likely to consider (31b) false just because these propositions are false (and not because Sharon is not literally a bulldozer, did not physically trample anything, and may not have gone through any red light).[24] If so, then the inferences here are explicated rather than implicated. This is why explicated inferences are implicit **in what the speaker says**, whereas implicatures are implied **by the act of saying** of the encoded message.

Here is an intuitive way to translate the functional independence criterion into a practical heuristic to determine the status of some communicated inference. We can ask ourselves whether the putative inference is an interpretation the speaker is interested in (indirectly) conveying in **addition** to the explicit content. If the answer is positive, it's an (external) implicature. But if it is a piece of information which cannot be seen as an independent, additional element, because it seems **inseparable** from the encoded message, it is explicated. In such cases we do not see the speaker as conveying both the explicit meaning and the derived meaning on top of it. Rather, the latter is a directly communicated explicature. In other words, while both implicatures and explicated inferences are implicit, implicatures in addition have a secondary, indirect status in discourse, whereas explicated inferences form part of the directly asserted message. Consider first cases which involve explicated inferences according to our analysis so far. It's fair to assume that regarding (16), we won't characterize the speaker as having said that (a) 'she has a nonzero amount of money,' and in addition that (b) 'possibly she has a substantial amount of money.' Instead, we would see the speaker as having conveyed only one message 'she has a substantial amount of money.' The same applies to $(25A_2)$ and to (31b). Thus, it's not the case that the readers of (31b) interpret it as: (i) '. . . the bulldozer (=machine) has done the work . . .' ('what is said'), and in addition, (ii) 'Sharon is like a bulldozer, i.e. ruthless' (implicated),[25] or that (i) 'it (the bulldozer =machine) goes through a red traffic light' ('what is said'), and, in addition, (ii) 'Sharon is like a bulldozer and he takes illegal actions' (implicated), etc. Instead, we incorporate the inferred interpretations here into one explicature, where the bulldozer is not a machine, no red light is actually crossed, etc.

Contrast the results of this "in addition" test for explicated inferences with those for cases of classical (particularized) conversational implicature. In (28a) above the addressors are implicating that it is harder to be admitted to the specific teachers' college advertised than to the university. We can roughly paraphrase (28a) by saying that the addressors here 'say' that 'if you were not . . . try the university,' and **in addition** they indirectly communicate that 'the studies at the

---

[24] In fact, one may consider that Sharon literally crossed a red light as true and still find (31b) false.
[25] Note that the Hebrew pronoun *hu* is used for both animate and inanimate masculine nouns, and 'bulldozer' is masculine in Hebrew.

college are harder, etc'. We can clearly separate out the implicature from the explicature. Similarly, Josh in (30) is not explicating his answer to JS. He is implicating it. What he explicates is 'I could tell you ...' And **in addition** he implicates that 'yes, you can use your old ...' Going back to (25), it's not that the speaker is saying 'I ate a house turkey sandwich,' and **in addition** indirectly saying that 'the eating took place recently today.' Rather, she is saying 'I ate a house turkey sandwich recently today,' and in addition she is indirectly communicating 'I am not hungry and not interested in eating now'. In other words, despite the fact that explicatures contain pragmatic enrichments, these play a different role from that of implicatures.

Explicatures and implicatures are then also different in that explicatures are directly communicated by the speaker, but implicatures are indirect meanings. For Relevance theoreticians, explicated inferences count as explicitly communicated assumptions (Bach here disagrees). There are some psycholinguistic findings compatible with this distinction. Gibbs (2004) reports different reading times for the same sentence, where in one context only explicated inferences were required (relevant), and in another context, conversational implicatures were strongly conveyed (only the implicature rendered the speaker's utterance relevant). He finds that when implicatures were necessary for the coherence of the discourse (this was verified in a separate experiment), reading time was longer. In other words, subjects take extra time to process implicatures, and it takes them longer than it takes them to process explicatures, although they too involve pragmatic inferencing.

Another test for distinguishing between explicated inferences and implicatures proposed by Carston (1988, 2002a: chapter 2) and Recanati (1989, 2001) is the embedding/scope criterion, which we already mentioned in section 3.1.[26] A putative inference is explicated if it falls within the scope of logical operators. The rationale is that logical operators have scope only on explicitly stated materials. It turns out that while implicatures do not show such interpretative sensitivity, explicated inferences do fall under the scope of logical operators, which shows that they have a "direct" presence, despite being implicit. We have already seen that some *and*-associated inferences pass this test. Consider again example (14) from chapter 3, which is the embedding of (24a) under a conditional operator:

(32)   ~If I eat the local food and get deathly ill I should stop going to Mexico.

The question here concerns the status of the causal interpretation sometimes associated with clauses conjoined by *and*. Quite clearly, the reason given by the speaker (in the antecedent) for having to stop going to Mexico (in the consequent) is the inferred causal connection between eating the local food and getting deathly ill. This is why it is roughly equivalent to (33a), where we embed the enriched proposition under the same conditional, but different from (33b), where we embed the reverse order of the constituents under the same conditional:

---

[26] But Carston (2004a) notes that this criterion too is not a foolproof test for explicated status, noting some putative implicatures which seem to interact with logical operators.

(33) a.   ~ If I eat the local food and as a result I get deathly ill I should stop going to
             Mexico.

    b.   ~ If I get deathly ill and eat the local food I should stop going to Mexico.

These facts point to the potentially explicated (rather than implicated) status of the causal interpretation here.[27] The content of the antecedent of the conditional here includes the inferred causal connection.

Let's now examine what we propose to consider JS's (33a) implicated inference. To see the behavior of a conversational implicature under a conditional, consider a shorter version of (30) above:

(34)   ~JS: Can I use my old Marker M48 bindings on new skis?
             JOSH: Skiing Magazine doesn't indemnify me.

Josh in (34) seems to implicate (35):

(35)   I don't dare tell you that you can use your old Marker M48 bindings on new skis.

Now, let's see if this implicature embeds under a conditional:

(36)   ?? If Skiing Magazine doesn't indemnify Josh, he's a coward.

It doesn't. (36) doesn't make sense because the consequent ('he's a coward') is only relevant to the implicature ('Josh doesn't dare tell JS that he can use his old bindings'). Since the conditional cannot apply to the implicature, the utterance is incoherent. In order for the conditional to apply to (35), we must explicate the implicature, as in:

(37)   If Josh doesn't dare tell JS that he can use his old Marker M48 bindings on
             new skis, he's a coward.

In other words, whereas the explicature stands for both the semantic meaning and the explicated inferences, it does not stand for the implicatures. This is why when the consequent is relevant to the inference, the explicature case is coherent (37), but the implicature case (36) isn't.[28]

We get a similar result if we submit the above two interpretations to negation (see Carston, 2004a). Contrast the following:

---

[27] But, as was emphasized in section 3.1, the status of some putative inference is not invariant in different contexts. Such causal interpretations may sometimes only be implicated (in which case they are external).

[28] We have applied the test as Carston (2002a: 2.6.3) applies it, namely by embedding only the implicature under the conditional, but actually, the counterpart of the explicature is the conveyed meaning. This too fails the test, however. Note that although the antecedents in (i) are equivalent to the 'said' + the implicated, the result is incoherent, for unlike explicated inferences, implicated inferences do not simply combine with 'said' aspects to create one coherent proposition:

    (i)   If Skiing Magazine doesn't indemnify Josh, and if Josh doesn't dare tell JS that he
            can use his old Marker M48 bindings on new skis, he's a coward.

    (i) here seems to specify two separate conditions for the consequence, as opposed to the one condition specified in (37).

(38) a.   ~KEN: So I eat the local food and get deathly ill.
            JOANNE: No, you don't eat the local food and get deathly ill.
    b.   ~JS: Can I use my old Marker M48 bindings on new skis?
            JOSH: Skiing Magazine doesn't indemnify me.
            MAYA: No! Skiing Magazine does indemnify you.

Note that in (38a) Joanne's denial of Ken's utterance may apply to the causal relation as well. But Maya's denial of JS's utterance in (38b) does not apply to the implicated 'Josh doesn't dare tell JS he can use his old Marker M48 bindings on new skis'. So, Joanne can continue with (39a), but Maya cannot continue with (39b):

(39) ~a.   There is no connection between your eating the local food and your getting deathly ill.
    ~b.   You do dare tell JS that he can use his old Marker M48 bindings on new skis.

The coherence of the sequence of (38a) and (39a) and the incoherence of the sequence of (38b) and (39b) once again testify that the causal connection in (24a) constitutes part of the proposition expressed, whereas the inference from (34) does not. The former is explicated, the latter an implicature.

Here's an attested example where it is the explicated inference that is treated as justifying *otherwise*, as well as contrastive stress on *I*:

(40)   J: ^You$_i$ sliced the ^bread.
        M$_i$:   Of ^course, otherwise ^I$_i$ would have had to slice it.   (July 13, 2006)

How is M's *I would have . . .* a different alternative from *You sliced . . .* when both refer to M slicing the bread? M has just returned from the bakery with a loaf of bread. What J explicates is that M sliced the bread **indirectly** (she had the bread sliced by the store people with their machine). M is then treating this interpretation as standing in a contrast to her slicing the bread (by hand, at home). What is crucial for us is that the inferred interpretation of *slice* ('slice indirectly') justifies the use of *otherwise*. There is then a good reason to distinguish between explicated and implicated inferences.

To sum up, we have seen that (i) the proposition expressed must have an independent discoursal and inferential role, that (ii) explicated inferences are inseparable from the semantic meaning but that (iii) implicatures are external to the semantic meaning. These assumptions and their practical tests, various ways of testing whether some inference affects/doesn't affect the truth-conditional content of the proposition expressed, the "in addition" test, speakers' intuitions re (in)separability, etc., all predict rather well whether some inference (in some specific context) is implicated or explicated.

Still, researchers no longer see inference levels as so different from each other as they initially did. While Recanati was one of the first to argue that even saturations (completions required for 'what is said$_{min}$') do require access to speakers' intentions (a "wide context"), he has recently argued that explicated inferences may only seem to rely on speakers' intentions. Instead of a full-fledged reasoning process, Recanati (especially 2002a) argues that explicated inferences (primary processes for him) are unconscious and automatic because they actually rely on associations. Spreading activation is said to be responsible for explicated inferences. These inferences are inferential only in a very weak sense, in the same sense in which perception is inferential. These ideas, which remain to be corroborated by psycholinguistic evidence, somewhat reduce the distinction between the minimalists' and maximalists' idea about the inferences that form part of 'what is said.' Unconscious and automatic inferences are not as cognitively demanding as calculations of speaker intentions. In this respect they seem closer to the automatic trivial context completions assumed by the minimalists.

Moreover, a complementary argument now has it that implicated inferences are not after all so different from explicated ones either. Recanati (2002a) does not believe that implicatures are necessarily slow, effortful, and under voluntary control. They too are spontaneous and more or less automatic. Carston (2002b) takes an even more radical position regarding implicatures. First, since Blakemore (1987), Relevance theoreticians have maintained that implicature generation is not as unconstrained as it may seem: at least sometimes it is guided by (procedural) linguistic expressions (e.g. *after all*). More recently, they have argued that implicatures are not consciously arrived at by addressees. Instead, they are automatically derived within a domain-specific module (see Wilson, 2005). According to Relevance theory, there is no cognitive difference between explicated and implicated inferences: both rely on the same kind of (wide) context, both are guided (constrained) by the principle of Relevance, both are not necessarily determinate (Carston, 2002a: chapter 5). They are, moreover, not necessarily derived sequentially (explicatures preceding implicatures), but rather, simultaneously, mutually constraining each other (see Wilson, 2003, Wilson and Sperber, 2004). Nonetheless, regardless of this changed outlook, a crucial difference remains between implicatures and explicated inferences for both Relevance theory and for Recanati. Implicatures and explicated inferences play different roles in our mental life and in discourse. Explicatures are logically prior to implicatures according to Relevance theory.

Table 7.1 sums up the differences between explicated and implicated inferences, all sharing features of inferences (implicitness, cancelability and some indeterminacy).[29] A distinction between strong and weak implicatures (see again section 1.3) has been added for completeness.

The crucial difference between explicated and implicated inferences is the feature here dubbed "directness," which is related to the inseparability of explicated inferences from the directly communicated semantic meaning. It is a reflex of the scope and functional independence principles. The next two features distinguish also between strong and nonstrong implicatures. The former are like

---

[29] Burton-Roberts (2005) argues that explicatures cannot be cancelable, for the speaker would be contradicting herself if they were (consider *You can call me later but not today*, where supposedly an explicated element is canceled). What is meant by the claim that explicated inferences are cancelable is perhaps better characterized as not unequivocal, open-ended, or suchlike.

Table 7.1 *Distinguishing explicated and implicated inferences*

	Explicated inferences	Strong implicatures	Nonstrong implicatures
Explicit	−	−	−
Cancelable	+	+	+
Indeterminate	+	+	+
Direct/inseparable	+	−	−
Interactionally Necessary	+	+	−
Truth-conditional	+	+/−	−

explicated inferences in that they are interactionally necessary (the utterance cannot be seen as relevant otherwise – see (51), (52) below). This is not the case for nonstrong implicatures. But note that even when it is the (strong) implicature that constitutes the relevant contribution to the discourse, the explicature must be computed. First, it serves as a premise in deriving the implicature. Second, as shown by Gibbs' (2004) results (see below), subjects asked about 'what is said' invariably selected both the explicature and the implicature, rather than just the implicature in strong implicature cases. Finally, whereas explicated inferences contribute to the truth conditions of the proposition expressed, nonstrong implicatures do not. Strong implicatures, however, may pattern with explicated inferences on this matter (see the results for (52) below).

The upshot of section 7.3.2 is that a maximalist position is not only intuitively satisfying, it is also coherent and consistent with a 'what is said' versus implicature distinction.

7.4   A mini–max 'what is said'

Maximalist approaches, as we have seen, opt for representing the intuitively meant content of the utterance (to the exclusion of implicatures). The price they pay is a heavy pragmatic "intrusion" into the basic-level meaning we assume as 'what is said.' The approach discussed in section 7.4 proposes that there is actually no price to be paid for the assumption of a 'what is said$_{max}$'. It is argued that although the relevant concept is the (maximalist) intuitive proposition expressed, the contextual completions needed are all grammatically mandated (including cases that have been classified as 'free enrichments'). They are saturations in fact, so that the completions required to fill the rather large gap between semantic and truth-evaluable meanings do constitute part of (a minimalist) 'what is said' after all. This approach actually denies that there is an inherent conflict between a minimalist and a maximalist 'what is said,' for a minimalist contextual contribution can provide an intuitively satisfying concept of 'what is said.' An advantage of this approach is that it preserves the principle of the compositionality of meaning (according to which the total meaning is a composite of all the linguistic components) at the 'what is said$_{max}$' level (and not only at the linguistic semantic level). This is impossible on the 'what is said$_{max}$' approach, where some enrichments are based on unarticulated constituents (i.e. missing interpretative aspects the completion of which is part of the proposition expressed, although they are not grammatically triggered – see Perry, 1993).

Recall that such an inclusive approach was the strategy adopted by Grice for reference and ambiguity resolutions.[30] In fact, there is agreement in the field that we have to assume at least some grammatically "unarticulated constituents," namely, semantic constituents of interpretations for which no overt constituents appear and no linguistic rule mandates their retrieval (but note that different researchers apply this analysis to somewhat different phenomena). In other words, there are cases where contextual inferences provide semantic constituents which do not correspond to the "Syntactic Correlation Constraint" (recall Bach's criterion). One example triggering this move was Perry's (1993: 206) *It is raining*, where we must contextually supply some location for the raining to be taking place, even though no grammatical reflex of this value is hypothesized. Otherwise, the statement would come out true virtually always (it must rain somewhere at any given point in time – Recanati, 2002b). Bach (1994), Recanati (2001), and Carston (2002a) have all referred to such completions, although to varying degrees.

Stanley (2000) has presented an extreme version of the inclusive Gricean approach, relegating to grammatically mandated completions a variety of contextual interpretations which most researchers view as optional and pragmatic (free enrichments). In fact, for Stanley (2000: 431), "**all truth-conditional effects** of context are traceable to logical form (emphasis added)." This is how 'what is said' is guaranteed to include all the intuitively relevant truth conditions of the proposition ('what is said$_{max}$'). Of course, for this analysis to work, many covert variables must be imposed on linguistic representations. Imposing on the language system inferences which are only conceptually/pragmatically mandated is not a trivial step theoretically. In order to motivate this highly abstract analysis, Stanley demonstrates that, indeed, these unarticulated constituents interact with sentential operators (recall the scope principle as a criterion for explicated inferences). In other words, these supposedly unarticulated constituents behave as if they were articulated, specifically, as if they were under the scope of overt operators. Here's one relevant example:

(41)   But um, basically, it's like ultimately each time I've been a nice guy this year
          I've been stung.   (LSAC)

Note that the times of 'being stung' (no temporal indicator appears) must vary with the times of 'being a nice guy' (the speaker claims to have been stung each time following each occasion of being a nice guy). Such a binding relation is said to testify to the presence of the temporal specification (a contextually supplied

---

[30] Levinson (2000b: 3.274) dubs approaches of this type "Enlarged indexicality" approaches.

value for a linguistic variable) for 'I've been a nice guy' in the logical form (the linguistic semantic meaning representation) of the sentence. Since the unarticulated constituent interacts with overt sentential constituents, the argument is that it plays a grammatical, and not merely a pragmatic role. Hence, its derivation must be seen as saturation, rather than as 'free enrichment.'

Both minimalists and maximalists have convincingly argued against this proposal, however, and proposed alternative analyses for Stanley's data.[31] Bach shows that the contextual enrichments are not of the automatic context retrieval type one would expect from semantic meaning. Wilson and Sperber demonstrate that there's no limit on the number of hidden variables we might need to postulate (they show how each context calls for reliance on some different "variable"), which renders the proposal psychologically implausible.[32] Consider the following:

(42)   JD: We can walk to Erez,
                 and have breakfast there.
           MA: But we're having lunch at my parents,
                 and we're going out with RG tonight. ((LINES OMITTED))
           JD: Okay, **We'll have breakfast another day**.
           MA: Maybe tomorrow.   (Sept. 7, 2005, 7:20 a.m.)

Although a locative is not obligatory with *have breakfast*, it's clear that JD and MA do not here make a decision to have breakfast another day but not on the day the conversation took place. What they decided to do was have breakfast **out** (at Erez cafe) another day and not that day. Instead of imposing obligatory automatic enrichments of so many hidden variables (this is what Stanley's analysis commits us to), Sperber and Wilson propose that such completions are selectively performed as needed, as in (42) (determined by considerations of Relevance).[33] The same locative enrichment makes absolutely no sense in the following:

(43)   A: You should eat sometime today, you know.
           B: I will eat at some point. **I had breakfast**.   (LSAC)

In addition, argues Carston (2004b), it is not feasible to explain all 'free enrichments' by reference to unarticulated constituents grammatically marked for completion. How can concept adaptation (as discussed above regarding the examples in (21)) be seen as obligatory filling in a value for a linguistic variable, when sometimes the very lexical denotation has to be relaxed? Finally, Carston (2004b) points out that Stanley (2000) cannot account for subsentential utterances

---

[31] See Berg (1993), Levinson (2000b: chapter 3), Bach (2000, 2001), Wilson and Sperber (1998, 2002), Ariel (2002a, 2002b), Recanati (2002b), and Carston (2002a: 2.7).

[32] As Carston (2004b) notes, declaring these unarticulated constituents as grammatically but only optionally added on cannot solve the problem here, since it would mean that truly obligatory cases of contextual enrichments (e.g. when syntactic deletions are involved) are also only optionally performed.

[33] Recanati (2002b) and Carston (2004b) explain the interpretative pattern noted in (41) above as resulting from 'free enrichment' nonetheless. The representation of the value for the "missing" variable only comes about when the bound variable interpretation is intended. It does not form part of the linguistic semantic representation, but of the referential semantic representation.

such as the final sentence in (44), which we fill in with something like the material specified in parentheses:

(44)   ... I am indebted to those attending either that presentation or the later one in Lansing, and to ((13 names follow – MA)) for their comments, suggestions, and complaints. Needless to say,. . . ((**all remaining errors are my own** – MA))   (Horn, 2006)

The completions are quite open-ended. Note that even when we know what the general content is, there is no specific completion which is clearly intended, or at least, retrieved:

(45)   M: Grey.   (April 28, 2007)

The context for (45) is that the addressee is standing in front of a door, hesitating which key to use. Can we decide which of the following M intends?:

(46) a.   It's the grey key for this door.
     b.   Use the grey key to open this door.
     c.   The grey key opens this door.

Most probably not. If we cannot determine what it is, it cannot be grammatical. Thus, the attempt to make the maximalist–minimalist gap in 'what is said' concepts disappear seems unsuccessful.

A minimalist–maximalist 'what is said' is not feasible, then. Given the arguments against 'what is said$_{min}$' (section 7.2), it seems that we are left with 'what is said$_{max}$' as the only viable option for 'what is said.' Still, in section 7.6 we will see that whereas 'what is said$_{max}$' is the common grammar/pragmatics interface, other, both more minimal and more maximal representations are also functional interface points. Section 7.6 discusses different attempts to hold on to both minimalist and maximalist concepts of 'what is said.' But let's first turn to a different set of inclusion–exclusion decisions (section 7.5).

7.5   'What is said' as less than semantic meaning

Up till now, we have concentrated on cases where 'what is said' is arguably richer than the encoded semantic meaning. But there is another gap between the semantic meaning and 'what is said,' one equally assumed by minimalists and maximalists, and it goes in the opposite direction. As mentioned at the outset in section 7.1, Grice (1989) and others following him excluded conventional implicatures from 'what is said.' Conventional implicatures constitute an exceptional category of meaning for most researchers, who were keen on equating the conventional with the truth-conditional (see Ariel, forthcoming: chapter 2). Conventional implicatures, such as the contrastive interpretation associated with *but*, specify conventional form–function correlations (and hence are semantic), but they are not seen as contributing to the truth conditions of the proposition expressed. They are used to generate implicatures, and are therefore extragrammatical. Consider the following:

(47)   LYNNE: (H) That's not bad,
                but sometimes you can get it really bad.   (SBC: 001)

The accepted assumption regarding Lynne's 'what is said' is that it is restricted to the conjunction of her two propositions, namely, 'that's not bad, **and** sometimes you can get it really bad'. The contrast between the two propositions is only represented at the conveyed level, where implicatures are combined with 'what is said.' Since they make no contribution to the truth conditions of the proposition expressed, and since the interpretations involved are implicit, they were excluded from 'what is said,' despite their encoded status. Conventional implicatures are then examples of cases where 'what is said' is leaner than the semantic meaning (as here defined).

Bach (1999) has recently argued against this analysis. According to him, there are no conventional implicatures. The *but* contrast, for example, does contribute to the truth conditions of the proposition expressed, it counts as a (subsidiary) proposition, and hence, as part of 'what is said.' As Bach notes, this is even clearer in the case of *therefore*:

(48)   A: There are some people who just don't read those things and **therefore**
             don't build up those expectations but there are other people who do read
             them and still don't build up the expectations and that's a different
             question. Why do some people build them up
         B: Mhm.
         A: and other people not build them up?   (LSAC)

The consequence interpretation associated with *therefore* here seems to affect the truth conditions of the proposition. The whole point in A's utterances revolves around the consequential connection between '(not) reading those things' and 'building up expectations.' *Therefore* does contribute to the truth conditions of A's propositions, and so should form part of 'what is said.' Thus, for some implicit interpretations, Bach diverges from Grice's excluding line for conventional implicatures, and proposes an inclusive line (see Ariel, forthcoming: chapter 9 for supporting evidence).

But even for Bach there are conventional interpretations which are excluded from 'what is said.' So again, for such cases, 'what is said' is more minimal than the semantic meaning. Consider utterance modifiers (e.g. *confidentially, between you and me*), as in:

(49)   **Just between you and me**, oh you don't need a, you don't need a
         collateral.   (LSAC)

Bach here proposes the excluding strategy, because utterance modifiers do not modify the propositional content of the utterance. While they are part of the sentence syntactically, they are external to it semantically. For Bach they perform second-order speech acts (something like 'I'm **telling** you confidentially' for (49)). Wilson and Sperber (1993) have a natural slot for utterance modifiers in their higher-level explicatures, where the proposition expressed is embedded under a higher-level description, often an illocutionary force indicator. So, for Wilson and Sperber, utterance modifiers are part of higher-level explicatures.

While either of these solutions may be able to account for clear-cut synchronic facts about the interpretation of utterance modifiers, we should note that not all cases are absolutely clear. Utterance modifiers can be analyzed either as internal or as external to 'what is said' in some cases, and this can be explained by reference to their history of use. External utterance modifiers typically develop out of 'what is said' internal sentential adverbs (see Traugott, 1982, 1989; Traugott and Dasher, 2002 on the semanticization path from meanings based in real-world situations to meanings based in the metalinguistic situation). We need to be able to account for this development. The solution seems to be that when internal, these adverbs form part of 'what is said' ('what is said$_{min}$' for Bach, the explicature for Relevance theory). Gradually, these expressions are reanalyzed as metalinguistic and external to 'what is said,' first-person speech act verbs providing the intermediate link most probably. Consider (50):

(50) a.　　Well I knew her from back when we were in Junior High and I'm just, this is just **between you and me**, she was mean, I remember her　　(LSAC)

　　b.　　He was all, all but I'll tell you, **between you and me**,　　(LSAC)

Just as it is clear that *between you and me* is an utterance modifier in (49), it is clear that it is part of (anybody's) 'what is said' in (50a). Perhaps (50b), where *between you and me* is still part of 'what is said,' is the mediating use. We must make sure that the grammar/pragmatics interface we assume be able to account for semanticizations, and what we know about the development of utterance modifiers is that they develop out of sentence-internal adverbs, which means that they must have formed part of 'what is said' initially. They cannot start out as part of the higher-level explicature, in other words. But once they are higher-level speech acts/explicatures, they are linguistically encoded elements which don't (necessarily) form part of 'what is said.' As such, they show that 'what is said' can be more minimal than the encoded meaning.

Silverstein (2001) draws our attention to a different sort of case where linguistically marked functions should probably not be considered part of 'what is said.' He notes that while Kiksht speakers can indicate negative and positive attitudes by employing forms expressing a diminutive or augmentation (via various phonological changes in how they pronounce certain words), such meanings are unavailable to any conscious metapragmatic discourse on the speakers' part. Silverstein's attempts to have his informants repeat those forms failed, even when he played his tape back to them. The same is true for class distinctions in pronunciations. Although these are all conventional form–function correlations, they seem not to enter a 'what is said' representation. If so, there are (rather rare) cases where 'what is said' is more minimal than the linguistic code.

7.6　Syncretic approaches to 'what is said'

Syncretic approaches constitute another attempt to reconcile minimalist and maximalist concepts of 'what is said.' Whereas Stanley (2000) argues that 'what is said$_{max}$' is one with 'what is said$_{min}$', syncretic views see them as widely apart. They take the position that in addition to the bare semantic representation, on the one hand, and the total interface level of the conveyed meaning on the other hand, there is more than just one meaning representation. On Bach's (1994) version, there is a minimalist 'what is said' in the spirit of the proposals in section 7.2 and a maximalist meaning level, the impliciture, in the spirit of the proposals in section 7.3.[34] Indeed, as pointed out by Recanati (2004), at least some minimalist positions are compatible with some maximalist positions. On my analysis too, while the default grammar/pragmatics interface is 'what is said$_{max}$', there is a range of interface levels with varying degrees of inferential enrichments (Ariel, 2002b).

Bach (1994, 2001) and, following him, Horn (2004, 2006) have adopted Grice's exclusive strategy for their concept of 'what is said,' so theirs is a minimalist position, as presented in section 7.2. Fully recognizing the extent of the gap between linguistic semantic meaning and truth-conditional meaning, however, instead of expanding 'what is said' to fit our maximalist intuitive concept, they chose to lower even further the demands made on 'what is said,' on the one hand, and to define a separate meaning level, the impliciture, as the meaning level actually communicated by the speaker on the other hand. For example, for sentences interpreted figuratively, the literal, implausible meaning is their 'what is said,' even though it is clearly nonmeant (Bach, 2006). The intended figurative interpretation is the impliciture (rather than the implicature, as Grice saw it). 'What is said' and the impliciture of the same sentence (in the same context) may therefore have distinct truth conditions. In fact, Bach's 'what is said' need not necessarily express a complete, truth-evaluable proposition. Thus, for cases such as (3) (as well as for *and* interpreted as 'and then'), Bach proposes that the incomplete 'what is said$_{min}$' is enriched with missing conceptual portions to create the impliciture. Just like explicatures, implicitures too may not just be developments of 'what is said$_{min}$', they may replace it when the speaker's intention is to communicate something other than her 'what is said$_{min}$'. Unlike Relevance theorists, however, Bach insists that any inferred material is inexplicit (hence his choice of the term impliciture).[35]

In short, Bach's view assumes two 'what is said' concepts: a minimalist 'what is said' (as discussed in section 7.2) and a maximalist impliciture (as discussed in section 7.3). (Another advocate of this approach is Soames, 2002: chapter 3.) Contra Stanley's (2000) attempt to merge the maximalist and minimalist 'what is said' concepts, Bach insists that these are two distinct meaning levels with distinct properties and functions which coexist next to each other. We have already reviewed Recanati's (1989, 2001) and Relevance theoreticians' (most prominently Carston, 1988 and onwards) arguments against positing a minimalist

---

[34] Note that Bach's maximalist term is impliciture, not implicature. See section 3.2.2 again.

[35] I followed Bach in assigning an inexplicit status to explicated inferences in table 7.1. Note that many speakers who refuse to refer to God by name have no problem referring to God by a pronoun. Now, of course, the explicated representation is 'God' in either case, but the implicitness of the reference when a pronoun is used is crucial. See also (55) below. Explicated inferences should indeed count as implicit interpretations.

'what is said.' Is there then a reason to adopt both a minimalist and a maximalist 'what is said'? Natural interactions teach us that there is.

The concept we are after in this chapter is a basic-level interpretation. But what counts as basic? How can we tell what Recanati's "Availability Principle" predicts regarding 'what is said'? One way to determine what basic-level is is to turn to natural interactions (Ariel, 2002b). 'What is said' should perhaps follow the basic level of communicated meaning in actual interactions, what is taken as the privileged interactional interpretation. The Privileged Interactional Interpretation is the meaning which the speaker is seen as minimally and necessarily committed to, i.e. the one by which she is judged as telling the truth or being sincere. It is also the meaning which contains the message that the addressee should take to be the relevant contribution made by the speaker. It is the information the addressee would be likely to (dis)agree with when responding with *yeah* or *no*. Note that it is not necessarily the most minimal meaning (although it can be, but it can also be uncooperatively enriched). It is the meaning which has a significant interactional status, because it is the one which serves as the basis for the contextual effects of the utterance. Now, if 'what is said' should correspond to the Privileged Interactional Interpretation, which of the concepts so far considered fits the bill? While we can define 'what is said' however we like (as above), if we are after a motivated concept, the Privileged Interactional Interpretation criterion offers a natural definition for 'what is said.'

Unlike the various concepts of 'what is said' considered so far, Privileged Interactional Interpretations are not constructed in a 'one size fits all' fashion. There is no fixed formula for their construction, as there is for 'what is said$_{min}$' or 'what is said$_{max}$'. Such interpretations are subjective and variable across speakers and contexts. The Privileged Interactional Interpretation is the one deemed contextually appropriate by some participant (either the speaker or the addressee), not even necessarily by all participants.[36] As we see below, interlocutors don't seem to follow any one definition of 'what is said' absolutely consistently. There is a need for positing both minimalist and maximalist concepts of 'what is said,' because Privileged Interactional Interpretations can be minimalist or maximalist. Moreover, even one minimalist and one maximalist 'what is said' do not exhaust the options available to interlocutors. Neither minimalist nor maximalist Privileged Interactional Interpretations come in one mold. Now, it should be emphasized that the common Privileged Interactional Interpretation is 'what is said$_{max}$' (see again the judges' rulings regarding *a three-year experience* and *an Israeli*). But this is not the case invariably. For example, although the district court decision regarding Sheinbein's case was maximalist, in that he was declared a non-Israeli according to the enriched definition of the term, the supreme court later reversed

[36] We cannot accept Recanati's (2004: 56) defense of a pragmatic (maximalist) 'what is said' as nonsubjective, because the latter is simply "what a **normal interpreter** would understand as being said, in the context at hand." Not just wise guys (see below) sometimes disagree about 'what is said.' Moreover, even 'wise-guy' interpretations should be accounted for, because there is a principle behind their derivation.

that decision, and reverted to the minimalist concept.[37] Although rarely so, Privileged Interactional Interpretations do testify to the potential availability of representations both more minimal and more maximal than 'what is said$_{max}$' (psycholinguistic evidence supports such an assumption too). This is why we should opt for a syncretic approach. Let's review a few such discourse cases.

First, Privileged Interactional Interpretations may (rarely) involve strongly implicated implicatures, which are excluded not only from the minimalists' but also from the maximalists' 'what is said.' Consider (51):

(51)   R: And Haim Getzl (=John Doe) who is a company director pretends to
                   know that the balance sheet is going to be good so he starts buying
            S: OK that's a criminal offence
            R: Eh . . .
            S: It's a bit of a criminal offence
            R: **So he has a mother-in-law**
            S: For **this** you go to jail.   (Lotan 1990: 16)

Note that *this* in S's last turn refers to the implicated proposition from R's last turn, namely, 'Haim Getzl might (illegally) buy shares under his mother-in-law's name.' This is clearly an implicature and not an explicated inference (by the independence criterion).[38] But still, what S 'says' is not 'you go to jail for having a mother-in-law.' It is the implicature and not the explicature that S's reaction responds to. The strong implicature in (51) constitutes the Privileged Interactional Interpretation, and S's 'what is said' supports this position.[39] Here is another example (already cited in chapter 1) where a very strong implicature constitutes the Privileged Interactional Interpretation of the utterance. In this case we can also see the consequences of the status of the Privileged Interactional Interpretation for truth evaluation:

(52)   Boss: You have small children. How will you manage the long hours of
                   the job?
            HD: **I have a mother.**   (Originally Hebrew, June 14, 1996)

HD's explicature is true (she has a mother), but the very strong implicature ('HD's mother will take care of her children when she needs to work long hours') happens to be false here. (The mother never helps her out with the children.) This fact

---

[37] But as I note in Ariel (2002b), counting all decisions made by various legal authorities in this case, there were 3 votes for a minimalist interpretation and 4 for a maximalist interpretation. The supreme court decision was made by 3 against 2, the supreme court president himself holding a maximalist line in the minority.

[38] François Recanati (p.c.) thinks that the above interpretation is neither explicated nor implicated. Rather, for him, it is a proposition made salient in the discourse without being explicated or implicated. I am not sure what such interpretations could be, especially since R clearly intends S to entertain this proposition. Be that as it may, Recanati agrees that the interpretation at hand is not explicated, so at least my point that the Privileged Interactional Interpretation need not be the explicature is maintained.

[39] A minimalist might cling to 'what is said$_{min}$' here, viewing S's 'you go to jail for having a mother-in-law' as 'what is said.' It is then not clear how this can combine with an implicature to yield the desired interpretation.

rendered the speaker's utterance false for over half (15/27, 55.5 percent) of my subjects (11/27, 40.7 percent said HD's utterance is not a lie). Interestingly, HD herself introduced (52) as a story about how she **lied** in order to get a job.[40] So, it is the implicature here that carries the relevant message (having a mother is quite irrelevant), and even determines the truth value of the utterance for many.[41] Thus, while by definition (i.e. according to the way in which it is derived) 'my mother will take care of the children . . .' is an implicature, by its interactional status it functions like 'what is said.' In Ariel (2004b) I quote questionnaire results regarding the following exchange, where Maya strongly implicates 'not all':

(53)   IDDO: Dana solved all the problems.
            MAYA: More than half of them.

While most subjects determined that Maya's utterance was true when they were told that reality was such that 'Dana solved all the problems' (because *more than half* is compatible with 'all'), as many as 40 percent thought it was not true (because the 'not all' implicature is incompatible with 'all'). The latter subjects must have assigned the very strong 'not all' implicature a privileged interactional status which affected their truth evaluations.[42]

The following experiment demonstrates that conveyed meanings, i.e. explicatures and implicatures taken together, may (sometimes) constitute the Privileged Interactional Interpretations. If so, once again, then, implicatures can form part of the Privileged Interactional Interpretation. Gibbs (2004) asked subjects what they understood from a sentence such as *I drive a sports utility vehicle* in a context where the implicature from this proposition, that 'it's safe to drive such a car in stormy weather,' was extremely relevant, more so than the explicature. As answers, subjects could choose the explicature ('I drive a particular kind of car that is a sports utility vehicle'), the implicature ('the car is capable of handling stormy weather'), and a combination of the two ('I drive a particular kind of car that is a sports utility vehicle, that is capable of handling stormy weather'). Subjects overwhelmingly chose the combined option (92 percent of the questions). The explicature alone and the implicature alone were each selected in only a negligible minority of the cases (3 percent and 5 percent respectively). Thus, the implicature was treated on a par with the explicature here.

---

[40] Note incidentally that in (51) and (52) the strong implicatures entail the explicatures (e.g. in (52), 'My mother will take care of my children' entails 'I have a mother').

[41] Coleman and Kay (1981) report somewhat less dramatic results for a similar false implicature case (their story VI). Half as many of their subjects classified the strongly implicated false inference as a lie (26.9 percent). A majority (62.7 percent) classified it as true (10.4 percent chose 'can't say'). But, as they note, many of their subjects were linguistics students and professors. It's quite possible that this was a relevant factor. Be that as it may, if strong implicatures cannot affect truth conditions, there is no reason for over a third of the subjects (37.3 percent) to avoid the choice of 'not lie.'

[42] Sweetser (1987) and Meibauer (2005) too propose that what are here characterized as strong implicatures may render the speaker a liar should they be false. But Bernard Comrie (p.c.) rightly warns that there's a potential problem in comparing between judgments as 'false' and the more morally loaded judgment as 'lie.'

Indeed, Carston (2002a: chapter 5) concedes that both explicatures and implicatures can be communicated with more or with less commitment, and that not only explicatures, but also implicatures may constitute the main point of the utterance (the source of cognitive effects). She tentatively suggests that it may be the strength of the assumptions communicated, as well as how Relevant they are, that are important in discourse, much more than the technical distinction between implicatures and explicatures. The fact that Gibbs and Moise's (1997) subjects chose explicatures (rather than 'what is said$_{min}$') as paraphrases for 'what is said' can be seen as evidence that explicatures are very often the Privileged Interactional Interpretations, but not more than that. As Nicolle and Clark (1999: 337) argue, subjects "tend to select the paraphrase that comes closest to achieving the same set of communicated contextual effects as the original utterance." This constitutes the Privileged Interactional Interpretation. So, when it is the implicature rather than the explicature that is seen as the speaker's main intended message, subjects should include it under 'what is said.' This is what Nicolle and Clark found. Strong implicatures were often chosen by their subjects as 'what is said' (see also Bezuidenhout and Cutting, 2002). These paraphrases (whether corresponding to explicated or implicated interpretations) reflect Privileged Interactional Interpretations, rather than explicatures or implicatures per se. If we take Recanati's (1989) "Availability Principle" seriously, we see that interlocutors' intuitions do not always point to a single definition for 'what is said'.

Note that it's not invariably the case that the Privileged Interactional Interpretation is richer than the explicature, as we have seen so far. More minimal representations too can constitute the Privileged Interactional Interpretations sometimes. Recall that Recanati (2001) argued that there is no psychological reality to a partially pragmatic construct. While it is indeed usually dysfunctional to represent to ourselves an only partially pragmatically interpreted utterance, it is precisely what we do sometimes. Interlocutors who revert to 'wise-guy' interpretations may fail to infer, or else, "peel off," as it were, layers of pragmatic meanings, and derive a contextually inappropriate/unintended interpretation as the Privileged Interactional Interpretation (see section 1.3 and Ariel, 2002b). They may then opt for a minimalist 'what is said.' Consider (54) ((54b) was already quoted in section 1.3):

(54) a.   MA (San Francisco):   I'd like to leave a message for X
           Hotel Operator (New York): I'll connect you to their room.
           MA: No, no. I don't want to wake them up. **It's midnight** in New York!
           Operator: No, **it's not**.
           MA: What time is it there?
           Operator: **It's 11:53**.   (Oct. 13, 1998)

    b.   A municipal regulation determines that a piece of property which remains **empty** is exempt from city tax for six months. A, a lawyer who has moved into a new office, was astonished when city hall inspectors refused to declare his old office as **empty** because of a few chairs left behind. "What is **empty**," he wondered, "when the floor tiles have been pulled out?" ... The director of the city income department explained ... ((that)) **formally, empty is empty**, and it's possible to say that even if there is a rag in the office, it is considered **full**.   (Originally Hebrew, reported in the magazine *Tel Aviv*, May 14, 1993)

Note that the operator in (54a) insists on the semantic meaning of *midnight* ('12 a.m.'), rejecting the more contextually appropriate inferred meaning, 'about midnight, too late for calling up people.' In (54b) the city official is defending an unenriched interpretation of *empty*, and in Ariel (2002b) I quote similar examples where a judge confirmed the interpretation of a non-narrowed concept of *red*. Thus, despite the fact that *red* has a prototypical narrowing with respect to cars ('bright red'), the judge ruled that supplying a burgundy car when a red one was ordered was a legitimate step on a car dealer's part, which should be acceptable to the buyers. The reason is that a burgundy car is an instance of a 'red car.'[43] Similarly, in a different case, the police decided not to press charges against a right-wing activist who had issued a threat against a leftist, because the speech act he used was literally a recommendation/suggestion (see Ariel, 2002a: 4.1 for details). These are all cases where the contextually plausible interpretation (an explicature) was rejected in favor of an unreasonable unenriched interpretation, just because the unreasonable one can be backed by the linguistic semantic meaning. Note that the city official in (54b) has a good reason to be a wise-guy interpreter. But not so the operator in (54a), nor the judge and the police. And recall also that a large minority of my subjects did rule that HD did not lie in (52). There just isn't (always) one Privileged Interactional Interpretation (see Ariel, 2002b for additional examples of differing Privileged Interactional Interpretations among interlocutors).

   Here's a case (originally quoted in Ariel, 2002b), where a speaker (Lewinsky) finds even the minimalist 'what is said' representation to be too rich:

(55)   LEWINSKY: You know, he ((Vernon Jordan – MA)) asked me point-blank if I, you know, had a thing with **him**.
           TRIPP: He asked you point-blank. No, he didn't.
           LEWINSKY: Yes, he did.
           TRIPP: What did he say?
           LEWINSKY: He said, "Did you have an affair with **him**?"
           TRIPP: He said, "Did you have an affair with **the President**?" You're kidding.
           LEWINSKY: **Not "the P,"** but with **him**. I mean, obviously **that's what he meant**, he just didn't say the name.
                     (Oct. 16, 1997: *New York Times*, Oct. 4, 1998)

In other words, even providing the intended referent ('President Clinton'), a clear case of anybody's 'what is said$_{min}$', renders Tripp's representation of Jordan's utterance (as cited by Lewinsky) an unfaithful paraphrase. And recall (15), where the wise guy picks the partially wrong referent for *gum*.

---

[43] Out of 34 'Introduction to pragmatics' students asked about the judge's decision, 9 supported it, 9 were critical, and as many as 16 could not decide.

Note how the next speaker is selective and inconsistent in what enrichments he accepts and what enrichments he rejects. (56) demonstrates how a wise-guy interlocutor can refuse to select the appropriate disambiguated sense (of *look here*, intended in its discourse marker function here), which he is supposed to according to a 'what is said$_{min}$' concept, but he does accept the intended referent resolution (that *look here* applies to him):

(56)   BEN: What are you doing, criticizing me?
          GUS: No, I was just . . .
          BEN: You'll get a swipe round your ear hole if you don't watch your step.
          GUS: **Now look here**, Ben . . .
          BEN: **I'm not looking anywhere!**
          (Harold Pinter, *The Dumb Waiter*, pp. 15–16, quoted from Yus Ramos, 1998: 87)

The importance of 'wise-guy' interpretations is that they show that the bare semantic meaning (or at least, more minimal than 'what is said$_{min}$') does have psychological reality on occasion. For speakers to create 'wise-guy' interpretations they must be able to bring to consciousness the linguistic semantic meaning. Note that 'wise-guy' interpretations are not just any inappropriate interpretations. They are inappropriate in a very specific way: they fail to include the speaker's intended inferences. Wise guys either refuse to enrich the semantic meaning, or they enrich it with an inappropriate inference, or they pick the wrong sense of an ambiguous form. All of these divergences nevertheless abide by some legitimate meaning of the utterance, and require access to the linguistic semantic meaning stripped of added inferences, both 'what is said$_{min}$' and 'what is said$_{max}$' ones. 'Wise-guy' interpretations are acceptable (reluctantly, of course) just because they are compatible with some legitimate semantic meaning (see Ariel, 2002b on how other inappropriate interpretations are unacceptable).

Hence, while Recanati (2001) and Carston (2002a: chapter 5) are correct in observing that it would be an arbitrary decision for interlocutors to stop drawing inferences just to create a 'what is said$_{min}$', only to then go on inferencing and creating a 'what is said$_{max}$', interlocutors choose to do just the first step sometimes, and even less than that. We sometimes stop at less than 'what is said$_{min}$' even. At other times, we can simultaneously take more than one perspective on the Privileged Interactional Interpretation. For example, the mother in (7) and in (8) seems to see both 'what is said$_{min}$' and 'what is said$_{max}$', On the one hand, in (7) she thinks Iddo told the truth, because the explicature from his words is true, but on the other hand, she does point out that his 'what is said$_{min}$' is false. Similarly, while MS's intention in (6) is to lie, her 'what is said$_{min}$' is true. The interlocutors here are simultaneously aware of both representations.[44]

The following example (a Hebrew bumper sticker spotted March 20, 2007) shows the simultaneous relevance of the literal and the explicated:

---

[44] In fact, Coleman and Kay (1981) tested such a case (story IV), and found that most of their subjects (74.6 percent) thought that such a speaker did lie.

(57)   Gilead Shalit   Ehud Ulmert
         Uri Goldvaser   HA-BAYTA   Amir Peretz
         Eldad Regev   THE-HOME.TO   Dan Chalutz

Ha-bayta literally means 'to the home,' i.e. movement towards home. Its explicated meaning, however, is different on each side of the sticker. On the left we have the names of three Israeli soldiers kidnapped by Palestinians and Hezbollah. 'Home' here is explicated to 'come home' or 'bring them home,' implicating 'we miss you, we love you, we want you back with us.' On the right we have the names of the three Israeli leaders responsible for the Second Lebanon War (2006), considered a failure in Israel. 'Home' in this connection is explicated to 'go home' or 'send them home,' implicating just the opposite, 'we don't want you as our leaders, we don't want to see you in the public sphere,' etc. In other words, while the literal meaning is identical for both sides, the explicated meaning is the opposite. Now, the fact that the writer could simultaneously use one and the same predicate for two different explicated meanings would seem to vindicate the 'what is said$_{min}$' proponents, for it must be the common literal meaning that enables the coexistence of these two opposites. Note, however, that (57) feels rather like a pun (this was ascertained with a number of speakers). The only reason why it would feel like a pun, which is what we feel when the relevant expression is semantically ambiguous, is that the explicated meaning is not like any inferred meaning. Although inexplicit, it can function as if it were explicit. Once we get to the list on the right, we feel we need to reinterpret *ha-bayta*.[45]

In sum, the examples discussed in section 7.6 demonstrate that sometimes enriched explicatures may not be maximalist enough, and at other times, even the minimalist 'what is said' is not minimal enough as the Privileged Interactional Interpretation functional in natural discourse. Although rarely so, implicatures (more than 'what is said$_{max}$') and bare semantic meanings (less than 'what is said$_{min}$') constitute Privileged Interactional Interpretations. In other words, whereas there is an automatic construction of a Privileged Interactional Interpretation in discourse, there is no guarantee that the enrichment intended by the speaker, and/or the one inferred by various addressees, will invariably be the explicature/ 'what is said$_{max}$' defined by Relevance theory and Recanati. The very fact that we sometimes entertain less or more enriched meaning levels means that we can access a variety of meaning representations. For 'what is said' to have an intuitive basis, it cannot be pinned down to a single definition. It seems that the grammar/ pragmatics interface in discourse does not come in a single formula, dictating precisely how much pragmatic inferencing is to be introduced into the basic-level representation. It should be emphasized, however, that more often than not, it is the explicature which is the relevant Privileged Interactional Interpretation. Not only synchronic data point to that. In the next section I propose that linguists consider the possibility that semanticization points in this direction too.

---

[45] Since Hebrew is read right-to-left, I have here reversed the sides of the two lists above, so in English too, it's the leaders that are encountered second.

7.7   In conclusion: the grammar/pragmatics divide and interfaces

In part I we discussed the theoretical implications of a code/inference distinction. Adopting a code versus inference distinction, we applied it not just to clear cases of conversational implicatures, but mainly to various cases where deciding whether some form–function correlation is coded or inferred is not straightforward. As we saw, despite the fact that there is general agreement in the field on a code versus inference distinction, researchers do not necessarily classify specific phenomena in the same way. What some analyze as code, others analyze as inference. Moreover, since we now assume that there is more than one type of intended inference (implicatures and explicated inferences), as well as truth-compatible inferences, we need to distinguish between types of inferences, and not only between codes and inferences. These were the tasks of part I.

But after we've analyzed utterance use into the distinct processes that go into it (part I), we had to put all these components back together again. This was the goal of parts II and III. In part II the argument was made that despite the distinct cognitive make-up of codes on the one hand, and inferences on the other, codes and inferences do make contact, or we wouldn't be able to explain many cases of historical change. The fact that so much of the linguistic code can be pragmatically motivated stems from the origin of grammar, the extralinguistic factors guiding interlocutors. Codes commonly develop out of (salient, recurrent) speaker-intended inferences associated with specific forms. The arena where this process takes place is the salient discourse pattern. The salient discourse pattern or profile results from consistently skewed uses speakers make of their current grammar. If the emerging pattern is salient enough, it may bring into being new forms and new form–function correlations, a new grammar, in other words.

In part III we considered two points of synchronic grammar/pragmatics interface representations: the conveyed meaning and 'what is said.' We first reviewed the motivation for distinguishing between implicated and explicated inferences. We saw that the two play different discoursal roles, and should, therefore, be kept apart. We then devoted most of chapter 7 to introducing different 'what is said' concepts for Interactional grammar/pragmatics interface representations. The conclusion from section 7.6 was that although 'what is said$_{max}$' is most probably the default concept available to interlocutors, other, more minimal as well as more maximal representations play a role, at least sometimes.

As food for thought, I would like to end this book by calling linguists to re-examine the common assumption that it is (only) the conveyed meaning level which potentially gives rise to grammaticization/semanticization. Following Recanati's "Availability Principle," linguists should consider the possibility that specifically recurrent **explicated** inferences (rather than implicatures, or invited inferences) are the immediate source for grammatical (semantic) innovations. This does not at all mean that implicatures have no role in discourse and in semanticization. Quite the contrary. Speakers sometimes prefer to convey interpretations indirectly for a variety of reasons (lessened responsibility, humorous effect, etc.). However, 'what is said' and 'what is implicated' are kept apart (the conveyed meaning is merely the sum of the two). They do not necessarily merge together into one whole meaning, as is the case for the semantic meaning and explicated inferences, the 'what is said.' For this reason, the main locus for the grammar/pragmatics interface may be 'what is said,' which is why we may hypothesize that explicated, rather than implicated, inferences serve as the immediate impetus for most semanticizations and grammaticizations. Here are two examples for what this rethinking might involve.[46]

Since is often cited as a classical example for the potential semanticization of implicatures. Traugott and König (1991) have described the development of an additional, causal meaning out of the originally temporal *since* as a process of conventionalizing a recurrent invited inference. Indeed, initially, it is only reasonable to attribute an implicated (or, as Traugott and Dasher, 2002 prefer, invited inference) status to the causal interpretation associated with *since*. At this stage, the explicature associated with *since* must have been restricted to the temporal interpretation, and it was by implicature that interlocutors derived an additional, independent proposition, to the effect that a causal relation may be involved. In such cases, the causal inference is indirectly communicated in addition to the explicature and is quite easily cancelable. This would be similar to the interpretation of *ever since* in (58), where the speaker seems to implicate (rather than explicate) that the dog has been snoring **because** she ate (quite a bit), and not only that she has been snoring **since** the time she ate:

(58)   And she's been snoring **ever since** she ate.   (LSAC)

Now, once *since* could function as 'because' without the mediation of an inference from a temporal sequence to an explained chain of events, the causal interpretation must have become an independent, conventional meaning. Note that *ever since* cannot substitute for *since* in (59), precisely because, unlike *since*, it did not undergo this semanticization:

(59)   **Since/~?? ever since** you're not gonna do the paperwork today, I need to
         get you to sign this.   (LSAC)

Clearly, these are two stages in the development of causal *since*. But we can suggest an additional phase between being implicated and being coded, an explicated inference phase, in which 'because' is already directly 'said' when *since* is used, but it is still cancelable (see table 7.1 above). The point is that at this intermediate stage, the causal interpretation was no longer perceived as an independent interpretation external to the temporal 'what is said.' Rather, speakers were often enough seen as directly 'saying' 'because,' and not as 'saying' 'temporal since' and implicating 'because.' Nonetheless, it was still cancelable, as all explicated inferences are,

---

[46] See Ariel (2007b) for an in-depth analysis in this spirit of one case in Hebrew.

although not as easily as implicatures are.[47] Under this proposal, it could be the inseparability of the 'because' interpretation from the *since* utterance (explicature status) that paved the way for the reinterpretation of the meaning of *since*.

Next, let's examine an inference which may turn conventional, which is explicated, rather than implicated right from the start. *Gourmet* in *Gourmet Garage* (a sign on a garage spotted in Manhattan, May 2005) is a currently innovative source for a metaphorical interpretation.[48] Being a current innovation, this example can more clearly demonstrate the potential role of explicatures in semanticization. *Gourmet*'s lexical meaning is "a connoisseur in eating and drinking" (*The Shorter Oxford Dictionary*), but the relevant interpretation in the case at hand could not possibly be that. The meaning of *gourmet* here necessarily omits the eating and drinking aspect, generalizing the interpretation to nonspecific 'connoisseur,' or 'high class.' In this innovative example, the inferred ('high-class') interpretation could not possibly be indirectly communicated by the addressors in addition to their communicating (as the direct explicature) the linguistic semantic meaning, i.e. 'a garage which is a connoisseur in eating and drinking.' Rather, the inferred meaning of *gourmet garage* ('a high-class garage') replaces its literal meaning, and is therefore explicated, rather than implicated. Should *gourmet* be used often enough with such a loosened meaning (as its explicated interpretation) it could very well lead to a semanticization of the 'high-class' interpretation. This is what happened to the Hebrew distinction between *sug aleph* 'grade A' and *sug bet* 'grade B,' which were first applicable to manufactured goods, but are now applicable to anything of higher or lower quality or worth. A similar development has occurred in English for *first/ second rate*.

We've now come full circle. With this proposal, we have completed the mission undertaken in this textbook, namely, to take grammar and pragmatics apart, and to put them back together again. We started by drawing the grammar/pragmatics division of labor for contentious cases (part I). We proceeded by outlining the diachronic mechanisms by which pragmatic patterns sometimes cross the dividing line to become part of grammar (part II). We then examined synchronic grammar/pragmatics interface levels of representation (part III). We concluded chapter 7 by proposing that future research look into the possibility that the very same grammar/pragmatics interface representations functional in the ephemeral discourse time are also the input for the diachronic transfer of the pragmatic into the grammatical.

---

[47] Note that it may be difficult to tell cancelability from selecting one sense of an ambiguous term. In other words, if *since* is interpreted as 'temporal,' is it because that's the meaning we selected in context for the ambiguous *since*, or is it because 'causality' was a canceled implicature or one not even generated? There is a difference, however. Canceling a seemingly context-appropriate sense is harder if the item is ambiguous than if the canceled interpretation is merely the result of an explicated inference. In other words, the former requires more of a 'wise-guy' interlocutor than the latter.

[48] All 27 occurrences of *gourmet* in LSAC were literal.

References

Abbott, Barbara. 2000. Presuppositions as nonassertions. *Journal of Pragmatics* 32: 1419–1437.

2004. Definiteness and indefiniteness. In Laurence R. Horn and Gregory Ward, eds., *Handbook of pragmatics*. Oxford: Blackwell, 122–149.

Akatsuka, Noriko. 1986. Conditionals are discourse-bound. In Elizabeth Closs Traugott, Alice ter Meulen, Judy Snitzer Reilly, and Charles A. Ferguson, eds., *On conditionals*. Cambridge: Cambridge Univeristy Press, 333–351.

Akhtar, Nameera. 1998. Characterizing English-speaking children's understanding of SVO word order. In Eve V. Clark, ed., *Proceedings of the 29th Annual Child Language Research Forum*. Stanford: CSLI Publications, 161–169.

Ansaldo, Umberto. 1999. Comparative constructions in Sinitic: Areal typology and patterns of grammaticalization. PhD dissertation, Department of linguistics, Stockholm University.

Ariel, Mira. 1983. Linguistic marking of social prominence: The Hebrew *mi she* introducer. *Journal of Pragmatics* 7: 389–409.

1985. Givenness marking. PhD dissertation, Tel Aviv University.

1987. Reflexives and reciprocals. Unpublished MS, Tel Aviv University.

1990. *Accessing noun-phrase antecedents*. London: Routledge.

1991. The function of accessibility in a theory of grammar. *Journal of Pragmatics* 16: 443–463.

1994. Interpreting anaphoric expressions: A cognitive versus a pragmatic approach. *Journal of Linguistics* 30: 3–42.

1996. Referring expressions and the +/− coreference distinction. In Thorstein Fretheim and Jeanette K. Gundel, eds., *Reference and referent accessibility* (Pragmatics and Beyond New Series 38). Amsterdam: John Benjamins, 13–35.

1998a. The linguistic status of the "here and now." *Cognitive Linguistics* 9: 189–237.

1998b. Three grammaticalization paths for the development of person verbal agreement in Hebrew. In Jean-Pierre Koenig, ed., *Discourse and cognition: Bridging the gap*. Stanford: CSLI Publications, 93–111.

1998c. Discourse markers and form-function correlations. In Andreas H. Jucker and Yael Ziv, eds., *Discourse markers: Descriptions and theory* (Pragmatics and Beyond New Series 57). Amsterdam: John Benjamins, 223–259.

1999a. Cognitive universals and linguistic conventions: The case of resumptive pronouns. *Studies in Language* 23: 217–269.

1999b. Mapping so-called "pragmatic" phenomena according to a "linguistic–extralinguistic" distinction: The case of propositions marked "accessible". In Michael Darnell, Edith A. Moravcsik, Frederick Newmeyer, Michael Noonan, and Kathleen M. Wheatley, eds., *Functionalism and formalism in linguistics*, vol. 2:

Case studies (Studies in Language Companion Series 41). Amsterdam: John Benjamins, 11–38.

2000. The development of person agreement markers: From pronouns to higher accessibility markers. In Michael Barlow and Suzanne Kemmer, eds., *Usage-based models of language*. Stanford: CSLI Publications, 197–260.

2001. Accessibility theory: An overview. In Ted Sanders, Joost Schilperoord, and Wilbert Spooren, eds., *Text representation: Linguistic and psycholinguistic aspects*. Amsterdam: John Benjamins, 29–87.

2002a. The demise of a unique concept of literal meaning. *Journal of Pragmatics* 34: 361–402.

2002b. Privileged Interactional Interpretations. *Journal of Pragmatics* 34: 1003–1044.

2002c. The possessive NP construction: Discourse function and discourse profile. In *Berkeley Linguistics Society 28*. Berkeley: Berkeley Linguistics Society, 15–26.

2003. Does *most* mean 'more than half'? In *Berkeley Linguistics Society 29*. Berkeley: Berkeley Linguistics Society, 17–30.

2004a. Accessibility marking: Discourse functions, discourse profiles, and processing cues. *Discourse Processes* 37: 91–116.

2004b. Most. *Language* 80: 658–706.

2006a. The making of a construction: From reflexive marking to lower transitivity. Unpublished MS, Tel Aviv University.

2006b. A 'just that' lexical meaning for *most*. In Klaus von Heusinger and Ken Turner, eds., *Where semantics meets pragmatics* (Current Research in the Semantics/Pragmatics Interface). London: Elsevier, 49–91.

2007a. Relational and independent strategies in interpreting and conjunctions. Unpublished MS, Tel Aviv University.

2007b. *Xaval al ha-zman*: On the role of explicatures in semanticization. Unpublished MS, Tel Aviv University.

2007c. A grammar in every register? The case of definite descriptions. In Nancy Hedberg and Ron Zacharsky, eds., *The grammar–pragmatics interface: Essays in honor of Jeanette K. Gundel*. Amsterdam: John Benjamins, 265–292.

Forthcoming. *Defining pragmatics*. Cambridge: Cambridge University Press.

Arnold, Jennifer, Thomas Wasow, Anthony Losongco, and Ryan Ginstrom. 2000. Heaviness versus newness: The effects of structural complexity and discourse status on constituent ordering. *Language* 76: 28–55.

Aronoff, Mark. 1976. *Word formation in generative grammar*. Cambridge, MA: MIT Press.

1987. Review article of *Morphology: A study of the relation between meaning and form* by Joan L. Bybee. *Language* 63: 115–129.

1997. Gender as unnatural grammar. Paper presented at the Haifa University English Department colloquium, Haifa, June 4, 1997.

Aslin, Richard N., Jenny R. Saffran, and Elissa L. Newport. 1999. Statistical learning in linguistic and nonlinguistic domains. In Brian MacWhinney, ed., *The emergence of language*. Mahwah, NJ: Lawrence Erlbaum Associates, 359–380.

Atlas, Jay David. 1975. Frege's polymorphous concept of presupposition and its role in a theory of meaning. *Semantikos* 1: 29–44.

1977. Negation, ambiguity, and presupposition. *Linguistics and Philosophy* 1: 321–336.

2004. Presupposition. In Laurence R. Horn and Gregory Ward, eds., *Handbook of pragmatics*. Oxford: Blackwell, 29–52.

Atlas, Jay David and Stephen C. Levinson. 1981. *It*-clefts, informativeness, and logical form: Radical pragmatics (revised standard version). In Peter Cole, ed., *Radical pragmatics*. New York: Academic Press, 1–61.

Bach, Kent. 1994. Conversational impliciture. *Mind and Language* 9: 124–162.

1999. The myth of conventional implicature. *Linguistics and Philosophy* 22: 327–366.

2000. Quantification, qualification and context: A reply to Stanley and Szabo. *Mind and Language* 15: 262–283.

2001. You don't say? *Synthese* 128: 15–44.

2002. Semantic, pragmatic. In Joseph Keim Cambell, Michael O'Rourke, and David Shier, eds., *Meaning and truth*. New York: Seven Bridges Press, 284–292.

2004a. Pragmatics and the philosophy of language. In Laurence R. Horn and Gregory Ward, eds., *Handbook of pragmatics*. Oxford: Blackwell, 463–487.

2004b. Minding the gap. In Claudia Bianchi, ed., *The semantics/pragmatics distinction*. Stanford: CSLI Publications, 27–43.

2006. The top 10 misconceptions about implicature. In Betty J. Birner and Gregory Ward, eds., *Drawing the boundaries of meaning: Neo-Gricean studies in pragmatics and semantics in honor of Laurence R. Horn*. Amsterdam: John Benjamins, 21–30.

Baker, C. L. 1995. Contrast, discourse prominence, and intensification, with special reference to locally free reflexives in British English. *Language* 71: 63–101.

Bar-Hillel, Yehoshua. 1971. Out of the pragmatic wastebasket. *Linguistic Inquiry* 2: 401–407.

Bar-Lev, Zev and Arthur Palacas. 1980. Semantic command over pragmatic priority. *Lingua* 51: 137–146.

Bardenstein, Ruti. 2005. The pragmatics of diminutive quantifiers in Modern Hebrew. MA Thesis, Linguistics, Tel Aviv University.

Barwise, Jon and John Perry. 1983. *Situations and attitudes*. Cambridge, MA: MIT Press.

Bates, Elizabeth. 2001. Class notes from "Psycholinguistics: A cross-language perspective." LSA summer school, UC Santa Barbara.

Bates, Elizabeth and Judith C. Goodman. 1997. On the inseparability of grammar and the lexicon: Evidence from acquisition, aphasia and real-time processing. *Language and Cognitive Processes* 12: 507–584.

1999. On the emergence of grammar from the lexicon. In Brian MacWhinney, ed., *The emergence of language*. Mahwah, NJ: Lawrence Erlbaum Associates, 29–79.

Bates, Elizabeth and Brian MacWhinney. 1982. A functionalist approach to grammatical development. In Eric Wanner and Leila Gleitman, eds., *Language acquisition: The state of the art*. Cambridge: Cambridge Univeristy Press.

1989. Functionalism and the competition model. In Brian MacWhinney and Elizabeth Bates, eds., *The crosslinguistic study of sentence processing*. Cambridge: Cambridge University Press, 3–73.

Bazerman, Charles. 1988. *Shaping written knowledge: The genre and activity of the experimental article in science*. Madison: University of Wisconsin Press.

Bendavid, Abba. 1971. *Biblical Hebrew and Mishnaic Hebrew*, vol. 2. Jerusalem: Dvir.

Berg, Jonathan. 1993. Literal meaning and context. *Iyyun* 42: 397–411.

2002. Is semantics still possible? *Journal of Pragmatics* 34: 349–359.

Berkenfield, Catie. 2001. The role of frequency in the realization of English *that*. In Joan L. Bybee and Paul J. Hopper, eds., *Frequency and the emergence of linguistic structure* (Typological Studies in Language 45). Amsterdam: John Benjamins, 281–307.

Berlin, Adele, Marc Zvi Brettler and Michael Fishbane, eds. 2004. *The Jewish study Bible*. New York: Oxford University Press.

Berman, Ruth A. and Sharon Armon-Lotem. 1996. How grammatical are early verbs? In C. Martinot, ed., *Annales Littéraires de l'Université de Franche-Comté: Actes du Colloque International sur l'Acquisition de la syntaxe*, 17–56.

Bezuidenhout, Anne and J. Cooper Cutting. 2002. Literal meaning, minimal propositions, and pragmatic processing. *Journal of Pragmatics* 34: 433–456.

Biber, Douglas. 1995. *Dimensions of register variation: A cross-linguistic comparison*. Cambridge: Cambridge University Press.

Biber, Douglas, Stig Johansson, Geoffrey Leech, Susan Conrad, and Edward Finegan. 1999. *Longman grammar of spoken and written English*. Harlow, Essex: Longman.

Birner, Betty J. 1994. Information status and word order: An analysis of English inversion. *Language* 70: 233–259.

Birner, Betty J. and Gregory L. Ward. 1998. *Information status and noncanonical word order in English*. Amsterdam: John Benjamins.

Blakemore, Diane. 1987. *Semantic constraints on relevance*. Oxford: Blackwell.

Blakemore, Diane and Robyn Carston. 2005. The pragmatics of sentential coordination with *and*. *Lingua* 115: 569–589.

Bock, Kathryn J. 1986. Syntactic persistence in language production. *Cognitive Psychology* 18: 355–387.

Bock, Kathryn J. and Zenzi M. Griffin. 2000. The persistence of structural priming: Transient activation or implicit learning? *Journal of Experimental Psychology: General* 129: 177–192.

Bock, Kathryn J. and Anthony S. Kroch. 1989. *The isolability of syntactic processing*. In Greg N. Carlson and Michael K. Tanenhaus, eds., *Linguistic structure in language processing* (Studies in Theoretical Psycholinguistics). Dordrecht: Kluwer, 157–196.

Bock, Kathryn J. and Helga Loebell. 1990. Framing sentences. *Cognition* 5: 1–39.

Bod, Rens. 1998. *Beyond grammar: An experience-based theory of language* (CSLI Lecture Notes 88). Stanford: CSLI Publications.

2005. Exemplar-based syntax. Paper presented at the 2005 LSA meeting, Oakland, CA.

2006. Exemplar-based syntax: How to get productivity from examples? *The Linguistic Review,* special issue*: Exemplar-based models of language*, 23: 291–320.

Bod, Rens, Jennifer Hay, and Stefanie Jannedy. 2003a. Introduction. In Rens Bod, Jennifer Hay, and Stefanie Jannedy, eds., *Probabilistic linguistics*. Cambridge, MA: MIT Press, 1–10.

eds., 2003b. *Probabilistic linguistics*. Cambridge, MA: MIT Press.

Bolinger, Dwight L. 1972. *That's that*. The Hague: Mouton.

1985. Two views of accent. *Journal of Linguistics* 21: 79–123.

1989. *Intonation and its uses: Melody in grammar and discourse*. Stanford: Stanford University Press.

Borg, Emma. 2005a. Saying what you mean: Unarticulated constituents and communication. In Reinaldo Elugardo and Robert J. Stainton, eds., *Ellipsis and nonsentential speech*. Dordrecht: Kluwer, 237–262.

2005b. Pragmatic determinants of what is said. In Keith Brown, ed., *Encyclopedia of language and linguistics*, 2nd edition. Oxford: Elsevier, 737–740.

Borochovsky Bar-Abba, Esther. 2006. From speaking to the newspaper – an examination of parallel texts (in Hebrew). In Rina Ben-Shahar and Gideon Toury, eds., *Hebrew – a living language*. Tel Aviv: The Porter Institute and Ha-Kibbutz Ha-Meuchad, 7–32.

Boroditsky, Lera. 2000. Metaphoric structuring: understanding time through spatial metaphors. *Cognition* 75: 1–28.

Bowerman, Melissa. 1996. The origins of children's spatial semantic categories: Cognitive versus linguistic determinants. In John Gumperz and Stephen Levinson, eds., *Rethinking linguistic relativity*. Cambridge: Cambridge University Press, 145–176.

Boyland, Joyce Tang T., and John R. Anderson. 1998. Evidence that syntactic priming is long-lasting. In Morton Ann Gernsbacher and Sharon J. Derry, eds., *Proceedings of the 20th Annual Conference of the Cognitive Science Society*. Mahwah, NJ: Lawrence Erlbaum Associates.

Branigan, Holly P., Martin J. Pickering, and Alexander A. Cleland. 2000. Syntactic coordination in dialogue. *Cognition* 75: B13–B25.

Branigan, Holly P., Martin J. Pickering, Andrew J. Stewart, and Janet F. McLean. 2000. Syntactic priming in spoken production: Linguistic and temporal interference. *Memory and Cognition* 28: 1297–1302.

Bresnan, Joan. 2006. Is syntactic knowledge probabilistic? Experiments with the English dative alternation. Paper presented at *International conference on linguistic evidence*, Tübingen.

Bresnan, Joan and Jennifer Hay. To appear. Gradient grammar: An effect of animacy on the syntax of *give* in New Zealand and American English. Lingua, special issue: Animacy.

Bresnan, Joan, Anna Cueni, Tatiana Nikitina and R. Harald Baayen. 2007. Predicting the dative alternation. In Gerlof Boume, Irene Krämer, and Joost Zwarts, eds., *Cognitive foundations of interpretation*. Amsterdam: Royal Netherlands Academy of Science, 69–94.

Brinton, Laurel J. and Elizabeth Closs Traugott. 2005. *Lexicalization and Language Change*. Cambridge: Cambridge University Press.

Burton-Roberts, Noel. 2005. Robyn Carston on semantics, pragmatics and "encoding." *Journal of Linguistics* 41: 389–407.

Bybee, Joan. 1985a. Diagrammatic iconicity in stem-inflection relations. In John Haiman, ed., *Iconicity in syntax*. Amsterdam: John Benjamins, 11–49.

  1985b. *Morphology: A study of the relation between meaning and form* (Typological Studies in Language 9). Amsterdam: John Benjamins.

  1988. Semantic substance vs. contrast in the development of grammatical meaning. In *Proceedings of the 14th Annual Meeting of the Berkeley Linguistics Society*. Berkeley: Berkeley Linguistics Society, 247–264.

  1998. The emergent lexicon. In M. C. Gruber, D. Higgins, K. S. Olson, and T. Wysocki, eds., *Chicago Linguistic Society 34(2): The Panels*. Chicago: Chicago Linguistic Society, 421–435.

  2000. The phonology of the lexicon: Evidence from lexical diffusion. In Michael Barlow and Suzanne Kemmer, eds., *Usage-based models of language*. Stanford: CSLI Publications, 65–85.

  2001. *Phonology and language use* (Cambridge Studies in Linguistics 94). Cambridge: Cambridge University Press.

  2002. Sequentiality as the basis of constituent structure. In Talmy Givón and Bertram F. Malle, eds., *The evolution of language out of pre-language*. Amsterdam: John Benjamins, 109–134.

2003a. Mechanisms of change in grammaticization: The role of repetition. In Richard Janda and Brian D. Joseph, eds., *Handbook of historical linguistics*. Oxford: Blackwell, 602–623.

2003b. Cognitive processes in grammaticalization. In Michael Tomasello, ed., *The new psychology of language: Cognitive and functional approaches to language structure*, vol. 2. Mahwah, NJ: Lawrence Erlbaum Associates, 145–167.

2005. The impact of use on representation: Grammar is usage and usage is grammar. Presidential address at the 2005 LSA meeting, Oakland, CA.

Bybee, Joan L. and Paul J. Hopper, eds. 2001a. *Frequency and the emergence of linguistic structure* (Typological Studies in Language 45). Amsterdam: John Benjamins.

2001b. Introduction to frequency and the emergence of linguistic structure. In Joan L. Bybee and Paul J. Hopper, eds., *Frequency and the emergence of linguistic structure* (Typological Studies in Language 45). Amsterdam: John Benjamins, 1–20.

Bybee, Joan L. and William Pagliuca. 1985. Cross-linguistic comparison and the development of grammatical meaning. In Jacek Fisiak, ed., *Historical semantics: Historical word formation*. Berlin: de Gruyter, 59–83.

Bybee, Joan L. and Joanne Scheibman. 1999. The effect of usage on degrees of constituency: The reduction of *don't* in English. *Linguistics* 37: 575–596.

Bybee, Joan L., Revere D. Perkins and William Pagliuca. 1994. *The evolution of grammar: Tense, aspect, and modality in the languages of the world*. Chicago: University of Chicago Press.

Cappelen, Herman and Ernest Lepore. 2005. *Insensitive semantics: A defense of semantic minimalism and speech act pluralism*. Oxford: Blackwell.

Carden, Guy and William A. Stewart. 1988. Binding theory, bioprogram, and creolization: Evidence from Haitian Creole. *Journal of Pidgin and Creole Languages* 3: 1–67.

Carrel, Patricia L. and Gabriela Richter. 1981. On presuppositions and speaker-beliefs. *Papers in Linguistics: International Journal of Human Communication* 14: 47–69.

Carston, Robyn. 1984. Semantic and pragmatic analyses of *and*. Paper presented at the Linguistic Association of Great Britain, April 1984.

1988. Implicature, explicature and truth-theoretic semantics. In Ruth M. Kempson, ed., *Mental representations: The interface between language and reality*. Cambridge: Cambridge University Press, 155–181. (Reprinted in Kasher, ed., 1998, vol. 4: 436–479.)

1990. Quantity maxims and generalised implicature. *UCL Working Papers in Linguistics* 2:1–31. (Reprinted in *Lingua* 96:213–244.)

1993. Conjunction, explanation and Relevance. *Lingua* 90: 27–48.

1998a. Pragmatics and the explicit-implicit distinction. PhD dissertation, University of London.

1998b. Negation, "presupposition" and the semantics/pragmatics distinction. *Journal of Linguistics* 34: 309–350.

1999. Negation, "presupposition" and metarepresentation: A response to Noel Burton-Roberts. *Journal of Linguistics* 35: 365–389.

2002a. *Thoughts and utterances: The pragmatics of explicit communication*. Oxford: Blackwell.

2002b. Linguistic meaning, communicated meaning and cognitive pragmatics. *Mind and Language* 17: 127–148.

2004a. Truth-conditional content and conversational implicature. In Claudia Bianchi, ed., *The semantics/pragmatics distinction*. Stanford: CSLI Publications, 65–100.

2004b. Explicature and semantics. In Steven Davis and Brendan Gillon, eds., *Semantics: A reader*. Oxford: Oxford University Press, 817–845.

Chafe, Wallace L. 1976. Givenness, contrastiveness, definiteness, subjects, topics, and point of view. In Charles N. Li, ed., *Subject and Topic*. New York: Academic Press, 25–55.

1982. Integration and involvement in speaking, writing, and oral literature. In Deborah Tannen, ed., *Spoken and written language: Exploring orality and literacy* (Advances in Discourse Processes 9). Norwood, NJ: Ablex, 35–53.

1988. Linking intonation units in spoken English. In John Haiman and Sandra A. Thompson, eds., *Clause combining in grammar and discourse*. Amsterdam: John Benjamins, 1–27.

1994. *Discourse, consciousness, and time: The flow and displacement of consciousness experience in speaking and writing*. Chicago: University of Chicago Press.

Chafe, Wallace L. and Jane Danielewicz. 1987. Properties of spoken and written language. In Rosalind Horowitz and S. Jay Samuels, eds., *Comprehending oral and written language*. New York: Academic Press, 83–113.

Chang, Franklin, Gary S. Dell, Kathryn J. Bock, and Zenzi M. Griffin. 2000. Structural priming as implicit learning: A comparison of models of sentence production. *Journal of Psycholinguistic Research* 29: 217–229.

Chierchia, Gennaro and Sally McConnell-Ginet. 1990. *Meaning and grammar: An introduction to semantics*. Cambridge, MA: MIT Press.

Chomsky, Noam. 1965. *Aspects of the theory of syntax*. Cambridge, MA: MIT Press.

1972. *Language and mind*. New York: Harcourt Brace Jovanovich.

1981. *Lectures on government and binding: The Pisa lectures*. Dordrecht: Foris.

2001. *Beyond explanatory adequacy* (MIT Occasional Papers in Linguistics 20) Cambridge, MA: MIT Press.

Choueka, Yaakov. 1997. *Rav-Milim: A comprehensive dictionary of Modern Hebrew*. Tel Aviv: C.E.T and Miskal.

Cifuentes-Férez, Paula and Dedre Gentner. 2006. Naming motion events in Spanish and English. *Cognitive Linguistics* 17: 443–462.

Clancy, Patricia M. 1980. Referential choice in English and Japanese narrative discourse. In Wallace Chafe, ed., *The pear stories: Cognitive, cultural, and linguistic aspects of narrative production*, vol. 3. Norwood, NJ: Ablex, 127–202.

1989. Form and function in the acquisition of Korean *wh-* questions. *Journal of Child Language* 16: 323–347.

in press. Discourse-functional correlates of argument structure in Korean acquisition. In Naomi McGloin, ed., *Japanese/Korean linguistics*, 15. Stanford: CSLI Publications, 1–20.

Clark, Eve V. and Herbert H. Clark. 1979. When nouns surface as verbs. *Language* 55: 767–811.

Clark, Herbert H. 1996. *Using language*. Cambridge: Cambridge University Press.

1998. Communal lexicons. In Kirsten Malmkjaer and John Williams, eds., *Context in language learning and language understanding*. Cambridge: Cambridge University Press, 63–87.

Clark, Herbert H. and Catherine R. Marshall. 1981. Definite reference and mutual knowledge. In Aravind K. Joshi, Bonnie L. Webber, and Ivan A. Sag, eds., *Elements of discourse understanding*. Cambridge: Cambridge University Press, 10–63.

Clark, Herbert H. and Deanna Wilkes-Gibbs. 1986. Referring as a collaborative process. *Cognition* 22: 1–39.

Claudi, Ulrike and Bernd Heine. 1986. On the metaphorical base of grammar. *Studies in language* 10: 297–335.

Clausner, Timothy, Brends Rapp, and Yi-ching Su. 1996. Does frequency determine the storage of compounds? Evidence from Chinese. Poster presented at the 18th Annual Conference of the Cognitive Science Society '96, La Jolla, CA.

Cohen, Dana. 2004. Intensive reflexives – from sentence to discourse. PhD dissertation, the Hebrew University in Jerusalem.

Cohen, Jonathan L. 1971. Some remarks on Grice's view about the logical particles of natural language. In Yehoshua Bar-Hillel, ed., *Pragmatics of natural languages*. Dordrecht: Reidel, 50–68.

Cohen, Uriel. 2005. Acceptance of gapped sentences where verbs are adapted differently. Tel Aviv University seminar paper.

Cole, Peter. 1981. Preface. In Peter Cole, ed., *Radical pragmatics*. New York: Academic Press, xi–xiv.

Coleman, Linda and Paul Kay. 1981. Prototype semantics: The English word *lie*. *Language* 57: 26–44.

Comrie, Bernard. 1978. Ergativity. In Winfred P. Lehmann, ed., *Syntactic typology: Studies in the phenomenology of language*. Austin: University of Texas Press, 329–394.

   1980. *Language typology and linguistic universals*. Chicago: University of Chicago Press.

   1983. Form and function in explaining language universals. *Linguistics* 21: 87–103.

   1988. Topics, grammaticalized topics, and subjects. In *Berkeley Linguistics Society 14*. Berkeley: Berkeley Linguistics Society, 265–279.

   1994a. Language universals and linguistic typology: Data-bases and explanations. *Sprachtypologie und Universalienforschung* 46: 3–14.

   1994b. Coreference: Between grammar and discourse. In *Proceedings of the 18th Annual Meeting of the Kansai Linguistic Society (1993)*, 1–10.

   1997. Pragmatic binding: Demonstratives as anaphors in Dutch. In *Berkeley Linguistics Society 23*. Berkeley: Berkeley Linguistics Society, 50–61.

   1998. Reference-tracking: description and explanation. *Sprachtypologie und Universalienforschung* 51: 335–346.

   2003. On explaining language universals. In Michael Tomasello, ed., *The new psychology of language: Cognitive and functional approaches to language structure*, vol. 2. Mahwah, NJ: Lawrence Erlbaum Associates, 195–209.

Comrie, Bernard and Tania Kuteva. 2005a. Relativization strategies. In Martin Haspelmath, Matthew S. Dryer, David Gil, and Bernard Comrie, eds., *The world atlas of language structures*. Oxford: Oxford University Press, 494–501.

   2005b. The evolution of grammatical structures and "functional need" explanations. In Maggie Tallerman, ed., *Language origins: Perspectives on evolution*. Oxford: Oxford University Press, 185–207.

Cooper, William E. and John Robert Ross. 1975. Word order. In Robin E. Grossman, L. James San and Timothy J. Vance, eds., *Chicago Linguistic Society: Papers from the parasession on functionalism*. Chicago: Chicago Linguistic Society, 63–111.

Craig, Colette G. 1991. Ways to go in Rama: A case study in polygrammaticalization. In Elizabeth Closs Traugott and Bernd Heine, eds., *Approaches to grammaticalization*, vol. 2: *Focus on types of grammatical markers* (Typological Studies in Language 19:1, 19:2). Amsterdam: John Benjamins, 455–492.

Croft, William. 1990/2003. *Typology and universals* (Cambridge Textbooks in Linguistics). Cambridge: Cambridge University Press.

1991. *Syntactic categories and grammatical relations*. Chicago: The University of Chicago Press.

1993a. A noun is a noun is a noun – or is it? Some reflections on the universality of semantics. In *Berkeley Linguistics Society 19*. Berkeley: Berkeley Linguistics Society, 369–380.

1993b. Functional-typological theory in its historical and intellectual context. *Sprachtypologie und Universalienforschung* 46: 15–26.

2000. *Explaining language change: An evolutionary approach*. Harlow: Longman.

Croft, William, Hava Bat-Zeev Shyldkrot and Suzanne Kemmer. 1987. Diachronic semantic processes in the Middle Voice. In Anna Giacalone Ramat, Onofrio Carruba, and Giuliano Bernini, eds., *Papers from the 7th International Conference on Historical Linguistics*. Amsterdam: John Benjamins, 179–192.

Dahl, Östen. 2001. Inflationary effects in language and elsewhere. In Joan L. Bybee and Paul J. Hopper, eds., *Frequency and the emergence of linguistic structure* (Typological Studies in Language 45). Amsterdam: John Benjamins, 471–480.

Deane, Paul D. 1992. *Grammar in mind and brain*. Berlin: Mouton de Gruyter.

Delong, Katherine A., Thomas P. Urbach, and Marta Kutas. 2005. Probabilistic word pre-activation during language comprehension inferred from electrical brain activity. *Nature Neuroscience* 8: 1117–1121.

Deutscher, Guy. 2005. *The unfolding of language*. London: William Heinemann.

Diderot, D. 1751/1875. *Lettre sur les Sourds et muets. Oeuvres complètes de Diderot*, vol I. Paris: Garnier Frères.

Dik, Simon C. 1986. On the notion "functional explanation." *Belgian Journal of Linguistics* 1: 11–52.

Dixon, Robert M. W. 1979. Ergativity. *Language* 55: 59–138.

1982. *Where have all the adjectives gone?* Berlin: Walter de Gruyter.

1988. *A grammar of Boumaa Fijian*. Chicago: University of Chicago Press.

1994. *Ergativity*. Cambridge: Cambridge University Press.

Donohue, Mark. 2006. Argument structure and adjuncts: Perspectives from Northern New Guinea. Paper presented at *Berkeley Linguistics Society 32*, Berkeley.

Dowty, David. 2003. The dual analysis of adjuncts/complements in categorial grammar. In Ewald Lang, Claudia Maienborn, and Cathrine Fabricius-Hansen, eds., *Modifying adjuncts*. Berlin: Mouton de Gruyter.

Du Bois, John W. 1974. Syntax in mid-sentence. In *Berkeley studies in syntax and semantics*, vol. 1. Berkeley: Department of Linguistics and Institute of Human Learning, University of California, III-1–III-25.

1980. Beyond definiteness: The trace of identity in discourse. In Wallace L. Chafe, ed., *The pear stories: Cognitive, cultural and linguistic aspects of narrative production*. Norwood, NJ: Ablex, 203–274.

1985. Competing motivations. In John Haiman, ed., *Iconicity in syntax*. Amsterdam: John Benjamins, 343–365.

1987. The discourse basis of ergativity. *Language* 63: 805–855.

1998. Reference and identification: Definiteness from a discourse point of view. Talk given at Tel Aviv University colloquium, Dec. 29, 1998.

2003a. Argument structure: Grammar in use. In John W. Du Bois, Lorraine E. Kumpf, and William J. Ashby, eds., *Preferred argument structure: Grammar as architecture for function*. Amsterdam: John Benjamins, 11–60.

2003b. Discourse and grammar. In Michael Tomasello, ed., *The new psychology of language: Cognitive and functional approaches to language structure*, vol. 2. Mahwah, NJ: Lawrence Erlbaum Associates, 47–87.

2004. Dialogic syntax: The syntax of engagement. Talk given at the Linguistics Dept. Tel Aviv University, Jan. 22, 2004.

2007. The stance triangle. In Robert Englebretson, ed., *Stancetaking in discourse: Subjectivity, evaluation, interaction*. Amsterdam: John Benjamins, 139–182.

Du Bois, John W. and Robert Engelbretson. 2004. Santa Barbara Corpus of Spoken American English, Part 3. Philadelphia: Linguistic Data Consortium, University of Pennsylvania.

2005. Santa Barbara Corpus of Spoken American English, Part 4. Philadelphia: Linguistic Data Consortium, University of Pennsylvania.

Du Bois, John W., Wallace L. Chafe, Charles Meyer, and Sandra A. Thompson. 2000. Santa Barbara Corpus of Spoken American English, Part 1. Philadelphia: Linguistic Data Consortium, University of Pennsylvania.

Du Bois, John W., Wallace L. Chafe, Charles Meyer, Sandra A. Thompson, and Nii Martey. 2003. Santa Barbara Corpus of Spoken American English, Part 2. Philadelphia: Linguistic Data Consortium. University of Pennsylvania.

Du Bois, John W., Lorraine E. Kumpf, and William J. Ashby, eds. 2003. *Preferred argument structure: Grammar as architecture for function*. Amsterdam: John Benjamins.

Ducrot, Oswald. 1972. *Dire et ne pas dire: Principes de semantique linguistique*. Paris: Hermann.

Duranti, Alessandro. 1997 *Linguistic anthropology*. Cambridge: Cambridge University Press.

Durie, Mark. 1995a. Towards an understanding of linguistic evolution and the notion "X has a function Y." In Werner Abraham, Talmy Givón, and Sandra A. Thompson, eds., *Discourse grammar and typology* (Studies in Language Companion Series 27). Amsterdam: John Benjamins, 275–308.

1995b. Language, function and time. MS, University of Melbourne.

Eisenberg, Dana. 2005. Anaphoric expressions and the semantics of *and* conjunctions. Seminar paper, Tel Aviv University.

Elman, Jeffrey L. 2001. Connectionism and language acquisition. In Michael Tomasello and Elizabeth Bates, eds., *Language development: The essential readings* (Essential Readings in Developmental Psychology). Oxford: Blackwell, 295–306.

Engelbretson, Robert ed. 2007. *Stancetaking in discourse: Subjectivity, evaluation, interaction*. Amsterdam: John Benjamins.

Erman, Britt and Beatrice Warren. 2000. The idiom principle and the open choice principle. *Text* 20: 29–62.

Ernestus, Mirjam. 2005. Systematic analogical effects in regular past tense production in Dutch: Adult production and children's acquisition. Paper delivered at the 2005 LSA meeting, Oakland, CA.

Erteschik-Shir, Nomi and Shalom Lappin. 1979. Dominance and the functional explanation of island phenomena. *Theoretical Linguistics* 6: 41–85.

Even Shoshan, Avraham. 1982. *The new dictionary (Hebrew)*. Jerusalem: Kiryat Sefer.

Faltz, Leonard M. 1977/1985. *Reflexivization: A study in universal syntax*. New York: Garland.

Farmer, Ann Kathleen. 1980. On the interaction of morphology and syntax. PhD dissertation, MIT.

   1984. *Modularity in syntax: A study of Japanese and English* (Current Studies in Linguistics 9). Cambridge, MA: MIT Press.

Farr, J. M. 1905. *Intensives and reflexives in Anglo-Saxon and Early Middle English*. Baltimore: J. H. Furst.

Firth, John Rupert. 1957. A synopsis of linguistic theory 1930–1955. In John Rupert Firth, ed., *Studies in linguistic analysis: Special volume of the Philological Society*. Oxford: Blackwell, 1–32.

Fischer, Olga C. M. 2003. Principles of grammaticalization and linguistic reality. In Günter Rohdenburg and Britta Mondorf, eds., *Determinants of grammatical variation in English* (Topics in English Linguistics 43). Berlin: Mouton de Gruyter, 445–478.

Foley, William and Robert D. Van Valin, Jr. 1984. *Functional syntax and universal grammar*. Cambridge: Cambridge University Press.

Ford, Cecilia E. 1993. *Grammar in interaction*. Cambridge: Cambridge University Press.

Fox, Barbara A. 1987. The noun phrase accessibility hierarchy reinterpreted: Subject primacy or the absolutive hypothesis? *Language* 63: 856–870.

Frazier, Lyn. 1985. Syntactic complexity. In David R. Dowty, Lauri Karttunen, and Arnold M. Zwicky, eds., *Natural language parsing: Psychological, computational, and theoretical perspectives* (Studies in Natural Language Processing 1). Cambridge: Cambridge University Press, 129–189.

   1990. Exploring the architecture of the language-processing system. In Gerry T. M. Altmann, ed., *Cognitive models of speech processing: Psycholinguistic and computational perspectives* (ACL–MIT Press Series in Natural Language Processing). Cambridge, MA: MIT Press/Bradford Books, 409–433.

Frege, Gottlob. 1892. On sense and reference. In Peter Geach and Max Black, eds., *Translations from the philosophical writings of Gottlob Frege*, 1952. Oxford: Blackwell, 56–78.

Gahl, Susanne and Susan Garnsey. 2004. Knowledge of grammar, knowledge of usage: Syntactic probabilities affect pronunciation variation. *Language* 80: 748–755.

Gamut, L. T. F. 1991. *Logic, language, and meaning*, vol. 1: *Introduction to logic*. Chicago: University of Chicago Press.

Garrod, Simon and Anthony Anderson. 1987. Saying what you mean in dialogue: A study in conceptual and semantic coordination. *Cognition* 27: 181–218.

Gast, Volker. 2006. *The grammar of identity: Intensifiers and reflexives in Germanic languages*. London: Routledge.

Gazdar, Gerald. 1979a. *Pragmatics: Implicature, presupposition, and logical form*. New York: Academic Press.

   1979b. A solution to the projection problem. In Chooh-Kyr Oh and David A. Dinneen, eds., *Syntax and semantics*, vol. 11: *Presupposition*. New York: Academic Press. 57–89.

Geeraerts, Dirk and Stefan Grondelaers. 1995. Looking back at anger: Cultural traditions and metaphorical patterns. In Robert E. Maclaury and John R. Taylor, eds., *Language and the cognitive construal of the world*. Berlin: Mouton de Gruyter, 153–180.

Geis, Michael L. and Arnold M. Zwicky. 1971. On invited inferences. *Linguistic Inquiry* 2: 561–566.

Geluykens, Ronald. 1992. *From discourse process to grammatical construction: On left dislocation in English*. Amsterdam: John Benjamins.

Gernsbacher, Morton Ann and Suzanne Shroyer. 1989. The cataphoric use of the indefinite *this* in spoken narratives. *Memory and Cognition* 17: 536–540.

Giacalone Ramat, Anna and Paul J. Hopper. 1998. Introduction. In Anna Giacalone Ramat and Paul J. Hopper, eds., *The limits of grammaticalization*. Amsterdam: John Benjamins, 1–11.

Gibbs, Raymond W., Jr. 2004. Psycholinguistic experiments and linguistics–pragmatics. In Ira A. Noveck and Dan Sperber, eds., *Experimental pragmatics*. Basingstoke: Palgrave Macmillan, 172–186.

Gibbs, Raymond W., Jr. and Jessica F. Moise. 1997. Pragmatics in understanding what is said. *Cognition* 62: 51–74.

Giora, Rachel. 1997. Understanding figurative and literal language: The graded salience hypothesis. *Cognitive Linguistics* 8: 183–206.

2003. *On our mind: Salience, context, and figurative language*. New York: Oxford University Press.

Givón, Talmy. 1976. Topic, pronoun and grammatical agreement. In Charles N. Li, ed., *Subject and topic*. New York: Academic Press, 149–188.

ed. 1979a. *Discourse and syntax*. New York: Academic Press.

1979b. *On understanding grammar* (Perspectives in Neurolinguistics and Psycholinguistics). New York: Academic Press.

ed. 1983. *Topic continuity in discourse: A quantitative cross-language study*. Amsterdam: John Benjamins.

1984. *Syntax: A functional-typological introduction*, vol. 1. Amsterdam: John Benjamins.

1990. *Syntax: A functional-typological introduction*, vol. 2. Amsterdam: John Benjamins.

1991. Isomorphism in the grammatical code: Cognitive and biological considerations. *Studies in Language* 15: 85–114.

1992. The grammar of referential coherence as mental processing instructions. *Linguistics* 30: 5–55.

1993. *English grammar: A function-based introduction*, vols. 1 and 2. Amsterdam: John Benjamins.

1999. Generativity and variation: The notion "rule of grammar" revisited. In Brian MacWhinney, ed., *The emergence of language*. Mahwah, NJ: Lawrence Erlbaum Associates, 81–109.

2002. *Bio-linguistics: The Santa Barbara lectures*. Amsterdam: John Benjamins.

Goldberg, Adele E. 1995. *Constructions: A construction grammar approach to argument structure*. Chicago: University of Chicago Press.

2004. Pragmatics and argument structure. In Laurence R. Horn and Gregory Ward, eds., *The Handbook of pragmatics*. Oxford: Blackwell, 427–441.

2006. *Constructions at work*. Oxford: Oxford University Press.

Goldberg, Adele E. and Ray Jackendoff. 2004. The English resultative as a family of constructions. *Language* 80: 532–568.

Goldberg, Adele E., Devin M. Casenhiser, and Nitya Sethuraman. 2004. Learning argument structure generalizations. *Cognitive Linguistics* 15: 289–316.

Green, Mitchell S. 1995. Quantity, volubility, and some varieties of discourse. *Linguistics and Philosophy* 18: 83–112.

Grice, H. Paul. 1975. Logic and conversation. In Peter Cole and Jerry L. Morgan, eds., *Syntax and semantics*, vol. 3: *Speech acts*. New York: Academic Press, 41–58.

1981. Presupposition and conversational implicature. In Peter Cole, ed., *Radical pragmatics*. New York: Academic Press, 183–198.

1989. *Studies in the way of words*. Cambridge, MA: Harvard University Press.

Gries, Stefan Th. 2003. Towards a corpus-based indentification of prototypical instances of constructions. *Annual Review of Cognitive Linguistics* 1: 1–28.

2005. Syntactic priming: A corpus-based approach. *Journal of Psycholinguistic Research* 34: 365–399.

Gundel, Jeanette K., Nancy Hedberg, and Ron Zacharski. 1993. Cognitive status and the form of referring expressions in discourse. *Language* 69: 274–307.

Haiman, John. 1980. Dictionaries and encyclopedias. *Lingua* 50: 329–357.

1983. Iconic and economic motivation. *Language* 59: 781–819.

1985a. *Natural syntax: Iconicity and erosion* (Current Studies in Linguistics 44). Cambridge: Cambridge University Press.

ed. 1985b. *Iconicity in syntax*. Amsterdam: John Benjamins.

1994. Ritualization and the development of language. In William Pagliuca, ed., *Perspectives on grammaticalization* (Amsterdam Studies in the Theory and History of Linguistic Science IV: Current Issues in Linguistic Theory 109). Amsterdam: John Benjamins, 3–28.

1998. *Talk is cheap*. New York: Oxford University Press.

Halliday, M. A. K. and Ruqaiya Hasan. 1976. *Cohesion in English*. London: Longman.

Hare, Mary and Jeffrey L. Elman. 1995. Learning and morphological change. *Cognition* 56: 61–98.

Hare, Mary L., Michael Ford, and William D. Marslen-Wilson. 2001. Ambiguity and frequency effects in regular verb inflection. In Joan L. Bybee and Paul J. Hopper, eds., *Frequency and the emergence of linguistic structure* (Typological Studies in Language 45). Amsterdam: John Benjamins, 181–200.

Harnish, Robert M. and Ann K. Farmer. 1984. Pragmatics and the modularity of the linguistic system. *Lingua* 63: 255–277.

Harris, Alice C. and Lyle Campbell. 1995. *Historical syntax in cross-linguistic perspective*. Cambridge: Cambridge University Press.

Haspelmath, Martin. 1999a. Explaining article-possessor complementarity: Economic motivation in noun phrase syntax. *Language* 75: 227–243.

1999b. Why is grammaticalization irreversible? *Linguistics* 37: 1043–1068.

2004a. Does linguistic explanation presuppose linguistic description? *Studies in Language* 28: 554–579.

2004b. On directionality in language change with particular reference to grammaticalization. In Olga Fischer, Muriel Norde, and Harry Perridon, eds., *Up and down the cline: The nature of grammaticalization* (Typological Studies in Language 59). Amsterdam: John Benjamins, 17–44.

2004c. A frequentist explanation of some universals of reflexive marking. Paper presented at the "Reciprocity and reflexivity – description, typology and theory workshop," Free University of Berlin, October 2004.

2006a. Against markedness (and what to replace it with). *Journal of linguistics* 42: 25–70.

2006b. A Review of John W. Du Bois, Lorraine E. Kumpf, and William J. Ashby eds. *Preferred argument structure: Grammar as architecture for function*. Language 82: 908–912.

to appear. Frequency vs. iconicity in explaining grammatical asymmetries. *Cognitive Linguistics* 19.

Hawkins, John A. 1990. A parsing theory of word order universals. *Linguistic Inquiry* 21: 223–261.

1994. *A performance theory of order and constituency* (Cambridge Studies in Linguistics 73). Cambridge: Cambridge University Press.

2003. Efficiency and complexity in grammars: Three general principles. In John Moore and Maria Polinsky, eds., *The nature of explanation in linguistic theory*. Stanford: CSLI Publications, 121–152.

2004. *Efficiency and complexity in grammars*. Oxford: Oxford University Press.

Heim, Irene. 1983a. File change semantics and the familiarity theory of definiteness. In Rainer Bäuerle, Christoph Schwarze, and Arnim von Stechow, eds., *Meaning, use and interpretation of language*. Berlin: de Gruyter, 164–189.

1983b. On the projection problem for presuppositions. In Michael Barlow, Daniel P. Flickinger, and Michael T. Wescoat, eds., *Proceedings of the 2nd Annual West Coast Conference on Formal Linguistics*. Stanford: Stanford University Press, 114–125.

Heine, Bernd. 1993. *Auxiliaries: Cognitive forces and grammaticalization*. New York: Oxford University Press.

1994a. Principles of grammaticalization. MS, University of Cologne.

1994b. Grammaticalization as an explanatory parameter. In William Pagliuca, ed., *Perspectives on grammaticalization* (Amsterdam Studies in the Theory and History of Linguistic Science IV: Current Issues in Linguistic Theory 109). Amsterdam: John Benjamins, 255–287.

1997. *Cognitive foundations of grammar*. New York: Oxford University Press.

2003. Grammaticalization. In Brian D. Joseph and Richard D. Janda, eds., *The handbook of historical linguistics*. Oxford: Blackwell, 575–601.

2005. On reflexive forms in creoles. *Lingua* 115: 201–257.

Heine, Bernd and Tania Kuteva. 2002. *World lexicon of grammaticalization*. Cambridge: Cambridge University Press.

Heine, Bernd and Mechthild Reh. 1984. *Grammaticalization and reanalysis in African languages*. Hamburg: Helmut Buske.

Heine, Bernd, Ulrike Claudi, and Friederike Hünnemeyer. 1991a. From cognition to grammar: Evidence from African languages. In Elizabeth Closs Traugott and Bernd Heine, eds., *Approaches to grammaticalization*, vol. 1: *Focus on theoretical and methodological issues* (Typological Studies in Language 19:1). Amsterdam: John Benjamins, 149–187.

1991b. *Grammaticalization: A conceptual framework*. Chicago: University of Chicago Press.

Himmelmann, Nikolaus P. 2004. Lexicalization and grammaticalization: opposite or orthogonal? In Walter Bisang, Nikolaus P. Himmelmann, and Björn Wiemer, eds., *What makes grammaticalization? A look from its fringes and its components* (Trends in Linguistics. Studies and Monographs 158). Berlin: Mouton de Gruyter, 21–44.

Hirschberg, Julia Bell. 1991. *A theory of scalar implicature*. New York: Garland.

Hooper, Joan B. 1976. Word frequency in lexical diffusion and the source of morphopho-
nological change. In W. Christie, ed., *Current progress in historical linguistics*.
Amsterdam: North-Holland, 96–105.

Hopper, Paul J. 1987. Emergent grammar. In *Berkeley Linguistics Society 13*. Berkeley:
Berkeley Linguistics Society, 139–157.

1991. On some principles of grammaticization. In Elizabeth Closs Traugott and Bernd
Heine, eds., *Approaches to grammaticalization*, vol. 1: *Focus on theoretical and
methodological issues* (Typological Studies in Language 19:1). Amsterdam: John
Benjamins, 17–35.

Hopper, Paul J. and Sandra A. Thompson. 1980. Transitivity in grammar and discourse.
Language 56: 251–299.

1984. The discourse basis for lexical categories in universal grammar. *Language* 60:
703–752.

1993. Language universals, discourse pragmatics, and semantics. *Language Sciences*
15: 357–376.

2001. Grammatical fragments and social action in conversation. Paper delivered at the 7th
International Cognitive Linguistics Conference. UC Santa Barbara, July 22–27, 2001.

Hopper, Paul J. and Elizabeth Closs Traugott. 1993/2003. *Grammaticalization*.
Cambridge: Cambridge University Press.

Horn, Laurence R. 1972. On the semantic properties of the logical operators in English.
Mimeo, Indiana University Linguistics Club.

1984. A new taxonomy for pragmatic inference: Q-based and R-based implicatures. In
Deborah Schiffrin, ed., *Meaning, form, and use in context: Linguistic applications*
(Georgetown University Round Table on Languages and Linguistics). Washington,
DC: Georgetown University Press, 11–42.

1985. Metalinguistic negation and pragmatic ambiguity. *Language* 61: 121–174.

1989. *A natural history of negation*. Chicago: University of Chicago Press.

1992. The said and the unsaid. In Chris Barker and David Dowty, eds., *Proceedings of
the 2nd Conference on Semantics and Linguistic Theory (SALT II)*. Columbus: Ohio
State University Linguistics Department, 163–192.

1996. Presupposition and implicature. In Shalom Lappin, ed., *The handbook of con-
temporary semantic theory*. Oxford: Blackwell, 299–319.

2004. Implicature. In Laurence R. Horn and Gregory Ward, eds., *Handbook of pragmatics*. Oxford: Blackwell, 3–28.

2006. The Border Wars: a neo-Gricean perspective. In Ken Turner and Klaus von
Heusinger, eds., *Where semantics meets pragmatics*. London: Elsevier, 21–48.

2007. Toward a Fregean pragmatics: *Voraussetzung, Nebengedanke, Andeutung*. In
Istvan Kecskes and Laurence R. Horn, eds., *Explorations in pragmatics: Linguistic,
cognitive, and intercultural aspects*: Mouton, 39–69.

Howes, Davis H. and Richard L. Solomon. 1951. Visual duration threshold as a function of
word-probability. *Journal of Experimental Psychology* 41: 401–410.

Huang, Yan. 2000. *Anaphora: A cross-linguistic study*. Oxford: Oxford University Press.

Huddleston, Rodney. 1988. *English grammar: An outline*. Cambridge: Cambridge
University Press.

2002. The clause: complements. In Rodney Huddleston and Geoffrey K. Pullum, eds.,
The Cambridge grammar of the English language. Cambridge: Cambridge
University Press, 213–321.

Huddleston, Rodney and Geoffrey K. Pullum, eds. 2002. *The Cambridge grammar of the English language*. Cambridge: Cambridge University Press.

Huddleston, Rodney, John Payne, and Peter Peterson. 2002. Coordination and supplementation. In Rodney Huddleston and Geoffrey K. Pullum, eds., *The Cambridge grammar of the English language*. Cambridge: Cambridge University Press, 1273–1362.

Hundt, Marianne. 2001. What corpora tell us about the grammaticalisation of voice in get-constructions. *Studies in Language* 25: 49–87.

Hyman, Larry M. 1983. Form and substance in language universals. *Linguistics* 21: 67–85.

Itkonen, Esa. 2002. Grammaticalization as an analogue of hypothetico-deductive thinking. In Ilse Wischer and Gabriele Diewald, eds., *New reflections on grammaticalization*. Amsterdam: John Benjamins, 413–422.

Izre'el, Shlomo. 2002. A corpus of Spoken Israeli Hebrew (CoSIH): Text examples. *Leshonenu* 64:289–314 (in Hebrew).

Jakobson, Roman. 1971. Quest for the essence of language. In Roman Jakobson, ed., *Roman Jakobson selected writings*, vol. 2. The Hague: Mouton, 345–359.

Johnson, Keith. 1997. Speech perception without speaker normalization. In Keith Johnson and John W. Mullennix, eds., *Talker variability in speech processing*. San Diego: Academic Press, 145–165.

Johnson, Marcia K., John D. Bransford, and Susan K. Solomon. 1973. Memory for tacit implications of sentences. *Journal of Experimental Psychology* 98: 203–205.

Joseph, Brian D. 1992. Diachronic explanation: Putting speakers back into the picture. In Garry W. Davis and Gregory K. Iverson, eds., *Explanations in historical linguistics*. Amsterdam: John Benjamins, 123–144.

Joseph, Brian D. and Richard D. Janda, eds. 2003. *The handbook of historical linguistics*. Oxford: Blackwell.

Jung-Beeman, Mark. 2006. Bilateral brain processes involved in understanding natural language. Paper presented at "Brain and language: Theoretical and clinical perspectives," Bar-Ilan University.

Jurafsky, Daniel. 1996. Universal tendencies in the semantics of the diminutive. *Language* 72: 533–578.

Jurafsky, Daniel, Alan Bell, and Cynthia Girand. 2002. The role of the lemma in form variation. In Carlos Gussenhoven and Natasha Warner, eds., *Laboratory Phonology VII*. Berlin: Mouton de Gruyter, 3–34.

Jurafsky, Daniel, Alan Bell, Michelle Gregory, and William D. Raymond. 2001. Probabilistic relations between words: Evidence from reduction in lexicon production. In Joan L. Bybee and Paul J. Hopper, eds., *Frequency and the emergence of linguistic structure* (Typological Studies in Language 45). Amsterdam: John Benjamins, 229–254.

Kadmon, Nirit. 2001. *Formal pragmatics*. Oxford: Blackwell.

Kamp, Hans. 1995. Discourse representation theory. In Jef Verschueren, Jan-Ola Östman, Jan Blommaert and Chris Bulcaen, eds., *Handbook of pragmatics*. Amsterdam: John Benjamins, 253–257.

Kärkkäinen, Elise. 2003. *Epistemic stance in English conversation: A description of its interactional functions, with a focus on I think* (Pragmatics and Beyond New Series 115). Amsterdam: John Benjamins.

Karttunen, Lauri. 1973. Presuppositions of compound sentences. *Linguistic Inquiry* 4: 169–193.

1974. Presuppositions and linguistic context. *Theoretical Linguistics* 1: 3–44.

Karttunen, Lauri and Stanley Peters. 1979. Conventional implicature. In Choon-Kyu Oh and David A. Dinneen, eds., *Syntax and semantics*, vol. 11: *Presupposition*. New York: Academic Press, 1–56.

Kasher, Asa. 1976. Conversational maxims and rationality. In Asa Kasher, ed., *Language in focus: Foundations, methods and systems*. Dordrecht: Reidel, 197–216.

1982. Gricean inference revisited. *Philosophica* 29: 25–44.

ed. 1998. *Pragmatics: Critical concepts*. 6 vols. London: Routledge.

Katz, Jerrold J. 1972. *Semantic theory*. New York: Harper and Row.

Kautzsch, E. 1898. *Gesenius' Hebrew grammar*. Oxford: Clarendon Press.

Keenan, Edward L. 1971. Two kinds of presupposition in natural language. In Charles J. Fillmore and D. Terence Langendoen, eds., *Studies in linguistic semantics*. New York: Holt, Rinehart, and Winston, 45–52.

1996. Creating anaphors: An historical study of the English reflexive pronouns. Unpublished MS, UCLA.

2002. Explaining the creation of reflexive pronouns in English. In Donka Minkova and Robert Stockwell, eds., *Studies in the history of English*. Berlin: Mouton de Gruyter, 325–355.

2003. An historical explanation of some binding theoretic facts in English. In John Moore and Maria Polinsky, eds., *The nature of explanation in linguistic theory*. Stanford: CSLI Publications, 212–256.

Keenan, Edward L. and Bernard Comrie. 1977. Noun phrase accessibility and universal grammar. *Linguistic Inquiry* 8: 63–99.

Keenan (Ochs), Elinor. 1977. Why look at planned and unplanned discourse? In Elinor Keenan (Ochs) and T. Bennett, eds., *Discourse across time and space* (Southern California Occasional Papers in Linguistics 5). Los Angeles: University of Southern California, 1–42.

Keller, Rudi. 1994. *On language change*. London: Routledge.

Kemmer, Suzanne. 1993. *The middle voice* (Typological Studies in Language 23). Amsterdam: John Benjamins.

1995. Emphatic and reflexive *-self*: Expectations, viewpoint, and subjectivity. In Dieter Stein and Susan Wright, eds., *Subjectivity and subjectivisation: Linguistic perspectives*. Cambridge: Cambridge University Press, 55–82.

Kemmer, Suzanne and Michael Barlow. 1996. Emphatic *-self* in discourse. In Adele E. Goldberg, ed., *Conceptual structure, discourse, and language*. Stanford: CSLI Publications, 231–248.

2000. Introduction: A usage-based conception of language. In Michael Barlow and Suzanne Kemmer, eds., *Usage-based models of language*. Stanford: CSLI Publications, vii–xviii.

Kemmer, Suzanne and Arie Verhagen. 1994. The grammar of causatives and the conceptual structure of events. *Cognitive Linguistics* 5: 115–156.

Kempson, Ruth M. 1975. *Presupposition and the delimitation of semantics* (Cambridge Studies in Linguistics 15). Cambridge: Cambridge University Press.

1984. Weak crossover, logical form and pragmatics. Paper presented at GLOW, April 1984.

Kempson, Ruth M., Ronnie Cann, and Matthew Purver. To appear. Talking and listening: Dialogue and the grammar-pragmatics interface. In Martin Hackl and Robert Thornton, eds., *Asserting, meaning and implying*. Oxford: Oxford University Press.

Kiparsky, Paul. 1990. Strong reflexives in Germanic. Paper presented at Diachronic syntax, York.

Koenig, Jean-Pierre. 1991. Scalar predicates and negation: Punctual semantics and interval interpretations. In *Chicago Linguistic Society 27*. Chicago: Chicago Linguistic Society, 140–155.

König, Ekkehard and Peter Siemund. 2000. Intensifiers and reflexives: A typological perspective. In Zygmunt Frajzyngier and Traci S. Curl, eds., *Reflexives: Forms and functions*. Amsterdam: John Benjamins, 41–74.

König, Ekkehard and Peter Siemund (with Stephan Töpper). 2005. Intensifiers and reflexive pronouns. In Martin Haspelmath, Matthew Dryer, David Gil, and Bernard Comrie, eds., *The world atlas of language structures*. Oxford: Oxford University Press, 194–197.

Kövecses, Zoltán. 1995. Anger: Its language, conceptualization, and physiology in the light of cross-cultural evidence. In Robert E. Maclaury and John R. Taylor, eds., *Language and the cognitive construal of the world*. Berlin: Mouton de Gruyter, 181–196.

Krug, Manfred. 2000. *Emerging English modals: A corpus-based study of grammaticalization*. Berlin: Mouton de Gruyter.

2001. Frequency, iconicity, categorization: Evidence from emerging modals. In Joan L. Bybee and Paul J. Hopper, eds., *Frequency and the emergence of linguistic structure* (Typological Studies in Language 45). Amsterdam: John Benjamins, 309–335.

2003. Frequency as a determinant in grammatical variation and change. In Günter Rohdenburg and Britta Mondorf, eds., *Determinants of grammatical variation in English* (Topics in English Linguistics 43). Berlin: Mouton de Gruyter, 7–67.

Labov, William. 1973. The boundaries of words and their meanings. In Charles-James N. Bailey and Roger W. Shuy, eds., *New ways of analyzing variation in English*. Washington, DC: Georgetown University Press, 340–373.

1980. The social origins of sound change. In William Labov, ed., *Locating language in time and space* (Quantitative Analyses of Linguistic Structure 1). New York: Academic Press, 251–265.

1990. On the adequacy of natural languages, I: The development of tense. In John Victor Singler, ed., *Pidgin and creole tense-mood-aspect systems* (Creole Language Library 6). Amsterdam: John Benjamins, 1–58.

1994. *Principles of linguistic change*, vol. 1: *Internal factors*. Oxford: Blackwell.

2001. *Principles of linguistic change*, vol. 2: *Social factors*. Oxford: Blackwell.

Ladd, D. Robert. 1990. Intonation: Emotion vs. grammar. *Language* 66: 806–816.

Lakoff, George. 1987. *Women, fire, and dangerous things: What categories reveal about the mind*. Chicago: University of Chicago Press.

Lakoff, George and Mark Johnson. 1980. *Metaphors we live by*. Chicago: University of Chicago Press.

Lambrecht, Knud. 1984. A pragmatic constraint on lexical subjects in spoken French. In *Chicago Linguistic Society 20*. Chicago: Chicago Linguistic Society, 239–256.

1994. *Information structure and sentence form: Topic, focus, and the mental representations of discourse referents* (Cambridge Studies in Linguistics 71). Cambridge: Cambridge University Press.

Lancelot, Claude, Antoine Arnauld, Thomas Nugent, and R. C. Alston. 1660. *Grammaire générale et raisonnée*.

Landman, Fred. 2000. *Events and plurality*. Dordrecht: Kluwer.

Langacker, Ronald W. 1987. *Foundations of cognitive grammar*, vol. 1: *Theoretical prerequisites*. Stanford: Stanford University Press.

1991. *Concept, image, and symbol: The cognitive basis of grammar*. Berlin: Mouton de Gruyter.

1995. Raising and transparency. *Language* 71: 1–62.

2000. A dynamic usage-based model. In Michael Barlow and Suzanne Kemmer, eds., *Usage-based models of language*. Stanford: CSLI Publications, 1–63.

Lass, Roger. 1997. *Historical linguistics and language change* (Cambridge Studies in Linguistics 81). Cambridge: Cambridge University Press.

Levelt, Willem J. M. 1993. *Speaking: From intention to articulation*. Cambridge, MA: MIT Press.

Levelt, Willem J. M. and Stephanie Kelter. 1982. Surface form and memory in question answering. *Cognitive Psychology* 14: 78–106.

Levinson, Stephen C. 1983. *Pragmatics*. Cambridge: Cambridge University Press.

1987. Minimization and conversational inference. In Jef Verschueren and Marcella Bertuccelli-Papi, eds., *The pragmatic perspective* (Pragmatics and Beyond Companion Series 5). Amsterdam: John Benjamins, 61–129.

1991. Pragmatic reduction of the binding conditions revisited. *Journal of Linguistics* 27: 107–161.

1995. Three levels of meaning. In F. R. Palmer, ed., *Grammar and meaning*. Cambridge: Cambridge University Press, 90–115.

2000a. Maxim. *Journal of Linguistic Anthropology* 9: 144–147.

2000b. *Presumptive meanings: The theory of generalized conversational implicature*. Cambridge, MA: MIT Press.

Lewis, David K. 1968. *Convention: A philosophical study*. Cambridge, MA: Harvard University Press.

1979. Scorekeeping in a language game. In Rainer Bäuerle, Urs Egli, and Arnim von Stechow, eds., *Semantics from different points of view* (Springer Series in Language and Communication 6). New York: Springer-Verlag, 172–187.

Li, Charles N. 1975. Synchrony vs. diachrony in language structure. *Language* 51: 873–886.

Li, Charles N. and Sandra A. Thompson. 1974. An explanation of word order change SVO → SOV. *Foundations of Language* 12: 201–214.

1981. *Mandarin Chinese: A functional reference grammar*. Berkeley: University of California Press.

Liberman, Mark. 1973. Alternatives. In *Chicago Linguistic Society 9*. Chicago: Chicago Linguistic Society, 346–355.

Lichtenberk, Frantisek. 1991. Semantic change and heterosemy in grammaticalization. *Language* 67: 475–509.

Lord, Carol. 1976. Evidence for syntactic reanalysis: From verb to complementizer in Kwa. In Sanford B. Steever, Carol A. Walker, Salikoko S. Mufwene, and Robert Peter Ebert, eds., *Chicago Linguistic Society 12: Papers from the parasession on diachronic syntax*. Chicago: Chicago Linguistic Society, 179–191.

Lord, Carol and Kathleen Dahlgren. 1997. Participant and event anaphora in newspaper articles. In Joan Bybee, John Haiman, and Sandra A. Thompson, eds., *Essays on language function and language type dedicated to T. Givón*. Amsterdam: John Benjamins, 323–356.

Lordrup, Helge. 1999. Inalienables in Norwegian and binding theory. *Linguistics* 37: 365–388.

Lyons, Christopher. 1999. *Definiteness*. Cambridge: Cambridge University Press.

Lyutikova, Ekaterina A. 2000. Reflexives and emphasis in Tsaxur (Nakh-Dagestanian). In Zygmunt Frajzyngier and Traci S. Curl, eds., *Reflexives: Forms and functions*. Amsterdam: John Benjamins, 227–255.

MacDonald, Maryellen C. 1993. The interaction of lexical and syntactic ambiguity. *Journal of Memory and Language* 32: 692–715.

1999. Distributional information in language comprehension, production and acquisition: Three puzzles and a moral. In Brian MacWhinney, ed., *The emergence of language*. Mahwah, NJ: Lawrence Erlbaum Associates, 177–196.

Macmillan. 2002. *Macmillan English dictionary for advanced learners*. Oxford: Macmillan.

MacWhinney, Brian. 2000. Connectionism and language learning. In Michael Barlow and Suzanne Kemmer, eds., *Usage-based models of language*. Stanford: CSLI Publications, 121–149.

2001. Emergentist approaches to language. In Joan L. Bybee and Paul J. Hopper, eds., *Frequency and the emergence of linguistic structure* (Typological Studies in Language 45). Amsterdam: John Benjamins, 449–470.

MacWhinney, Brian and Elizabeth Bates. 1989. *The crosslinguistic study of sentence processing*. Cambridge: Cambridge University Press.

Magliano, Joseph P., W. B. Baggett, B. K. Johnson, and C. Arthur Graesser. 1993. The time course of generating causal antecedent and causal consequence inferences. *Discourse Processes* 16: 35–53.

Maling, Joan. 1984. Non-clause bounded reflexives in Icelandic. *Linguistics and Philosophy* 7: 211–241.

Mandelkern, Solomon. 1937. *Veteris Testamenti concordantiae (A concordance of the Old Testament)*. Jerusalem: Shocken.

Mann, William C. and Sandra A. Thompson. 1986. Relational propositions in discourse. *Discourse Processes* 9: 57–90.

Manning, Christopher D. 2003. Probabilistic syntax. In Rens Bod, Jennifer Hay, and Stefanie Jannedy, eds., *Probabilistic linguistics*. Cambridge, MA: MIT Press, 289–341.

Marantz, Alec P. 1984. *On the nature of grammatical relations* (Linguistic Inquiry Monographs 10). Cambridge, MA: MIT Press.

Matsuki, Keiko. 1995. Metaphors of anger in Japanese. In Robert E. Maclaury and John R. Taylor, eds., *Language and the cognitive construal of the world*. Berlin: Mouton de Gruyter, 137–152.

McClelland, James L. and David E. Rumelhart. 1986. *Parallel distributed processing*, vols. 1 and 2. Cambridge, MA: MIT Press.

Meibauer, Jorg. 2005. Lying and falsely implicating. *Journal of Pragmatics* 37: 1373–1399.

Meltzer, Yoram. 2005. *Xavlaz ze lo mila* ("A waste of time doesn't capture it"). *Haaretz*, May 6, 2005 (in Hebrew).

Michod, Richard E. 1999. *Darwinian dynamics: Evolutionary transitions in fitness and individuality*. Princeton: Princeton University Press.

Miller, Carolyn R. 1984. Genre as social action. *The Quarterly Journal of Speech* 70: 151–167.

Milroy, James and Lesley Milroy. 1985. Linguistic change, social network and speaker innovation. *Journal of Linguistics* 21: 339–384.

Mithun, Marianne. 1984. The evolution of noun incorporation. *Language* 60: 847–894.

1988. The grammaticization of coordination. In John Haiman and Sandra A. Thompson, eds., *Clause combining in grammar and discourse*. Amsterdam: John Benjamins, 331–359.

1989. Historical linguistics and linguistic theory: Reducing the arbitrary and constraining explanation. In *Berkeley Linguistics Society 15*. Berkeley: Berkeley Linguistics Society, 391–408.

1991a. Active/agent case marking and its motivations. *Language* 67: 510–546.

1991b. The role of motivation in the emergence of grammatical categories: The grammaticization of subjects. In Elizabeth Closs Traugott and Bernd Heine, eds., *Approaches to grammaticalization*, vol. 2: *Focus on types of grammatical markers* (Typological Studies in Language 19:2). Amsterdam: John Benjamins, 159–184.

2003. Functional perspectives on syntactic change. In Brian D. Joseph and Richard D. Janda, eds., *The handbook of historical linguistics*. Oxford: Blackwell, 552–572.

in press. Borrowed rhetorical constructions as starting points for grammaticalization. In Alexander Bergs and Gabriele Diewald, eds., *Constructions and language change*. Berlin: Mouton de Gruyter.

Moore, John and Maria Polinsky. 2003. Explanations in linguistics. In John Moore and Maria Polinsky, eds., *The nature of explanation in linguistic theory*. Stanford: CSLI Publications, 1–30.

Morgan, Jerry L. 1978. Two types of convention in indirect speech acts. In Peter Cole, ed., *Syntax and semantics*, vol. 9: *Pragmatics*. New York: Academic Press, 261–280.

Moscati, Sabatino, Anton Spitaler, Edward Ullendorff, and Wolfram von Soden. 1964. *An introduction to the comparative grammar of the Semitic languages*. Wiesbaden: Otto Harrassowitz.

Mufwene, Salikoko S. 2001. *The ecology of language evolution* (Cambridge Approaches to Language Contact). Cambridge: Cambridge University Press.

Myhill, John. 1997. *Should* and *ought*: the rise of individually oriented modality in American English. *English Language and Linguistics* 1: 3–23.

Newman, John and Sally Rice. 2004. Patterns of usage for English *sit*, *stand*, and *lie*: A cognitively inspired exploration in corpus linguistics. *Cognitive Linguistics* 15: 351–396.

Newmeyer, Frederick. 1991. Iconicity and generative grammar. *Language* 68: 756–796.

Nicolle, Steve and Billy Clark. 1999. Experimental pragmatics and what is said: A response to Gibbs and Moise. *Cognition* 69: 337–354.

Noordman, Leo G. M. and Wietzke Vonk. 1998. Memory-based processing in understanding causal information. *Discourse Processes* 26: 191–212.

Noveck, Ira A. 2001. When children are more logical than adults: Experimental investigations of scalar implicature. *Cognition* 78: 165–188.

Noveck, Ira A. and Andres Posada. 2003. Characterizing the time course of an implicature: An evoked potentials study. *Brain and Language* 85: 203–210.

Noveck, Ira A. and Florelle Chevaux. 2002. The pragmatic development of *and*. In Barbora Skarabela, ed., *Proceedings of the 26th Annual Boston University Conference on Language Development*. Somerville, MA: Cascadilla Press, 453–463.

Nuyts, Jan. 1992. *Aspects of a cognitive-pragmatic theory of language: On cognition, functionalism, and grammar* (Pragmatics and Beyond New Series 20). Amsterdam: John Benjamins.

Ochs, Elinor. 1996. Linguistic resources for socializing humanity. In John J. Gumperz and Stephen C. Levinson, eds., *Rethinking linguistic relativity*. Cambridge: Cambridge University Press, 407–437.

Onifer, William and David A. Swinney. 1981. Accessing lexical ambiguities during sentence comprehension: Effects of frequency of meaning and contextual bias. *Memory and Cognition* 9: 225–236.

Papafragou, Anna and Julien Musolino. 2003. Scalar implicatures: Experiments at the semantics–pragmatics interface. *Cognition* 86: 253–282.

Papafragou, Anna and Naomi Schwarz. 2005/6. "*Most* wanted." *Language Acquisition*, special issue: *The acquisition of quantification*, 13: 207–251.

Peirce, Charles Sanders. 1932/1965. The icon, index and symbol. In Charles Hartshorne and Paul Weiss, eds., *Collected papers of Charles Sanders Peirce*, vol. 2. Cambridge, MA: Harvard University Press, 156–173.

Perry, John. 1993. *The problem of the essential indexical and other essays*. New York: Oxford University Press.

Pierrehumbert, Janet B. 2001. Exemplar dynamics: Word frequency, lenition and contrast. In Joan L. Bybee and Paul J. Hopper, eds., *Frequency and the emergence of linguistic structure* (Typological Studies in Language 45). Amsterdam: John Benjamins, 137–157.

  2003. Probabilistic phonology: Discrimination and robustness. In John Moore and Maria Polinsky, eds., *The nature of explanation in linguistic theory*. Stanford: CSLI Publications, 177–228.

Posner, Roland. 1980. Semantics and pragmatics of sentence connectives in natural languages. In John R. Searle, Ferenc Kiefer, and Manfred Bierwisch, eds., *Speech act theory and pragmatics* (Synthese Language Library 10). Boston: Reidel, 169–203.

Potts, George R., Janice M. Keenan and Jonathan M. Golding. 1988. Assessing the occurrence of elaborative inferences: Lexical decision versus naming. *Journal of Memory and Language* 27: 399–415.

Prince, Ellen F. 1976. The syntax and semantics of Neg-Raising, with evidence from French. *Language* 52: 404–426.

  1978. On the function of existential presupposition in discourse. In *Chicago Linguistic Society 14*. Chicago: Chicago Linguistic Society, 362–376.

  1981. On the inferencing of indefinite *this* NPs. In Aravind K. Joshi, Bonnie L. Webber, and Ivan A. Sag, eds., *Elements of discourse understanding*. Cambridge: Cambridge University Press, 231–250.

  1988. Discourse analysis: A part of the study of linguistic competence. In Frederick J. Newmeyer and R. H. Robins, eds., *Linguistics: The Cambridge survey*, vol. 2: *Linguistic theory: Extensions and implications*. Cambridge: Cambridge University Press, 164–182.

  1998. On the limits of syntax, with reference to left-dislocation and topicalization. In Peter W. Culicover and Louise McNally, eds., *Syntax and semantics*, vol. 29: *The limits of syntax*. San Diego: Academic Press, 281–302.

Quirk, Randolph, Sidney Greenbaum, Geoffrey Leech, and Jan Svartvik. 1985. *A comprehensive grammar of the English language*. London: Longman.

Reboul, Anne. 1997. What (if anything) is accessibility? A relevance-oriented criticism of Ariel's accessibility theory of referring expressions. In John H. Connolly, Roel M. Vismans, Christopher S. Butler, and Richard A. Gatward, eds., *Discourse and pragmatics in functional grammar*. Berlin: Mouton de Gruyter, 91–108.

Recanati, François. 1989. The pragmatics of what is said. *Mind and Language* 4:295–328. (Reprinted in Steven Davis, ed., 1991. *Pragmatics: A reader*. New York: Oxford University Press, 97–120.)

1993. *Direct reference*. Oxford: Blackwell.

1995. The alleged priority of literal interpretation. *Cognitive Science* 19: 207–232.

2001. "What is said." *Synthese* 128: 75–91.

2002a. Does linguistic communication rest on inference? *Mind and Language* 17: 105–126.

2002b. Unarticulated constituents. *Linguistics and Philosophy* 25: 299–345.

2004. 'What is said' and the semantics/pragmatics distinction. In Claudia Bianchi and Carlo Penco, eds., *The semantics/pragmatics distinction. Proceedings from WOC 2002*. Stanford: CSLI Publications, 45–64.

2007. Truth conditional pragmatics. In Paolo Bouquet, Luciano Serafini, and Rich Thomason, eds., *Perspectives on Contexts*. Stanford: CSLI.

Reinhart, Tanya. 1983. *Anaphora and semantic interpretation*. Chicago: Chicago University Press.

1991. Elliptic conjunctions: Non-quantificational LF. In Asa Kasher, ed., *The Chomskyan turn*. Oxford: Blackwell, 360–384.

Reinhart, Tanya and Eric Reuland. 1993. Reflexivity. *Linguistic Inquiry* 24: 657–720.

Reinhart, Tanya and Tal Siloni. 2005. Thematic arity operations and parametric variation. *Linguistic Inquiry* 36: 389–436.

Romaine, Suzanne. 1999. The grammaticalization of the proximative in Tok Pisin. *Language* 75: 322–346.

Rosenbach, Anette. 2005. Animacy versus weight as determinants of grammatical variation in English. *Language* 81: 613–644.

Rosenbach, Anette and Gerhard Jäger. 2006. Priming as a driving force in grammaticalization: On the track of unidirectionality. Unpublished MS, Universities of Düsseldorf and Bielefeld.

Russell, Bertrand. 1905. On denoting. *Mind* 14: 479–493.

Sadock, Jerrold M. 1978. On testing for conversational implicature. In Peter Cole, ed., *Syntax and semantics*, vol. 9: *Pragmatics*. New York: Academic Press, 281–297. (Reprinted in Kasher, ed. 1998, vol. 4: 315–331.)

Saffran, Jenny R., Richard N. Aslin, and Elissa L. Newport. 1996. Statistical learning by 8-month-old infants. *Science* 274: 1926.

Sailer, M. 2002. The German incredulity response construction and the hierarchical organization of constructions. Paper presented at 2nd International Conference on Construction Grammar, Helsinki.

Salmon, Nathan. 1991. The pragmatic fallacy. *Philosophical Studies* 63: 83–97.

Sanders, Ted J. M. and Leo G. M. Noordman. 2001. The role of coherence relations and their linguistic markers in text processing. *Discourse Processes* 29: 37–60.

Saul, Jennifer M. 2002. What is said and psychological reality: Grice's project and relevance theorists' criticism. *Linguistics and Philosophy* 25: 347–372.

Scheibman, Joanne. 2002. *Point of view and grammar: Structural patterns of subjectivity in American English conversation* (Studies in Discourse and Grammar 11). Amsterdam: John Benjamins.

Schiffer, Stephen. 1972. *Meaning*. Oxford: Clarendon Press.

Schiffrin, Deborah. 1985. Multiple constraints on discourse options: a quantitative analysis of causal sequences. *Discourse Processes* 8: 281–301.

1986. The functions of *and* in discourse. *Journal of Pragmatics* 10: 41–66.

1987. *Discourse markers*. Cambridge: Cambridge University Press.

Schladt, Mathias. 2000. The typology and grammaticalization of reflexives. In Zygmunt Frajzyngier and Traci S. Curl, eds., *Reflexives: Forms and functions*. Amsterdam: John Benjamins, 103–124.

Searle, John R. 1980. The background of meaning. In John R. Searle, Ferenc Kiefer, and Manfred Bierwisch, eds., *Speech act theory and pragmatics* (Synthese Language Library 10). Boston: Reidel, 221–232.

1992. *The rediscovery of the mind*. Cambridge, MA: MIT Press.

Seidenberg, Mark S., Michael K. Tanenhaus, James M. Leiman, and Marie Bienkowski. 1982. Automatic access of the meanings of ambiguous words in context: Some limitations of knowledge-based processing. *Cognitive Psychology* 14: 489–537.

Shimizu, Makoto and Masaki Murata. 2004. Transitive verb plus reflexive pronoun/personal pronoun patterns in English and Japanese: Using a Japanese-English parallel corpus. Talk presented at ICAME, Verona, May 2004.

Shlonsky, Ur. 1992. Resumptive pronouns as a last resort. *Linguistic Inquiry* 23: 443–468.

Siemund, Peter. 2003. Varieties of English from a cross-linguistic perspective: Intensifiers and reflexives. In Günter Rohdenburg and Britta Mondorf, eds., *Determinants of grammatical variation in English* (Topics in English Linguistics 43). Berlin: Mouton de Gruyter, 479–506.

Silverstein, Michael. 1976. Shifters, linguistic categories, and cultural description. In Keith Basso and Henry A. Selby, eds., *Meaning in anthropology*. Albuquerque: University of New Mexico Press, 11–55.

2001. The limits of awareness. In Alessandro Duranti, ed., *Linguistic anthropology: A reader*. Oxford: Blackwell, 382–401.

Sinclair, John M. 1991. *Corpus, concordance collocation*. Oxford: Oxford University Press.

1992. Trust the text. In Martin Davies and Louise Ravelli, eds., *Advances in systemic linguistics: Recent theory and practice* (Open Linguistics Series). London: Pinter, 5–19.

Singer, Murray. 1979. Processes of inference during sentence encoding. *Memory and Cognition* 7: 192–200.

1980. The role of case-filling inferences in the coherence of brief passages. *Discourse Processes* 3: 185–200.

Singer, Murray and Fernanda Ferreira. 1983. Inferring consequences in story comprehension. *Journal of Verbal Learning and Verbal Behavior* 22: 437–448.

Smith, Mark. 2004. Light and heavy reflexives. *Linguistics* 42: 573–615.

Snow, Catherine E. 1999. Social perspectives on the emergence of language. In Brian MacWhinney, ed., *The emergence of language*. Mahwah, NJ: Lawrence Erlbaum Associates, 257–276.

Soames, Scott. 1979. A projection problem for speaker presuppositions. *Linguistic Inquiry* 10: 623–666.

1982. How presuppositions are inherited: A solution to the projection problem. *Linguistic Inquiry* 13: 483–545.

2002. *Beyond rigidity*. Oxford: Oxford University Press.

Solan, Lawrence M. 1983. *Pronominal reference: Child language and the theory of grammar* (Studies in Theoretical Psycholinguistics). Dordrecht: Reidel.

Solan, Zach, David Horn, Eytan Ruppin, and Shimon Edelman. 2005. Unsupervised learning of natural languages. *Proceedings of the National Academy of Science of the United States of America* 102: 11629–11634.

Sperber, Dan and Deirdre Wilson. 1986/1995. *Relevance*. Oxford: Blackwell.

1987. Précis of *Relevance: Communication and cognition*. *Behavioral & Brain Sciences* 10: 697–754.

Stainton, Robert J. 1994. Using non-sentences: An application of Relevance theory. *Pragmatics and Cognition* 2: 269–284.

Stalnaker, Robert C. 1974. Pragmatic presuppositions. In Milton K. Munitz and Peter K. Unger, eds., *Semantics and Philosophy*. New York: New York University Press, 197–214.

Stanley, Jason. 2000. Context and logical form. *Linguistics and Philosophy* 23: 391–434.

Stefanowitsch, Anatol and Stefan Th. Gries. 2003. Collostructions: Investigating the interaction of words and constructions. *International Journal of Corpus Linguistics* 8: 209–243.

Stern, Gustav. 1931. *Meaning and change of meaning* (Indiana University Studies in the History and Theory of Linguistics). Bloomington: Indiana University Press.

Stirling, Lesley and Rodney Huddleston. 2002. Deixis and anaphora. In Rodney Huddleston and Geoffrey K. Pullum, eds., *The Cambridge grammar of the English language*. Cambridge: Cambridge University Press, 1449–1564.

Strawson, Peter F. 1950. On referring. *Mind* 59: 320–344.

1952. *Introduction to logical theory*. London: Methuen.

1964/1974. Identifying reference and truth-values. In Farhang Zabeeh, E. D. Klemke, and Arthur Jacobson, eds., *Readings in semantics*. Urbana: University of Illinois Press, 194–216.

Swales, John M. 1990. *Genre analysis: English in academic and research settings* (Cambridge Applied Linguistics Series). Cambridge: Cambridge University Press.

Sweetser, Eve. 1987. The definition of "lie." In Dorothy Holland and Naomi Quinn, eds., *Cultural models in language and thought*. Cambridge: Cambridge University Press, 3–66.

1988. Grammaticalization and semantic bleaching. In *Berkeley Linguistics Society 14*. Berkeley, 389–405.

1990. From etymology to pragmatics: Metaphorical and cultural aspects of semantic structure (Cambridge Studies in Linguistics 54). Cambridge: Cambridge University Press.

Swinney, David A. 1979. Lexical access during sentence comprehension: (Re)consideration of context effects. *Journal of Verbal Learning and Verbal Behavior* 18: 645–659.

Talmy, Leonard. 1983. How language structures space. In Herbert L. Pick and Linda P. Acredolo, eds., *Spatial orientation: Theory, research, and application*. New York: Plenum Press, 225–282.

1985. Lexicalization patterns: Semantic structure in lexical forms. In Timothy Shopen, ed., *Language typology and syntactic description*, vol. 3: *Grammatical categories and the lexicon*. Cambridge: Cambridge University Press, 36–149.

1988. The relation of grammar to cognition. In Brygida Rudzka-Ostyn, ed., *Topics in Cognitive Linguistics (Amsterdam Studies in the Theory and History of Linguistic Science IV: Current Issues in Linguistic Theory 50)*. Amsterdam: John Benjamins, 165–205.

Terkel, Studs. 1974. *Working*. New York: Avon.

Thompson, Sandra A. 1990. Information flow and dative shift in English discourse. In Jerold A. Edmondson, Crawford Feagin, and Peter Mühlhäusler, eds., *Development and diversity: Language variation across time and space* (Summer Institute of Linguistics and the University of Texas at Arlington Publications in Linguistics 93). Dallas: Summer Institute of Linguistics and University of Texas at Arlington, 239–253.

1991. On addressing functional explanation in linguistics. *Language and Communication* 11: 93–96.

2002. Constructions and conversation. Unpublished MS, UC Santa Barbara.

Thompson, Sandra A. and Paul J. Hopper. 2001. Transitivity, clause structure, and argument structure: Evidence from conversation. In Joan L. Bybee and Paul J. Hopper, eds., *Frequency and the emergence of linguistic structure* (Typological Studies in Language 45). Amsterdam: John Benjamins, 27–60.

Tomasello, Michael. 1992. *First verbs: A case study of early grammatical development*. Cambridge: Cambridge University Press.

2000. The item-based nature of children's early syntactic development. *Trends in Cognitive Sciences* 4: 156–163.

2003a. *Constructing a language*. Cambridge, MA: Harvard University Press.

ed. 2003b. *The new psychology of language: Cognitive and functional approaches to language structure*, vol. 2. Mahwah, NJ: Lawrence Erlbaum Associates.

Toole, Janine. 1996. The effect of genre on referential choice. In Thorstein Fretheim and Jeanette K. Gundel, eds., *Reference and referent accessibility*. Amsterdam: John Benjamins, 263–290.

Tottie, Gunnel. 1991. Lexical diffusion in syntactic change: Frequency as a determinant of linguistic conservatism in the development of negation in English. In Dieter Kastovsky, ed., *Historical English syntax* (Topics in English Linguistics 2). Berlin: Mouton de Gruyter, 439–467.

Traugott, Elizabeth Closs. 1982. From propositional to textual and expressive meanings: Some semantic-pragmatic aspects of grammaticalization. In Winfred P. Lehmann and Yakov Malkiel, eds., *Perspectives on historical linguistics*. Amsterdam: John Benjamins, 245–271.

1988. Pragmatic strengthening and grammaticalization. In *Berkeley Linguistics Society 14*. Berkeley: Berkeley Linguistics Society, 406–416.

1989. On the rise of epistemic meanings in English: An example of subjectification in semantic change. *Language* 65: 31–55.

2003. Constructions in grammaticalizations. In Brian D. Joseph and Richard D. Janda, eds., *The handbook of historical linguistics*. Oxford: Blackwell, 624–647.

2004a. Historical pragmatics. In Laurence R. Horn and Gregory Ward, eds., *Handbook of pragmatics*. Oxford: Blackwell, 538–561.

2004b. Exaptation and grammaticalization. In Minoji Akimoto, ed., *Linguistic studies based on corpora*. Tokyo: Hituzi Syobo Publishing Co., 133–156.

Traugott, Elizabeth Closs and Richard B. Dasher. 2002. *Regularity in semantic change* (Cambridge Studies in Linguistics 97). Cambridge: Cambridge University Press.

Traugott, Elizabeth Closs and Bernd Heine, eds. 1991. *Approaches to grammaticalization*, vol. 1: *Focus on theoretical and methodological issues*; vol. 2: *Focus on types of grammatical markers* (Typological Studies in Language 19:1, 19:2). Amsterdam: John Benjamins.

Traugott, Elizabeth Closs and Ekkehard König. 1991. The semantics-pragmatics of grammaticalization revisited. In Elizabeth Closs Traugott and Bernd Heine, eds.,

Approaches to grammaticalization, vol. 1: *Focus on theoretical and methodological issues* (Typological Studies in Language 19:1). Amsterdam: John Benjamins, 189–219.

Travis, Charles. 1991. Annals of analysis: *Studies in the way of words*, by H. P. Grice. *Mind* 100: 237–264.

Trudgill, Peter. 1995. Grammaticalisation and social structure: Non-standard conjunction-formation in east Anglian English. In F. R. Palmer, ed., *Grammar and meaning*. Cambridge: Cambridge University Press, 136–145.

Turk, Monica J. 2004. Using *and* in conversational interaction. *Research on language and social interaction* 37: 219–250.

Verhagen, Arie. 2000. Interpreting usage: Construing the history of Dutch causal verbs. In Michael Barlow and Suzanne Kemmer, eds., *Usage-based models of language*. Stanford: CSLI Publications, 261–286.

Walker, Ralph C. S. 1975. Conversational implicatures. In Simon Blackburn, ed., *Meaning, reference and necessity: New studies in semantics*. Cambridge: Cambridge University Press, 133–181.

Ward, Gregory L. 1990. The discourse functions of VP preposing. *Language* 66: 742–763.

Wedel, Andrew Benjamin. 2004. Self-organization and categorical behavior in phonology. In *Berkeley Linguistics Society 29*. Berkeley: Berkeley Linguistics Society, 611–622.

Weiner, E. Judith and William Labov. 1983. Constraints on the agentless passive. *Journal of Linguistics* 19: 29–58.

Weinreich, Uriel, William Labov, and Marvin I. Herzog. 1968. Empirical foundations for a theory of language change. In Winfred P. Lehmann and Yakov Malkiel, eds., *Directions for historical linguistics: A symposium*. Austin: University of Texas Press, 98–195.

Werner, Heinz and Bernard Kaplan. 1963. *Symbol formation: An organismic-developmental approach to language and the expression of thought*. New York: Wiley and Sons.

Wierzbicka, Anna. 1985. "Oats" and "wheat": The fallacy of arbitrariness. In John Haiman, ed., *Iconicity in syntax*. Amsterdam: John Benjamins, 311–342.

Wilson, Deirdre. 1975. *Presuppositions and non-truth-conditional semantics*. New York: Academic Press.

1992. Reference and Relevance. *UCL Working Papers in Linguistics* 4: 165–191.

1995. Is there a maxim of truthfulness? *UCL Working Papers in Linguistics* 7: 197–212.

2003. Relevance and lexical pragmatics. *Italian Journal of Linguistics/Rivista di Linguistica*, special issue: *Pragmatics and the lexicon*, 15:273–291. (Reprinted in *UCL Working Papers in Linguistics* 16(2004), 343–360.)

2005. New directions for research on pragmatics and modularity. *Lingua* 115: 1129–1146.

Wilson, Deirdre and Dan Sperber. 1979. Ordered entailments: An alternative to presuppositional theories. In Choon-Kyu Oh and David A. Dinneen, eds., *Syntax and semantics*, vol. 11: *Presupposition*. New York: Academic Press, 299–323.

1993. Linguistic form and relevance. *Lingua* 90: 1–25.

1998. Pragmatics and time. In Robyn Carston and Seiji Uchida, eds., *Relevance theory: Applications and implications*. Amsterdam: John Benjamins, 1–22.

2002. Truthfulness and relevance. *Mind* 111: 583–632.

2004. Relevance theory. In Laurence R. Horn and Gregory Ward, ed., *Handbook of pragmatics*. Oxford: Blackwell, 607–632.

Witkowski, Stanley R. and Cecil H. Brown. 1983. Marking reversals and cultural importance. *Language* 59: 569–582.

Yus Ramos, Francisco. 1998. The "what-do-you-mean syndrome." A taxonomy of misunderstandings in Harold Pinter's plays. *Estudios Ingleses de la Universidad Complutense* 6: 81–100.

Zipf, George Kingsley. 1929. Relative frequency as a determinant of phonetic change. *Harvard Studies in Classical Philology* 15: 1–95.

Ziv, Yael. 1994. Left and right dislocations: Discourse functions and anaphora. *Journal of Pragmatics* 22: 629–645.

Zribi-Hertz, Anne. 1995. Emphatic or reflexive? On the endophoric character of French *lui-même* and similar complex pronouns. *Journal of Linguistics* 31: 333–374.

    2003. Réflexivité et disjonction référentielle en français et en anglais. In P. Miller and Anne Zribi-Hertz, eds., *Essais sur la grammaire comparée du français et de l'anglais*. Saint Denis: Presses Universitaires Vincennes, 142–169.

Zuraw, Kie. 2003. Probability in language change. In Rens Bod, Jennifer Hay, and Stefanie Jannedy, eds., *Probabilistic linguistics*. Cambridge, MA: MIT Press, 139–176.

Author index

Subject index